ROUSSEAU'S PLATONIC ENLIGHTENMENT

ROUSSEAU'S PLATONIC ENLIGHTENMENT

DAVID LAY WILLIAMS

FOREWORD BY PATRICK RILEY

The Pennsylvania State University Press
University Park, Pennsylvania

Library of Congress Cataloging-in-Publication Data
Williams, David Lay.
    Rousseau's Platonic Enlightenment / David Lay Williams ;
    foreword by Patrick Riley.
        p.   cm.
Includes bibliographical references and index.
ISBN-13: 978–0-271–02997–9 (cloth : alk. paper)
ISBN-13: 978-0-271-02998-6 (pbk: alk.paper)
1. Rousseau, Jean-Jacques, 1712–1778.
I. Title.

B2137.W55   2007
194—dc22
2007026766

The Pennsylvania State University Press
is a member of the Association of
American University Presses.

It is the policy of The Pennsylvania State
University Press to use acid-free paper.
This book is printed on Natures Natural,
containing 50% post-consumer waste,
and meets the minimum requirements of American
National Standard for Information
Sciences—Permanence of Paper for Printed
Library Material, ANSI Z39.48–1992.

For T. K. SEUNG

The late Judith N. Shklar, *doyenne* of American Rousseau studies, liked usually to stress Rousseau's "modernity," viewing him as a proto-Freudian and pre-Proustian psychologist and group psychologist diagnosing early modern mental illnesses (such as alienation, resentment, and nostalgia). But even she, who saw Rousseau as an eloquent *homme revolté* railing against misery and *inégalité*, always insisted too that the "citizen of Geneva" was the "heir of Plato"—not in detailed imitation, but in sheer radical boldness. For if Plato had insisted on sublimated love (*philo-sophia*) for quasi-mathematical "eternal moral verities" and on the rule of the wise, "golden" few, Rousseau had been no less startlingly innovative in insisting that natural egoists with self-loving "particular wills" must be transformed by "denaturing" education (supplied by Moses or Lycurgus or Numa) into citizens with a civic "general will" like that of the "Spartan mother" in *Emile,* who asks not whether her sons have survived but whether the city still lives. For Shklar, then, Plato and Rousseau, though separated by whole universes, shared what one wag has called "polis envy." In fact, she merely pointed to Rousseau's Platonism, leaving it to others to prove what she only claimed. (Perhaps she thought that Charles Hendel's magisterial *Jean-Jacques Rousseau: Moralist* [Oxford, 1934] had done enough to indicate a Platonic *provenance* for some of Rousseau's concerns.)

But the point is that, since 1934, we have had no comprehensive, careful "reading" of Rousseau as Plato-shaped. It is, therefore, a matter of the first importance in Rousseau scholarship that David Williams has now brilliantly undertaken the first serious study of Rousseau's Hellenophilia in seven decades. The wait has been long, but it is now justified by the results: Williams's book will immediately become the "standard" text and will join the company of Shklar and Hendel and Starobinski and Cassirer as a work that responsible Rousseau students need to know. Moreover, because Rousseau is arguably the greatest and boldest political philosopher of modernity—rivaled only by Hobbes, Kant, and Hegel—a freshly illuminating study of him *matters*.

As Williams shows very effectively, it is "no accident" that Rousseau especially revered (among his immediate French intellectual ancestors) Malebranche and Fénelon—for the oratorian priest and the archbishop had done most to convey Plato into early modern France. Malebranche's argument that we know only "ideas," which are seen "in God," that we cannot know the reality of a physical world or even of other minds, is obviously a form of hyper-Platonic "idealism" that would appeal to the Rousseau who thought that "materialism" (á la d'Holbach or Helvétius) was fatal to "morals" and to becoming "what one ought to be." Hence, it is not surprising that in Rousseau's early *Le Persifleur,* the spiritual heroes are not just Locke but also "Plato and Malebranche." And Fénelon, even more hyper-Platonic, was of even greater significance to Rousseau: the archbishop of Cambrai's reverence for the Greco-Roman polis, for subordinating "self-love" to "disinterested" love of *le bien général,* led him to write the great didactic novel *Telemachus, Son of Ulysses*—the story of the denaturing transformation of Ulysses' son from a thoughtless egoist into a responsible statesman (through the ministrations of Minerva), which Rousseau so loved and admired that he made it the only modern book recommended to Emile (after his own transformative education) when he reaches adulthood at the end of Rousseau's greatest single work. (And Williams shows, too, that Rousseau's admiration for Leibniz—in the *Lettre à Voltaire sur la providence*—is also grounded in modern Platonism, for Leibniz did for German Platonism what Malebranche and Fénelon did for the French version.)

But if Rousseau had only been "influenced" by Malebranche and (especially) Fénelon, making a minor contribution to the great "quarrel between the ancients and the moderns" that dominated French thought from the seventeenth century to the death of Benjamin Constant, he would now be thought of as a secondary embroiderer of French-Platonic themes. In fact, however—as David Williams shows so fully and carefully—Rousseau's social thought makes "Platonism" central from 1750, from the *Discourse on the Arts and Sciences,* which made his reputation, in which Rousseau treats Socrates as a civic saint and martyr who willingly sacrificed himself (as a victim of judicial murder) for the general good of the Athenian polis. (Rousseau's Greek heroes are usually Spartan, and at his hands the self-sacrificing Socrates is more Spartan than Athenian.) Moreover, if Rousseau began his career as a political theorist with a Spartanized Socratic Platonism, he later crowned the *Social Contract* and *Government of Poland* with yet another encomium of "the general good of the body politic" that owes much to Plato's notion, in book 5 of the *Republic,* that in a body politic, the particular good of any "member" (such as a finger) must lovingly subordinate itself to *le bien général*—a theme then taken over by St. Paul in 1 Corinthians 12 and by Pascal in the *Pensées* before finally reaching Rousseau himself. (Not only does Williams show how much sheer Platonism there is in Rousseau's published works, but he also— through a first-ever contextual integration of Rousseau's marginalia to Plato's texts left behind in Britain when Rousseau gave up his Hume-provided refuge and returned to France—shows that Rousseau was constantly reading and interpreting Plato's words throughout the 1760s, his most important decade.)

It would have been praiseworthy enough if David Williams had only revealed, often for the first time, the full weight of Platonism in Rousseau: but, meritoriously, Williams reminds us that no less a figure than Immanuel Kant called Rousseau "the Newton of the moral world" who had taught him to "honor mankind," and that the same Kant had made crucial use of Rousseau's central idea—"the general will one has as a citizen"—in many of his most important political and moral writings. But while some appreciators of the Rousseau-Kant *rapport* have pointed out Kant's use of *volonté générale* in the 1797 *Metaphysik der Sitten,* no earlier commentator has shown remotely so fully how Kant used Rousseauean notions in his precritical works before 1781. Indeed, one of the glories of Williams's new study is a first-ever (once again) full appreciation of Rousseau's significance for Kant over a thirty-year period. Nothing to match this superb chapter has ever appeared in *Kant-Studien,* or in the *Annales de la société Jean-Jacques Rousseau,* or even in Ernst Cassirer's Kantianizing reading of Rousseau in *Rousseau, Kant, and Goethe.* For a Plato-Rousseau scholar to throw so much light on Kant on the two-hundredth anniversary of his death (1804) is an unlooked-for bonus that makes an already valuable book absolutely invaluable—the more so because Williams rightly resists the famous claim of Lewis White Beck that Kant's practical philosophy is "deepened Rousseau." To have got the Rousseau-Kant rapport exactly right is a welcome added attraction crowning an already splendid effort.

In short, David Williams's study of Rousseau's Platonism is the one we have been awaiting since the days of Hendel and Cassirer, and Williams can be rightly glad to find himself in that exalted company.

Patrick Riley
Oakeshott Professor of Political Science and Moral Philosophy
The University of Wisconsin–Madison
December 2004

Citations of Rousseau's works include volume and page numbers from the Pléiade *Œuvres complètes* (*OC*). Citations of Kant's works, with the exception of the *First Critique,* include volume and page numbers from the Prussian Academy edition of *Kants gesammelte Schriften* (*KGS*).

WORKS OF JEAN-JACQUES ROUSSEAU

Confessions	*The Confessions,* 1781
Dialogues	*Rousseau, Judge of Jean-Jacques: Dialogues,* 1776
FD	*Discourse on the Arts and Sciences* [*First Discourse*], 1751
GM	*Geneva Manuscript,* 1756
"Imitation"	"On Theatrical Imitation: An Essay Drawn from Plato's Dialogues," 1764
Julie	*Julie; Or, the New Heloise: Letters of Two Lovers Who Live in a Small Town at the Foot of the Alps,* 1761
Letters	*Letters Written from the Mountain,* 1764
Letter to d'Alembert	*Letter to M. d'Alembert on the Theater,* 1758
"Letter to Voltaire"	"Letter from J. J. Rousseau to M. de Voltaire, 18 August 1756"
OC	*Œuvres complètes,* 1959–95
Poland	*Considerations on the Government of Poland,* 1772
Political Economy	*Discourse on Political Economy,* 1755
Reveries	*Reveries of the Solitary Walker,* 1778
SC	*Of the Social Contract,* 1762

SD	*Discourse on the Origin and the Foundations of Inequality Among Men* [*Second Discourse*], 1755
"State of War"	"The State of War," 1758

OTHER WORKS

Capital	Karl Marx, *Capital*, 1867
Communist Manifesto	Karl Marx and Friedrich Engels, *The Communist Manifesto*, 1848
DP	Michel Foucault, *Discipline and Punish*, 1975
FC	Immanuel Kant, *Critique of Pure Reason* [*First Critique*], 1781
Groundwork	Immanuel Kant, *Groundwork of the Metaphysics of Morals*, 1785
KGS	Immanuel Kant, *Kants gesammelte Schriften*, 1902–
Leviathan	Thomas Hobbes, *Leviathan*, 1651
MM	Immanuel Kant, *Metaphysics of Morals*, 1797

For the better part of the last century, scholars have predominantly come to view Jean-Jacques Rousseau as a Hobbesian. After all, he employs the social contract that Hobbes popularized. Beyond this, he is well attuned to the human passions that both necessitate the social contract and provide the motives to agree to it. Further, he explicitly acknowledges the undeniable brilliance of Hobbes. Perhaps the greatest reason for linking him to the revolutionary from Malmesbury, however, is the context of his intellectual emergence. While the Enlightenment means many things to many people, one of its essential features is the reemergence of the century-long latent philosophy of Thomas Hobbes. A central part of this revival was Hobbes's materialist metaphysics, to wit, what exists must be composed of matter, and, conversely, what is supposed to be immaterial cannot be said to exist. In Hobbes's day this position provoked strong reaction, particularly among the significant set of moderns who read his materialism as rejecting the hallowed objects of Western metaphysics—God, the soul, free will, and immaterial ideas, such as justice. Indeed, it was the greatest of insults in the seventeenth century to be labeled a "Hobbist."

Hobbism thus remained largely silent in the decades immediately following Hobbes's death, but a century after its articulation in the *Leviathan* it resurfaced in the intellectual world of the Enlightenment, where it would prove to be the essential foundation for that world's two most important dimensions: science and morals. In the scientific realm, Hobbes's work was positively revelatory. Freed from the Aristotelian task of seeking purposes and immaterial causes of natural phenomena, natural philosophers could instead focus on discovering their material cause and effect, which is to say, they would begin to conduct modern science.

Hobbes was equally influential in morals and politics. The hub of this activity was in mid-eighteenth-century Paris, home to Claude Helvétius, Paul-Henry Dietrich von (Baron) d'Holbach, and Denis Diderot. Rather than locating morality in immaterial concepts, such as freedom, God, or the idea of justice or the good, they sought to ground it in material substance. In Hobbes's own work, this metaphysical constraint in morals and politics generated some of his most shocking innovations. Among these was his dismissal of free will. Because all human beings are material, their behavior is completely determined by matter. Matter does not choose their behavior. Their actions are determined just as anything else in the natural world—by cause and effect. Parallel to this was Hobbes's stark moral relativism. For him, that which is preferred by an individual is good; that which is shunned is evil. Because different people or cultures can prefer or shun different objects, Hobbes's ethics are relative to individuals or cultures. It is also, in a sense, proto-utilitarian. People seek that which provides pleasure or happiness; they shun that which is painful or makes them unhappy. Materialism likewise shapes his politics. In the absence of an independent immaterial standard of justice that could serve as the foundation of a civil society, foundations must instead be constructed. He thus defines justice as merely the upholding of agreements, or contract. Above this there can be no higher political standard. This is the doctrine of positivism. The implications of the metaphysical assumption of materialism are thus far ranging—one can deduce from it the ancillary doctrines of determinism in human behavior, relativism and utilitarianism in ethics, and positivism in politics.

Helvétius, d'Holbach, and Diderot followed Hobbes closely in these respects. They described human behavior as being completely determined. There is no immaterial soul or conscience providing motives independent of our physical impulses. Thus, in a world where physical impulses were everything, morality became a matter of satisfying preferences and generating pleasure. The philosophes were essential precursors to the philosophy of Jeremy Bentham, likewise a materialist, who developed the elaborate moral and political theory of utilitarianism. That which is preferred is good; that which is preferred is pleasure. Therefore, pleasure is the good. Although its measures are sometimes contested, pleasure is a kind of material phenomenon. Thus, utilitarianism—the doctrine that takes the greatest pleasure as the greatest good—is almost the inevitable choice of materialists who aspire to moral philosophy.

The movement toward the acceptance of Hobbesian materialism proceeded at different paces in natural and moral philosophy. In natural philosophy its progress was rapid, because its applications were readily apparent. The moral realm, however, was considerably different. Whereas Helvétius, d'Holbach, and Diderot were confident of the truth of relativist and utilitarian consequences drawn from their materialist assumptions, none of them expected their ideas to be met with wide approval. Therefore, none published materialist tracts in his own name. The authorship of Helvétius's *De l'esprit* was anonymous, although a badly kept secret, ultimately resulting in three public retractions of the work. D'Holbach's *System of Nature* was published without any connection to his name and reputation. In the case of Diderot's *D'Alembert's Dream,* he destroyed what he believed to be the only extant copy in order to prevent posthumous persecution.

The anonymity of the Enlightenment materialist tracts suggests great opposition from another tradition—and in fact, one of those most hostile to the reemerging Hobbesian materialism was Jean-Jacques Rousseau. He had come to Paris in 1741 with fifteen louis in his pockets, concerned primarily with making a name for himself as a musical innovator. He achieved this in part, having written one of the most wildly successful operas of his age. By the time this had happened, however, his interests and priorities had radically shifted. His early friendship with Denis Diderot brought him into the circle of budding materialists. Rousseau was at once entranced and repulsed, suitably impressed by its opulence and intellectual freedom yet shocked by its frank materialism. The tension did not last long, as his disgust quickly overwhelmed his youthful awe, and he would in the end not only reject the materialism of his new friends but also attempt to steer Europe away from doctrines he would later describe as "rootless" and "fruitless." They were rootless insofar as they had no foundations in anything permanent or eternal. They were fruitless inasmuch as they could not yield a morality consistent with his deepest intuitions.

If Rousseau rejected materialism and utilitarianism, of course, then he must have grounded his system elsewhere. Where did he look? In what source did he find inspiration? History is our most useful guide in this respect, because this was not the first time that materialism had come to inform the intellectual class. The most notorious materialists prior to Hobbes were the pre-Socratic and sophistic philosophers of ancient Greece. Beginning with Thales, a series of early thinkers speculated that the world could be best understood as matter—whether it be water, air, fire, or atoms. Most significant of the pre-Socratic materialists was Heraclitus, who held everything to be a manifestation of fire, a metaphor for change. Fire is the transformation of matter, for example, from wood to smoke and ash. All matter constantly changes. Metal becomes rust; rust becomes dirt. Ice becomes water; water becomes steam. Food becomes living human flesh; human beings become dirt. Everything, Heraclitus held, is in flux.

On the heels of the pre-Socratic natural philosophers came the sophists, who applied Heraclitean principles to the moral realm. No morality is stable.

It likewise is constantly changing. As Protagoras famously asserted, "Human beings are the measure of all things." Different lands have different morals. Different individuals believe different things to be right or wrong. The same people may even change their views from one time to another. There is no universal or eternal morality. The moral world has all the flux and instability of the natural world. All that matters in discourse is persuasion. Truth is an afterthought.

The doctrines of the pre-Socratics and sophists did not go unchallenged. Parmenides objected to Heraclitus by locating reality not in change or "becoming," but rather in "being"—that which is eternal and unchanging. Similarly, Socrates opposed the sophists. Morals were not, for him, simply a matter of *doxa,* or opinion. Winning an argument was not a simple matter of persuasion. Rather, it was a matter of arriving at a universal truth. Of course, the greatest response to both the pre-Socratics and the sophists came from Socrates' student, Plato. His theory of the forms remains, in many respects, the most elaborate answer to the challenges of materialism and relativism.[1] For him, the forms are the ultimate reality, eternal and unchanging, incapable of being created by fiat or agreement. They are the bases of critiques and foundations of moral maxims and political communities.

Two millennia later, Rousseau would assume Plato's role in the very same debate. He devoted virtually an entire career to fighting the advocates of materialism in modern Europe. In fact, he viewed his program as a heroic defense against those doctrines that threatened forever to undermine the bases of morals and politics. "I admit in good faith that when my adversaries' works no longer survive," he once wrote, "my own will be perfectly useless" (Rousseau 1994a, 45/*OC,* III:516). Just as Plato constructed his theory of the immaterial and transcendent forms to combat rampant materialism and relativism, so Rousseau likewise appealed to "eternal truths admitted at all times by all wise men, recognized by all nations, and engraved on the human heart in indelible characters" (*Reveries,* 25/*OC,* I:1021). It is in this context that we can begin to appreciate the fact that Rousseau would refer to Plato as "divine," a "genius," "profound," and indeed nothing less than his "master," while both Hobbes and the philosophes merited the label "sophists"—people who were, in his estimation, "not even concerned with whether [their arguments] were true or false" (18/I:1013). Rousseau's place in modernity is indeed deeply analogous to Plato's in antiquity.

1. That Plato was actually a "Platonist" in this respect has been challenged by some scholars, most notably Allan Bloom in his introduction to the *Republic.* Following George Klosko (1986b), I instead take Plato at his word when he claims to be endorsing Platonic doctrines.

Before advancing any further, it is important to establish what is meant herein by "Platonism." This includes five substantive areas: metaphysical, ontological, epistemic, political, and institutional.

Metaphysical

Perhaps the doctrine most clearly identified with Platonism is a belief in the existence of immaterial ideas. For Plato, this is the doctrine of the forms. The forms are metaphysically different from the material world in which we conduct our daily lives. They take no material shape. They have no material properties. They are perceptible only through the intellect. For Plato, the soul is also of this character. It is separable from the material body, suggesting its immateriality. This is not to say that Platonism implies the doctrine of idealism—that ideas constitute the entirety of substance. Plato acknowledges the existence of both material and immaterial substance (*Phaedo*, 79a). On his account, human beings are composed of both body (material) and soul (immaterial). This is the doctrine of *metaphysical dualism*, and it is central to both Plato and Rousseau.

Ontological

It is one thing to assert the existence of something like the forms or the soul. It is another to know what they are like. Plato provides several attributes of his immaterial substances. First, they are invariable (*Phaedo*, 78c). These ideas do not change in attributes or character from one generation or location to the next. They are absolutely constant or transcendent. In Kantian language, they are necessary a priori truths. Given this quality, they are in no way subject to human creation or alteration. Human beings neither create Platonic ideas nor are capable of changing them as they might see fit. The Platonic idea of Justice is not, for example, created by agreement in the same way that modern or contemporary understandings of justice sometimes suggest. People may agree to that which is just, but this has nothing to do with the ontological status of justice itself. In many respects, this represents the core essence of Platonism, as discussed throughout this book. There are many variants of eternal standards throughout the canon of Western political thought, such as natural law, natural rights, and moral realism, but they all derive from the Platonic impetus to place the ultimate norms beyond artifice and contingency.

I thus regard them all as Platonic, insofar as Plato was the founder of this ambition. This ontological dimension of Platonism is especially important in understanding Rousseau's aims as a political philosopher.

A second important ontological feature of Platonism is less orthodox. It is also, I would argue, more specifically Platonic. This is that the immaterial ideas are indeterminate.[2] That is, the content of any given Platonic idea is not spelled out in concrete detail like a legal code. As an analogy, consider the game of chess. While the goal of a chess match is always to corner the opponent's king, there is nothing in the rulebook that explains how this is to be done. The method by which to achieve this will always be contingent upon the myriad circumstances that arise in the context of an individual game. Sometimes it will be wise to take the opponent's rook; sometimes it will appear suicidal to do so. It all depends on context—*almost.* Although context is a necessary variable to consider in the process, it does not function alone. This is because the player must always be informed by a strategy that leads to the ultimate goal—cornering the king. This means that whereas the individual moves are shaped by context, they are not arbitrary. Such is the case with Plato's ideas. We are given an indeterminate idea, for example, of justice. This becomes the goal of any state aspiring to be just. But the means by which it might be pursued will depend, in large part, on the practical circumstances. This is why the Athenian Stranger, for example, pursues detailed knowledge of the Magnesia before drawing up its laws (*Laws,* 704a–709d). The indeterminacy of the ideas in ontological Platonism implies the necessity of this kind of contextual knowledge.

Epistemic

The epistemic dimension of Platonism is that these immaterial ideas are indeed knowable under the right circumstances. Fundamental among the right circumstances is the elimination of distractions. Many things, according to Plato, keep the intellect from knowing the ideas. In the *Phaedo,* he cites all bodily pleasures as such hindrances. This would obviously include sexual appetites and passions, and it further extends to other passions, such as love or anger. Beyond this (but related for Plato), an interest in fashion can prevent

2. I do not argue that this is Plato's account of the forms throughout all his writings. Rather, it is only in the mature dialogues that the indeterminacy of the forms truly emerges. I am indebted to T. K. Seung's *Plato Rediscovered* for this interpretation. See Seung (1996, 185–214; 1993, 194–99).

the would-be philosopher from attaining knowledge of the immaterial ideas (*Phaedo,* 64d).

The senses are also generally prone to divert the quest for genuine knowledge. Because the ideas are themselves immaterial, and the senses are only good for the perception of material phenomena, there is no obvious way in which they can be useful. To the contrary, they are profoundly deceiving. The idea of justice can no more be seen with the eyes than the idea of an immortal soul. Some may falsely associate materially perceptible phenomena with the ideas, but this is, for Plato, a terrible mistake. This is the case with the proto-utilitarianism of Callicles in the *Gorgias,* which locates the good in pleasure seeking (*Gorgias,* 492a–498c). This leads to the absurd conclusion, for Plato, that fools could and do have knowledge of the most lofty object of philosophic contemplation, such as the good. Such is the faulty logic of those attached to the material world. For this reason, Socrates says that he eagerly awaits his death—he anticipates its epistemic liberation of the intellect from the body.

This raises the question of how one might know the ideas, then, if not through the senses. For Plato, the "ideas can be thought [*noeisthai*] but not seen" (*Republic,* 507).[3] To know something without sensing it is to know by virtue of the intellect or understanding. This is the foundation of the modern epistemological school of rationalism. Plato elaborates on this mode of knowledge in his simile of the divided line (509d–511e). There are two classes of entities upon which we can devote our focused attention. They are either part of the "intelligible order" or "the world of the eyeball." The latter is the realm of material artifacts, and our five senses are the appropriate tools for examining them. Above this, however, exists the intelligible realm, where we find such things as first principles. Our senses are useless here. It is only the mind that provides access to this kind of knowledge.

Plato does not give an extended account of just how one employs the mind to come to these truths. This is undoubtedly related to the fact that, on his account, it is virtually impossible to do so in the context of a written book. Anything like a comprehensive knowledge of the ideas is the result of an extended journey accessible to the few. In order to be considered even a candidate for this kind of knowledge, an individual must possess an ease of learning, good memory, quick wits, intelligence, youthful spiritedness, and high-mindedness (*Republic,* 503c). And this is just to start the process. The rare individu-

---

3. "[T]here certainly are . . . self-existent ideas unperceived by sense, and apprehended only by the mind" (*Timaeus,* 51d).

als wielding these talents then commence an extended education that takes them through decades of intense study. This includes attention to physical training, music, poetry, mathematics, geometry, trigonometry, and astronomy, culminating in dialectic. This formal education ends at age thirty-five, but not even at this point can these talented, extensively trained individuals know the good. They must then go out into the world and gain fifteen years' worth of experiences. It is only then, at age fifty, that, if all has miraculously gone according to plan, the student can be said to have genuine philosophic wisdom. And even at this stage, Plato cautions against epistemological corruption. With all their training, talent, and wisdom, philosophers can still fall prey to the natural influences of family and property that threaten what is good for the community for the sake of what is good only for select individuals. Thus, to protect philosophers' epistemological purity, Plato recommends that they adopt a monkish existence, one without families or property.

Political

Putting the good into practice through political institutions is the lofty goal of Plato's politics. The ideas are not merely the objects of contemplation for the few gifted enough to know them. Rather, they are to guide how we conduct our lives. Indeed—at least for Plato's Socrates in the *Parmenides*—out of all the ideas, we can have the greatest epistemic certainty about the political, moral, and aesthetic ones (*Parmenides,* 130bc).[4] The component of Platonism I mean to describe here is the goal of making such ideas—particularly the ideas of justice and goodness—relevant to politics. For Plato, any legislator "worth his salt, could have no other object in view in his legislation than the supreme virtue. This supreme virtue is what Theognis speaks of as loyalty in peril, and we may call it complete justice [*dikaiosunen*]" (*Laws,* 630c). This is likewise the goal of the philosopher-rulers in the *Republic,* who are chosen specifically because of their access to knowledge of these ideas. One cannot do what is right without knowing what is right. Thus, the supreme qualification for ruling is knowledge of this kind. It is important to keep in mind, however, that the knowledge of the rulers is far from the complete story. Implementing these ideas in the imperfect material world is the goal of the political dimensions of Platonism.

4. He contrasts these areas of certainty with the possibility of forms for objects and phenomena such as fire, water, hair, mud, and dirt.

Institutional

There is, of course, another element of political Platonism—the specific recommendations that Plato makes in regard to political institutions and laws. Although a subset of political Platonism, properly speaking, it can stand as a distinct category. Institutional Platonism is necessarily the most wide-ranging category of Platonism, because his two most comprehensive works, the *Republic* and the *Laws,* are specifically concerned with the questions of institutions and laws. This includes several of his most famous (and infamous) programs and innovations from the *Republic,* such as philosopher-rulers, the eligibility of women for political office, and the abolition of family and property for political rulers. But this is only the beginning. It extends well beyond these doctrines. Plato's interests in these matters range from the big questions, such as who should rule, to the legal minutiae of educational curriculum, marriage laws, and pollution regulations.

Alfred North Whitehead's dictum that the "safest general characterization of the European philosophical tradition is that it consists in a series of footnotes to Plato" is quoted frequently enough to threaten it with being a tired cliché. But even if it were to attain such a dubious status, the great virtue of clichés is their proximity to the truth. The fact is that Plato wielded enormous influence in modern Europe. The rediscovery of dialogues as important as the *Republic, Theaetetus,* and *Symposium* had helped fuel the humanism of the Renaissance (Mercer 2002, 26). Starting with Marsilio Ficino's Latin translation of the dialogues in the sixteenth century, Platonic doctrines spread throughout Europe, including Italy, Germany, England, and France, and to figures as central to modernity as Descartes, Leibniz, Cudworth, and Malebranche. Although they were faithful to many of the above doctrines of Plato, they had particular points of emphasis that helped characterize what I will call in this book "modern European Platonism." These doctrines included faith in God, immortality of the soul, free will, and the existence of immaterial ideas.

Faith in God

While a faith in God is not central among Plato's doctrines, it is a significant component of the philosophies of his intellectual descendants. St. Augustine was the most famous of the early philosophers of this type, but perhaps the most important figure in modern European Platonism was Ficino, whose translation of Plato's dialogues made the works accessible to a wide Western audience for the first time. Beyond his work as a translator, however, Ficino worked in his own research to fuse Platonism with his religious faith. This is embodied in the very title of his most substantial work, *Platonic Theology,* where he explicitly drew from Plato's Cave to argue that "our minds bear the same relationship to God as our sight to the light of the Sun" (Ficino [1469–73] 2001, 9). In a similar spirit, one finds a significant role for God in the works of Descartes, Leibniz, and Malebranche, each of whom believes that it is possible to locate God with a Platonic rationalist epistemology (through the mind, rather than the senses).

Immortality of the Soul

The immortality of the soul is an important element of both Plato's work and that of his admirers. Plato offers his best-known argument for the immortality of the soul in the *Phaedo.* He separates human existence into two separate realms—body (material) and soul (immaterial). According to Plato, the soul precedes the existence of the body, which is demonstrated through the doctrine of recollection, and it continues after the body perishes, which is deduced from its immaterial and eternal nature. Varieties of this argument are enthusiastically endorsed by the modern European Platonists. Descartes, for example, states that one of the two primary purposes of his *Meditations* is to prove the immortality of the soul,[5] on which he argues the very existence of morality is contingent. Similar positions are likewise found in Leibniz and Malebranche.

Freedom of the Will

St. Augustine is often cited as the founder of all questions regarding a free will, but his concern here, as in many of his substantive doctrines, is preceded by Plato's. In the context of fending off the doctrine of materialism, Plato remarks, "To say that it is because of them [bones and sinews] that I do what I am doing, and not through choice of what is best—although my actions are controlled by mind—would be a very lax and inaccurate form of expression"

---

5. The other purpose is the first tenet of modern European Platonism cited above: the existence of God.

(*Phaedo*, 99ab).[6] The freedom of the will thus stems from his dualism. It is only by virtue of an immaterial component of the individual that one can resist the causality of the material world. Descartes, in this respect, is typical of the Platonic doctrine and representative of the modern European Platonists. He establishes a clear metaphysical dualism in order to claim that "the will is by its nature free in such a way that it can never be constrained" (Descartes [1649] 1989, 41). This doctrine is embraced in a similar fashion by Cudworth, Leibniz, and Malebranche.

Immaterial Ideas

Each of the above three doctrines assumes the existence of some immaterial component, whether it be God or the soul. Thus, is it no surprise that immaterial ideas are a crucial element of modern European Platonism. Here the greatest example is found in Leibniz, who on occasion rejects material substance as logically impossible. Further, he holds that "the essences of things and the truth of the first principles are immutable" ([1710] 1985, 242). These truths, for Leibniz, are not only free from human contingency but also free from divine contingency. God himself cannot change the truths of morality and justice. They are eternal and transcendent. This is consistent with his broader theory of immaterial monads that resist physical characterization. These principles are discovered without reference to the senses or the material world, but are rather found "written on the heart" (Leibniz [1706] 1988, 69).

That Rousseau shared in both the doctrines of Plato and his modern European advocates is easy enough to sketch. I will only outline the doctrines here in this Preface, saving their elaboration and arguments for subsequent chapters. On the metaphysical dimension of Platonism, Rousseau clearly believed in the existence of immaterial substance. For him, the soul was just one example (e.g., [1763] 2001, 28/*OC*, IV:936). Likewise, there is an idea of justice that exists independently of all human convention (*SC*, 66/*OC*, III:378). Ontologically, the idea of justice itself is universal (*SC*, 66/*OC*, III:378) and eternal (*Emile*, 259/*OC*, IV:556). Epistemologically, such ideas cannot be known directly through the senses. Rather, the senses function to obscure moral knowledge of the first principles, such as justice and goodness (*Emile*, 292/ *OC*, IV:603; *Reveries*, 26/*OC*, I:1022). Instead of turning outward, Rousseau

6. See also the *Laws*, 903c.

has us look to the "inner sense" of the Savoyard Vicar, resembling Plato's turn away from the five senses to unshakable truths that can be known independently by the mind. These truths are written on the heart as conscience (*FD*, 28/*OC*, III:30). Finally, Rousseau is concerned that these ideas play a role in politics. For Rousseau, the purpose of the law is nothing other than "bring [ing] justice back to its object" (*SC*, 66/*OC*, III:378). Thus, the immaterial idea of justice has everything to do with politics. Similar affinities can be found with the modern European Platonists. Rousseau was adamant in his faith in God, free will, the immortality of the soul, and, again, the existence of ideas independent of human manipulation.

It is important to address here that I will *not* be making the case in this book that Rousseau is an *institutional* Platonist.[7] This is for several reasons. First, it is difficult to argue that the institutional views of *any two thinkers*, especially from vastly different eras, can be shared on questions of institutional and legal detail. It is the nature of these concerns that substantive proposals should differ in the same way that the manner in which two people do anything involving detail differs. Consider, for example, how two different individuals from the same neighborhood might drive to work at the same office. One might take the highway; the other, the back roads. One might drink coffee and eat a doughnut in the car, while the other might eat before getting behind the wheel. One might drive at the speed limit; the other might be less concerned with such a restriction. One might listen to a shock jock; the other might listen to the news. One might turn on the air conditioning; the other might open the windows. One might actively cut off merging cars; the other might be especially aware of the presence and needs of other motorists. The point is this: once we get into questions of detail, there will always be differences to uncover. Such differences absolutely exist between Plato and Rousseau.

Second, I am *not* making the case that Rousseau is an institutional Platonist because Rousseau himself, on occasion, pointed to these differences. One example is in his marginal notes to his personal copy of Plato's *Laws*, where the Athenian Stranger recommends that the children of master/slave couplings should either belong to the slave's owner or be shipped off to another land altogether (*Laws*, 930d). Rousseau expresses his disagreement simply and unambiguously by writing "*mal*" in the margins. Third, there are obvious and substantial disagreements between Rousseau and Plato that cannot help but

7. Although I do not make this case, a strong argument for this position has been outlined in Silverthorne (1973), based largely on Rousseau's interest in Plato's *Laws*.

be noticed. One such example is in Plato's tolerance of the institution of slavery and Rousseau's absolute abhorrence of it. There is no respect in which their views on this matter can be reconciled at the level of institutional Platonism. Likewise, for all of Rousseau's abilities to break free of convention, he did not join Plato in his belief that women were fit to rule.

Finally, another reason that Rousseau and Plato must necessarily differ on the institutional dimension is ironically explained by something that they share: *ontological* Platonism. As long as both thinkers remain committed to the belief that the highest principles of politics are abstract and indeterminate, their application of these principles (even if identical) will vary according to circumstance. And, to be sure, Plato and Rousseau lived in vastly different circumstances. Returning to the chess analogy, it is as if Rousseau and Plato were sitting down to finish matches begun by two separate individuals. Each game has taken its own idiosyncratic twists and turns, leaving both Plato and Rousseau considerably different boards. Thus, their strategies would necessarily have to deviate, even as their ultimate goals remain the same. One may need to sacrifice a rook, another a couple of pawns—but in both cases they are striving to corner their opponent's king. Likewise with politics. Each exists in a different time, with radically different circumstances. When Rousseau writes his constitutional proposal for Poland, for example, he must necessarily take into consideration the proximity of Prussia on one side and Russia on the other, but when Plato's Athenian Stranger draws up the laws of Magnesia, there is no such threat. These circumstances must necessarily force changes in the details. This, however, does not suggest differences at the highest levels of abstraction, where Plato and Rousseau's similarities become most sympathetic to one another.

Of course, to identify Rousseau's Platonic affiliations is one thing—to know why this is important is yet another. In beginning to answer this question, it is useful to focus on the most important elements of Platonism for his purposes. Here we see a combination of the metaphysical, ontological, and political dimensions: *the commitment to transcendent ideas as the ultimate authority for moral and political arguments.* And we can now contrast Platonic transcendentalism with Hobbesian positivism. Are there eternal, transcendent norms relevant to the critique and construction of political communities? On this question, Plato argues that there are such norms; Hobbes posits that there are not. Plato's theory of the ideas is perhaps the most elaborate affirmative answer to the question ever devised. For him, there are independently existing ideas that inform our knowledge of everything, including and especially politics. Hobbes's materialist positivism, on the other hand, is perhaps the most adamantly negative response. All political institutions or ideas are dependent upon agreement and sovereign will, and nothing more.

Whether one sides with Plato or Hobbes on this question determines a great deal about the content of a political theory. Platonists will have specific or at least circumscribed options with respect to the articulation of its ideas. They would not, for example, permit a state in which physical pleasure is the ultimate end. Nor would they promote any political society that systematically seeks to celebrate and promote its least intelligent and least virtuous members. A Hobbesian or positivist account, on the other hand, could be interpreted as permitting anything on which human agreement is possible. If a community can agree to it, it is permissible. Further, Hobbes's system of a sovereign Leviathan means that once the initial agreement is reached, all matters are to be decided by that office. Defining justice by convention opens a world of possibilities, with all its implications. Norms may issue either from the agreement of many or the will of one, but in both cases their content is empty until filled by the will.

The consequences following from the choice between Plato and Hobbes are enormous. The great danger in Hobbesian positivism is its very lack of content. This is true in spite of Hobbes's humane intentions. Having witnessed the horrors of war, he was highly keen to devise a method to end violence and by which peace could be more reliable. Indeed, the establishment and preservation of peace is his first law of nature. The problem for his theory, however, is that without any stable, noncontingent substance to guide the formation of his institutions and policies, anything can happen. With a government in good hands, this could be a good thing. With a government in bad hands, this is potentially devastating. As Gustav Radbruch concluded at the fall of the Third Reich, "This view of the nature of a law and its validity [Hobbesian positivism] . . . has rendered the jurist as well as the people defenseless against laws, however arbitrary, cruel, or criminal they may be" ([1945] 1973, 327). This question remains equally resonant today. Hobbesian doctrines—by virtue of rejecting Platonic premises listed above—leave many at a loss to condemn recent atrocities in Sudan. On this interpretation of the Hobbesian worldview, there is nothing transcendently unjust in slaughtering innocent thousands and displacing millions of others from their homes, even if it is sad and painful. That is because there is nothing transcendent at all. At a moral level, it comes down to the physical appetites and aversions of those witnessing or considering such events. For those who are able to push genocide out of their minds, it is of little consequence one way or another. At a political level, such matters are merely a question of the content of preexisting contracts and power relations. Was there an agreement not to kill others based on their race? Further, who has the power? If one is being pursued and killed by those of a greater recognized political power, is there any right to refuse the exercise of those powers?

Those who find positivism inadequate to the high charge of moral judgment can turn instead to Platonism, as Rousseau did. Platonic transcendent norms provide an alternative and more intuitive form of judgment. They do not appeal to the standards of an existing government or society in forming our judgments. Nor do they appeal to personal taste. Rather, they appeal to ontologically independent norms that apply to all similarly situated rational creatures. And with these norms in tow, Rousseau could find fault with flatterers, those influenced by opinion, those obsessed with luxury, those consumed by their own vanity, those driven by power, and those willfully ignorant of the needs of their fellow citizens. This is not to deny the inevitable epistemic and ontological issues raised by Platonism. What is the content of Platonic ideas? And how can one be sure of knowing them? Those questions may still be raised. Platonism does, however, provide a vibrant alternative to a system with known and obvious flaws.

Thus, it is a matter of great importance whether Rousseau tends to side more with Hobbes or Plato on these questions.[8] If scholars such as Leo Strauss are correct in asserting that Rousseau's affinities in this regard are more modern than ancient, one might reasonably charge him with all the critiques that have accompanied the works of Thomas Hobbes and the philosophes themselves. If they are incorrect, however, and Rousseau is instead a Platonist, this reveals an entirely different thinker—one with deep metaphysical commitments. That Rousseau was aware of the importance of metaphysics in this

8. To be sure, many argue that there is a considerable middle ground between Hobbes and Plato on this particular question—specifically, that it is possible to reject Platonic metaphysics while retaining eternal or transcendent norms. Such arguments can be found in the works of John Rawls and Jürgen Habermas, for example. Habermas suggests that moral and political norms can be "universal" without necessarily being transcendent. The difficulty with this approach, even as its ambitions are admirable in removing metaphysical ambiguities from political theory, is that its norms end up having to become either contingent or Platonic in the strong sense. If we take him at his word that his norms are purely material, then we must assume that they are capable of changing—that whatever people agree to be "just" will change according to time and circumstance. This heads down the slippery slope of relativism. On the other hand, one might ask Habermas what values guide the ideal speech situation, for example. If one interprets the values of liberty and equality as important, regardless of cultural circumstances, then he has asserted principles with value that preexist human artifice, in which case they are essentially Platonic. See Williams (1999) for a full argument to this effect. Similar arguments analyzing Rawls can be found in Seung (1993, chaps. 1–3). The point here is that a middle ground between Plato and Hobbes is difficult to sustain.

regard is easy enough to discover. This is precisely why he was so concerned with the materialist metaphysics of the philosophes. On his own account, belief in the wrong metaphysical doctrines, materialist ones, would lead to succumbing to the passions, "fanaticism," "shameless libertinage," "youth without discipline," "kings without law," and "no social bond of any kind other than strength" (*Dialogues*, 241–42/*OC*, I:970–71). For all his protestations to the contrary,[9] Rousseau was deeply concerned with metaphysics and their moral and political effects. It is this Rousseau that I hope to reveal throughout this book.

Why write this book now? Why should our attention be drawn to a debate that took place more than two centuries years ago? It is because, in spite of Rousseau's best efforts, history has repeated itself. We live in an age where materialism has prospered. This has had undeniable benefits in the realms of science and technology. Unfettered by the constraints of immaterial teleology, it has brought distant families together for the holidays, large libraries of information to offices in Dubuque, Iowa, and the Metropolitan Opera to living rooms in Stevens Point, Wisconsin. At the same time, however, we live in an age where university students regularly cheat on assignments without so much as a flicker of conscience, athletes take harmful and illegal drugs to gain an unfair competitive advantage against their foes, corporations in America have been allowed to plunder the life savings of thousands, and genocide has gone ignored in Africa and elsewhere. In examining Rousseau's understanding of his era, we might very well find some commonalities with our own. As Alexander Nehamas has recently reminded us, "The sophists are still alive and well" (2004, 14). To this extent, we should perhaps commence the awesome task of diagnosing our ills and eventually treating them. Philosophy can offer no greater challenge to civic life. And in this respect Rousseau remains among the greatest of philosophers.

---

9. On each occasion that Rousseau appears dismissive of metaphysics, one will note that he is speaking specifically of the materialist metaphysics of the philosophes. See, for example, the *Reveries*, 25/*OC*, I:1022, and the *Emile*, 274/*OC*, IV:576.

ACKNOWLEDGMENTS

Nearly every scholar of modern political philosophy acknowledges the importance of Jean-Jacques Rousseau, yet there is little consensus on the substance
of his contributions. There are many reasons for this, including the wide range
of Rousseau's works, his reveling in paradox, and the diverse contexts in which
he has been interpreted. One of the great things about great thinkers is that
they attract these divergent approaches from which we can all learn and glean
some truth. This has certainly been the case in my study of Rousseau's Platonism. Although there are many interpretations with which I disagree, I have
profited enormously from engaging with all of them. In this respect, I have
been particularly stimulated by grappling with the works of Roger D. Masters
and Arthur Melzer, which have challenged me on almost every page to
sharpen my arguments in order to meet their significant claims.

Of course, I have not been completely alone in my interpretation that
Rousseau is a Platonist. The book from which I have drawn my greatest inspiration is Charles Hendel's *Jean-Jacques Rousseau: Moralist.* Hendel was the first
to assemble a substantial case that Rousseau was a Platonist, and his work
continues to be indispensable. Because Hendel has already argued for a reading of Rousseau as a Platonist, the burden is on me to explain why another
one, some seventy years later, is required. Happily, an answer is found in the
preface to Hendel's work. He did not see his book as a systematic argument
for Rousseau's Platonism so much as a broad (and deep) survey of Rousseau's
works with one eye fixed on the Plato connection. His ambition to write a
substantial argument for the connection (to be entitled *Rousseau the Platonist*)
was never fulfilled. This book is meant to make this connection explicit and
offer the best case possible for interpreting Rousseau through a Platonic lens,
while at the same time placing him in a broader historical and philosophical

context. Platonic ideas provide a leitmotiv by which we can understand the origins of Rousseau's program and his legacy to this day. I am not certain that Hendel would agree with this approach, but I would like to think that he would be sympathetic to my goals.

Over the course of writing this book, I have incurred many debts. At Penn State University Press, I would like to thank Sandy Thatcher for his confidence in my Platonic reading of Rousseau, as well as Joe Parsons and Laura Reed-Morrisson for their careful editing. I have greatly profited from discussing the book's themes with Michael McLendon, Jon Bloch, Rixey Ruffin, Jonathan Marks, Larry Cooper, Richard Boyd, Matthew Simpson, Sharon Vaughan, A. P. Martinich, David Sorkin, and Andrew Laird. Michael, Jonathan, and Larry read every chapter with great care and helped to sharpen the book's arguments in more ways than I can recount here. I have profited in other respects from Blake Hestir, Ian Offord, Alek Toumei, Richard Galvin, and Charles Lockhart. In yet other ways, I have benefited from the many good friends and colleagues who have tolerated and even encouraged my sometimes single-minded pursuit of making sense of Rousseau. These include Sean Phillips, Mark Hawley, Michael and Carey Cairo, Michael Nelson, David and Nikki Arnold, James and Toni Sage, Donald Fadner, Ed Miller, Jianwei Wang, Justus Paul, Lance Grahn, Karin Fry, Dôna Warren, Corinne Dempsey, David Chan, Scott Wallace, Frank Thames, Doug Forbes, Tracy Hofer, Anna Law, Tim and Julie Johnson, Ken Abrams, and Greg Summers. In a similar spirit, I have likewise benefited from family, including Richard and Julianne Williams, Carol Fletcher, Larry and Julia Weiser, and especially my wife, Jennifer Weiser, who has humored my references to Rousseau on almost every social occasion of the past five years.

I would like to make special mention of two mentors. I discussed the ideas that formed the kernel of this book with Patrick Riley several years ago without even thinking of a book. It was he who suggested that I had something more substantial than a conference paper and encouraged me to pursue this project to its conclusion. I subsequently had the opportunity to discuss with him virtually all of its arguments in detail and have profited from these conversations at Husnus more than this book can convey. Finally, I need to express the gratitude I owe my dissertation supervisor, T. K. Seung. Although this book is not my dissertation, I learned everything I needed to know to write this book from working with him. Professor Seung was a student at Yale during the final years of Charles Hendel's tenure there, and, though he did not study Rousseau or Plato with Hendel, I would like to think that somehow the spirit of this connection was conveyed and passed on. At any rate, not only did Seung read all of this book and offer countless suggestions for its improvement, but he also served as its inspiration. I count myself very fortunate to have worked with him, and it is in his honor that I dedicate this book.

Significant parts of Chapters 4 and 6 have been previously published as "Justice and the General Will: Affirming Rousseau's Ancient Orientation," *Journal of the History of Ideas* 66, no. 3 (2005): 383–411, and "Modern Theorist of Tyranny? Lessons from Rousseau's System of Checks and Balances," *Polity* 37, no. 4 (2005): 443–65. I thank them, respectively, for their permission to use some of those materials in this work. Finally, I must acknowledge my debt to the Institute for Research in the Humanities at the University of Wisconsin–Madison. It gave me a home for a full year to complete this project, and it goes without saying that I could not have completed the book without the Institute's generous support.

ONE

THE CONTEXT, PART I:
METAPHYSICS AND POLITICS IN HOBBES AND LOCKE

One of the oldest maxims of competition and warfare is to respect thine enemy, and Jean-Jacques Rousseau had perhaps no enemy greater than Thomas Hobbes. It is unsurprising then that Rousseau referred to him as "one of the finest geniuses that ever lived" ("State of War," 164/*OC,* III:611). Although Hobbes was born more than a century before Rousseau and lived in a different land, his doctrines were the ones that most aroused, agitated, and ultimately engaged Rousseau. Virtually his entire career would—in one respect or another—be dedicated to correcting, amending, or refuting the teachings of Hobbes. The most obvious of these is Rousseau's corrections of Hobbes's state of nature, but this is only the tip of the iceberg. Hobbes's state of nature both assumes and sets the stage for the doctrines that would most deeply concern and offend the *citoyen de Génève:* his metaphysics and politics. Hobbes's materialism and positivism were not his own inventions. Rather, they were present millennia earlier among the pre-Socratics and Sophists, such as Democritus, Protagoras, Gorgias, and Thrasymachus. These ideas had, however, remained relatively latent for a considerable period of time. The ascendancy of Christianity and its subsequent control over the European universities had largely kept the doctrines from gaining a foothold in the minds of educated people everywhere.

All this changed with the publication of the works of Thomas Hobbes. "Man is nothing but matter in motion": this sloganistic version of Hobbes's metaphysics is still repeated in virtually every undergraduate modern philosophy course.[1] It is not, however, a phrase that should ever lose force by virtue

---

1. The slogan sums up Hobbes's intentions as described in his own introduction to *Leviathan:* "For what is the *heart,* but a *spring;* and the *nerves,* but so many *strings;* and the *joints,* but so many *wheels,* giving motion to the whole body, such as what was intended by the artificer?"

of its continuous repetition. Rather, its repetition is a direct consequence of its enduring impact on those who practiced philosophy in Hobbes's enormous wake. His materialism, a direct and conscious affront to the metaphysics taught and practiced in the schools of his day (*Leviathan,* 1.5),[2] would play no small part in modernity's scientific discoveries and the separation of the church from philosophic and naturalistic inquiry.[3] This revolutionary system constituted, in the words of Huntington Cairns, nothing less than "a transformation of the metaphysical and scientific bases of Western thought" (1949, 248).

Hobbes's materialism had consequences beyond that of opening up the doors to Newton. Indeed, it had profound effects in political philosophy as well. Perhaps nowhere was this more true than in his own political thought. If the only substance of the universe is matter—and we nevertheless must by necessity learn to live together for mutual peace and prosperity—how do we establish communal society? On what principles, if not abstract metaphysics, can we ground the legitimacy of the state? For the Scholastics and ancients, against whom Hobbes sets himself, the answers range from Plato's forms to Augustine's God. If there are no preexisting standards of right and wrong, no God upon whom one can rely for cosmic justice, and the only reliable fact of the world one can assume is the baseness of human nature, where does one turn? For the materialistic Hobbes, the answer is contract. Because matter is the only substance, one must agree by convention to obey the commands of a sovereign. One consequence of this politics by agreement, according to Hobbes, is the necessity of complete obedience. One must under all circumstances do whatever the sovereign asks, regardless of content.[4]

Although Hobbes's admirers have ranged from covertly sympathetic Enlightenment thinkers to aspiring tyrants of the twentieth century, the overt reaction of most early modern philosophers was that of utter horror. Blaise Pascal, in the *Pensées,* remarked of the Hobbesian metaphysics, "Anyone who considers himself in this [materialistic] way will be terrified at himself, and, seeing his mass, as given to him by nature, supporting him between these two abysses of infinity and nothingness, will tremble" ([1660] 1966, 61). Leibniz, who protested against materialism generally, found Hobbes and Spinoza to be co-conspirators against freedom. He wrote in the *Theodicy,* "I think one must not reproach any but the adherents of Hobbes and Spinoza with destroying

---

2. References are to chapter and paragraph number.
3. This is likely true even if it were contrary to Hobbes's own intentions.
4. This has the notable exception of suicide.

freedom. . . . Hobbes made everything material and subject to mathematical laws alone" ([1710] 1985, §371).

Concern about the Hobbesian philosophy was not limited to metaphysical matters. Hobbes's system of complete obedience to a Leviathan yielded two enormously important replies in the political systems of John Locke and Jean-Jacques Rousseau. For Locke, how could one make the assumption that human nature was nothing but nasty selfishness and still want to elevate one such person to a position of unrivaled power? For Rousseau, Hobbes's political doctrine was nothing short of a reinvention of the old Thrasymachian mantra: might equals right.[5] Both Locke and Rousseau ultimately present significant and distinct challenges to the Hobbesian system. This in itself is not a particularly ambitious thesis; many (but by no means all) commentators have understood Locke and Rousseau to do precisely this. I will go on, however, to argue that, to oppose themselves adequately to Hobbes, they must either systematically or implicitly offer alternative and original ontologies to support their political challenges. That is, the metaphysics of modern political philosophy underwent two significant changes, in part, to meet the sizable challenge of Hobbes. This chapter explores the philosophy of Hobbes and Locke's response. Chapter 4 will outline Rousseau's. In examining the philosophy of Hobbes and Locke, we shall find just how difficult it is to construct a coherent and desirable philosophy on the twin modern pillars of empiricism and materialism. Although both thinkers are eager to avoid the inevitable epistemic and ontological issues associated with ancient philosophy, they ultimately appear to beg these very same questions themselves.

1. Thomas Hobbes

When he writes, "that which is not body is no part of the universe" (*Leviathan*, 46.15), Hobbes leaves little room to question his break from the ancient and medieval philosophies in which he was schooled. There are two possible levels at which one could conceivably understand this materialism to influence his politics. The first is at the level of human nature. The second is at the level of contract.

---

5. The obviously disturbing consequences stemming from this doctrine associated with Hobbes's philosophy are in many senses contrary to Hobbes's own intentions. Headley Bull has described his "deeply pacific . . . approach . . . at least in the values from which it sprang" (1983, 729).

I.I. METAPHYSICS AND MORAL PSYCHOLOGY

The traditional view of Hobbes is that his materialistic modern science mandated his view of the rapaciousness of human nature. That is, if the only substance of the universe must necessarily be matter, it is not surprising that we should find the selfish pleasure seekers Hobbes describes in his characterizations of human nature. The argument follows a fairly well-defined logic. All substance is material. If everything is material, then so must be human beings. As D. D. Raphael has summarized, for Hobbes "*life* is simply a form of *internal* motion in matter" (1977, 22). If human beings are material, their minds must also be material. This leads Hobbes to a thoroughgoing empiricism. Thus, preceding Locke by several years, he is the first to declare that "the original of [all perception] is that which we call SENSE" (*Leviathan,* 1.2). The perception of objects can be accounted for strictly in terms of the natural sciences. Unlike Descartes, for example, there is no reference to an immaterial God or other suprasensible objects. Instead, we find a carefully constructed system of motions, pressures, and counter-pressures against the sensory organs, generating our perceptions: "So that sense in all cases is nothing else but original fancy, caused (as I have said) by the pressure, that is, by the motion of external things upon the eyes, ears, and other organs, thereunto ordained" (*Leviathan,* 1.4). Subsequent thoughts, such as memory or imagination, are nothing other than decaying sensation.

Sensation, however, is largely a passive activity. Human beings are also engaged in active ones. Hobbes describes these in similarly mechanistic terms. All activity begins with desire, which is for him a form of motion. The desire to eat, for example, begins with physical pangs of hunger, relayed from the stomach to the brain. The brain then employs the senses and body to search for objects that will cease the pain. On finding food, the body consumes it and the pain is relieved—a purely mechanistic process.

The first psychological element in the process, for Hobbes, is that of desire. Desire, however, must be understood in conjunction with aversion as the two primary forces behind human behavior. He writes, "This endeavor, when it is toward something which causes it, is called APPETITE or DESIRE, the latter being the general name, and the other oftentimes restrained to signify the desire of food, namely *hunger* and *thirst.* And when the endeavor is fromward something, it is generally called AVERSION" (*Leviathan,* 1.2). With the introduction and characterization of these two motives Hobbes apparently means to constitute the mechanization of motives previously thought of as "irreducible" and "nonmaterialistic" (Martinich 2002, 41).

Desires and aversions, in turn, constitute the essence of human motivations in the state of nature. We either desire food, possessions, power, and glory or seek to avoid pain and death—or worst of all, a painful death. These two motives then take Hobbes to his famous state of nature, synonymous with a state of war, where one finds "the life of man, solitary, poor, nasty, brutish, and short" (*Leviathan*, 13.9). We thus have an evidently clean path from Hobbes's materialistic account of man to his state of nature.

The question for twentieth-century Hobbes scholars, however, was whether this materialism was *necessary* to complete his political program. Leo Strauss makes a persuasive case that, whereas Hobbes was indeed convinced of the truth of his materialism, it was not a necessary component of his moral psychology. This is the case for at least two reasons. First, he argues that although Hobbes seems careful to link his political psychology with his metaphysics in the *Leviathan*, his psychology was in place long before he discovered, much less fully formulated, his metaphysics. His view of human nature is present in his 1629 translation of and introduction to Thucydides' *Peloponnesian War*. He does not "discover" Euclid until 1630 (Martinich 1999, 84–86) and does not take a serious interest in science until some time after this (Strauss [1936] 1952, 29).

Second, it is obvious that no geometry, natural science, or materialism is necessary to develop Hobbes's moral psychology. After all, sheep are made of the same materials as are wolves or, for that matter, human beings. Nevertheless, the psychological predisposition of each creature is significantly different. One therefore need not attribute Hobbesian selfishness and vanity to material. In fact, as Bertram Jessup argued, there is no way to arrive at this assumption deductively from the precepts of materialism (1948, 212). Rather, according to Strauss, Hobbes constructs his view of human nature from history and "first-hand experience of human life" ([1936] 1952, 29). It is in this respect that the influence of Thucydides is most profound on Hobbes. Hobbes finds in Thucydides an unrivaled proper emphasis on the passions—something that would become a central assumption in his own works. The passions are, in fact, one of his defining features of humanity: "men are continually in competition for honour and dignity, which these creatures [bees and ants] are not; and consequently amongst men there ariseth on that ground that envy and hatred and finally war; but amongst these [insects] not so" (*Leviathan*, 17.7). Strauss thus persuasively argues that, although Hobbes was later interested in connecting his materialism with his moral psychology, the two components of his system developed entirely independently ([1936] 1952, 112).

I.2. METAPHYSICS, MORAL PHILOSOPHY, AND THE SOCIAL CONTRACT

Strauss, however, exaggerates when he suggests that Hobbes's metaphysics has *nothing* to do with his politics ([1936] 1952, 6). He is correct to separate Hobbes's materialism from his moral *psychology,* but one should question whether it is advisable to exclude considerations of Hobbes's materialism from his moral *philosophy.* Moral psychology and moral philosophy are two entirely separate matters. If one does not believe in suprasensible objects, one can still identify certain patterns of human behavior. If one does not believe in suprasensible objects of some kind, however, it is difficult to establish transcendent moral principles. John Wild correctly asserts, "Hobbes, being a materialist, cannot accept any such [moral] realistic conception, for materialism always leads to subjectivism. . . . This conclusion, I think can hardly be seriously questioned" (1953, 127). Although there is clear evidence that Hobbes held his view of human nature before he had recorded a commitment to materialism, it is not so clear that he developed his theories of contract and justice before doing so. And in this respect, one can find a clear link between his metaphysics and his politics.

Hobbes's materialism has a profound and inextricable link to his ethics and politics. In ethics, he clearly intends to draw a connection between his metaphysics and his understanding of the good. Chapter 6 of *Leviathan* is intended to make this conclusion obvious. Hobbes here describes "good" and "evil" as speech determined by "passions," which are in turn created by "motions," and because people are subject to different motions they have different emotions and, finally, distinct conceptions of good and evil: "But whatsoever is the object of any man's appetite and desire, that is it which he for his part calleth *good:* and the object of his hate and aversion, *evil.*"[6] This is the very definition of a relativistic ethics. Each person has his or her own set of ethical norms, formed independently of any incorporeal idea (which for Hobbes is nonsense) or similar notion. We simply call that which we desire "good," regardless of its consequences for either ourselves or others. Hobbes's relativism goes hand in hand with his materialism.

His politics are similarly affected by his materialism. His metaphysics dictates, for example, that there can be no such thing as justice prior to the establishment of a Leviathan (*Leviathan,* 13.13). Justice can exist only once law is established and is for Hobbes, in fact, mere compliance with the law: "A Just Action is that which is not against the Law" ([1681] 1971, 72). Hobbes's doc-

---

6. *Leviathan,* 6.7. Plato associates this approach to ethics with the Sophists (*Republic,* 493bc).

trine is in this respect the model of contemporary legal positivism, where no moral standards are acknowledged relevant to the task of statutory construction or interpretation. Hence, Hobbes is the modern antithesis of Plato. Whereas Plato's criterion for legislative authority in the *Republic* is knowledge of the transcendent ideas, for Hobbes, "It is not Wisdom, but Authority that makes a Law" ([1681] 1971, 55).

If there is no abstract transcendent idea of justice preceding the existence of society, society must turn elsewhere for its foundation. T. K. Seung suggests that there are two fundamental options (1992, 144). First, there is the imposition of norms by force. This is apparently the model accepted by Machiavelli in *The Prince*. His advice on how to execute proper conquering suggests a politics of power, force, and conquest. The second option (in the absence of transcendent norms) Seung identifies as agreement. This is Hobbes's method. As Seung says, it is his only choice because, by virtue of his declaration of natural equality, he rules out the Machiavellian option. As a consequence, Hobbes carefully constructs a society built on agreement. This is, of course, the foundation of his social contract—the agreement each citizen suffering in the state of nature makes to surrender his right to everything on the condition that others do the same: "The mutual transferring of right is that which men call CONTRACT" (*Leviathan*, 14.9).

Hobbes's laws of nature thus appear to be rules of prudence rather than those dictated by the order of things. In his own words, each law of nature is "a precept or general rule, found out by reason, by which a man is forbidden to do that which is destructive of his life, or taketh away the means of preserving the same, and to omit that by which he thinketh it may be best preserved" (*Leviathan*, 14.3). The definition here implies a degree of contingency not found in the natural law theory of St. Thomas Aquinas, for example, where the first principles are immutable and generated by God. That which may preserve one's life seems to vary according to time and circumstance.

1.3. ADVANTAGES OF THE HOBBESIAN POLITICAL ONTOLOGY

This ability to meet the exigencies of time and circumstances, according to Charles Hendel, is one of the prime motivations behind Hobbes's politics.

> Hobbes had railed against the Platonists of his day because they thought of laws as if they were fixed and unalterable principles in the heavens, and above titular "sovereigns" as well as ordinary men. He repudiated their ideas of "natural laws" and "rights" and "funda-

mental laws." Such laws were a feudal straight-lacing of the body-politic; they prevented its "representative" from meeting the exigencies of public affairs in a changing, nationalistic world with intelligence and resolution; they were a fatal restriction on the new power of sovereignty which was to save the day. (Hendel 1934, 1:169)

Although it is clear that Hobbes had some admiration for Plato himself—he called him "the best philosopher of the Greeks" (*Leviathan,* 46.10)—it is obvious that he was unimpressed with contemporary Platonism. Platonism, at least as conceived in the position attributed above to Hobbes, involved an unwavering commitment to a fairly rigid set of specific principles, even sometimes in the face of exceptions demanded by very real, if practical, circumstances. A metaphysics working against politics appeared to be, for Hobbes, no metaphysics at all. And, to the extent that one can envision obvious exceptions to many apparent moral rules (e.g., a rule against lying that makes one turn over hidden enemies of the Nazis), it seems that Hobbes has offered by virtue of his materialism a genuine advance in political ontology. Without the "feudal straight-lacing" of preexisting moral rules, the sovereign is free to meet exigencies with all the imaginable resources of the state.

In this sense, if we are to believe Hendel, one might want to take Strauss's original argument one step further than Strauss himself did. One could say not only that Hobbes's understanding of moral psychology and his politics precede his metaphysics, but also that these things might very well have been the forces that *determined* his metaphysics. Without the constraints of a rigid moral code as mandated by a metaphysical superstructure, sovereigns are free to meet all the challenges that various cultures and times impose on their peculiar governments.

1.4. INCOHERENCES IN HOBBES'S METAPHYSICS AND POLITICS

Although Hobbes presents a system that is at once friendly to natural science and at the same time amenable to the exigencies of the real political world, it is not clear that he is able to pull it off without some difficulties. The most obvious respect in which one finds problems of consistency in Hobbes's political system is in the relative priority and ontological status of his natural laws. On the one hand, he writes that justice (one of the natural laws) does not exist prior to the establishment of civil society, but on the other he writes elsewhere that the laws of nature are "immutable and eternal" (*Leviathan,* 15.38). This is not the only occasion on which Hobbes makes such a claim. Citing the authority of scripture, in *The Elements of Law,* he tells us that "the law of nature is unalterable."[7]

Such claims for the transcendence of law are not out of place in Plato, Augustine, or Aquinas, but it is surprising to find them in Hobbes. His materialism seems to preclude them. This is because the material world is contingent and hence not subject to immutable or eternal principles. As Heraclitus said of the natural world, "It is not possible to step twice into the same river." Everything is in flux. Rocks become sand, caterpillars become butterflies, children become adults, ponds become lakes, ice becomes water, water becomes vapor. All material changes. It is the nature of extended substance. The problem for Hobbes is that, because everything is material, so must be the laws of nature. They therefore are incapable of being immutable or eternal. This is precisely why both Plato and Rousseau ultimately turn away from the material realm to ground their ethics and politics. They both acknowledge the existence of material objects, as does Hobbes. But, unlike Hobbes, they consciously perceive the material realm in a Heraclitean fashion. For Plato, "concrete instances" of objects, such as clothes, animals, or specific human beings, are "never free from variation"—the visible is "never . . . the same" (*Phaedo,* 78d–79a). For Rousseau, "Everything is in continual flux on earth. Nothing on it retains a constant and static form" (*Reveries,* 46/*OC,* I:1046). In the absence of any constancy in the material world, both Plato and Rousseau turned to the immaterial one—a realm where ideas could remain constant and eternal.

It is for this reason that many interpret Hobbes's laws of nature not as divine commands or transcendent moral imperatives, but rather as rules of prudence. It is because his materialism appears to rule out this very possibility. It also comes from his very derivation of the laws of nature. Because he defines the laws as the best means for preserving one's life (*Leviathan,* 14.3), and the preservation of one's life is a matter of prudence, the laws of nature themselves must be rules of prudence.[8] The problem with rules of prudence, however, is that they cannot be "immutable" or "eternal." What is prudent for one person might not be for another. While it may well serve the purpose of promoting the survival of a corporate employee to avoid abusive language, it was probably not necessary for Alexander the Great. For that matter, it hardly

---

7. Hobbes ([1640] 1994, 18.4). References are to chapter and paragraph number.

8. As Patrick Riley notes, in Hobbes "any Platonic notion of natural justice is made impossible" (1982, 28). A more extensive argument that Hobbes's laws of nature are in fact rules of prudence can be found in F. W. N. Watkins's *Hobbes's System of Ideas: A Study in the Significance of Philosophical Theories* (1973, 82–99) and Steven Darwall's *The British Moralists and the Internal "Ought"* (1995, 79).

seems necessary for a powerful figure such as Alexander to respect the Hobbesian notion of justice. Why obey a contract if that contract fails to serve one's interest? This question is regularly asked by professional athletes who sign relatively cheap contracts, only to find themselves soon to be underpaid by the subsequent standards of the market. Would it not be prudent to escape such a contract, or even violate it, if the opportunity were available? As Machiavelli might have asked, "What would Cesare Borgia do?" Undoubtedly, prudence would never hold one down to "immutable" or "eternal" laws of conduct. Such is the nature of prudence. As its ultimate concerns are empirical, its rules must be contingent. They cannot be otherwise. Thus, regardless of Hobbes's claims, his laws of nature cannot be eternal or immutable.

How Hobbes actually meant to reconcile these alternating claims of transcendence and contingency is unclear. This logical inconsistency would lead to practical difficulties in many instances. How does one know what is right when one has contracted for a killing? The law of justice (performance of contract) would suggest that the killing is right; the natural law of complaisance and Hobbes's recommendation that we follow the Golden Rule would suggest otherwise. As his system stands, there is no apparent reason to choose one interpretation over the other.

A second related difficulty in Hobbes is how he means to connect his natural laws with his positive ones. Although it is abundantly clear that Hobbes has laws of nature, and that they are important to him, it is less clear what relation they have to those laws that govern the day-to-day affairs of the citizens. On at least one occasion, Hobbes suggests that the natural law and civil law are identical: "The law of nature and the civil law contain each other and are of equal extent" (*Leviathan,* 26.8). This sentence appears at once unambiguous, bold, and shockingly contrary to the received interpretation of Hobbes qua positivist. It appears unambiguous, for the obvious reason that there is no other way to read it than that positive and natural law are identical. It is bold because it apparently goes beyond the naturalistic sentiments of even St. Thomas Aquinas, who was careful to distinguish natural law from human law. It is shockingly contrary to Hobbes's reputation as a positivist because it evidently explicitly rejects the positivist demand of separation of moral and legal questions.

Is Hobbes then actually an antipositivist—that is, a Platonist? Although there is clearly evidence here for that claim (Martinich 1992; Bobbio 1994; Murphy 1995), there remains the traditional evidence to the contrary. As we will see, both Locke and Rousseau read him as a positivist and had good reasons for doing so. First, as already revealed, Hobbes embraced—at least on occasion—a position resembling moral relativism. Second, his definition of justice is conventional. Third, although at times he claims an identical relation of the natural to the civil laws, his arguments at other times make this seem impossible. Consider his claim that civil law is nothing other than a command (*Leviathan*, 26.2). If the civil law is merely a command, and commands can be of any kind (Hobbes does not carefully restrict the commands issuable by the sovereign), it clearly seems possible that the civil laws could come into conflict with the natural laws. In this case, these two types of law are obviously not identical.

Speculating on why these difficulties persist in Hobbes is a tricky question. There are at least three possible answers. First, Hobbes could have simply been trying to mislead the reader by intentionally introducing contradictions into his writings. This answer, however, places Hobbes on the level of Descartes's "malignant demon," and this seems highly improbable, because no obvious ends can be achieved by such deception in a book like Hobbes's. Second, Hobbes was somewhat careless in his editing. This is certainly plausible. Third, Hobbes was torn between the "science" of positivism and the distinctive force granted by divine or natural law. This is perhaps the most plausible explanation. Hobbes was clearly in love with science: positivism—from Hobbes through Kelsen and beyond—makes the law most closely resemble science. It presents clear and empirically demonstrable ways to prove the validity of any given law. There is every reason to believe that Hobbes would be drawn to it the same way he was to Euclid and materialism. On the other hand, Hobbes's desire for law to have supernatural force might have inclined him to a more traditional natural law. It is therefore highly plausible that his writings alternatively reveal a bias toward one system or the other. This would explain how the irreconcilable positions both find their way into his work.

I.5. DISADVANTAGES OF THE HOBBESIAN POLITICAL ONTOLOGY

Regardless of what Hobbes may have ultimately intended to have preferred—positivism or some version of natural law theory—there is no disputing how history has read him: as the prototype of modern positivism. Strauss describes Hobbes as having "no cosmic support" for his doctrines ([1953] 1965, 175). This results in the boundless authority of the sovereign. Because justice (upholding of a contract) appears to be a matter of convention, and the Leviathan does not take part in the social contract, it is impossible for the sovereign to be unjust: "whatsoever he [the sovereign] doth, can be no injury to any of his Subjects nor ought he to be by any of them accused of injustice" (*Levia-*

than, 18.6). Gottfried Leibniz recorded his fear of the consequences stemming from Hobbes's conclusions: "Mr. Hobbes will say . . . that this person [the Leviathan] will have an absolute right over us after he conquers us, since one cannot complain of this conqueror for the reasons which we have just pointed out [the impunity of the Leviathan against charges of injustice]" (Leibniz [1702–3] 1988, 57). And it is in this respect that Hobbes has come to be associated with the varieties of European authoritarianism that emerged in his wake. If materialism implies positivism, then how could anything else follow? Traditional theories of natural law or Platonism, on the other hand, imply limits to the behavior of the ruler by having independent standards of justice by which the ruler's behavior can be judged and, if necessary, rebuked. Authoritarianism thrives on a metaphysics that places no restrictions on behavior. Regardless of what the ultimately correct interpretation of Hobbes was, this was clearly the dominant one throughout modern Europe, and it was precisely the fear of this "Hobbist" Hobbes that inspired Locke and Rousseau to spend considerable effort in constructing alternative ontologies to make room for a more friendly politics.

2. John Locke

Locke's political philosophy is often rightly seen as a direct response to Sir Robert Filmer's doctrines (Laslett [1960] 1988, 67). The evidence is obvious. The first of his *Two Treatises of Government* is, after all, a point-by-point refutation of Filmer's *Patriarcha.* It might be a slightly overzealous commitment to the Locke-Filmer relationship, however, that would lead one to dismiss the possibility that Locke was also concerned with Filmer's contemporary and fellow advocate of monarchy—Hobbes. Although Hobbes might not have been quite so prominent at the time as Filmer, he was certainly casting his own shadow over Locke's generation. As already mentioned, both Leibniz and Pascal deeply feared the consequences of Hobbesian materialism. There is likewise strong evidence to suggest that Locke was similarly concerned about Hobbism. According to Mark Goldie, "He was anxious not to be associated with a view which contemporaries attributed to Hobbes: that natural law is so ineffable and ineffectual that it must dissolve into positive law" (1997, xxii).

But as Hobbes lived in an age of scientific discovery, so did Locke. It is sometimes forgotten that he spent his early years as a physician. Further, he was good friends with one of the most esteemed scientists of his or any other age—Isaac Newton. So perhaps as a consequence, however repulsed he may have been by Hobbes's politics, he was attracted to Hobbes's empiricism—the assumption that all knowledge originates with the senses. Locke is often cited as the modern founder of the school of empiricism, and he certainly has good claim for being so: "This great source of most of the ideas we have, depending wholly on the senses, and derived by them to the understanding, I call SENSATION."[9] This position is perhaps most famously represented by his rejection of innate ideas—that we lack access to ideas independent of sensation.

Although empiricism certainly does not imply materialism, as one sees in the work of George Berkeley, it commonly leads one in that direction. At the very least, it makes some uncomfortable with the existence of immaterial entities, such as Platonic ideas. It is in this respect that we begin to see Hobbes's imprints in Locke's work. So, whereas Locke was obviously concerned about Hobbes's materialistic positivism and the politics he felt that followed, he was at the same time attempting to build a system that Hobbesians might appreciate. In some respects, Locke's efforts are obviously a failure, as seen in his essays on natural law. But his legacy is far more complex. At times, he appears to be operating with completely different assumptions in different works, a move facilitated by anonymous publishing. In particular, one finds in the *Second Treatise* a work that offers a viable alternative to Hobbesian politics in terms of its metaphysics, epistemology, and especially its politics. In fact, I will argue that Locke's concern with Hobbesian politics led him, in the *Second Treatise,* to offer not only an alternative system of politics but also an alternative to his own epistemology and metaphysics found in his other writings.[10]

2.I. LOCKEAN POLITICS

There is a great difference in method between Hobbes and Locke. Whereas Hobbes carefully connects the dots between his metaphysics and his politics

9. See Locke ([1690] 1959, II.i.3). All references to Locke's *Essay Concerning Human Understanding* are to book, chapter, and paragraph number. Locke's apparent qualification ("most of the ideas") is not meant to retract his strict empiricism. It is merely an indication that some ideas come from reflection, itself a mode of experience.

10. The most obvious place to turn in Locke's writings for an answer to the questions raised by the Hobbesian metaphysics is his *Essays on the Law of Nature.* Doing this, however, poses some problems. First, because Locke chose never to publish the *Essays,* one must be cautious in attributing the views within it to the broader Lockean system. Second, the work is a relatively immature one, predating his most significant intellectual achievements by more than twenty years. Third, there is sound evidence to suggest that there are certain issues on which Locke clearly changes his mind between the writing of his *Essays* and his more mature works, such as his rejecting hedonism in the former and embracing it in the latter (von Leyden 1954, 77). These reasons do not necessarily exclude, however, any appropriation of Locke's *Essays.*

in his *Leviathan,* Locke separates his works according to these very same categories. His two most significant works—*An Essay Concerning Human Understanding* and *Two Treatises of Government*—appear plausibly as if they could have been written by two different authors. This sense is buttressed by the fact that Locke published the *Two Treatises* anonymously. Because both works were published in 1690, however, it is not unfair for contemporary readers to desire to read them together and endeavor to systematize. I will begin with Locke's political doctrines as outlined in the *Second Treatise* and then work my way back to his *Essay* in an attempt to see whether his work can be conceived in part as a reaction to Hobbes.

Locke's politics represent an obvious alternative to the severe absolutism one finds in Hobbes's *Leviathan.* Whereas Hobbes's men are necessarily determined, Locke's citizens are free. Whereas Hobbes's government and sovereign are one and the same, Locke distinguishes his sovereign people from their delegates in the government. Whereas Hobbes's government can act with impunity, Locke places strict limits on the legitimate sphere of state activity. Whereas the Leviathan can commit no act of injustice, Locke's government is capable of and accountable for violations of the law of nature. Whereas Hobbes absolutely prohibits revolution, Locke cautiously endorses it as a politically viable alternative under extreme circumstances generated by a tyrannical government.

In light of the obvious contrasts between the two, it is surprising to discover that many argue, as Peter Laslett does, that Locke "did not reply to *Leviathan* because it was irrelevant to his purposes as a writer of political principle" ([1960] 1988, 83). If Locke's purposes include establishing the freedom of men, placing sovereignty in the people, establishing transcendent laws of nature, holding government accountable for its actions, and providing for the possibility of just revolution, it would seem that Hobbes is very relevant indeed, because in every case he holds the opposite view. Although his immediate political aims and animus against Filmer should not and cannot be discounted, the repeated contrast with Hobbes likewise cannot be ignored. This contrast is amplified by Locke's own sentiments. Tyrrell's letters to Locke in 1690, for example, reveal that Locke's *Essay* generated charges of Hobbism. These accusations were neither meant to be, nor were they received as, compliments. Rather, they were the source of "ill feeling all round" (von Leyden 1954, 13). Perhaps the most harmful charge of this kind was from Isaac Newton, who wrote, "I beg your pardon for my having hard thoughts of you for it, and for representing that you struck at the heart of morality in a principle you laid down in your book on ideas, and designed to pursue in another book, and that I took you for a Hobbist" (Newton, quoted in Cranston 1957, 372). Locke's response, while sympathetic to Newton's personal troubles at the time,[11] strongly objects to this accusation, reporting that "I cannot but be mightily troubled that you should have had so many wrong and unjust thoughts of me" and that he would be happy to meet with Newton on any occasion to dissuade him of these insidious charges (Locke, quoted in Cranston 1957, 373). If nothing else can be gained from this, it seems reasonable to assume that at a minimum, Locke was both familiar with Hobbes's doctrines and (at least publicly) meant to preserve his distance from them.

Locke's earliest confrontation with Hobbesian doctrines appears in his *Essays on the Law of Nature,* specifically in the sixth essay, where he takes up three points related to his predecessor. Locke first addresses the Hobbesian notion that the laws of nature might be based upon self-preservation, given that some universal source must be found to ground these laws. Making an obvious allusion to Hobbes, he tells us that "there are some who trace the whole law of nature back to each person's self-preservation."[12] According to Locke, however, following this doctrine would have grave consequences: "if the source and origin of all this law is the care and preservation of oneself, virtue would seem to be not so much man's duty as his convenience" ([1664] 1997, VI.1). That is to say, the Hobbesian system of natural law becomes optional for the individual. If a particular law does not serve the immediate interest of the moral agent, it becomes at that instant disposable. Locke's unstated, but implied, conclusion is that optional or disposable laws are as good as no laws at all. The natural law must therefore be based on something beyond mere self-preservation.

The second Hobbesian doctrine subject to Locke's ire is that force creates all obligations. Responding to the same fear implicit in his later response to Newton, Locke argues in the *Essays* that force cannot serve as a legitimate foundation of the state: "not all obligation seems to consist in, and ultimately to be limited by, that power which can coerce offenders and punish the wicked" (VI.4). Contrary to the classic Hobbist doctrine of legal positivism, Locke argues that, although force might be necessary for constraint, it is not the source of our duty to obey the law. Rather, this is found in the inherent moral propriety of the law itself: "all obligation binds conscience and lays a bond on the mind itself, so that not fear of punishment, but a rational appre-

11. Newton had, according to Maurice Cranston, "some sort of nervous breakdown in 1693, following an illness the year before" (1957, 372).
12. Locke ([1664] 1997, VI.1). References are to essay and paragraph number.

hension of what is right, puts us under an obligation." To do anything else, according to one of Locke's more memorable lines, is to submit oneself "to the service of a pirate" (VI.4).[13]

To remedy this, on Locke's account, we get his third argument against Hobbism—that the positive law must be related to the natural law if it is to possess legitimacy. As discussed above in section 1.4, Hobbes himself argued this at times, but it is clearly not the doctrine that had become popularly associated with the *Leviathan*. The popularly received Hobbes was that of law being the command of the sovereign. For reasons discussed earlier, this is the very definition of positivism, and it rightly generated concern by apparently authorizing the arbitrariness of dictators. In this spirit, Locke asserted in the *Essays on the Law of Nature*, "If natural law is not binding on men, neither can any human positive law be binding" ([1664] 1997, VI.14). He makes the connection even more explicit later in the same paragraph: "the binding force of civil law is dependent on the natural law; and we are not so much coerced into rendering obedience to the magistrate by the power of the civil law as bound to obedience by natural right." The effect of this is that Locke unambiguously rejects the doctrine of legal positivism. Positive laws must be grounded in the natural law if they are to be valid. In this respect, he carefully distinguishes himself from Hobbes (the "Hobbist") who asserts that law is nothing other than a command. In Locke's system, commands may be issued, but this is not a sufficient condition for their validity.

This assumption that civil laws must be connected to the natural law would play a substantial role in Locke's mature political thought. In almost every dimension in which he could be said to be different from Hobbes, it is in relation to his effort to reject the Hobbist doctrine of positivism. Consider three elements of the *Second Treatise*: (1) the existence of the natural law in the state of nature, (2) the notion of limited government, and (3) the right of revolution. In each category, Locke makes assumptions concerning the natural law inconsistent with Hobbism.

First, Locke asserts in the *Second Treatise* that "the *State of Nature* has a Law of Nature to govern it" ([1690] 1988, §6). This stands in distinction to Hobbes's conception of the state of nature, where the residents are not bound

---

13. Locke repeats this complaint later in the *Essay*, this time explicitly citing Hobbes: "That men should keep their compacts is certainly a great and undeniable rule in morality. But yet, if a Christian, who has the view of happiness and misery in another life, be asked why a man must keep his word, he will give this as a reason:—Because God, who has the power of eternal life and death, requires it of us. But if a Hobbist be asked why? He will answer:—Because the public requires it, and the Leviathan will punish you if you do not" ([1690] 1959, I.ii.5).

by the laws of nature or anything else for that matter, with the exception of the external constraints of those who aim to harm them.[14] Although Locke insists on the existence of these norms, he famously denies the steadfast obedience of the people to them. It is on this basis that he thus justifies the flight from the state of nature to civil society. The purpose of civil government, according to Locke, is to protect rights grounded in the law of nature, only tenuously guarded in the state of nature: "For though the Law of Nature be plain and intelligible to all rational Creatures; yet Men being biassed by their Interest, as well as ignorant for want of study of it, are not apt to allow of it as a Law binding them in the application of it to their particular cases" (§124).

Second, Locke's conception of the natural law is necessary for his understanding of a limited government. The actions of the legislature, for example, are carefully circumscribed by Locke to "be conformable to the Law of Nature . . . [such that] no Humane Sanction can be good, or valid against it" (§135). Likewise, Locke insists that no government can create right simply by the introduction of force (§§19, 172, 175, 180–87, 196).[15] In whatever ways he might have altered his thought between 1664 and 1690, in this respect Locke remains consistent and true to his assertion in the *Essays* that positive laws must necessarily be linked to natural ones. And, if we are to believe Mark Goldie's (1997, xxii) and Wolfgang von Leyden's (1954, 53) reasonable claim that this argument was directed against Hobbes in 1664, there is some ground for understanding this same argument of Locke's similarly in 1688.

Third and related to the above paragraph, Locke's conception of the natural law in the *Second Treatise* is also essential for his justification of revolution. The people reserve this remarkable right "[w]hensoever . . . the *Legislative* shall transgress this fundamental Rule of Society [the natural right to property]; and either by Ambition, Fear, Folly or Corruption, *endeavor to grasp* themselves, *or put into the hands of any other an Absolute Power* over the Lives, Liberties, and Estates of the People" (Locke [1690] 1988, §222). Locke makes it clear that this right of revolution is inextricably linked to his law of nature as sketched out in chapter 2, being that no one ought to harm others in their

14. The existence of a natural law in the Lockean state of nature contrasted to the absence thereof in Hobbes's leads to important consequences in the events that take place in it. Specifically, whereas Hobbes holds that the state of nature and state of war are synonymous, Locke understands them to be logically distinct. That Locke was aware of this contrast with Hobbes is evident in his own observations in the *Second Treatise:* "however some Men have confounded [the state of nature and the state of war, they] are as far distant, as a State of Peace, Good Will, Mutual Assistance, and Preservation, and a State of Enmity, Malice, Violence, and Mutual Destruction are from one another" ([1690] 1988, §19). This has already been noted in the literature (Zuckert 1994, 220).

15. These passages have been noted previously in Myers (1998, 152).

life, health, liberty, or possessions. As soon as the government violates these eternal laws in the manner he describes in chapter 19, the people thus gain the additional right of replacing it with one more friendly to the law of nature. Again, the contrast with Hobbes is striking, because Hobbes specifically prohibits rebellion of any kind on the basis that it would be the violation of contract and hence by definition unjust (*Leviathan,* 18.3). Hobbes's reliance on convention for his norms makes this case. Locke's understanding of natural law as independent and prior to convention makes possible a relatively coherent theory of rebellion, by contrast.[16]

2.2. THE ONTOLOGY OF LOCKE'S NATURAL LAW

Locke's conception of the natural law differs considerably from that of his ancient and medieval predecessors, as he formulates his principles in terms of rights. John Yolton describes at least thirteen distinct natural laws appearing in his work (1958, 488):

1. Love and respect and worship God.
2. Obey your superiors.
3. Tell the truth and keep your promises.
4. Be mild and pure of character and be friendly.
5. Do not offend or injure, without cease, any person's health, life, liberty, or possessions.
6. Be candid and friendly in talking about other people.
7. Do not kill or steal.
8. Love your neighbor and your parents.
9. Console a distressed neighbor.
10. Feed the hungry.
11. "Whosoever sheddeth man's blood, by man shall his blood be shed."
12. That property is mine which I have acquired through my labor so long as I can use it before it spoils.
13. Parents are to preserve, nourish, and educate their children.

---

16. One could conceivably argue that Locke derives his principles of limited sovereignty and right of revolution from prudence, as Hobbes is frequently interpreted. This is Leo Strauss's version of Locke (Strauss [1953] 1965 and 1958). Many of Strauss's specific arguments are met forcefully and effectively in Yolton (1958). Further, a prudential reading of Locke is difficult to sustain in the face of his claim that the laws of nature are "eternal." Prudential laws, by their nature, cannot be eternal. Prudential laws must change according to circumstance. Eternal laws must always remain constant. Further, the prudential interpretation is difficult to sustain because the presumed ground of prudence—self-preservation—is explicitly denied by Locke as a foundation for natural law.

What is striking about these rights is both their primacy and determinacy. These rules are highly determinate, when compared with those found in St. Thomas Aquinas, for example. On the one hand, Aquinas begins with an indeterminate *summum bonum* and then proceeds to construct determinate laws designed for particular circumstances. Locke, on the other hand, speaks of no such vague principles. As Yolton notes, "He nowhere formulates a general maxim which he calls the 'law of nature.' There is no such single and general law. The law of nature turns out to be a list of laws" (1958, 488). His laws are determinate and apparently meant to apply to all times and circumstances. Locke makes this clear in the *Essays on the Law of Nature,* noting that specific prohibitions against theft, debauchery, and slander "are binding on all men in the world equally" regardless of context ([1664] 1997, VII.8).

The determinacy of Locke's rights is related to their primacy, as well. Because the natural rights are not derived, they must stand at the front of his ontological pedigree: "it is clearly impossible to derive these precepts from any single principle, whether it be innate, the light of reason, or a standard agreed upon by men" (Yolton 1958, 488).

Beyond primacy and determinacy, the most fundamental ontological question to be asked of a theory of natural law is whether it is intended to derive from transcendent norms whose status is impervious to conditions of time, place, or circumstance. Locke's own words appear unambiguously in the *Essays* to support a "yes" answer to this question. He declares these laws to include precepts that are "permanent," "absolute," based upon "the eternal order of things," and recognized by "all men in the world . . . unanimously" ([1664] 1997, VII.3, VII.8, VII.10, I.9).

Despite the apparent lack of ambiguity here, dissension dominates among Locke scholars on this issue. Lockean scholarship is divided, as noted by Peter C. Myers (1998), into two fundamental camps. The first consists of Cambridge Skinnerians, who argue that Locke's overt words are faithful representations of his intentions. Locke declared the transcendence of his natural laws because he believed it. The second camp, the Straussians, dispute Locke's sincerity.[17] Locke's words were mere esotericism, veiling an elaborate defense of Hobbesian positivism.[18]

---

17. This view is expressed in Strauss ([1953] 1965, 202–51). Substantial replies can be found in Yolton (1958) and Dunn (1968).

18. Other important issues of contention exist between the Skinnerians and Straussians related to this matter—such as whether Locke was addressing the specific political concerns of his day (Skinnerians) or was consciously addressing posterity (Straussians). A satisfactory answer to such questions extends well beyond the scope of this chapter.

Much of the fuel igniting the Locke-as-positivist fire has been Locke's own arguments against innate ideas, because innate ideas have generally been associated with theories of transcendent natural law (Budziszewski 1997, 61). His claims—as numerous as they are legendary—sprawl throughout the first book of the *Essay Concerning Human Understanding.* Locke extends his argument from the denial of innate speculative principles (e.g., "It is impossible for the same thing to be and not to be") to the denial of innate practical principles (e.g., "That one should do as he would be done unto") as well.[19] That he denies innate principles, however, does not necessarily mean that he rules out self-evident ones (Yolton 1958; White 1978).

Locke is careful to distinguish the fictional notion of innate ideas against the real self-evident ones. The doctrine of innate ideas is defined, in the *Essay,* as the "established opinion amongst some men, that there are in the understanding certain innate principles; some primary notions, characters, as it were stamped upon the mind of man; which the soul receives in its very first being, and brings into the world with it" ([1690] 1959, I.i.1). Yolton (1958, 479) has characterized this as "the naïve form" of innatism, as found in Henry More and Nathaniel Culverwel. Locke's dismissal of this doctrine is thorough and unambiguous both in the *Essays on the Law of Nature* and the *Essay Concerning Human Understanding.*

Both Yolton and White argue, however, that even though Locke has no place for this naïve form of innatism, he clearly has a place for self-evident propositions.[20] In the *Essay,* these include propositions "where that agreement or disagreement is perceived immediately by itself, without the intervention or help of any other."[21] Locke's illustrations of self-evidence include mathematics, being, identity, and difference. He does not extend his examples to include practical principles, such as we might find in the laws of nature. To this extent, Locke is consistent with his claim in the *Essays* that the laws of nature can only be derived empirically, rather than being found written on the hearts of individuals ([1664] 1997, II.1 and 9).

Can transcendent laws of nature actually be derived empirically? This is much easier said than done. Locke's argument is quite sketchy and does not

19. See Locke ([1690] 1959, I.i.4, I.ii.4).
20. Significantly, Locke insists on self-evident "propositions" rather than self-evident "ideas."
21. See Locke ([1690] 1959, IV.vii.2). Locke's definition of "intuition" in the *Essay* is almost identical: "the mind perceiv[ing] the agreement or disagreement of two ideas immediately by themselves, without the intervention of any other" (IV.ii.1). Arthur Lovejoy argues that Locke's reliance on intuition renders him "essentially a Platonist" ([1936] 1963, 362 n. 2). As we will see, however, this assessment is careful to make this association only with regard to his speculative, rather than practical, principles.

exist in any work he chose to publish. It appears in the fourth article of the *Essays*. There he explains that two faculties combine to derive the natural law: sense and reason. Reason is, for Locke, a "discursive faculty" by which a person advances from known facts to unknown ones. For this process to take place, however, one must naturally begin with a set of known facts. This is the role of the senses, because "reason can achieve nothing more than a labourer can working in darkness behind shuttered windows" ([1664] 1997, IV.1). He emphasizes this necessity of a foundation for reason on more than one occasion, drawing upon mathematics as a close analogy. Thus, sense provides the foundation of knowledge from which reason then builds the edifice of the natural law. Once Locke establishes the role of sense in his political epistemology, however, he proceeds to argue that given the natural beauty and order of the world, "there must be a powerful and wise creator of all these things" (IV.4). This is what Kant would later dismiss, in his *Critique of Pure Reason* (or *First Critique*), as the "Physico-Theological" proof for the existence of God on the basis of its reliance on unsustainable rational arguments (*FC*, 621A–630A). From the existence of God, Locke constructs standard rationalistic arguments to the effect that God can only create with purpose and that this purpose is for man to act in accordance with the natural law. Locke's argument is obviously problematic. Judgments concerning the beauty of the world, for example, are not purely empirical, as he suggests. Rather, a judgment of beauty requires the comparison of sense data with a rational concept, and, if one were to reject rational concepts and admit relative conceptions of beauty, for some people God may exist, and for others, God does not. This would subsequently imply that the natural laws apply to some and not others. This clearly contradicts Locke's intentions, because he earlier claimed the necessary transcendence of the laws.

One cannot be certain whether Locke was aware of these obvious problems. It is not unreasonable, however, to assume that he was. If he were, this might explain one important mystery in Lockean scholarship: his steadfast refusal to publish the *Essays*. Not only did he refuse to publish them, but he also went so far as to *conceal* them to the best of his ability, successfully hiding them from public view until centuries after his death (Horwitz 1987, 28–29). He never discussed them in his published or unpublished writings or even in his correspondence. Robert Horwitz speculates that Locke may have held back publishing the *Essays* in 1681–82 for political reasons (1987, 35), but by this time fifteen years had already lapsed since the manuscript had been completed. Locke thus must have had other reasons for carefully withholding it from the public, and the recognition of evident flaws would certainly provide motivation.

If Locke's refusal to publish or acknowledge the *Essays* makes contemporary scholars reluctant to find a foundation for his natural laws, we must turn to his *Second Treatise*. Any foundation to be found here, however, is not so explicit as that in the *Essays*. There are two instances in which Locke gives a suggestion of a foundation sufficient to ground his ultimate edifice of natural rights. They are the infamously perplexing sections 11 and 136. In recounting and endorsing the biblical account of the right to punish murderers with death, Locke tells us that its proof is "writ in the Hearts of all Mankind" ([1690] 1988, §11).[22] Later, in outlining the duties of the legislature, he tells us, "For the Law of Nature being unwritten, . . . [is] no where to be found but in the minds of Men" (§136). These two passages have proved befuddling to Locke scholars, because there is no obvious way to reconcile them with his unambiguous dismissal of innate ideas in the *Essay*—published the very same year. Yet Locke's employment and endorsement here of innate ideas seems likewise unambiguous.

I cannot pretend to offer a substantial account of what might explain Locke's motives for the existence of contradictory passages. Once again, however, it may be instructive to consider authorial ownership. Locke published the *Two Treatises* anonymously. The Cambridge school tends to suggest that Locke's anonymity was inspired by personal tendencies of secrecy. The Straussians, by contrast, suggest that Locke was attempting to avoid political persecution. A third option, however, deserves consideration. Perhaps it was the case that Locke's failure to build a successful empirical foundation for the natural law in his *Essays* persuaded him that innate ideas were really a necessary component of an epistemically consistent moral philosophy. The problem was that he was still completely committed to empiricism, which had no room for innate ideas. The solution? Locke could write two epistemologically independent works, claiming ownership of only one to avoid the otherwise inevitable charges of inconsistency with the other. Thus, whereas he could publish what he understood to be a thoroughgoing empirical doctrine in the *Essay*, he was free to employ innate ideas in the *Second Treatise*. Without those innate ideas in the latter work, he would not otherwise be able to justify the radical and central claims that were obviously important to him.

22. Locke's reference is to God's command, "Whoever sheds the blood of man, by man shall his blood be shed" (Gen. 9:6). That the law of nature is written on the heart does not occur until later: "They show that what the law requires is written on their hearts" (Rom. 2:15).

If this were Locke's actual decision, it would give him in some sense the best of both worlds. He would have all the empirical rigor and internal consistency of Hobbes and at the same time could offer an alternative to the unappealing positivism associated with Hobbism that bothered him so clearly. This would be an ingenious solution if it were not for the fact that Locke had to cheat to accomplish it.

2.3. ADVANTAGES OF LOCKEAN POLITICAL ONTOLOGY

Locke's conception of determinate transcendent rights has obvious advantages. First, the transcendence of his natural rights allows him to avoid the problems of Hobbist positivism. That Locke was keen to address this particular problem is already amply evident. The universality of his rights provides the necessary leverage to critique unjust commands of the sovereign and, when necessary, depose a tyrannical one. Their transcendence simultaneously provides a moral authority to the law absent in strictly positivist systems.

Second, the determinacy of the natural rights also provides substantial benefit. Whereas the vague indeterminacy of a *summum bonum* lends itself to greater contextual fit, its content will remain uncertain to many. Nevertheless, the determinacy of Locke's natural rights lends itself to crystal-clear promulgation. The laws are simple and understandable by most. A natural law commanding "do good and avoid evil" strikes many as a truism and virtually devoid of content. A natural right commanding that people ought not harm others in their property, however, is largely understandable. As John Finnis notes, "The strength of rights-talk is that . . . it can express precisely the various aspects of a decision involving more than one person, indicating just what is and what is not required of each person concerned" (1980, 210–11). It is this determinacy, perhaps more than anything else, that has made appeals to Lockean natural rights dominant in the twentieth and twenty-first centuries. This is no doubt one reason that the Universal Declaration of Human Rights takes the form of rights rather than general principles. The violation of concrete rights is relatively easy to discern and measure when compared to a violation of general or aggregate good.

Third, the determinacy of the natural law also places seemingly clear limits on governmental behavior. Strict and determinate laws of nature can be the best friend of limited government. Locke is particularly clear on this point, noting that it is the abuse of natural rights that justifies overthrowing a regime. The existence of delineated natural rights allows the government to know exactly what type of behavior is proscribed and will not be tolerated by the people.

Fourth, and related to this, is a final, more controversial, advantage of Locke's system of natural rights—its inalienability. Substantial attention has been given to the question of the inalienability of Locke's rights in the past half-century. Although there is strong evidence to suggest that Locke does not always rely on a conception of rights as inviolable (Kendall 1965; Simmons 1983), there are also persuasive grounds to believe that he does so at least on occasion (Glenn 1984). To the extent that Locke does employ inalienable rights, this places an even more emphatic limitation on governmental behavior. If rights are inviolable, the grounds of rebellion and regime change are more determinate and obvious.

2.4. DISADVANTAGES OF LOCKEAN POLITICAL ONTOLOGY

Parts of what makes natural rights appealing also provide difficulties. First, although the determinacy of rights allows for seemingly easy access and testability, it is less clear that it can address the problem of context. This was part of the problem that Hobbes had hoped to avoid with his positivism (see section 1.3 above). The inalienability of rights could conceivably place a straightjacket upon governments, rendering them impotent in times of emergency or crisis. If the right to life were inviolable, how could a government conceivably ask its citizens to sacrifice their lives in times of war? Further, mundane tasks, like the collection of taxes, might be difficult if the right to property is characterized as inalienable (Vaughan 1960, 168). John Gray, for example, has argued that "it is an unavoidable failure of any Lockean theory of the minimum state—that it cannot account for the necessity of taxation in terms consistent with the inviolability of the basic Lockean rights" (1995, 73).

This position might plausibly be viewed as a straw man, because it is not likely something that Locke himself would advocate. Locke does suggest, after all, that rebellions are justified, and revolutions are almost always accomplished only at the cost of tremendous bloodshed. The problem is that Locke does not suggest in any detail the extent to which his rights might be limited by other concerns. Could executive prerogative, for example, be employed to violate natural rights in addition to positive ones? And if rights are to have the bite he would like, it would seem that they need an aura of inalienability. It is unclear how Locke might reconcile these notions.

A third problem with Locke's conception of rights is that, even though they are determinate, he still suggests that many lack access to them. Those for whom the laws of nature are out of reach include children ([1690] 1988, §59), the mentally ill (§60), and the deliberately ignorant, the ill-raised, and the unintelligent ([1664] 1997, I.ii). Morton White refers to this as Locke's "epistemological elitism" (1987, 216). Locke never makes clear exactly what proportion of the population might have access to knowledge of natural rights.

Finally, there are the inevitable questions concerning how we might actually know natural rights. As discussed above, Locke had rigorously objected to the employment of innate ideas but nevertheless apparently relied on them periodically. Such behavior suggests that Locke did not have a substantially developed account of the epistemic access to natural rights. Did he or did he not mean to rest his natural law on some version of innate ideas?

Conclusions

There are many good reasons to treat Hobbes and Locke as distinct from one another. They have different views of the state of nature; they have different notions of equality; they have different notions of liberty; they have different laws of nature; they place sovereignty in different places; their attitudes toward rebellion are opposite in important respects; they differ widely on the separation of powers; and they have different views of human nature.

On the other hand, they appear to share one important assumption: Hobbes claims that all knowledge comes from the senses but then asserts the existence of eternal or immutable ideas. Likewise, Locke is an empiricist but nevertheless asserts that the laws of nature are written on the heart. In other words, they both desire a clean empiricist epistemology consistent with advances in natural science but at the same time want their politics to have the force that can be gained by reference to eternal or immutable ideas or laws of nature.

Thus, modern philosophy had hit something of a roadblock. The allure of modern science had led many philosophers to think more "scientifically." Empirical science had already brought about extraordinary advances over theological and intuition-based approaches from previous centuries. It had done much to overturn arguments based on groundless teleology and revealed discoveries still considered valid today. The only problem was that, whereas this epistemology offered a very workable metaphysics for the sciences, it burdened the normative realm. Materialism is necessarily bound up with contingency and change. The problem is that contingency and change do not provide the foundations most want to ground their politics and morals.

Rousseau was, contrary to his reputation, sensitive and accommodating to the discoveries of the natural science. Even in his famous attack against the sciences, he referred to Newton as a man of "vast genius." He went on to argue that such figures should "find honorable asylum in [royal] courts" (*FD,* 26–27/*OC,* III:29). The world has plenty of room and indeed need for scientific minds of the first rank. It is thus not surprising to find that the education of Emile includes extensive training in scientific method with a commitment to experiment that would make Francis Bacon proud. At the same time, however, he does not suggest that the scientists' mode of inquiry should be employed by the moralist. Different modes of thought demand different approaches, and, to the extent that Rousseau is aware of this, we can begin to appreciate how he stands out from those with whom he is often associated. Despite his employment of a social contract, Rousseau is neither Hobbes nor Locke. For that matter, he is not Condillac. Rousseau understands that, if one is to get eternal and immutable moral and political laws, one must start outside the world of contingency. In this respect, we can begin to see not only that he is a Platonist but also that this Platonism distinguishes him from his most famous associates in the social contract tradition.

TWO

THE CONTEXT, PART 2:
MATERIALISM AND PLATONISM IN MODERN EUROPE

It has become fashionable to suggest that Jean-Jacques Rousseau was a man of his time. In certain respects, this cannot be disputed. As many of the greatest intellectuals of his milieu had, he for a time regularly participated in the salon culture of Paris. As others of his age did, he challenged standard views of politics, religion, and culture. And as still others had done, he turned to a particularly modern device—the social contract—to solve the classic problems of politics. On the other hand, suggesting that Rousseau was a man of his time presents immediate and almost intuitive difficulties. Although he participated in the salon culture, he ultimate fled it in disgust, and although he called into question standard views in politics, he appealed to even more ancient models as alternatives. Finally, despite his reliance on modern devices to solve tricky political problems, he did so to secure what he described as ancient values.

Perhaps the most modern view of all attributed to Rousseau is the suggestion that he was a materialist (Strauss 1953; Melzer 1990; Hulliung 1994). Materialism was a growing specter in modernity. Beginning in earnest with Hobbes, the doctrine holds that "that which is not body is no part of the universe" (*Leviathan,* 46.15). The very notion of immaterial substance, crucial to idealists from Plato through Leibniz, was characterized as oxymoronic. This rejection was enthusiastically endorsed by some of the most distinguished members of the French Enlightenment approximately a century after the publication of the *Leviathan.* Most notoriously, Julien de La Mettrie's conclusion that both body and mind were the same substance led him to declare boldly that "man is a machine" (La Mettrie [1748] 1994, 30). He was joined in this belief by the likes of Helvétius, d'Holbach, and Diderot.

Of course, this begs the question of what the real zeitgeist of the Enlightenment was. While all of us are, in a sense, products of our time, a proper understanding of a given individual requires a thorough understanding of that time. The prominence of thinkers such as Diderot, d'Holbach, La Mettrie, and Helvétius in Rousseau's lifetime cannot be denied. They remain some of the most memorable and significant figures of the Parisian salon culture. Indeed, if it were not for them, we could imagine scientific and cultural history evolving along very different lines. The imperative to understand Rousseau's milieu better, however, requires knowledge of a different tradition, as well: that of the less-noted, but nevertheless extremely important, modern European Platonists. Though perhaps less organized as a movement and less exotic to contemporary historians, the modern Platonists featured their own roster of imposing minds, including Ficino, the Cambridge Platonists, Descartes, Leibniz, Malebranche, and Fénelon.

The two camps represent opposite views on fundamental metaphysical issues. The materialists deny the existence of immaterial substance; the Platonists embrace it. The materialists assert that human behavior is predetermined by matter in motion; the Platonists embrace the doctrine of free will. The materialists find the notion of an immaterial God dubious; the Platonists are open to it. This chapter outlines some of the most prominent figures from both sides for the purpose of illuminating the metaphysical debates leading up to and dominating Rousseau's Europe. In some cases, figures are mentioned because they contribute to the general intellectual environment of Rousseau's period. In other cases, we shall see that Rousseau not only read these figures carefully but also had close and personal relationships with them. Understanding the issues that he would eventually take on requires this history.

1. Platonism on the Continent

There are two reasons to reject the assumption that Rousseau was operating in a climate hostile to Platonism. First, it is simply false that Platonism was dead in Europe. Second, it tempts one to misread radically the doctrines of Rousseau himself. His Europe was a place largely sympathetic to idealism. Platonism was not a fringe movement in one corner of the Continent. It was in fact a widespread mode of thinking in modern Europe, found in all corners—England, Germany, Italy, and indeed France. That Rousseau was a Platonist should not be surprising in context. Rather, it is by all rights to be expected. The Platonic milieu included many of the central figures of modern philosophy—Descartes, Malebranche, and Leibniz, all of whom were familiar to Rousseau.

I.I. ITALIAN RENAISSANCE PLATONISTS

The earliest known school of Platonism in modern Europe is where one might logically expect it: in Renaissance Italy, where the rediscovery of Plato's dialogues soon created enthusiastic followers. Its hub was the Florentine Academy, led by Marsilio Ficino (1433–1499), which fancied itself a modern-day Platonic academy. There were readings of and public lectures on Plato, celebrations of Plato's birthday, and invited guests from across the Continent on themes Platonic. As Paul Kristeller notes, Ficino had many sources for his Platonism, including not only Plato himself but also the ancient neoplatonists, medieval Arabic and Latin philosophers (e.g., Boethius, Augustine, Alfarabi, and Avicenna), and some figures from earlier fifteenth-century Europe (Bessarion and Cusanus).

Ficino's cosmology posited a particularly medieval neoplatonic hierarchy of being, stemming from shapeless matter at the bottom to God at the top. Midway in the chain of being was humanity, which he distinguished by its soul and the dignity accorded to it. Like Plato, Ficino advocated turning away from shadowy images as a source of truth. In a clear depiction of epistemic Platonism, Kristeller summarizes in Ficino that the mind "is capable of turning away from the body and the external world, and of concentrating upon its own inner substance. Thus purifying itself from things external, the soul enters the contemplative life and attains a higher knowledge, discovering the incorporeal or intelligible world that is closed to it while engaging in ordinary experience and in the troubles of external life" (Kristeller 1964, 44).

Ficino gives Plato a central role in much of his published work. He wrote separate commentaries on the *Symposium* and the *Philebus* in 1469 and translated all of the dialogues into Latin to bring Plato's writings to a larger audience. Each dialogue was prefaced by a substantial introductory interpretation.[1] Further, his multivolume magnum opus was entitled *Platonic Theology*. The very opening of the book leaves little room for doubt about his Platonic loyalties: "Noble-souled Lorenzo [d'Medici]! Plato, the father of philosophers, realizing that our minds bear the same relationship to God as our sight to the light of the Sun, and that therefore they can never understand anything without the

---

1. Ficino's translations of Plato eventually became an extensively annotated portion of Rousseau's library, now available at the British Library.

light of God, considered it just and pious that, as the human mind receives everything from God, so it should restore everything to God" ([1469–73] 2001, 1:9). Drawing upon Augustine, he presses on to note that with only slight modifications, Platonists would be Christians. Finally, he concludes his introduction with explicit references to Platonic metaphysics, epistemology, and the allegory of the cave: "I believe that those for whom the objects of thought are confined to the objects of bodily sensation and who in their wretchedness prefer shadows of things to things themselves, once they are impressed by the arguments of Plato, will contemplate the higher objects which transcend the senses, and find happiness in putting these things before their shadows" (11). Ficino's Platonism was explicit, thorough, and extensively influential in modern Europe.

I.2. CAMBRIDGE PLATONISTS

If only for the obvious reason of their name (given to them only in the nineteenth century), perhaps the most famous Platonists of the early modern period were the Cambridge Platonists. Although hardly an official organization or a self-defined clique, the Cambridge Platonists were consistent in their reliance on Plato and Platonism for solutions to the problems of modern philosophy. They reigned at Cambridge in the middle of the seventeenth century and had undoubted influence on the practice of philosophy throughout the Continent, one of their greatest admirers being Leibniz. The most significant figures to emerge from this movement were Henry More (1614–1687), Ralph Cudworth (1618–1689), and Benjamin Whichcote (1609–1683).

As Sarah Hutton has noted, although not definable as Platonists in the strict sense of adopting every element of Plato's doctrines and no others, they were nevertheless committed to central aspects of his thought. These included beliefs in the immortality of the soul, the principle of metaphysical dualism, and the eternality of moral principles and truth (Hutton 2002, 308–9). They further asserted the existence of an immaterial God and the freedom of the will. Whichcote, for example, argued that ethical principles were to be found in the reason rather than the will of God, in reasoning somewhat reminiscent of Plato in the *Euthyphro*. Underlying this was a "Platonic metaphysics, according to which God is the sum of all perfections" (Hutton 2002, 311).

Henry More held similar doctrines, but did so more with an eye to combating what he perceived as his most dangerous contemporaries. Taking on Hobbes and Spinoza, More rejected voluntarism and asserted the existence of an immaterial God, the immortality of an immaterial soul, and a thoroughgoing dualism on which he rested his ethics. Confronting Hobbes directly, and consequently embracing metaphysical Platonism, he insisted that the very same Hobbesian demonstrations for the existence of material substance could also be employed to prove immaterial substance (Hutton 2002, 314). The immaterial soul subsequently became a central element in his ethics, which likewise had strong Platonic elements: "Knowledge of virtue is attainable by reason, and the pursuit of virtue entails the control of the passions of the soul" (315). Platonic epistemology here supports the Platonic virtue of *sophrosune*, or self-mastery.

Perhaps the most influential Cambridge Platonist was Ralph Cudworth. He was likely at the same time the most committed Platonist. This is clear from the very title of perhaps his most enduring works: *A Treatise on Eternal and Immutable Morality* and *Of Freewill.* The latter is directed against his natural and mortal intellectual rival, Thomas Hobbes. Contrary to Hobbesian determinism, Cudworth asserts that "From hence, alone, it appears that rational beings, or human souls, can extend themselves further than [their] necessary natures, or can act further than they suffer, that they can actively change themselves and determine themselves contingently or fortuitously, when they are not necessarily determined by causes antecedent" (Cudworth [1731] 1996, 164). With this freedom, human beings are at liberty to choose the highest good. Without freedom, there can be no morality whatsoever.

This highest good is likewise defined in contrast to the morality of Hobbes. Whereas Hobbes defined good and evil as contingent upon individual desires and aversions, Cudworth was repelled by relativistic ethics. Hobbesian definitions are dismissed as "vulgar" (Cudworth [1731] 1996, 9) and are grouped with similarly voluntaristic theological definitions of right and justice. He asserts that such affronts can only be combated with a strong appeal to ontological Platonism; hence the appeal that "the natures of essences of all things being immutable, therefore upon the supposition that there is any thing really just or unjust, due or unlawful, there must of necessity be something so both naturally and immutably, which no law, decree, will, nor custom can alter" (29). In this respect, he follows Plato's lead, to the point of recounting the Athenian's deconstruction of Protagoras (from the *Theaetetus*) line by line. The ultimate and eternal principles of morality, for Cudworth, are known without recourse to the corrupting influence of the senses and therefore rely, contrary to Locke's tabula rasa, on an innatist Platonic epistemology.

1.3. DESCARTES

Although René Descartes (1596–1650) often goes beyond Platonism, there are several clear Platonic elements in his thought—most of which can be linked with epistemic Platonism. Christia Mercer describes his *Meditations on a First Philosophy* as "a handbook on how to escape the shadows of the cave and discover the illuminating truth beyond" (2002, 37). She notes three respects in which Descartes can specifically be identified as Platonic. First, he identifies certain truths as innate: in the *Third Meditation,* he writes, "the faculty which I have of conceiving what is called in general a thing, or a truth, or a thought, seems to me to derive from nowhere else than my own nature" ([1641] 1968, 116). The most significant truth of this kind for Descartes is awareness of the existence of God. Second, Descartes complains of the corrupting influence of sensory data on the acquisition of such truths. His famous initial skepticism in the *Meditations* uses a profound skepticism about the senses as its departure point. And third, he insists that it is the intellect alone that considers these truths (Mercer 2002, 37–38). Although Descartes does not cite Plato in his *Meditations,* it would be incorrect to assume that his work is devoid of Platonism. According to Mercer, he "was not explicit about his Platonist epistemology because there was no reason to be: his contemporaries were thoroughly familiar with that tradition, and could recognize this part of his philosophy for what it is" (2002, 38). This was apparently true for the great German Platonist Leibniz, who said of Descartes that "most of his metaphysics is already found, partly in Plato and Aristotle and partly in the scholastics" (Leibniz 1969, 189).

1.4. GERMAN PRE-LEIBNIZIANS

Platonism was also prominent in Germany. This was especially the case in Leipzig, home to two Platonist scholars, Johann Adam Scherzer (1628–1683) and Jakob Thomasius (1622–1684). Thomasius was a professor of rhetoric, dialectic, and moral philosophy and was among the most influential teachers of the young Leibniz (Mercer 2001, 32). And, although he also had strong Aristotelian elements, he had significant Platonic leanings. Epistemologically, Thomasius held that true knowledge was only possible through the understanding. The object of the understanding was nothing less than eternal forms or ideas (Mercer 2001, 202).

Scherzer—like Thomasius, a teacher of the young Leibniz—was a professor of philosophy, Hebrew, and theology in Leipzig. Drawing on Ficino, Plotinus, Philo, Proclus, Augustine, and Reuchlin, in addition to Plato, Scherzer committed himself to seek the "bare truth." Claiming to follow Plato in book 2 of the *Republic,* he argues that God "remains simple while being 'most beautiful . . . and most good'" (Mercer 2001, 201). Beyond this, he follows metaphysical Platonism in the distinction of the world of perfect ideas from the world of artifacts. The former resides in the mind of God and contains Platonic ideas. The latter is defined by its imperfection.

Thomasius and Scherzer were scarcely the only German Platonists of the day. Leibniz is known to be influenced either in reading or in person by other Platonists such as Althanasius Kircher, Johann Heinrich Alsted, and Erhard Weigel. By all accounts, Platonism was a robust tradition in modern Germany, just as was the case in Italy, England, and France.

1.5. LEIBNIZ

The most significant modern German Platonist, of course, was Gottfried Wilhelm von Leibniz (1646–1716). Indeed, Patrick Riley has written that "Leibniz' thought is quite inconceivable without its almost-dominant Platonic component" (1996, 33). Having studied with many significant Platonists of the period, Leibniz was very conscious of his own Platonism.[2] As a young man, he wrote to his former teacher, Thomasius, that they shared a common ambition with the metaphysical goals of Plato—to help their "contemporaries 'escape from the shadows' of materialism" (Mercer 2001, 206). Just as Plato had to fight off the pre-Socratic materialists, so, too, was there a contemporary need to fight off a similar challenge from Hobbes. Leibniz would view Hobbes as his "principal philosophical antagonist" (Riley [1972] 1988, 1) and developed the Platonist teachings of his predecessors to combat his materialism and the politics extending from it.[3]

Leibniz opposed Hobbes on at least two significant and related fronts. First, he opposed Hobbesian metaphysics—materialism—and its accompanying determinism. Second, he rejected Hobbes's politics—positivism—which he saw as a consequence of materialism. With regard to the former, Leibniz posits early in the *Theodicy* the necessity of freedom for morality. In its absence, "morality is destroyed and all justice, divine and human, shaken" ([1710] 1985, §3). This is for him one of the most disturbing facets of Hobbes. Although there appear to be unresolved tensions between freedom and his

---

2. G. MacDonald Ross has written that Leibniz's "great philosophic hero was Plato" (1984, 74).

3. Leibniz's interest in Plato was scarcely a passing fancy. Like Ficino, he translated Platonic dialogues to make them accessible to broader audiences and firmly held Platonist doctrines throughout his career (Mercer 2001).

doctrine of preestablished harmony, Leibniz is committed to the existence of freedom. In the closest thing he offers to a resolution of this tension, he notes that freedom involves resistance in the face of inclination: "There is always a prevailing reason which prompts the will to its choice, and for the maintenance of freedom for the will it suffices that this reason should incline without necessitating. That is also the opinion of all the ancients, of Plato, of Aristotle, of St. Augustine. The will is never prompted to action save by representation of the good, which prevails over the opposite representations" (148). Thus, we are prompted to be good, but we must make that decision ultimately ourselves, if our actions are to have moral content.

The second respect in which Leibniz represents a Platonic reaction against Hobbes is in the nature of normative standards. For Hobbes, normative standards are completely voluntaristic—contingent upon the choice or whim of a recognized authority. Leibniz rejects such claims, even when they might be based on the will of God. Following Plato's *Euthyphro* closely, he notes, "It is agreed that whatever God wills is good and just. But there remains the question whether it is good and just because God wills it or whether God wills it because it is good and just." Leibniz rejects the former view, because, as he puts it in "Meditation on the Common Concept of Justice," it would "destroy the justice of God" ([1702–3] 1988, 45–46). If God's will were to define justice, it would have no value as an attribute. A "just God" would be tautological. If, by contrast, God were to conform its will to justice, one could rightly praise its justice.[4] Leibniz later draws on a second Platonic dialogue, the *Republic*. Specifically, he notes the similarity of the refuted definition of justice with that advocated by Thrasymachus. Defining justice as the consequence of an arbitrary will is the essence of justice as the interest of the stronger.[5] Leibniz finds the same definition, and consequently the same problems, in Hobbes as well (Leibniz [1702–3] 1988, 47). Indeed, he rejects all forms of positivism. His "Opinion on the Principles of Pufendorf" takes on Hobbes again, in addition to its identified target.

It is obvious, according to Leibniz, that the common understanding of justice is anything but positive. When people reflect on the justices and injustices

---

4. Leibniz makes a similar argument in his *Discourse on Metaphysics:* "In saying . . . that things are not good according to any standard of goodness, but simply by the will of God, it seems to me that one destroys, without realizing it, all the love of God and all his glory; for why praise him for what he has done, if he would be equally praiseworthy doing the contrary? Where will be his justice and his wisdom if he has only a certain despotic power, if arbitrary will take the place of reasonableness, and if in accord with the definition of tyrants, justice consists in that which is pleasing to the most powerful?" ([1686] 1902, 5).

5. Leibniz repeats this observation subsequently in the preface to his *Theodicy* ([1710] 1985, 59).

they encounter in their daily lives, their intuitions do not lead them to reflect upon the content of the will of the strongest. If someone has pointlessly destroyed my garden, I need not ask what the authorities think before I issue my charge of "injustice!" This is because justice is, for Leibniz, an idea. More specifically, it is a Platonic idea: "Neither the norm of conduct itself, nor the essence of the just, depends on [God's] free decision, but rather on eternal truths, objects of the divine intellect. . . . And indeed, justice follows certain rules of equality and of proportion [which are] no less founded in the immutable nature of things and in the divine ideas, than are the principles of arithmetic and of geometry" (Leibniz [1702–3] 1988, 71).[6] These words, written to dismiss Samuel Pufendorf's *De Officio Hominis et Civis,* speak to all positivist lawyers, including and perhaps especially Hobbes. Thus, Leibniz not only shares metaphysical and ontological assumptions with Plato, but also, like Plato, holds these views to be directly relevant to politics.

Another Platonist aspect of Leibniz's thought is epistemological. Just as Plato suggested that the eternal truths, or ideas, reside within us and are there to those undistracted by the shadows of the material world, so does Leibniz find the natural law "written in our hearts" ([1702–3] 1988, 69). Combining Christian theology with Platonism, he finds in each individual an "inner light"—knowledge of the existence of God, from which all other knowledge can be derived. To see this inner light, one must close oneself off from the distraction of the external world (Mercer 2002, 41). This recommendation recalls Plato's warning to mistrust the senses as a source of truth.

1.6. MALEBRANCHE

The undisputed greatest Platonist of modern France was Nicolas Malebranche (1638–1715). Impressed in his late twenties by the writings of Descartes, he soon began vigorously pursing a program to fuse the philosophies of Descartes and the medieval neoplatonist Augustine. This resulted in his two best-known doctrines: occasionalism and his notion of vision in God. Both doctrines rely heavily on a role for God in metaphysics.

Occasionalism suggests that there are two causes for every event. First, there is the "occasional" cause—that which we perceive. Second, there is the real cause—that is, God. Malebranche's own example is of a pinprick. The pricking of a pin on a finger is the occasional cause of our pain. This, however, is only a perceived cause. The real cause is God's will. God has willed first

---

6. This is also cited in Riley (1996, 16).

the pinprick and then, second, the sensation of pain. God is ultimately for Malebranche the primary causal agent of the universe.

Given that God wills all, we can then deduce that the very contents of our minds are its products. Thus begins his doctrine of vision in God. Every-one—if undistracted by sensory data—has ideas. According to Malebranche, these ideas reside in God. God can, however, make them accessible to us through the intellect, a notion echoing epistemological Platonism, and, as is the case with the ontological Plato, they are both eternal and immutable: "It would not be difficult to prove, as St. Augustine has done, that there would not be any sciences, any demonstrated truths, any clear difference between the just and unjust, in a word, any necessary truths or laws known by all minds, if that which is contemplated by all intelligence . . . was not, by its nature, absolutely immutable, eternal, and necessary."[7] Both the Platonic elements and Platonic lineage here are obvious. Ideas as eternal and immutable are part of the classic Platonic ontology, and these notions were largely passed on to Malebranche through the Augustinian tradition of his divinity training. As Steven Nadler has said, "Malebranche . . . simply sees himself as a traditional-ist on the matter of ideas, upholding the original (i.e., Platonic) philosophic understanding of the term" (1992, 10). Like his epistemic Platonist predeces-sors, Malebranche was concerned with preventing corruption in the under-standing of the ideas. The senses, though neither true nor false in themselves, can confuse or distract individuals from a proper accessing of the ideas: "a man who judges all things by his senses and loves only what flatters him, is in the most wretched state of mind possible. In this state he is infinitely removed from the truth and from his good. But when a man judges things only accord-ing to the mind's pure ideas, when he carefully avoids the noisy confusion of creatures, and, when entering into himself, he listens to his sovereign Master with his senses and passions silent, it is impossible for him to fall into error" (Malebranche [1674] 1997, xxxvii).

1.7. FÉNELON

One of the more memorable doctrines of Rousseau's *Emile* is his concern about the use of books in education. In an age when parents, teachers, and legislators are all promoting reading for young people, this strikes us as a pecu-liar doctrine. His reasons, perhaps at first alien, are not as absurd as common sense might initially suggest. What concerns him is that books do not instruct

7. Malebranche ([1685] 1959–66, lettre I, 6:199), quoted in Nadler (1992, 103).

nearly as well as experience. It is one thing to read Hobbes's warnings concerning human nature; it is another to experience this for oneself. For all that a book might instruct about a subject, one gains considerably more by actually experiencing it. This is even more dramatic with the natural and mathematical sciences. Learning a formula from a book is one thing, but discovering it through need and experience offers distinct advantages—the mind is an active participant in learning, and, as a consequence, the lessons are more likely to be retained. It is likely for this reason that parents tell their children to turn off the television and go outside. Television is undoubtedly the contemporary analogue to what Rousseau called "the plague of childhood" (*Emile*, 116/*OC*, IV:357).

Nevertheless, Rousseau makes a few exceptions. The first comes in adolescence: *Robinson Crusoe*. Its selection is consistent with many themes in Emile's education. Robinson is a natural, rather than artificial, man. Everything that he learns or accomplishes is on the basis of his own exploration and experiments. He is for Rousseau the perfect role model for the adolescent, who likewise is to learn through his own experiments and experiences: "I want him [Emile] to think that he is Robinson himself" (*Emile*, 185/*OC*, IV:455). A later—and only modern—book, however, has been less understood both on its own terms and in its importance to Rousseau: François de Fénelon's *Telemachus* (*Emile*, 467/*OC*, IV:762).[8]

Written in 1699 as a study in statesmanship for his pupil, the duc de Bourgogne, the grandson of Louis XIV, it became second in popularity only to the Bible in eighteenth-century France. It was less popular with Louis XIV, however, who viewed its emphasis on republican virtues as an attack on his rule and character. Shortly after its publication, Fénelon was dismissed from his tutorial post and divested of his pension. He was never to return to Versailles or Paris.

The book itself traces the adventures of young Telemachus, son of Ulysses. Accompanied by his tutor, he retraces many steps of his famous father in the hope of finding him. He begins his escapades as a well-intentioned, but somewhat unrefined, adolescent. He wants to be good, but inexperience, ignorance, and lack of self-control occasionally mislead him. It is only through the guidance of his wise Mentor that he escapes early troubles. As the story progresses and experiences accumulate, however, he begins asserting himself in the manner befitting a prince and eventually, indeed, a king.

---

8. This is only beginning to be redressed, largely due to the efforts of Patrick Riley. He has in the past decade provided a new translation of *Telemachus* and written of its importance to Rousseau (Riley 2001).

Throughout the story, Fénelon emphasizes the virtues necessary not only for being a king, but simply for being a good person. Among them are courage, wisdom, self-control, and justice. Each virtue is the subject of repeated and extended discussions. The virtue of courage is cited as one of the attributes of his admirable father, and Telemachus gets his own opportunity to exercise it in a great battle. The virtue of wisdom is most present in the sagacious Mentor. It is a virtue that requires time and experience to develop—one that he begins truly to appreciate toward the end of his adventures. The Mentor is confident at the novel's conclusion that "the gods love you, and are preparing a reign of full wisdom for you" (Fénelon [1699] 1994, 302). The virtue with which he struggles most is moderation or self-control. He comes very close to abandoning himself to passion on the island of Calypso. Tempted by beautiful nymphs to abandon his quest and his duties, it is only by force that the Mentor is able to push him, literally, off the island. In subsequent lessons, the Mentor stresses the need for young Telemachus not to succumb to flattery. It is only a means by which the crafty subvert the public good through the weakness of the prince. Self-control is needed to resist flatterers and do good. It is necessary for overcoming virtually all obstacles: self-interest, passion, pride, vanity, laziness, luxury, fear, and so forth. His eventual mastery of this virtue is represented by his refusal to give up his quest and duties, despite his passionate affection for Antiope (314).[9] Justice is perhaps the least elaborated, but most ubiquitous, virtue in the book. The Mentor first notes its presence in Egypt, where it is exercised to protect the poor from the rich. It returns, however, with great frequency in numerous contexts. Narbal reports that his heart "loves only justice" (43). Telemachus himself realizes that true greatness resides in justice (218). Toward the end, it is identified as one of the "true pillars of power" (281).

These virtues will look familiar to any reader of Plato. They are the four virtues of the soul, as outlined in the *Republic*. This is hardly coincidental. Although the historical context of *Telemachus* prohibits any references to Plato himself by the fact of its predating his birth by many centuries, it carries the Athenian's stamp on every page. As Patrick Riley has intimated, this should not be surprising: Fénelon "loved the *Symposium* and the *Phaedrus* with nonconcupiscent passion" (2001, 86). In Fénelon's *Lettre à l'Académie* he took the side of the ancients in their quarrel with the moderns, arguing that Socrates had contributed substantially to the perfection of morals ([1714] 1970, 132).

9. This is paralleled in the observation that Emile would "prefer duty to her [Sophie] and . . . to everything else" (*Emile*, 439/*OC,* IV:809–10).

Fénelon leaves other important clues, beyond the simple assertion of the Platonic virtues, that he is committed to Platonism. It is a highly unlikely coincidence, for example, that the *Telemachus* begins in a cave. This is true both literally and metaphorically for Telemachus. He is literally in the cave of Calypso. Metaphorically, he is possessed of a heart that is "touched only by . . . self-interest" (Fénelon [1699] 1994, 311). In the literal cave, he is tempted by sexual desire, fancy clothes, and luxury, believing these things to be of genuine value. He can only escape with the assistance of the wise Mentor, who literally pushes him out for his own good. Metaphorically (and Platonically), these same temptations are shadows on the cave wall, preventing him from knowing true virtue. The Mentor is a philosopher who has dutifully taken on the role of going back into the cave to assist the less enlightened. Telemachus only escapes from this metaphorical cave in the end, when he has seen the light of true virtue and has practiced it out of disinterested love.

Even if these similarities to Plato were thought to be spurious, Fénelon leaves little room for doubt in the following passage:

> Then Mentor and he began to discourse together of that supreme power that formed the heaven and earth; of that simple, infinite, unchangeable light, which, though imparted to all, is never exhausted; of that sovereign, universal truth, which illuminates every mind, as the sun enlightens every body. "The man," he said, "who has never seen the light, is as blind as the man that is born without the sense of seeing. He passes his days in profound darkness, like those to whom the sun does not shine for several months of the year; he fancies that he is wise, though he is a fool; that he sees everything, though he is altogether blind; he dies without having ever seen anything: at least all he perceives is only a false and dismal light, vain shadows and phantoms that have no reality. Thus are all the men who are led astray by sensual pleasure, or the delusions of the imagination. There are not true men on earth but those who consult, who love, and who are guided by that eternal reason; it is she that inspires our good thoughts, and reproves our bad." (55–56)

The Platonic vocabulary is unmistakable—unchangeable light, universal truth, illumination, the sun, wisdom, darkness, false lights, vain shadows and phantoms, eternal reason, and so forth. Whereas Fénelon's book is hardly the metaphysical treatise one finds in Leibniz or Malebranche, its commitment to the central Platonic ontological doctrine of transcendence and its attendant virtues,[10] in addition to epistemic Platonism, appears beyond question. This is likely why Rousseau saw fit to send Emile, as a young adult, into the world with it in hand. Emile is not trained to be a philosopher in the contemporary sense. He has no need for the works of Malebranche—however divine they may be in Rousseau's estimation—because they explore details that would be of minimal use for the everyday citizen. *Telemachus,* on the other hand, carries a largely implicit assumption of the central teachings of these works, while emphasizing their most practical relevance—the virtues that should guide us in our daily lives.[11]

1.8. BERNARD LAMY

Also close to Rousseau's heart were the writings of Father Bernard Lamy (1640–1715), an Oratorian priest, student of Malebranche, correspondent of Fénelon, and author of *Dialogues on the Sciences.* Rousseau was drawn to Lamy while a young man at Les Charmettes. In Lamy's *Dialogues on the Sciences,* Rousseau found teachings against the dangers of passion, vanity, pride, and selfishness, all of which would become central concerns in his own mature work. It is little surprise, then, that he "read it and reread it a hundred times; I resolved to make it my guide" (*Confessions,* 194/*OC,* I:232).

The substance of Lamy's teachings derives largely from his own teacher, Malebranche. One finds in his work an Augustinian or Christianized Plato: "one sees things in Plato that approach the force of our religion. . . . [H]e speaks with dignity of God, of the immortality of the soul, and of spirituality. His morals are elevated and disengaged with the sensible. . . . His morals are exquisite, and little different from that of the Christians" (Lamy [1683] 1966, 250–51).[12] Like his teacher, Lamy is drawn to the transcendent and metaphysical elements of Plato.

It is therefore perhaps no surprise that, in his view, an obsession with the material world would lead to our downfall. A fixation on concupiscence, according to Lamy, leads to disorder of the soul and of the state. Again following Malebranche, he held that the general will was the will of God and that particular wills were the wills of misguided and selfish humans, stemming from their material elements. This doctrine, as Patrick Riley has noted, is extremely close to the one Rousseau develops in his mature political writings.

10. See Riley (1994, xxvii–xxviii).
11. In this light, it is revealing to discover the virtues praised in the dedication to the *Second Discourse:* justice, wisdom, and moderation (121/*OC,* III:118–19).
12. Attention to these passages is given in Lee (2001, 263–64).

According to Charles Hendel, it is in reading Lamy that Rousseau developed both his reliance on immaterial ideas and the conscience:

> Thus early . . . he [Rousseau] was impressed with the reality of ideas that are "spiritual" in character, distinct from the ideas within the soul itself, and wanting only to be given their release through meditation in order to show their reality and power. Conscience is the mind of man governing him by means of its inner laws. And man's lack of conscience, as he knew in his own heart, is due more to a refusal to listen than to an utter absence of such ideals. (Hendel 1934, 1:7)

One sees, then, the Platonic elements in Rousseau's influences and their clear imprint on his own philosophy. From an early age, he was drawn to texts that emphasized both Platonic metaphysics and virtues. It is thus more than reasonable to suppose that the mark of Plato lurks in all his most important works.

2. Materialists

While the prevalence of a Platonic and dualist school of thought cannot be disputed in modern Europe, it had met a significant new challenge by the mid-eighteenth century: materialism. Although it was in fact a school as old as almost any other, stemming back to the early Greek Atomists, it had been largely suppressed in Europe throughout the Christian era. This changed in most dramatic fashion with the works of Hobbes, most significantly the *Leviathan* in 1651. The immediate reaction was overwhelmingly negative. Even Isaac Newton, whom we might now be tempted to think sympathetic to his materialism, had used the adjective "Hobbist" as a vicious epithet against Locke. The seed, however, had been planted, and approximately a century later a new wave of materialists emerged in Paris. The most significant of these were Julien de La Mettrie, Paul-Henry Dietrich von (Baron) d'Holbach, Claude Helvétius, and Denis Diderot. Inspired by Hobbes's doctrines, they pushed materialism further into new and perhaps unexpected areas, such as animal rights and sexual ethics. Perhaps less surprising, they abandoned Hobbes's attempts to reconcile theism and materialism, suggesting and even on occasion advocating explicit atheism. This was, of course, one of the early concerns about the doctrine of materialism. Even though Hobbes professed his faith, his readers charged that his system necessitated atheism. Now that very charge was embraced by the defenders of materialism.

2.1. LA METTRIE

Julien de La Mettrie (1709–1751) was not a philosopher by profession or training. He was a physician.[13] As such, he was drawn to the works of Descartes. It was not the *Meditations,* the *Discourse on Method,* or the *Passions of the Soul* that drew his attention; these works by virtue of their theism and dualism were, if anything, antithetical to La Mettrie's ultimate directions. Rather, it was Descartes's *Treatise on Man* that fascinated him. Descartes had famously separated thinking and extended substance. This is nothing other than the mind/body distinction. Humans were granted the status of thinking (and hence free) subjects, whereas plants and animals were merely extension. They were nothing other than machines, albeit extremely complex ones. Human beings, however, also had a mechanical element. They were not simply souls—they were also attached to bodies. The *Treatise on Man* focused on both of these.

La Mettrie took Descartes's principles one step further: he removed the immaterial element from human beings. As he put it in *Man a Machine,* to assume that people were two substances was the great "mistake" of contemporary philosophy (La Mettrie [1748] 1944, 27). Significantly, he cites Leibniz, Malebranche, and Fénelon as his adversaries. We are "only one single diversely modified substance"—material (76). His ground for this is a simple empiricism. Absent sense data about the soul, we cannot assert its existence. What we *can* observe, however, are the effects of the body on the mind. He cites a litany of examples to suggest that our behavior is not motivated so much by a soul as by material causes. Opium, coffee, food, climate, and the menstrual cycle all affect human behavior, he suggests, in fairly predictable and scientifically discernable ways. Opium, for example, as a material substance, has the capacity to transport an individual "into a state of happiness" (32). That our very mood is affected not by any activity of an immaterial substance, but rather by the most simple and explainable physical process, is suggestive of this one-substance worldview, according to La Mettrie.

---

13. It was in fact his chosen profession that, in his own estimation, made him a superior philosopher to his contemporaries: "Physician-philosophers probe and illuminate the labyrinth that is man. They alone have revealed man's springs hidden under coverings that obscure so many other marvels." Theologian-philosophers like Malebranche, by contrast, speak "shamelessly on something they are incapable of understanding" (La Mettrie [1748] 1994, 29).

His materialism has several intriguing consequences. First, he erases the line between animals and human beings. Because all creatures are made of the same substance, he argues, they must ultimately have similar capacities. Focusing on orangutans, he suggests that with simple improvements in their hearing and proper training, they could easily learn human languages. In fact, the primary difference between man and animals, he suggests, is in their degree of training. Were human beings and orangutans to attend the same classrooms, one might expect similar performance. Further, to the extent that there is a natural law, it is as known by animals as it is human beings, according to La Mettrie: "Its imprint is so firm in all animals that I have no doubt whatsoever that the wildest and most ferocious have moments of repentance" (51).[14]

The second surprising revelation carries over from his discussion of animals: that there is a natural law. He finds it in sentiment: "It is a feeling that teaches us what we must not do on the basis of what we would not like someone else to do to us" (53). His understanding of the natural law, however, does not purport to contradict his materialism. To the contrary, he firmly believes that the two are part of the same system. The "soul" is merely the name we attach to our material thinking faculty. It need not be free to accommodate morality. Rather, he attaches morality to an instinctual conscience. It is in this light that one can see how he bridges the gap between human beings and animals. La Mettrie does not offer anything like a theory of the good. He hints in his conclusion, however, that the materialist outlook will contribute to happiness: "Whoever thinks in this way will be wise, just, and tranquil about his fate, and consequently happy" (75). This is not a developed theory of utilitarianism, as one sees in Helvétius or especially Bentham. It does, however, suggest the beginnings of a morality based on something detached from free will and immateriality—things Rousseau found indispensable. It is therefore unsurprising to see La Mettrie cite Leibniz, Malebranche, and Fénelon as his fundamental opponents.

2.2. HELVÉTIUS

Like La Mettrie, Claude A. Helvétius (1715–1771) came from a medical background. His father was a royal physician. This had at least three important consequences for his life and thought. First, it fostered his materialism. Second, it afforded him the leisure to pursue his thought. And third, the connec-

14. This contradicts his earlier dismissal of innate ideas: "I would certainly not take a quarter of the trouble that Mr. Locke does to attack such chimeras. Really, why bother to write a big book to prove a doctrine that was set up as an axiom three thousand years ago?" (La Mettrie [1748] 1994, 46).

tions made through his father afforded him some protection in the face of violent opposition to his work. It is difficult to gauge just how extensive this last matter was, insofar as he still experienced considerable public opposition and condemnation of his work (Smith 1965).

His most significant and notorious work was the anonymously published *De l'esprit* (1758). Standing on the epistemological shoulders of Locke and Condillac, he hoped to give a more philosophically firm foundation to the metaphysics of La Mettrie. That is, Helvétius brought together what he saw as the natural marriage of empiricism and materialism. In this sense, we can agree with Judith Shklar that he was "Hobbes' most ardent disciple" (1969, 79). The book brought immediate censure from numerous sources, including the church, the state, and prominent thinkers of the period. As we will see later, Rousseau was among his harshest critics. His authorship being poorly concealed, he was forced to retract the book publicly at least three times.

Helvétius asserts in *De l'esprit* that there are only two sources of ideas: sensation and memory. Sensation is the faculty of receiving the impression of physical objects. Memory is simply continued, weakened sensation. Because memory is then merely a continuation of sensation, "Sensibility alone produces all our ideas" ([1758] 1809, 7).[15] The faculty of judgment is likewise another form of sensibility.[16] Although such arguments were consistent with those of the respected Locke, Helvétius's claims were still striking in an age where recourse to Platonic or innate ideas remained commonplace. Notably, Helvétius took no recourse to God and throughout his life remained an agnostic (Kors 1976, 58).

There was a similar agnosticism in *De l'esprit* toward the existence of a free will: "no idea can be formed of the word Liberty, when applied to the will. It must be considered a mystery . . . and allow that it is a subject only proper for theology" ([1758] 1809, 31–32). This also follows from his empiricism. Because there is no physical sensation of the will, philosophy can say absolutely nothing on the subject. In the absence of a will, all human behavior thus must be understandable in terms of what is observable: the seeking of pleasure and avoidance of pain. Anticipating and indeed influencing Bentham, Helvétius holds that human actions are explicable in only these terms. We are slaves of pleasure and pain. It is in this respect that Helvétius became

15. This is obviously reminiscent of Hobbes's claim that "The original of [all perception] is that which we call SENSE" (*Leviathan*, 1.2).

16. The derivation of many of Helvétius's substantive doctrines from sensation is persuasively outlined in John O'Neal's *The Authority of Experience: Sensationist Theory in the French Enlightenment* (1996, chap. 3).

known as a determinist. This conforms closely to Hobbes's account of human action. All of our actions are based on the principle of self-interest. We do not make our own moral choices. They are made for us by the balance of pleasure and pain. Thus, the only manner by which to alter the decision of a human being is to alter the pleasure/pain calculus.

This leads Helvétius to a proto-utilitarian principle of legislation. We cannot alter the minds of people or persuade them to act for the common good, so we must change their behavior by altering their incentives: "the reformation of manners is to begin by the reformation of the laws" ([1758] 1809, 123). The function of law is to make the cost for performing a socially undesirable act more painful than the act is itself pleasurable. By altering incentives, we alter human behavior, because behavior is completely predictable by virtue of its determinism.

Helvétius's moral system is similarly proto-utilitarian. Because there can be no proof of the "unintelligible dreams of the Platonists" (102), we must turn to what is observable with our senses: happiness. Virtue, on his account, is therefore the promotion of the greatest general happiness in a community. Likewise, justice is defined as "the practice of actions useful to the greater number" (178). Because we have no free will, however, we cannot consciously choose to be virtuous or just. We can only make rational calculations that will best serve our self-interest. It is the function of the law to promote the greatest happiness for all, so virtuous actions ultimately result from our acting in accordance with the laws.

2.3. D'HOLBACH

Like Helvétius, Paul-Henry Dietrich von (Baron) d'Holbach (1723–1789) came from a wealthy family. This not only afforded him the luxury to pursue his writing, unfettered to any patron, but also allowed him regularly to host meetings of what Rousseau would later dub the *coterie holbachique* (*Confessions*, 333/ *OC*, I:401). From the late 1740s to the end of his life, Baron d'Holbach hosted some of the most remarkable minds of all modern Europe—including Rousseau, Diderot, Raynal, Helvétius, Grimm, Hume, Smith, Saint-Lambert, Naigeon, and Marmontel, among others—and although many misconceptions exist concerning the supposed uniformity of thought at the meetings (see Kors 1976), it is undoubtedly the case that it was a forum in which d'Holbach could express, explore, and test his particular brand of materialism. Perhaps more cautious than Helvétius, he published his works in genuine anonymity. To ensure this anonymity, there was a code of honor among the members of his coterie that forbade members from attributing his voluminous works and associated ideas to him (Kors 1976, 13–14). To further protect his secret life as a materialist, determinist, and atheist, he regularly attended church services.

Eschewing the cautious agnosticism of Helvétius, d'Holbach, in his *System of Nature,* sided with La Mettrie in asserting a one-substance metaphysics: "The universe, that vast assemblage of every thing that exists, presents only matter and motion" (d'Holbach [1770] 1999, 13). This principle extended to human beings. No less than stones, people are purely material. "MAN," for him, is nothing more than "the result of a certain combination of matter" (14). Any attempt to attribute ideal or spiritual dimensions is foolishness. For d'Holbach, such fictions were not harmless. Religious doctrines supposing immaterial substance pose a great danger. Substituting authority for reason, they contribute to the rise of tyranny and authoritarianism. This has characterized the condition of humankind too long, he argued. In his eyes, his system was more than a new metaphysics—it was a mode of liberation designed to promote the permanent happiness and progress of the species.

As was the case with La Mettrie and Helvétius, materialism leads d'Holbach to determinism, or as he sometimes called it, "fatalism." Just as his culture pretended to see immaterial substance, so in its predominantly Catholic doctrines it also mistakenly asserted the freedom of the will. There can be no such thing, according to d'Holbach. Because men are purely material creatures, their behavior is accounted for in purely material terms: "Man's life is a line that nature commands him to describe upon the surface of the earth, without his ever being able to swerve from it, even for an instant" (135). We are determined from two causes. The first is natural—that which we get through our genetic composition. The most dominant of these are echoes of Hobbes, the desire to preserve one's life and the promotion of self-interest. The second is environmental—that which we get through our various forms of education—and, even though we can be educated in ways that modify our behavior, this does not render us free. Whether we choose education, or it is thrust upon us by others, this too has been determined by something other than a free will. Thus, for d'Holbach every bit as much as La Mettrie, man is truly a machine.

One consequence of his materialism and determinism is to be found in his ethics. Following Helvétius, he cannot rely on the free will to make moral evaluations. Rather, d'Holbach appeals to that which is empirically observable—happiness. Thus, utility becomes the standard of ethics: "Utility . . . ought to be the only standard of the judgment of man. To be useful is to contribute to the happiness of his fellow creatures; to be prejudicial, is to further their misery" (218). As a proto-Benthamite, he measures happiness as continued pleasure. Moral systems resting on anything else, for d'Holbach, are based on at least two chimeras. First, they suppose the existence of immaterial ideas. Second, they assume a free will.

Virtue likewise consists in promoting general happiness. Our motives, however, are always selfish. The trick for institutions, such as law, is to make socially desirable behavior coincide with our self-interest. Thus, the aim of the law is to render socially undesirable behavior against the interest of individuals through the attachment of penalties sufficient to alter behavior: as d'Holbach put it in *System of Nature,* "Morals would be a vain science if it did not incontestably prove to man that *his interest consists in being virtuous*" (221).

What most distinguishes d'Holbach from his materialistic predecessors is his explicit atheism. Whereas Hobbes attempted to portray a material God, and La Mettrie and Helvétius were publicly agnostic, d'Holbach went further to insist repeatedly that God was a fiction. His argument was simple: if God exists, it must be immaterial. There are no immaterial substances. Therefore, God does not exist. He also rejected arguments for God on the basis of first causes, popular with contemporary deists. D'Holbach argued that there was no first cause. Rather, material has "existed from all eternity" (23). There is no need of God as a cosmically causal agent.

2.4. DIDEROT

The most illustrious and well known of the French Enlightenment materialists was undoubtedly Denis Diderot (1713–1784). He was also, paradoxically, the least invested and least public of the materialists. By "least invested" I mean that Diderot's interests were broader than those of La Mettrie and d'Holbach, for example, who are now known almost exclusively for their materialism. He had wide-ranging interests, most fittingly symbolized by his editorship of the *Encyclopédie.* He was the least publicly a materialist for the simple reason that he did not publish any of his materialist works during his lifetime. In fact, at the time of his death he assumed that the solitary copy of his most significant materialist treatise, *D'Alembert's Dream,* had been burned. It was only by chance that this work was ever known to anyone outside his circle of closest friends.

D'Alembert's Dream takes a considerably different form from those of the works of La Mettrie, Helvétius, and d'Holbach. Diderot's materialism is delivered as a dialogue. It opens as a conversation between Diderot and d'Alembert on the existence of God and materialism. Although the character of d'Alembert acknowledges difficulties attached to an immaterial God, he has a more difficult time wrapping his mind around the materialism he holds necessarily to follow from atheism. If one dismisses God altogether, he says, "then you will have to admit that stones can think" (Diderot [1830] 1956, 92). Diderot responds that the difference between man and stone is not as great as most suppose. In fact, one can be transformed into the other. A marble statue can be ground up, planted with seeds, fed to human beings and hence become human. There is thus nothing significantly separating one material from another, other than its particular organization. Therefore, Diderot argues that human beings are purely material. Echoing Hobbes, he finds in them nothing but a conglomeration of fibers, possessing senses like "vibrating strings" (100).[17]

If the difference between a person and a statue is negligible, the difference between a person and other animals is even less so. A baby chick comes from a purely mechanical process, argues Diderot. An egg is mixed with a germ, which in turn is heated (a form of motion), and a life emerges from it. Likewise is the origin of human beings. Thus, Diderot concludes, "if you admit that there is no difference between you and the animals except in degree of organization, you will show reason and common sense as well as good faith" (102). All creatures, be they living or otherwise, are made up of the same substance. To think anything else is, on his account, "[t]heologico-metaphysical fiddle-faddle" (103).

Following his materialist predecessors, Diderot likewise derives determinism from his materialism. There is no free will. What others call a "will" is in reality the outcome of a series of impulses.[18] More so than Helvétius and d'Holbach, who hold some hope for education in the shaping of virtuous individuals, Diderot is a biological determinist: "A person has either a good or a bad heredity, and once born he is insensibly drawn into the general current that carries one person along to glory and another to a shameful end" (161).

Diderot's ethics similarly derive from his materialism and determinism. Because there is no free will and no external ideas on which to rest standards, there is only pleasure, and, in this respect, Diderot is perhaps the most radical of the eighteenth-century materialists. He not only endorses onanism but also appears to condone interspecies sex. The only standard is pleasure. As long as pleasure is present, it is evidently virtuous. Thus, chastity cannot be a virtue,

17. See the introduction to Hobbes's *Leviathan*.
18. See *Leviathan*, 6.53.

because no pleasure is derived from it.[19] He is a thoroughgoing utilitarian, every bit as much as Bentham, and probably more so than J. S. Mill.

3. Rousseau's Relationships with the Platonists and Materialists

Whereas Rousseau's works speak to the ages, it is also the case that a careful, historically sensitive reading of his writings is ultimately necessary to appreciate the origin of and faithfully interpret these otherwise timeless pieces. He was a man who lived in a particular age, in a particular culture, who read particular books, and had specific friends and enemies. All of these factors contributed to the formation of his most significant ideas. He entered some of the most engaging and vital debates of his day, and his answers were in many respects wholly original.

It has often been noted that Rousseau was an active participant in the Enlightenment. This begs the question, however, of how to define this movement properly. For quite some time, many historians of political thought have asserted that it was the age of materialism and atheism. This view, however, is inaccurate or at least incomplete. As historians have demonstrated, the views of La Mettrie, Helvétius, d'Holbach, and Diderot were far from the only, or even the dominant, voices (e.g., Bradley and Van Kley 2001; Sorkin 2003, 2005). They existed, to be sure, but there are reasons why their works were published anonymously, if they were published at all. This is because there were other, more dominant, currents of the Enlightenment that, though revolutionary in their use of reason and faith in the idea of progress, were traditional in respect to metaphysics and morals. As the historian of the *coterie holbachique* itself has acknowledged, not even in the heart of materialist Paris, the d'Holbach salon, was there consensus on materialism and atheism. For all those who passed through his salon, d'Holbach was alone with Naigeon, Diderot, and an occasional visit from Helvétius in his radical materialism (Kors 1976, 41–81). This is a far cry from the suggestion that Rousseau's status as a modern automatically implies a commitment to materialism and positivism. In fact, just the opposite is true. To understand Rousseau's metaphysical commitments properly, we must understand two important elements of his education: the impression on him made by Plato and the modern Platonists and his complex relationship with the materialists.

19. This is quite possibly a response to Rousseau's portrait of chastity as the great virtue practiced by Julie and Saint Preux in *Julie*.

4. Rousseau's Familiarity with the Modern Platonists

There is little doubt that Rousseau was intimately familiar with a number of the modern European Platonists, and though he does not make reference to each and every figure of the movement, he cites many and is considerably sympathetic with the views of others. Further, regardless of whether he was intimately familiar with the works of all of the Platonists, he participated in a milieu that was in large part shaped by their various contributions. The modern Platonists can be placed in three categories with respect to their influence on Rousseau: (1) those with little or no direct influence, (2) those plausibly with some, and (3) those likely with extensive influence.

Some authors can be dismissed as having little or no direct influence on the thought of Rousseau. First, because of Rousseau's unfamiliarity with the English language, it is unlikely that he ever read the Cambridge Platonists.[20] Second, because of the mostly regional fame of the German pre-Leibnizian Platonists and Rousseau's lack of competency in German, it is unlikely that Rousseau was familiar with the works of Scherzer and Thomasius. Nowhere do his writings express any direct familiarity with their specific works or doctrines. It is known, however, that Thomasius and Scherzer had significant influence over Leibniz, who was to influence Rousseau both directly and indirectly.

In the category of those with plausibly some influence over Rousseau is Ficino. Rousseau never cites the work of Ficino, but we do know that his copies of Plato were Ficino's Latin translations and, further, that Rousseau studied these with great care, as is obvious from his extensive markings. Ficino introduces each dialogue with an essay of his own. It is likely that Rousseau read, or at least perused, the prefatory essays at least in part, and it is not inconceivable that his respect for these works led him to Ficino's other writings on matters Platonic. He had both the language skills and the interest.

The remaining category is of those who likely had a substantial effect on Rousseau's development. This includes Descartes, Leibniz, Malebranche, Lamy, and Fénelon. In each instance, Rousseau's tributes are both explicit and implicit. Descartes, for example, is cited as having "vast genius" in "no need of masters" (*FD*, 26/*OC*, III:29), on par with no less than Isaac Newton. Rousseau indicates that his exposure to Descartes goes back at least as far as

---

20. Their works also, however, existed in Latin, which Rousseau could read. Thus, it is not inconceivable that he stumbled across their work, though there is no direct evidence of such being the case.

Les Charmettes, where he was introduced to the rationalist's ideas through a physician and amateur philosopher, Jean-Baptiste Salomon (Cranston [1982] 1991, 120–21). In the evenings, he would often occupy himself by reading the works of Descartes (*Confessions*, 199/*OC*, I:237). He implicitly endorses Cartesian doctrines on several occasions. He employs, for example, Descartes's term "immense Being" *(Être immense)* to describe God (Rousseau [1769] 1997, 276/ *OC*, IV:1137; *Emile*, 285/*OC*, IV:592; see also Descartes [1641] 1968, 136).[21] More significantly, he follows Descartes's mind/body distinction, offered in *The Passions of the Soul* (e.g., articles 24–25). Rousseau unambiguously held that we are both flesh and spirit ([1769] 1997, 274–75/*OC*, IV:1135–37). Finally, he accepts Descartes's characterization of animals as automatons or machines (*SD*, 140/*OC*, III:141; see Descartes [1637] 1968, 73), albeit machines with the morally relevant capacity to sense pain. Human beings, on the other hand, are creatures with a soul and free will. What unites all these appropriations from Descartes is their immateriality. Not the "immense Being," the soul, or freedom has any material essence for Descartes or Rousseau.

One finds even larger imprints of Leibniz, whom Rousseau also encountered in his studies at Les Charmettes. As was the case with Descartes, Rousseau is not stingy with praise: Leibniz "died laden with goods and honors, and . . . even deserved more" (Rousseau [1751] 1997b, 82/*OC*, III:92).[22] The most obvious place in which Rousseau adopted Leibniz's peculiar doctrine is in his "Letter to Voltaire." Devastated by the Lisbon earthquake of 1755 that killed thousands, Voltaire wrote a long poem on the disaster, using the opportunity to jab at Leibniz's doctrine that we live in the best of all possible worlds. How could the best of all possible worlds, reasoned Voltaire, include the senseless killing of multitudes?

Rousseau's passionate response was sent some five months later, and it constitutes nothing less than a thorough defense of Leibniz. He reasoned that Leibniz's doctrine was still perfectly sensible, even in the wake of such horrors. Beginning with the existence of God ("Letter to Voltaire," 242/*OC*, IV:1070), we can believe that it is either good or bad. If God is good, it will prevent all the evils it can, consistent with the freedom of human beings. If God is evil, then it will inflict cruelties on human civilization, willy-nilly. The difference between Rousseau's and Voltaire's theology, according to Rousseau, is on specifically this point. Rousseau's God is good; Voltaire's is evil. Voltaire's God "could have prevented all your evils: hence do not hope that they will ever

---

21. See Butterworth, Cook, and Marshall (2000, 335).
22. See also Hendel (1934, 1:134).

end; for there is no understanding why you exist, if not to suffer and to die" (233/IV:1060). In fact, Rousseau elsewhere says that Voltaire's God is nothing less than the Devil (*Confessions*, 360/*OC*, I:429), because inflicting unnecessary pain and anguish would be its modus operandi.

The true explanation for the deaths in Lisbon, according to Rousseau, was the poor use of human freedom. God had made people free (as Leibniz maintains), but they put that freedom into building large structures in densely populated areas. Had they rather lived in smaller communities with greater numbers of simple single-story homes, they would have been spared all the suffering Rousseau and Voltaire agree was tragic. Nature had not built those houses. It was man. Man himself was therefore to account for the evils of Lisbon. God was innocent of the charges Voltaire implied. Thus, Rousseau defends Leibniz's goal, as he put it in the *Theodicy*, to "banish from men the false ideas that represent God to them as an absolute prince employing a despotic power, unfitted to be loved and unworthy of being loved" ([1710] 1985, 127).[23]

The defense of Leibnizian doctrines in the "Letter to Voltaire" is not limited to the "best of all possible worlds." Just as Leibniz rejected the materialism of Hobbes, so Rousseau rejects the materialism of his contemporaries. Responding to the Diderotian claim that all matter is organized as a result of chance and the force of numbers, Rousseau responds, "no one has ever explained the generation of organized bodies and the perpetuity of seeds in terms of materialism" ("Letter to Voltaire," 243/*OC*, IV:1071). In rejecting such reasoning, he admits that he is turning up his nose at reasoning and taking recourse to "proof of sentiment," an epistemological principle that would later inform his Savoyard Vicar.

Rousseau likewise admired the works of Malebranche and Lamy. He placed Malebranche in the pantheon of the profound metaphysicians, along with Plato (*OC*, I:1111), and also read his works while at Les Charmettes. As has already been noted, Lamy was read by Rousseau a "hundred times" (*Confessions*, 194/*OC*, I:232). Rousseau thus read both outspoken Platonists and undoubtedly absorbed much of their teachings. One of the most obvious places in which Rousseau's familiarity with Malebranche's doctrines is evident is in his *Essay on the Origin of Languages*. Here he employs Malebranche's notion of an occasional cause: "Whoever wishes to philosophize about the force of sensations must . . . begin by setting the purely sensory impressions

---

23. Rousseau would later claim that *Candide* was Voltaire's ultimate response to his letter (*Confessions*, 361/*OC*, I:430).

apart from the intellectual and moral impressions we receive by way of the senses, but of which the senses are only the occasional causes: let him avoid the error of attributing to sensible objects a power which they either lack or derive from the affections of the soul which they represent to us" (Rousseau 1997, 289–90/*OC*, V:420–21). He warns us here not to assume that we get our moral ideas from our senses—such as thinking that being wronged is something that can be measured empirically, as the materialists and utilitarians suggest. They have, Rousseau argues, confused the occasional cause (the empirical phenomenon) with the actual cause (the inner sentiment). In one respect, he differs from Malebranche. He does not immediately attribute the real cause to God and places it in "intellectual impressions." This, however, is also related to Malebranche and Lamy. Malebranche cautions, in the spirit of Plato, against relying on the senses for genuine knowledge; Lamy likewise affirms the existence of immaterial ideas that transcend sense perception. Rousseau thus understood Malebranche's general theory, imbibed his vocabulary, and used it to attack figures Malebranche and Lamy no doubt would attack themselves.

Lamy and Malebranche also assert the existence of "eternal verities." This is something that Rousseau would affirm throughout his career. Much more will be said about this in Chapter 3.

It is worth observing one important respect in which Rousseau would distance himself from both Malebranche and Leibniz. This emerges in his attack against philosophy and science generally in the *First Discourse*. Toward the beginning of Part II, he lists a series of achievements by the learned men of modernity. Included in this list of accomplishments are "how man sees everything in God [and] how there is correspondence without communication between soul and body, as there would be between two clocks" (*FD*, 17/*OC*, III:18).[24] This is a clear reference to Malebranche's "vision in God" and Leibniz's "pre-established harmony." Rousseau acknowledges that these doctrines represent "much sublime knowledge" (17/III:19), yet he nevertheless is concerned that they also represent much idle metaphysical speculation and openly wonders how much such reflections might contribute to making good citizens.

It is in this regard that Rousseau is especially attracted to Fénelon, who combines the substantive moral views of his fellow Platonists without the unnecessary abstraction. Rousseau had identified *Telemachus* as a book for

24. It is worth noting that also included in this list are some of Kepler's laws of planetary motion—the veracity of which Rousseau would likely not question.

Emile to take with him into the real world. He would later describe Fénelon as one of those who had "opened their hearts to genuine charity" (*Confessions,* 519/*OC,* I:620). Subsequently, he would also identify him as one who "did honor to modern times" (*Dialogues,* 158/*OC,* I:863). He was extremely fond of *Telemachus.* Its emphasis on the practical virtues combined with a faith in eternal verities would nicely summarize the central lessons of *Emile.* It is worth noting, however, that he strongly opposed Fénelon's belief in perdition. Rousseau remarked that the presence of Hell in the work of an otherwise virtuous and wise man was simply "astonishing" (*étonnemens*) (*Confessions,* 192/*OC,* I:229).

5. Rousseau and the Philosophes

Rousseau's relations with the materialists were complex, and the personal and intellectual dimensions must be sharply distinguished. Personally, Rousseau was very fond (at least early in his career) of some of the most vigorous materialists of his age. He attended their salons, visited them in prison, and even relied on them for money. Intellectually, by contrast, he despised their teachings. Virtually everything they taught contradicted his ultimate arbiter in such matters—the "inner sentiment"—and it will be seen that it was in opposition to their program that he formulated many of his most significant doctrines.[25]

Rousseau's introduction to the materialists came through his friendship with Denis Diderot. He met Diderot in 1742, shortly after his move to Paris. They bonded quickly, discussing science, philosophy, and music, and frequently played chess with one another at the Café Mangins. During these early times, Diderot was not yet an atheist or materialist, holding views approximating Rousseau's deism. According to Cranston, "as young men their minds were in such harmony that they planned literary projects together as partners, not rivals, in the search for fame" ([1982] 1991, 162–63). They remained close for the next several years, and Rousseau even visited Diderot in prison in 1749.

It was shortly after this time that Diderot fell in with d'Holbach, and, although they were of different temperaments, they became fast friends (Kors 1976, 14). It was d'Holbach's salon that rapidly became home to the *coterie holbachique* (*Confessions,* 414/*OC,* I:492). Rousseau's first impressions of d'Holbach were decidedly negative. He was at first put off by his wealth and

---

25. An excellent account of these dynamics can be found in Garrard (2003).

was apologetic for his friendship (310–11/I:369). Nevertheless, Rousseau found himself a regular at the baron's house and was actively engaged in its lively discussions. The coterie met twice a week, on Sundays and Thursdays. The core consisted of Rousseau, d'Holbach, Diderot, Grimm, Morellet, Le Roy, Raynal, Marmontel, Roux, and Saint-Lambert (Kors 1976, 11–24). They were supplemented by semiregulars and visitors, including Helvétius.

The relationship with d'Holbach and others in the clique, however, suffered two breaks, the last of which was permanent. The first occurred on the heels of his success as an operatic composer. When it became obvious that *Le devin du village* was going to be a sensation, Rousseau began to perceive his friends' "jealousies," manifested in secret "clusters" and "whispers." It seemed to Rousseau that while his friends could bear his successes as a man of letters, they "could not forgive me for having written an Opera nor for the brilliant success the work had, because none of them was in a condition to forge ahead in the same career nor to aspire to the same honors" (*Confessions,* 324/*OC,* I:386–87). Shortly after this, he resolved not to return to the salon again, though at the same time to speak "honorably" of d'Holbach in polite company.

Rousseau violated his resolution when he learned of the death of the baron's wife in 1754. He had been particularly fond of his old hostess and wrote an affectionate letter to the widower upon learning of the depth of his grief. "This sad event," Rousseau later recorded, "made me forget all his wrongs," and soon he was back in the fold (*Confessions,* 333–34/*OC,* I:397). During this time, he also accepted money from d'Holbach. The amiability lasted until Rousseau failed to accompany Mme d'Épinay on a journey to Paris. Diderot and the other members expressed deep offense at his apparent lack of chivalry. From Rousseau's perspective, they had embarked on a mission to sour his reputation "from top to bottom" (413/I:492–93), and his ties with the d'Holbach clique never recovered.

Less is known about Rousseau's relations with Helvétius. This is largely because his relations with him were far less extensive. We do know that Rousseau had some personal acquaintance with him. He mentions having attended Helvétius's carnival ball in February 1755 and reportedly found it delightful (Cranston 1991, 2–3). Further, Marmontel's letters suggest that Helvétius was at least occasionally present at the early meetings with Rousseau of the d'Holbach coterie (Kors 1976, 32). Rousseau was at least well enough acquainted with Helvétius to have kind words to say about him in his own letters. In a letter to Deleyre, he wrote that Helvétius had "quit his job as a tax farmer, tied his fortunes to an honest girl whom he has made happy, and has on more than one occasion helped people in need: his actions speak louder than his writings. My dear Deleyre, let us try to have as much said about us" ([1758] 1967, 160).

That Rousseau could have personal respect for those adhering to a materialist worldview is most evident in the character of Wolmar in *Julie*. Wolmar is a confirmed atheist and materialist. He is also a model of wisdom (*Julie*, 481–82/*OC*, II:588). So, while this character is well known to have been based on Saint-Lambert, it could equally be said to describe Rousseau's sentiments about Helvétius.

It is also the case that Rousseau spent a great deal of time with nonmaterialists. In fact, as Alan Kors has demonstrated, it is a mistake to characterize the d'Holbach clique—the very heart of the movement—as a block of atheists and materialists (1976, 74–81). One regular deist at the salon, the Abbé Raynal, was described by Rousseau as "a warm friend" (*Confessions*, 310/*OC*, I:369). Raynal had argued, among other things, that God was the origin of justice and that we should exercise some caution with respect to metaphysics.[26] He was deeply impressed by the Chinese Confucian tradition, which to him was "nothing but the natural law, which should be the foundation of all the religions of the earth, the foundation of every society, the rule of all governments" (Kors 1976, 80).

Another antimaterialist acquaintance of Rousseau's at the baron's salon was Marmontel. He was a deist who held that "religion and honor are the supporters of innocence, the restraints upon vice, the motives of virtue, and the counterpoises to human passions: to deprive man of these aids is to abandon him to himself" (Marmontel 1767, 231–33). His epistemology revolved around two principles: the light of faith and the light of feeling. Neither reason nor experience could provide access to the most important truths. The inner voice, the oracle of such knowledge, becomes for him synonymous with conscience: "leave me my conscience; it is my guide and support. Without it I no longer know the true, the just nor the honest; . . . it is then that I am blind" (231–33). As Kors has noted, the role of conscience, the inner voice, is remarkably consistent with Rousseau (1976, 78).[27]

Conclusions

It is time to stop and take stock of the history thus far traversed and understand exactly how materialism developed and why it was so attractive to its

---

26. The first sentiment is echoed in *Emile*, 284/*OC*, IV:591 and *SC*, 66/*OC*, III:378; the second can also be found in *Emile* (274/*OC*, IV:577).
27. See *Emile*, 286–87/*OC*, IV:594–96.

proponents, even in the face of vigorous opponents such as Leibniz and Malebranche. There are at least two forces in the seventeenth century that make the appeals to materialism and positivism attractive to Hobbes. First, as has already been discussed, he lived at the cusp of the transformation of the natural sciences. As a good friend of one of the leaders of this metamorphosis, Francis Bacon, he was keenly aware of the power of this burgeoning mode of inquiry. Bacon had carefully excised the "Idols of the Mind" from natural philosophy—obstacles and prejudices that had held up scientific inquiry for the better portion of recorded European history, as he saw it. In doing so, he argued that he had opened the gates seemingly to the limitless potential to improve life on earth. Bacon called one of these idols the "Idol of the Theater"—prejudices engulfing entire cultures to their own detriment. To be sure, foremost in Bacon's mind was the vast prejudice of Aristotelian scholasticism with its commitment to theological and immaterial principles. But further, in this regard, Bacon would have his problems with Plato, who had "intermingled his philosophy with theology" (Bacon [1605] 2002, 146). Likewise for Hobbes, Plato had committed the philosophic sin of introducing immaterial ideas to address real-world problems. As Hobbes might have viewed things, science had languished for centuries under the old Platonic assumptions. Now it had the opportunity to move forward absent of the old prejudices.

Politics had likewise come to an apparent impasse immediately preceding and during the life of Thomas Hobbes. The relative consensus on religious matters of the Middle Ages had given way to chaos in the wake of Martin Luther. Conflicts between Protestants and Catholics and between various sects of Protestantism revealed this eroding consensus. These conflicts were particularly visible in Hobbes's England, where quarrels between Anglicans and Catholics, on the one hand, and Anglicans and Presbyterians, on the other, had paved the way for civil war. As Ross Harrison argues (2003), Hobbes viewed this tension as inescapable until the comprehensive views characterizing religion were extirpated from politics. Immaterial ideas are inherently controversial. Because there is no definitive way to assess their existence and nature, interpretations of them will necessarily vary. And if politics were to be based on these controversial ideas, Hobbes reasoned, they would likewise necessarily be characterized by conflict. This is the respect in which Hobbes's turn away from Platonism can be understood in its most charitable and effective light.

Understanding the context for Thomas Hobbes helps shed some light on the motives of the philosophes. As central figures in the Enlightenment, they were the great champions of modern natural science. Like Hobbes, they had grown weary of immaterial explanations for natural phenomena. It was their considered view that this flimsy metaphysics had represented one of the greatest barriers to progress. History was on an upward trajectory. Science and the accumulation of worldly wisdom were on an inevitable path to the improvement of life on earth. In this light, it made no sense to return to antiquity for inspiration. It was part of what might only be considered the regrettable past. To be sure, there was proof in the pudding. Very little progress was made in numerous areas of human learning between the heady days of ancient Athens and the period immediately preceding the Renaissance. The fact that such progress had been made between the Renaissance and the middle of the eighteenth century testified to a fundamental rejection of the past and an embrace of a bold new vision of the world—one fueled by the achievements of Bacon and Hobbes. Thus, Hobbesian materialism seemed like the champion metaphysics, the one obviously most deserving of canonization in the *Encyclopédie.*

Furthermore, if Hobbesian metaphysics were true, it appeared obvious to the philosophes that its assumptions had to be carried over to the realm of politics and ethics. Philosophic consistency seemed to demand it. Thus, morality was no longer contingent upon such things as free will and abstract ideas of the good. Continued reliance on such outmoded concepts threatened to stunt moral growth just as much as the natural sciences were slowed by scholasticism. Likewise in politics, immaterial abstraction had proven detrimental to progress. Filmer, for example, had used abstractions in the Bible to argue that the political power of existing kings had come from God—an argument that would prove popular with kings everywhere, but decidedly unpopular with the growing commercial middle class.[28] To strike such immaterial fictions would pave the way for a more forward-looking and humane politics, they reasoned. Baron d'Holbach insisted, for example, that politics "should found its principles upon nature; that is to say, should conform itself to the [material] essence of man" ([1770] 1999, 102). Without recourse to this metaphysical truth, he argued, societies have "contained nothing but a vile heap of slaves" (104). If human beings were materially determined creatures, he reasoned, then their behavior could be counted on to follow from simple incentives of pleasure and pain in order to promote the general good of the community.

It was in response to reading such texts, and living in the culture that informed them, that Rousseau would compose all of his most significant works. But it must also be kept firmly in mind that, despite the growing

---

28. This association between immaterial ideas and divine king theory was made explicitly by d'Holbach ([1770] 1999, 104).

prominence of the materialists, there was an equally vibrant community of scholars who contested these assumptions, finding Plato of more solace than Hobbes. Thus, it would be difficult to make many assumptions about Rousseau's beliefs solely on the basis of the epoch in which he lived. A few things, however, should be clear. First, Rousseau grew up in a Europe largely friendly to Platonism. Many of the most respected philosophers preceding him on the Continent were Platonists, either explicitly or implicitly. Second, we know for a fact that Rousseau read many of these thinkers with great enthusiasm, sometimes a "hundred times." Third, we also know that the intellectual fashions in the Parisian salons were just beginning to open up to Hobbesian materialism. Fourth, Rousseau would befriend and then subsequently alienate some of this movement's most central figures. History can tell us these things with certainty. What was happening in Rousseau's head all along is the domain of speculation or theory. A sound theory, however, can be developed from a close examination of Rousseau's own words. His texts betray a thinker more than a little uneasy with the trends emerging in his Paris of the 1750s. The form and substance of his response to the intellectual doctrines of his one-time materialist friends is addressed in Chapter 3.

THREE

METAPHYSICS AND MORALITY:
THE PLATONISM OF THE SAVOYARD VICAR

Late in life Rousseau reflected on the philosophes, the growing group of materialist philosophers who were once his close friends. Perhaps his advanced age fostered the candor of his remarks, because he described them as "[a]rdent missionaries of atheism and very imperious dogmatists" (*Reveries*, 21/*OC*, I:1016). He added, so there would be no doubt, "I never adopted their dismal doctrine" (25/I:1016). At the same time, however, he recognized the significance of their claims. The denial of God, free will, the soul, and transcendent ideas would, if widely adopted, change the very bases of moral and political society. This was, in fact, their goal. They wanted to build a politics and morality on materialist assumptions. As Baron d'Holbach proudly declared, he was attempting to "build up an altar whose foundations shall be consolidated by morality, reason, and justice" (d'Holbach [1770] 1999, 5). These were not arguments that could merely be brushed aside. They demanded an answer, and Rousseau saw himself as the one to provide it. This answer came in the voice of the Savoyard Vicar, whose Profession of Faith takes up a sizable portion of book 4 of the *Emile*.

He described the task of the vicar as combating the "rootless" and "fruitless" morality of the materialists (*Reveries*, 26/*OC*, I:1022). It was "rootless" insofar as they had denied the traditional and proper (from Rousseau's perspective) foundations of morality—God, free will, the soul, and transcendent ideas. It was "fruitless" insofar as their attempt to construct a proto-utilitarian model of morality promised only to serve "secret and cruel" purposes (26/I:1022) instead of the genuine good of the whole community. A morality grounded in nothing could serve nothing—except perhaps the base interests of those behind its construction.

A rooted and fruitful morality, on the other hand, would have to return to the teachings of the early modern European Platonists. The vicar would thus reclaim the doctrines found in those he read so voraciously in his youth— Plato, Descartes, Leibniz, Malebranche, Fénelon, and Lamy. In taking on the materialist philosophes, he would aim to place the Platonic tenets of his heroes on what he perceived to be the firmest possible foundations. The Savoyard Vicar derives his principles from "inner sentiment" in order to affirm faiths in the foundations of morality. He was doing nothing less than attacking the most serious modern threat to morality as he knew it. Without proper foundations, morality would eventually cease to exist altogether as we slowly receded back into the amoral despotic end of political time, he described at the end of the *Second Discourse* (the *Discourse on Inequality*). Rousseau best describes his fears toward the end of his *Dialogues:* "Men nurtured from childhood by an intolerant impiety pushed to fanaticism, by fearless and shameless libertinage; youth without discipline, women without morals, peoples without faith, Kings without law, without a Superior whom they fear and free of any kind of limit, all the duties of conscience destroyed, patriotism and attachment to the Prince extinguished in all hearts, and finally no social bond other than strength" (*Dialogues*, 242/*OC*, I:971).

Drawing in large part from the background established in Chapter 2, this chapter puts the vicar's doctrines in context. Rousseau was not writing in a historical vacuum. The very futures of philosophy and, consequently, society were at stake in this contest with the materialists. Hobbism was making inroads into respectable society. It was no longer the ravings of a long-deceased British philosopher, but was now a regular topic of conversation at the Paris salons. From here, no doubt, Rousseau envisioned it extending from husbands to wives, from citizens to statesmen, from city to country, and from nation to nation. To halt *this* was the task of the vicar. In this context, we can begin to appreciate why Rousseau would characterize the vicar's doctrines as the "immovable rule of my conduct and faith" (*Reveries*, 23/*OC*, I:1018). This chapter establishes Rousseau's commitment to the central doctrines of modern Platonic metaphysics—the existence of God, free will, an immaterial soul, and transcendent ideas. Further, he establishes these principles with a Platonic epistemology, suspicious of the distraction of the senses, relying instead on "inner sentiment."

1. Doubt About the Authenticity or Relevance of the Vicar to Rousseau

Rousseau introduces the Savoyard Vicar in book 4 of his *Emile*. The monologue takes up approximately seventy Pléiade pages and fifty-seven pages of the most frequently cited English translation, by any measure a substantial work. It is divided into roughly two halves. The first is an attack against materialism.[1] The second half constitutes his objections to the practices of contemporary Christianity. Rousseau was, by his own account, far more concerned with the success of the first half than with the second, because it constituted "the longer, [and] the more important" portion, as he put it in the *Letter to Beaumont* ([1763] 2001, 75/*OC*, IV:996). It is thus ironic that it was the second, rather than the first, that brought him the most trouble, ultimately leading to his exile.

Some have denied that the views of the vicar are Rousseau's. Arthur Melzer, for example, dismisses the vicar *en tout* in his *Natural Goodness of Man*. He offers three reasons to support this claim. First, if Rousseau meant to embrace these views, he would express them in his own voice, rather than in that of the vicar. Second, he suggests that Rousseau's own metaphysical views "flatly contradict" those of the vicar. And third, the vicar's epistemic reliance on "inner sentiment" contradicts his appeals elsewhere to reason (Melzer 1990, 30).[2] As this book suggests, these arguments can be defused. First, if the vicar's views are not Rousseau's, one would need to explain why these arguments appear repeatedly in his works, most commonly in his own voice, including in his correspondence and in the *Reveries,* which Rousseau characterized as being written only for himself. Further, there are other highly plausible reasons that Rousseau would place the doctrines of the vicar in a voice other than his own—particularly because of the second half's threats to received Christian doctrines. Second, it is far from clear that the vicar's teachings "flatly contradict" his other writings. In fact, the vicar's views appear consonant and complementary to his other metaphysical and political works. As will be demonstrated in Chapter 4, transcendent ideas are essential for understanding the focus of his constructive politics—the general will. And third, there is no reason to assume that reason and sentiment are incapable of functioning together. The vicar himself notes the close relationship of sentiment and reason (*Emile*, 290/*OC*, IV:600). Further, sentiment is nothing other than intuition and, as T. K. Seung (1993) has demonstrated, is the common

1. If there were any room for debate on the object of this half, Rousseau himself described it as an assault on the materialist philosophy of Helvétius (*Letters*, 138/*OC*, III:693); see also Smith (1965, 172–84).

2. Although Melzer dismisses the authenticity of the vicar in the *Natural Goodness of Man*, he subsequently takes up the vicar extensively and argues that Rousseau has established a "new religion of sincerity" while repeating his earlier skepticism concerning the vicar's voice as the voice of Rousseau (Melzer 1996, 355).

building block on which reasoned systems are constructed in thinkers from Plato to Rawls. As Leibniz suggested, all systems must ultimately assume first principles. The vicar's tenets are precisely these first principles. Moreover, the Profession of Faith is scarcely the only occasion on which Rousseau relies on sentiment for arguments of this type. The appeal to inner sentiment is ubiquitous in his works (e.g., "Letter to Voltaire," 243/*OC,* IV:1071; [1769] 1997, 283/*OC,* IV:1145; *Dialogues,* 22/*OC,* I:687).

Victor Gourevitch is likewise skeptical in attributing the views of the Savoyard Vicar to Rousseau. He points to Rousseau's discussion of the vicar in the *Reveries* and notes that it comes "in the context of his most comprehensive and candid discussion of lying" (1998, 554). This, however, is not quite accurate. Rousseau does discuss lying, but this does not occur until the fourth walk. The discussion of the vicar comes in the third walk, and in the context of confronting the menace of materialism. Further, because Rousseau's justification for telling untruths is that they must serve justice, it would be strange that he would intentionally undermine the very standard of justice itself. Finally, this doctrine suggests reading Rousseau as having an esoteric teaching—that is, making one set of claims for the unwashed masses and yet another for those clever enough to find the subtext (e.g, Strauss 1972; Gourevitch 1994). On this reading, Rousseau knows that the masses need religion to be kept in order and has concocted fanciful arguments to persuade them of these myths. At a deeper level, however, he would be as skeptical or agnostic as his philosophe compatriots. Christopher Kelly provides strong evidence for resisting such interpretations of Rousseau (2003, 148–54). He notes that Rousseau identifies the practice of esoteric writing in Pythagoras, in China, and among his contemporaries and refers to it as a "fatal doctrine" that "def[ies] reason, truth, and time itself because it has its source in human pride" (Rousseau [1751] 1997c, 42/*OC,* III:46). Rousseau, Kelly observes, is particularly concerned about this practice among the philosophes in the *Reveries:* "this other secret and cruel morality, the esoteric [*intérieure*] doctrine of all their interests, for which the other [exoteric] only serves as a mask, which is the only one they have so skillfully practiced . . . is of no use for defense and is good only for aggression" (*Reveries,* 26/*OC,* I:1022). Thus, Rousseau not only was aware of the practice of secret doctrines but also was on the record as being opposed to it.[3] From this and other considerations, Kelly reasonably concludes that Rousseau is among the most open and sincere writers of his day.

3. Rousseau also explicitly states in the *Dialogues* (through the voice of "Rousseau") that Jean-Jacques was "without a secret aim" in his works (53/*OC,* I:728).

2. The Existence of God

As discussed in Chapter 2, the idea of God was under sustained attack by the new French materialists. La Mettrie did not explicitly deny the existence of God in his *L'homme machine*. Nor did he affirm it. The same can be said of Helvétius, who had no role for a God in his theory. D'Holbach pushed the materialist position one step further by explicitly arguing not only that there was no God but also that the very notion was hostile to an enlightened and peaceful society. His argument rested on the eternality of matter in motion. According to d'Holbach, there are two possible types of movement: acquired motion, caused by some external force, and spontaneous motion, which is internally caused. The problem with theological explanations of the world, for d'Holbach, is that spontaneous motion is mythological. All matter and motion is eternal (d'Holbach [1770] 1999, 16–26). Therefore, God is unnecessary as an explanation for either.

In this context, we can understand the introduction to the vicar's argument. It is framed in such a way as to leave little doubt that it was responding to precisely d'Holbachian concerns.[4] Like d'Holbach, the vicar distinguishes two kinds of movement: communicated and spontaneous. Unlike d'Holbach, however, he holds that movement must have a first cause. Because such a cause must exist, there must have been at least one instance of spontaneous movement in the history of the universe. A first cause by definition cannot be a communicated movement.

Further, in light of the Newtonian orderliness of motions, reasons the vicar, they must have been initiated by some intelligence. This leads him to one of his three articles of faith: "If moved matter shows me a will, matter moved according to certain laws shows me an intelligence" (*Emile,* 275/*OC,* IV:578). This is nothing less than God. The intelligent designer is likely a response to Diderot, who speculated in his *Philosophical Thoughts* that all order is the consequence of chance.[5] Rousseau references Diderot by noting that the materialists find all order the consequence of "combination and chance." He is unimpressed by such arguments, remarking, "if someone were to come to me and say that print thrown around at random had produced the

4. D'Holbach's *System of Nature* was not published until some eight years after *Emile,* so Rousseau cannot be said to be responding to the book. It is likely, however, that Rousseau was familiar with d'Holbach's arguments, because they were a frequent topic of conversation at the salon.

5. Leo Damrosch, in sketching some of the fundamental differences between Rousseau and Diderot, notes that in comparison with his old friend, Rousseau "held firmly to belief in God and the soul" (2005, 295).

Aeneid all in order, I would not deign to take a step to verify the lie" (*Emile*, 275–76/*OC*, IV:580).[6] The universe cannot be explained by random chance, even with numerous opportunities for repeating experiments. It is too intricate for such facile explanations. Rousseau rounds out his discussion of God with an adumbration of its attributes, including intelligence, power, will, and goodness.[7]

The vicar's Profession of Faith is not the only occasion on which Rousseau expressed a faith in God. It is likewise found in his "Letter to Voltaire."

> I believe in God just as strongly as I believe in any other truth, because to believe and not to believe are the things that least depend on me, because the state of doubt is too violent a state for my soul, because when my reason wavers, my faith cannot long remain in suspense, and decides without it; and finally because a thousand things I like better draw me toward the more consoling side and add the weight of hope to the equilibrium of reason. ("Letter to Voltaire," 242–43/*OC*, IV:1070–71)

Rousseau's argument for the existence of God is less elaborate here than it is in the *Emile*, but it is largely the same in substance. Setting the pattern that would be adopted by the vicar, Rousseau argues that materialism is insufficient to explain the phenomenon of motion. Materialism, according to the letter, is simply incapable of explaining the organization or motion of matter. Their intricacies evince intelligent design, and, even if materialists could offer convincing arguments, he would not be persuaded. This is because they would conflict with his "*proof of sentiment*" or the "invincible disposition of my soul" (243/IV:1071).

3. Free Will

As has already been established, the materialists uniformly rejected free will. If there is no such thing as spontaneous movement, all human behavior must be the effect of some external cause. Freedom of the will was perhaps most explicitly denied in the "dangerous" (Rousseau, *Letters*, 138/*OC*, III:693; [1758]

---

6. Lest one doubt that this is the voice of Rousseau, consider his 1759 "Letter to Voltaire": "if someone were to tell me that, with one fortuitous throw of characters, the *Henriade* was composed, I would unhesitatingly deny it" (243/*OC*, IV:1071).

7. It is an assumption of God's goodness that later causes Rousseau to reject divine perdition.

1967, 160) teachings of Helvétius: "no idea can be formed of the word Liberty, when applied to the will" (Helvétius [1758] 1809, 31–32). That Rousseau rejected determinism in favor of a robust conception of a free will is difficult to dispute. As D. W. Smith has noted, Rousseau's Savoyard Vicar is in large part a response to Helvétius's determinism. Helvétius himself viewed the vicar as a response to his materialist determinism and wrote his *De l'homme* to meet Rousseau's challenge (Smith, 174).

The vicar introduces the topic of free will by directly questioning the materialists' common sense: "The more I reflect on thought and on the nature of the human mind, the more I find that the reasoning of the materialists resembles that of the deaf man. They are indeed deaf to the inner voice crying out to them in a tone difficult not to recognize" (*Emile,* 280/*OC,* IV:585). This "inner voice" is at the core of Rousseau's epistemology of sentiment. Sentiment is intuition. It is written in the heart and, when healthy, is resistant to sophistic reasoning. The materialists, however, do not have a healthy sentiment. Rather, they have become "deaf" to their own inner voice. Instead of recognizing the most obvious first principles, they have perverted their reason to accept the most counterintuitive claims.

Healthy sentiment confirms our autonomy. According to the vicar, it only takes a moment's reflection to arrive at this, his third article of faith: "To suppose some act, some effect, which does not arrive from an active principle is truly to suppose effects without cause; it is to fall into a vicious circle. Either there is no first impulse, or every first impulse has no prior cause; and there is no true will without freedom. Man is therefore free in his actions and as such is animated by an immaterial substance" (*Emile,* 280–81/*OC,* IV:566–67).

This is one of the most persistent motifs in all of Rousseau's work. It is also one of the most necessary. His earliest significant treatment comes in the *Second Discourse,* where he distinguishes human beings from animals:

> I see in any animal nothing but an ingenious machine to which nature has given senses in order to wind itself up and, to a point, protect itself against everything that tends to destroy or disturb it. I perceive precisely the same thing in the human machine, with this difference that Nature alone does everything in the operations of the Beast, whereas man contributes to his operations in his capacity as a free agent. The one chooses or rejects by instinct, the other by an act of freedom; as a result the Beast cannot deviate from the Rule prescribed to it even when it would be to its advantage to do so, while man often deviates from it to his detriment. Thus a Pigeon would

starve to death next to a Bowl filled with the choicest meats, and a Cat atop heaps of fruit or grain, although each could very well have found nourishment in the food it disdains if it had occurred to it to try some; thus dissolute men abandon themselves to excesses which bring them fever and death; because the Mind depraves the senses; and the will continues to speak when Nature is silent. (140/*OC*, III:141)

This passage is revealing in at least two important respects. First, it suggests—in opposition to Melzer's claim that the vicar's views are contradicted elsewhere in Rousseau's work—that there is great consistency between the views of the vicar and of Rousseau.[8] Freedom is decidedly a defining characteristic of human beings, and this point is clearly established in Rousseau's own voice. Second, Rousseau likely chose to contrast animals with human beings in reply to La Mettrie's (and subsequently Diderot's) view that there is little or no difference between animals and human beings. The fact that he chooses to employ the word "machine" with reference to animals likely testifies to the fact that he had La Mettrie in mind.[9] The erasure of the line between human beings and animals was perhaps an inevitable consequence of materialism. Once the autonomy of human beings is denied, La Mettrie is perhaps obliged to say that a trained ape "would be a real man" (La Mettrie [1748] 1994, 41). Rousseau thus attempts in the *Second Discourse* to reclaim the distinctness of human beings by reclaiming their freedom.[10]

Leo Strauss challenges the significance of this passage by suggesting that Rousseau dispenses with moral freedom in favor of perfectibility as the defining feature of human nature.[11] To support his interpretation, he points to Rousseau's admission that, "even if the difficulties surrounding all these ques-

8. It is worth noting that elsewhere Melzer acknowledges the importance of a free will to Rousseau's larger program (1990, 19).

9. Rousseau later makes a joking allusion to La Mettrie by noting, in the context of a critique of materialism, that "a sweet tooth is the dominant vice only of people who feel nothing" (1997, 289/ *OC*, V:418). It was rumored that La Mettrie met his fate in 1751 from complications of gluttony (see Gourevitch 1997, 405).

10. Rousseau also later responds to La Mettrie's effacing of the line between humans and animals. In his *Letter to d'Alembert*, he remarks, "Man is not a dog or a wolf. It is only necessary in his species to establish the first relations of society to give his sentiments a morality unknown to beasts. The animals have a heart and passions; but the holy image of the decent and the fair enters only the heart of man" (86–87/*OC*, V:79). Thus, Rousseau goes beyond claims of freedom specifically to introduce notions of morality and fairness in distinguishing animals from humans, concepts directly opposed to La Mettrie's materialism.

11. This argument is later echoed by Roger Masters (1968, 69–71).

tions left some room for disagreement about this difference between man and animal, there is another very specific property that distinguishes between them" (*SD,* 141/*OC,* III:142). This is perfectibility. Because "difficulties" persist in these matters, Strauss infers, Rousseau has no intention of resting his arguments on dualism. Perfectibility is thus offered as a bridge to unify both dualists and materialists in the *Second Discourse.* This, however, in no way implies an abandonment of free will. It is rather to defer more substantial arguments for freedom to another occasion and to move on with the present business of explaining the origins of inequality. If Strauss were right, he would then have to explain all the other instances in which Rousseau makes similar arguments for free will.

One example of this is his "Letter to Franquières." In words remarkably reminiscent of the vicar's, Rousseau challenges his correspondent:

> How can you fail to be sensible [to the fact] that this same law of necessity which, according to you, alone regulates how the world and all events proceed, also regulates all the actions of men, all the thoughts of their heads, all the sentiments of their hearts, that nothing is free, that all is forced, necessary, inevitable; that all movements of man, directed by blind matter, depend on his will only because his will depends on necessity: that there are in consequence neither virtues nor vices, neither merit nor demerit, nor [any] morality in human conduct, and that for you the words honest man or scoundrel must be devoid of all sense? Yet they are not so, I am quite certain of it. For all your arguments, your honest heart protests against your sad philosophy. You are sensible to the sentiment of freedom, to the charm of virtue in spite of yourself, and this is how on all sides this forceful and salutary voice of the internal sentiment recalls everyone whom his misguided reason leads astray to the bosom of truth and virtue. Bless this holy and beneficent voice, Sir, which returns you to the duties of man and which the fashionable philosophy would end up making you forget. Yield to your arguments only when you feel that they agree with the dictamen of your conscience, and whenever you feel that they contradict it, you may be sure that it is they that deceive you. ([1769] 1997, 283/*OC,* IV:1145)

Rousseau not only echoes here the vicar's third article of faith in remarkably faithful fashion but also elaborates that this freedom is absolutely necessary for morality to exist in any meaningful sense. This places a substantial obstacle in the path of those, such as Roger Masters, who suggest that the vicar's dualist metaphysics is "detachable" from Rousseau's general doctrines (Masters 1968, 73–89; see O'Hagan 2004, 80–84). This interpretation is available only to those who eliminate morality altogether from Rousseau's doctrines, and that, too, is refuted by the "Letter to Franquières." Further, because a central purpose of the *Social Contract* is to endow human beings with the capacity for morality they previously lacked (53/*OC,* III:364), morality grounded in free will seems to be at the very core of not only his metaphysical speculations but also his politics.

One text stands in opposition to this interpretation. Rousseau notably writes a "Fragment on Freedom" between the composition of his first and second discourses, a period during which he was still largely friendly with the philosophes. Here his thought reflects an uncharacteristic agnosticism on an important metaphysical matter: "I have no idea if the acts of my will are in my own power or if they follow an outside impetus, and I care very little about knowing that, since this knowledge could not influence my behavior in this life, and, if there is another as I believe, I am convinced that the same means by which I can create my current happiness must also earn my immortal felicity" (1994b, 12). This passage is fascinating for at least two reasons. First, it is his first recorded engagement with the important question of the freedom of the will. Second, it contradicts virtually everything else he ever wrote on moral or metaphysical freedom. This latter point begs to be addressed.

Rousseau is often charged with being a philosopher of contradiction, even though that is rarely the case. In light of the foregoing discussion, however, this is one occasion on which it is unambiguously true. How does one make sense of this obvious contradiction? There are a few possibilities. First, we might assume that Rousseau has a secret doctrine of agnosticism or even determinism. This interpretation, however, is difficult to sustain in light of the many occasions on which Rousseau asserts the freedom of the will (as noted above). This commitment to moral or metaphysical freedom continues through his very last works, including the *Dialogues* (e.g., 140/*OC,* I:841–42) and the *Reveries* (e.g., 76–77/*OC,* I:1052–53). Further, as already noted, Rousseau despised the notion of secret teachings—a practice generally at odds with his overwhelming sincerity. Even Arthur Melzer, who is generally skeptical about Rousseau's metaphysical commitments, argues that he denies the Christian doctrine of original sin primarily to protect the more important doctrine of free will (1990, 19). Second, one might argue that Rousseau holds contradictory views. Sometimes he believes in free will; at other times, he is skeptical.

The problem with this interpretation, however, is that the "Fragment on Freedom" is the only occasion on which he expresses this level of doubt, so if he maintains both contradictory positions, they are played out in his mind rather than in his writings.

The third interpretive possibility is that Rousseau was undecided on this question for a period of time before settling the matter. This is attractive for several reasons. First, Rousseau's early indecision on freedom is reflected by the fact that he did not publish the fragment. If he felt certain about an agnostic or skeptical position, he would have likely said so in a published work. Second, Rousseau's fragment is likely written in 1750 or 1751, and everything written thereafter supports the existence of metaphysical freedom. Thus, the chronology of Rousseau's work best fits this interpretation. Third, Rousseau's period of indecision corresponds to the time he spent in the salons and with Diderot. It is only after the publication of his *Second Discourse* that the break with the philosophes becomes permanent. Thus, the chronology of Rousseau's life best fits this interpretation. It is not uncommon for thoughtful persons, such as Rousseau, to ponder difficult questions, such as the existence of a free will. It is also not uncommon for one to consider carefully the positions of one's close associates, such as the determinism of the philosophes. Ultimately, however, Rousseau appears to have settled this in his mind no later than 1754, when he wrote the *Second Discourse,* and he never appeared to depart from it again.[12] Indeed, strong evidence for this interpretation also exists in his "Preface to Narcissus," written in the winter of 1752–53, where he acknowledged that he had "not always had the good fortune to think as I do now." Rather, he had "[l]ong been seduced by the prejudices of my century" ([1752–53] 1997, 94/*OC,* II:962). These remarks are perfectly placed between the apparent

---

12. One would be remiss not to point out that this very question of freedom vs. determinism is confronted directly by Plato in his *Phaedo,* with similar results to those found by Rousseau:

> to say that it is because of them [bones and sinews] that I do what I am doing, and not through choice of what is best—although my actions are controlled by mind—would be a very lax and inaccurate form of expression. Fancy being unable to distinguish between the cause of a thing and the condition without which it could not be a cause! It is this latter, as it seems to me, that most people, groping in the dark, call a cause—attaching to it a name to which it has no right. That is why one person surrounds the earth with a vortex, and so keeps it in place by means of the heavens, and another props it up on a pedestal of air, as though it were a wide platter. As for a power which keeps things disposed at any given moment in the best possible way, they neither look for it nor believe that it has any supernatural force. They imagine that they will someday find a more mighty and immortal and all-sustaining Atlas, and they do not think that anything is really bound and held together by goodness or moral obligation. (*Phaedo,* 99a–c)

agnosticism of the "Fragment on Freedom" and the decisive commitment to free will in the *Second Discourse.*

4. Immateriality of the Soul

The soul was yet another battleground in mid-eighteenth-century France. La Mettrie once said that the physician who merits the most confidence is the one who "ignores the soul and all the anxieties this chimera raises in fools and ignoramuses" (La Mettrie [1748] 1994, 70). Ironically, this does not stop La Mettrie himself from defining and discussing the soul. He labels it "the part in us that thinks" (59). True to his metaphysics, however, he characterizes it as a material substance. D'Holbach follows suit. If there is a soul, on his account, it "forms a part of the body" ([1770] 1999, 70). As a consequence, it dies and decays along with the rest of the body.

Rousseau is deeply concerned by these teachings. If the soul dies along with the body, good deeds would never be vindicated. Unrewarded virtue, however, is inconsistent with the existence of a good and loving God: "If I had no proof of the immateriality of the soul other than the triumph of the wicked and the oppression of the just in this world, that alone would be enough to prevent me from doubting it" (*Emile,* 283/*OC,* IV:589–90). Without a soul surviving the body, we would live in the cruelest of all possible worlds, rather than in the best, as he asserts in his "Letter to Voltaire." It is therefore an inevitable deduction from the existence of a just God, according to the vicar. Rousseau also upholds the immateriality of the soul in his *Letter to Beaumont.* Echoing Descartes, he writes that human beings are composed of two substances: body and soul. The body is animated by appetites, whereas the soul is animated by conscience ([1763] 2001, 28/*OC,* IV:936). In this respect, Rousseau also echoes the language of Plato. Just as Plato saw the dominance of the appetite as the downfall of the soul, so Rousseau refers to the "illusion" of the body (*Emile,* 283/*OC,* IV:591).

Whether the soul lives eternally, however, is a different matter. Although sentiment speaks unambiguously to Rousseau on the existence of an immaterial soul, it does not do so on eternal life. On this specific question, Shklar might be correct in calling him an "agnostic" (1969, 108).[13] Even though he

---

13. In the face of the evidence, however, it is difficult to agree with Judith Shklar that he was a "*complete* agnostic" (emphasis added). It is worth noting here that the vicar's views are slightly modified from those Rousseau offered in the "Letter to Voltaire," where he asserted that "All the subtleties of metaphysics will not make me doubt for one moment the immortality of the soul and a beneficent Providence" (246/*OC,* IV:1075). If one agrees that the voice of the vicar is in fact the voice of Rous-

admits a lack of certainty, he still is inclined to believe the soul is immortal: "whereas I can conceive how the body wears out and is destroyed by the division of its parts, I cannot conceive of a similar destruction of the thinking being" (*Emile*, 283/*OC*, IV:590). That this is Rousseau's own view is confirmed by the fact that the character of Saint Preux, the character based on himself (*Confessions*, 362/*OC*, I:430), clearly believes that the soul is immortal (*Julie*, 311/*OC*, II:379; see also 318/ II:387). In fact, the word "soul" appears so frequently in *Julie* that one can scarcely turn a page without finding it.

5. Platonic Ideas

Because the materialists assert that all substance is matter, they can hardly appeal to Platonic ideas in their morals and politics. This, of course, is of little concern to them. Ideas existing immaterially and independently of the empirical world are, according to Helvétius, "unintelligible dreams" ([1758] 1809, 102) and "platonic chimera[s]" (188). Likewise, d'Holbach characterizes them as "chimerical" and "imaginary" ([1770] 1999, 221). Insofar as we have ideas, they come from society, in particular education (Helvétius [1758] 1809, 123). In light of their denial of transcendent standards in morals and politics, the materialists turn to utilitarianism. Pleasure or happiness is for them a tangible, physical, and empirically verifiable phenomenon. It can therefore serve as the basis of their value system. The greatest amount of pleasure thus becomes the societal and legal standard of justice, and, because pleasures are contingent, this standard changes from one society to another. This leads Helvétius to observe that different cultures have different standards of justice (83). This is virtually an inevitable consequence when first principles are contingent.

Rousseau's approach could scarcely be more different. With the establishment of God, free will, and the immateriality of the soul, the vicar turns his attention to what is perhaps his ultimate concern: morality. In doing so, he retains the epistemological framework of sentiment: "I do not draw these rules from the principles of a high philosophy, but find them written by nature with ineffaceable characters in the depth of my heart" (*Emile*, 286/*OC*, IV:594). This is the method of intellectual intuition, and it is scarcely the only

---

seau, there has been moderation of Rousseau's metaphysical claim from an immortal soul to an immaterial soul. The vicar's view is less radical. If one were to argue that the vicar's views were not actually Rousseau's, this evidence suggests that Rousseau actually had more extensive metaphysical commitments than are expressed in the Profession of Faith.

occasion on which Rousseau appeals to the moral principles being written on the heart. It is a dominant theme throughout his works. It is in his *First Discourse:* "Are not your principles engraved in all hearts, and is it not enough in order to learn your Laws to return into oneself and to listen to the voice of one's conscience in the silence of the passions?" (28/*OC,* III:30). It is in his "State of War": "If natural law were inscribed only in human reason, it would have little capacity to guide most of our actions, but it is also engraved in the human heart in indelible characters" (166/*OC,* III:602). It is in his *Lettres morales:* "There is . . . found in all souls an innate principle of justice and of moral truth, anterior to all national prejudices, to all maxims of education" (*OC,* IV:1108). It is in the voice of Saint Preux: "we all sense what is right" (*Julie,* 47/*OC,* II:58), and "He [God] has given him [man] freedom to do good, conscience to will it, and reason to choose it. He has constituted him the sole judge of his own acts. He has written it in his heart" (315/II:383–84). It is also in the voice of Julie: virtue's "timeless source lies in the heart of the just man" (126/II:155). Likewise, in the *Dialogues:* "Those innate feelings [of justice and moral truth] that nature has engraved in all hearts to console man in his misery and encourage him to virtue, by means of art, intrigues, and sophisms, become stifled" (242/*OC,* I:972). It appears in the *Reveries* as well: there are "eternal truths which have been accepted at all times and by all wise men, recognized by all nations, and indelibly engraved on the human heart" (25/*OC,* I:1021). It even appears later in the *Emile,* in the voice of Rousseau: there are eternal laws of nature "written in the depth of his heart by conscience and reason" (473/*OC,* IV:857; see also 253/IV:548).

Returning to the vicar for the moment, there is a name for those laws of nature written on the heart. It is conscience. Rousseau writes: "There is in the depth of souls . . . an innate principle of justice and virtue according to which, in spite of our own maxims, we judge our actions and those of others to be good or bad. It is to this principle that I give the name *conscience*" (*Emile,* 289/*OC,* IV:598). Conscience is the final component of the vicar's great attack on materialism.

In this respect, it is important to see that Rousseau is operating with two separate conceptions of nature. Each speaks to us, but in very different terms. The first natural voice is that of instinct and inclination. This is the only voice that speaks to savage man. In the state of nature, this is perfectly acceptable and indeed agreeable. Nature tells us to eat, and we eat. Nature tells us to drink, and we drink. At this stage, it is directed wholly at sustaining the body. Once in civil society, however, it becomes more problematic, though not to say necessarily bad. Nature may tell us to relieve the procreative urge, but the object of this desire may not be appropriate. We may be hungry, but that does not mean that we should take vegetables from someone else's garden. In some manifestations, this voice of nature is synonymous with the passions: something that is not in itself bad, but must be carefully watched (*Emile*, 445/*OC*, IV:819).

This voice of inclination is countered by a second natural voice: conscience.[14] Conscience tells us what is good. Insofar as we act in accordance with its voice, we are virtuous. Most often, it operates contrary to the voice of instinct and inclination. As Rousseau remarks in the *Reveries*, there is no virtue "in following our inclinations . . . [for] virtue consists in overcoming them when duty commands to do what duty prescribes" (51/*OC*, I:1052–53). In fact, Rousseau's understanding of freedom is contingent upon the battle between these two voices of nature. Those who act only by instinct or inclination are slaves. Those who act in accordance with duty and conscience are free (56/ I:1059).

Unlike the voice of instinct and inclination, conscience exists and operates only in the social sphere (Rousseau [1763] 2001, 28/*OC*, IV:936–37). Because there is no social interaction in the state of nature, it is absent. It only becomes relevant once people begin interacting. This is consistent with Rousseau's characterization of conscience as a principle of justice.

Beyond this, conscience is a universal, indeed transcendent, principle:[15] "All the duties of the natural law . . . are recalled to it in the name of the eternal justice which imposes them on me and sees me fulfill them" (*Emile*, 292/*OC*, IV:603). This is yet another reply to the materialists who, ruling out the existence of Platonic and nonempirical ideas, necessarily hold moral principles to be contingent. In *De l'esprit*, Helvétius supposes, for example, that "were I to run through all the nations, I should everywhere find a different behavior" ([1758] 1809, 83). And although Rousseau admits that in practice there is great diversity of mores (see *Letter to d'Alembert*, 16/*OC*, V:17), his principle of conscience and of eternal justice leads him to very different conclusions when it comes to the foundational principles: "Cast your eyes on all the nations of the world, go through all the histories. Among so many inhuman and bizarre cults, among this prodigious diversity of morals and characters, you will find everywhere the same ideas of justice and decency, everywhere the same notions of good and bad" (*Emile*, 288/*OC*, IV:597–98; see also the *Lettres morales*/*OC*, IV:1102–3). It is the eternal laws of nature,

14. Cooper holds that this voice is indeed a natural one (1999, 80–105).
15. See Cooper (1999, 83–84).

justice, and conscience that make this necessarily the case. And it is especially
in this respect that Rousseau is a Platonist.

Like other positions of the vicar, the commitment to eternal norms is confirmed elsewhere in Rousseau's works, and in his own voice. Within the *Emile,*
Rousseau reasserts the principle in book 5: "the eternal laws of nature and
order do exist" (473/*OC,* IV:857). It is in the *Social Contract:* "What is good
and conformable to order is so by the nature of things and independently of
human convention. . . . No doubt there is a universal justice" (66/*OC,*
III:378).[16] It is in the *Reveries:* there are "eternal truths admitted at all times
by all wise men, recognized by all nations, and engraved on the human heart
in indelible characters" (25/*OC,* I:1021). He speaks of "universal justice" in his
Letter to d'Alembert (66/*OC,* V:61). It is also in the voice of the respectable
Milord Edward from *Julie:* "It is in the interest of universal justice that these
abuses be set aright" (159/*OC,* II:194). It is in the voice of Saint Preux: there
are "eternal truths of morality" (*Julie,* 69/*OC,* II:84), and "the rules of morality do not depend on the customs of Peoples" (199/II:243).

6. On Rousseau's Supposed Rejection of Natural Law and Transcendent Ideas

Even though Rousseau clearly declares allegiance to eternal laws of nature and
justice, some have argued that he ultimately rejected these very principles.
They most commonly point to three things. First, they suggest that the voice
of the vicar is simply inconsistent with the voice of Rousseau (Melzer 1990,
30; 1996, 355) or is irrelevant to his larger moral and political program (Masters
1968, 73–89). As the above should sufficiently demonstrate, the central components of the vicar's attack on materialism are fully supported by other texts
in Rousseau's oeuvre and are commonly expressed in his own voice. As for the
relevance of the vicar's views to his political program, this will be substantially
addressed in Chapter 4. Second, some have suggested that Rousseau rejected
the universality of moral principles and of natural law in the preface to his
Second Discourse. And third, others have found what they believe to be a substantial rejection of these principles in the first draft of the *Social Contract,* the
Geneva Manuscript. I address these last two concerns next.

---

16. This passage clearly echoes the voice of Usbek from Montesquieu's *Persian Letters:* "I think
that justice is eternal and independent of human conventions" ([1721] 1964, 140).

6.1. THE PREFACE TO THE *SECOND DISCOURSE* AND NATURAL LAW

Rousseau opens his discussion of natural law in the preface to the *Second Discourse* by noting the profound disagreement among ancient, Roman, and particularly modern thinkers. The moderns are engaged in far-ranging metaphysical speculation so abstruse that scarcely anyone can discern their meanings.[17] Thus, the only point of accord among them appears to be that one must be a "profound Metaphysician" to be able to understand the natural law. Beyond this, however, Rousseau finds more agreement. The moderns derive their fundamental precepts from convention and utility:

> One begins by looking for the rules about which it would be appropriate for men to agree among themselves for the sake of the common utility; and then give the name natural Law to the collection of these rules, with no further proof than the good which, in one's view, would result from universal compliance with them. That is certainly a very convenient way of framing definitions, and of explaining the nature of things by almost arbitrary conformities. (*SD*, 127/*OC*, III:125)

There is little doubt here that Rousseau is rejecting at least one mode of natural law theory. The question is whether he "sweeps away the idea of natural Law, root and branch," as some have suggested (Vaughan [1915] 1962, 16; see also 424).

On this point, the work of Helena Rosenblatt has been particularly insightful. In *Rousseau and Geneva* (1997), she places the preface in its proper political, and consequently philosophical, context. She points to the very object of the *Second Discourse*'s dedication. It reads, "The Republic of Geneva: Mag-

17. It is worth noting, of course, that Rousseau does not leave ancient natural law theory unscathed in his critique. He notes that the "Ancient Philosophers . . . seem deliberately to have set out to contradict one another on the most fundamental principles, the Roman jurists indiscriminately subject man and all other animals to the same natural Law which Nature imposes upon itself, rather than that which it prescribes; or rather, because of the particular sense in which these Jurists understand the word Law, which they seem on this occasion to have taken only for the expression of the general relations established by nature among all animate being, for their common preservation" (*SD*, 126/*OC*, III:124). The fact that Rousseau is suspicious of a subset of Ancients does not threaten my overall thesis. First, he is speaking of the Romans and not remotely of Plato. Second, he is not concerned with broad principles of Platonism as outlined in this book, but rather a specific question of the subjects of the natural law. Third, he removes himself from Rome and goes back to Athens, of which he has a far greater opinion: "I shall suppose myself in the Lyceum of Athens, repeating the Lessons of my Masters, with the likes of Plato and Xenocrates as my Judges, and Mankind as my audience" (*SD*, 133/*OC*, III:133).

nificent, Most Honored, and *Sovereign* Lords" (*SD*, 114/*OC*, III:111, emphasis added). As they are subsequently identified, this is the general council of Geneva (117/III:115), rather than the magistrates, who are identified as "MAG-NIFICENT AND MOST HONORED LORDS"—a description very obviously absent of the word "sovereign" (119/III:117). This was a highly significant distinction, given the contentiousness of sovereignty in eighteenth-century Geneva.

Geneva, like much of the rest of modern Europe, was experiencing growing pains with the emergence of the bourgeoisie. Political lines had been drawn in this provincial city. One either supported the sovereignty of the magistrates (representing the patrician class) or that of the general council (representing the people, or the bourgeoisie). Each faction grounded its arguments in philosophy. The magistrates rested on the philosophy of Hobbes, Grotius, Pufendorf, Barbayrec, and Burlamaqui. Although there are differences of detail in these philosophers, the general story is roughly consistent. Individuals are fundamentally selfish, and hence dangerous. This contributes to an altogether undesirable state of nature that in turn leads these same selfish people to devise, out of utility, a social contract by which they establish a government. It is the job of government to restrain individuals so that peace may be obtained and afterward preserved. To accomplish this end, the people transfer their original sovereignty to the government. This consequently leads to the establishment of an absolute sovereign, independent of the people—precisely the argument the magistrates of Geneva hoped its citizens would find persuasive.

Supporters of the general council, on the other hand, naturally found different inspirations. One of its most vocal supporters had been engaged with scholarly disputes on natural law before being recruited to defend his principles in the real world: Antoine Léger. Léger refuted the notion that self-interest and utility could compose the foundations of moral and political society. This is because self-interest and utility are contingent factors, incapable of providing firm ground on which to build: "I will not dwell upon the *material*, or what man has which is *accidental*, but I will seek . . . what his *essence* consists of" (Léger, quoted in Rosenblatt 1997, 120). Self-interest and utility are contingent. People desire different things. Some may desire peace; some may desire conflict. To assume that all desire the same things is foolish, on Léger's reasoning. On the other hand, there are things that are universal in a noncontingent or necessary sense. These include the fact that human beings possess both a free will and a conscience, and, to the extent that justice exists, it presupposes the existence of both these things. Thus, concluding the opposite of Hobbes and his disciples, Léger found "an objective order and truth laid down by God anterior to all human needs, wants, conventions, or contracts" (Rosenblatt 1997, 120). God communicates this order to us through conscience.

These themes were developed by Antoine Léger's son, Michel Léger, in his *Représentations* of 1734. This document detailed the bourgeois grievances with the existing Genevan government. Léger connected the free will outlined by his predecessors with popular sovereignty: "the People of Geneva is free and sovereign." In practice, this meant that the people had the right to approve or deny the creation of new taxes. In theory, the fact that we are free implies that we must be sovereign. Any individual or body that would exercise this above us would be instituting nothing less than slavery. Also consistent with the elder Léger, he rejected utilitarian appeals: "it is not a question of deciding here what is suitable, but what is owing and what is just" (Léger, quoted in Rosenblatt 1997, 132).

In this context, Rousseau's dedication to the general council takes on a special significance. It is far from mere perfunctory homage. He is choosing sides, and, in doing so, he is revealing his sympathies, both political and philosophical. He identifies them not merely as worthy subjects, but as a "free People" (*SD*, 119/*OC*, III:117). Following the Légers, Rousseau finds that free people must also be sovereign. Addressing the magistrates' concern that too much popular liberty would disturb the Hobbesian peace, he finds that "they mistake unbridled license for freedom, which is its very opposite" (115/III:113). This freedom, which has no place in the work of Hobbes, is central to Rousseau and the defenders of the general council. It is the ability to legislate for oneself. Stemming from it is the right of a people to create its own laws: "I should have sought out a Country where the right of legislation was common to all Citizens" (116/III:113–14).

It is also in this context that Rousseau's attack on modern natural law can be most clearly understood. In attacking Hobbes, Grotius, and Pufendorf, Rousseau is pulling out the foundation from the magistrates. The heart of the *Second Discourse* is a critique of social contract theory, as expounded by Hobbes, Grotius, Pufendorf, and their Genevan disciples. Hobbes's reliance on contingent features of human behavior is just the first misstep. Perhaps even more disturbing for Rousseau is Pufendorf's insistence that freedom can be surrendered in a social contract: "Pufendorf says that just as one transfers one's goods to another by convention and Contracts, so too can one divest oneself of one's freedom in favor of someone else. This seems to me to be a very bad argument" (*SD*, 179/*OC*, III:183). Freedom in this sense is not a commodity to be traded. Nor is it a contingent element of human nature. It is the very essence of humanity (140/III:141). The moment it is surrendered, we do not have, as Hobbes and Pufendorf suggest, a state. Rather, we have instituted slavery. Such is not the proper goal of either a philosopher or statesman.

It is noteworthy that in Rousseau's onslaught against Hobbes and his disciples, he is, at the same time, possibly speaking to his French materialist nemeses. Because materialism entails determinism, it has no room for freedom in Rousseau's sense. Every action is caused, and hence no eternal laws can be derived, despite the materialists' best efforts.[18] Further, Rousseau explicitly rejects the utilitarianism associated with materialism (SD, 127/OC, III:125).

Nevertheless, some still maintain that Rousseau rejects all natural law theory. Marc E. Plattner, for example, acknowledges his attack as initially focused on modern natural law theory but concludes that it ultimately extends to a critique of all natural law. He draws this inference from Rousseau's definition of the essential conditions for natural law. Rousseau outlines two: (1) that we must be able to submit to it knowingly and (2) that it must be able to speak to us immediately with the "voice of nature" (SD, 127/OC, III:125). Plattner points to the fact that savages have no conscious understanding of the voice of nature. They are, in Rousseau's own words, stupid. As a consequence, they are completely incapable of meeting either criterion. Thus, Rousseau established conditions for the existence of natural law that he knew were unattainable, according to Plattner: "In short, according to Rousseau's own criteria, properly speaking *there can be no natural law*" (Plattner 1979, 106).

Rousseau's criteria for natural law, however, deserve closer scrutiny with regard to his own works. Let us consider the first criterion—that we must be able to submit to the natural law knowingly. Although Plattner is correct to insist that no one in the state of nature could perform this task for lack of reason, it is not savage man who is ultimately engaging in this task for Rousseau. Agreement to the natural law does occur in Rousseau's theory—it is in his own version of the social contract. For him, the social contract is an agreement—perfectly understood by its participants—to follow the general will in all things. The general will itself, however, rests upon the transcendent notion of justice (*Political Economy*, 12/OC, III:250–51; SC, 66/OC, III:378). Thus, the very point of the *Social Contract* is to meet the first criterion. As he says in his defense of the *Social Contract*, the contract must have "nothing contrary

---

18. La Mettrie, for example, does attempt to establish a natural law consistent with his materialism. He grounds it in the "feeling that teaches us what we must not do on the basis of what we would not like someone else to do to us" (La Mettrie [1748] 1994, 53). This "feeling," however, is either contingent, in which case so are the natural laws, or it is transcendent, which would introduce assumptions foreign to materialism.

to the natural Laws," because these laws ultimately give the necessary moral force to the contract itself (*Letters*, 231/*OC*, III:807).

The second criterion—that the natural law should speak to us with the "voice of nature"—is also lacking in the state of nature, as Plattner notes. Whether it is present in the state of nature, however, is irrelevant to the question of its presence under germane social conditions. As was noted earlier, the "voice of nature" is a significant component of Rousseau's philosophy; it is "conscience." And though it may not exist in the state of nature, this does not mean it is not natural. It is, as Laurence Cooper has persuasively argued, the most natural thing about us in civil society (1999, 80–105). It is, in fact, the "voice of nature" within us.

Rousseau's rejection of modern natural law theory is thus not a rejection of natural law theory altogether. It is instead an attempt to thwart those who would pervert its name in the pursuit of political power. As Rosenblatt concludes, "when Rousseau attacked the modern natural law school, it was in the name of a higher law, and a higher purpose for man," one that embraced "the eternal standard of justice" (1997, 177, 176). When Rousseau writes the *Social Contract* some years later, it is likely that this Genevan dispute was still firmly in mind.[19] This is why he pointedly anchors his own constructive theory in something permanent and noncontingent, as opposed to the Hobbesian magistrates: "What is good and conformable to order is so by the nature of things and independently of human conventions" (*SC, 66/OC,* III:378).

6.2. THE *GENEVA MANUSCRIPT*

A second place Rousseau scholars turn to argue that he rejected natural law is the *Geneva Manuscript,* the unpublished first draft of the *Social Contract,* written in 1756. And, as was the case with the preface to the *Second Discourse,* this, too, requires contextualization. As has been well established, Rousseau wrote the *Geneva Manuscript* to respond to Diderot's 1755 *Encyclopédie* entry on natural right. Diderot's essay represents both a challenge to Rousseau's *Second Discourse* and a call to reconsider the doctrines of Samuel Pufendorf (Wokler 1994, 385–87). In this respect, we may view Diderot's essay and the *Geneva Manuscript* as a continuation of the debates informing Rousseau's critique of modern natural law theory in the *Second Discourse.*

Diderot's essay itself makes several key assumptions. First, human beings

---

19. Rousseau, after all, identifies himself on the title page as a "Citizen of Geneva" (*SC,* 39/*OC,* III:347).

possess a metaphysical or moral freedom.[20] Without freedom, there can be no moral acts or attributes on either a personal or political level. Second, we are selfish creatures. On these two assumptions, he is consistent with Rousseau. He apparently, however, departs from Rousseau on the next two. Third, he insists that we are capable in the state of nature of universalizing our maxims, in almost proto-Kantian fashion (even though it is unclear that even Kant would grant human beings this power outside civil society). The fourth assumption is related: we are capable of reason in the state of nature. From these assumptions, he draws the conclusion that natural human beings are quite capable of discerning and agreeing to a social contract on the principles of what he calls the general will, the standard of justice. Similar to what Rousseau would subsequently say, Diderot defines the general will as always good and the source of all duties. It is the source of enlightenment and prefers no particular individuals to the general good ([1755] 1992, 17–21).

Diderot's short essay is a commentary on both Hobbes and Rousseau. Against Hobbes, Diderot asserts the existence of a free will. Without it, consent to the social contract would be meaningless.[21] Against Rousseau, he holds that natural human beings are capable of high levels of reason and abstract thought (see Rousseau, *SD,* 151/*OC,* III:153–54). Further, he assumes against both Hobbes and Rousseau that there is a standard of justice present in the state of nature, accessible to all individuals (see *SD,* 154/*OC,* III:157).

Rousseau would take up these issues in the *Geneva Manuscript.* Although much of this text was ultimately incorporated into the *Social Contract,* two chapters were dropped, either in part or in whole. Book 1, chapter 2, was omitted virtually entirely. This chapter nevertheless gives an important glimpse into Rousseau's mind upon reading Diderot's essay. He places Diderot on the side of Pufendorf, insofar as both assume the existence and accessibility of the natural law in the state of nature. Echoing and advancing themes from the *Second Discourse,* he maintains that natural man—without government, law, and order—is a stupid creature, unfamiliar with such lofty institutions and ideas. Rousseau challenges Diderot's claim that savages can access and agree to the general will. Individuals have no meaningful connections to a whole and there is no communication between persons. Under such circumstances, the only motivation available is self-interest. Further, without social inter-

20. This is obviously at odds with his later writings, specifically *D'Alembert's Dream* (Diderot [1830] 1956, 123, 140, 160–61).
21. In this respect, Diderot's assumptions concerning free will (again, later to be rejected by him) would help meet Patrick Riley's challenge to Hobbes that his social contract's legitimacy is contingent upon a freedom he denies his citizens.

course, individual understanding is incapable of development. And, without the development of the understanding, morality itself is impossible. Therefore, "we would never have enjoyed the soul's most delicious sentiment, which is the love of virtue" (*GM,* 159/*OC,* III:283).

Because human beings are selfish—though certainly not evil, because moral attributions to individuals at this stage are still impossible—and they at the same time lack the faculty of reason, the "so-called social treaty dictated by nature is a true illusion" (159/III:284). The institution of any social contract rests upon appealing to the motives and faculties possessed by the uncivilized individuals. This is a practical question. How can selfish and unsophisticated persons agree to something as important and ennobling as the social contract, which will in turn transform them into persons who will subsequently experience the "soul's most delicious sentiment"? Rousseau presents the problem in the voice of an "independent man": " 'I admit that I see in this the rule [the general will] that I can consult, but I do not yet see,' our independent man will say, 'the reason for subjecting myself to this rule. It is not a matter of teaching me what justice is, but of showing me what interest I have in being just' " (161/III:286). The question of the independent man is a legitimate one. As Rousseau himself would admit later, both in the *Geneva Manuscript* and in the *Social Contract,* agreeing to the rules of justice is a tricky business. Those alone in following its rules, while others act according to their own self-interests, are exposed to the worst kinds of misery (*GM,* 189–90/*OC,* III:327; *SC,* 66/*OC,* III:378). To persuade the independents to join the social contract, we have no choice but to appeal to their self-interest. The formation of society is not a natural act, contrary to the reasoning of both Diderot and Pufendorf. It is an artificial act. It is an agreement.[22]

This theme is expanded in the unused portions of book 2, chapter 4, of the *Geneva Manuscript,* where Rousseau promises to show the "true foundations of justice and natural right" (*GM,* 190/*OC,* III:328). Here he outlines what follows from the initial contract. The fundamental law it issues is that every-

22. Here, Rousseau might very well be drawing lessons from Hobbes. According to J. W. N. Watkins, Hobbes has "two contrasting and disconnected systems" (1973, 58). A. P. Martinich interprets these as two systems of natural law: one of obligation and one of motivation. The system of obligation (i.e., what makes them binding) descends from the divine commands of God. The system of motivation (i.e., what makes us agree to the natural laws) is fueled by the desire for self-preservation. In like manner, Rousseau gives special attention to the motivation question in the *Geneva Manuscript.* But this should not be conflated with his separate account of its normative foundations, which is the focus of his final draft. This analogy with Hobbes, of course, only works if one assumes, as Martinich does, that Hobbes is sincere in his theological foundations for the natural law (Martinich 2005, 210–11).

one must prefer the greatest good of all. To the extent that people do just this in obedience to the laws, they are acting in accordance with positive right. Should they follow this principle in the absence of laws, they are acting virtuously. With laws in place, we no longer fear doing good only to be wronged in return. Rather, we can freely develop what Rousseau calls "rules of rational natural right," which is "different from natural right properly so called, for the latter is based on nothing but a true but very vague sentiment that is often stifled by love of ourselves" (191/III:329). He appears to suggest that political right is entirely severed from natural right. This interpretation would seem confirmed by the following paragraph: "This is how the first concepts of the just and unjust are formed in us, for the law comes before justice, and not justice law; and if the law cannot be unjust, it is not because justice is its basis, which might not always be true; but because it is contrary to nature for one to want to injure oneself; which is true without exception" (191/III:329).

Several commentators have pointed to this passage in suggesting that Rousseau is a confirmed Hobbesian positivist, holding that his understanding of political justice is conventional (e.g., Masters 1968; Melzer 1983, 1990). This paragraph offers the best evidence for this interpretation. It must, however, be read with great caution. One thing we must remind ourselves of in reading it is that it did not find its way into Rousseau's final draft. In this spirit, it is important to recall Charles Hendel's caution in reading the unpublished chapters of the first draft: "Rousseau was here exploring still, and not yet master of his own thought" and was "uncertain of the way in which to represent his own ideas" (1934, 1:182, 133). Indeed, all drafts have this character, and we should not assume Rousseau to be an exception. This does not eliminate the fact, however, that Rousseau said what he did. It thus remains to determine what led him to say what he did, and why he ultimately removed these paragraphs from the final draft of the *Social Contract*.

The first interpretive problem in understanding these passages is reconciling them with the very opening of the chapter: "Whatever is good and in accordance with order is so by the nature of things, independently of all human convention. All justice comes from God; He alone is its source. . . . There is without a doubt a universal justice for man emanating from reason alone" (*GM*, 189/*OC*, III:326). This presents an obvious difficulty for positivist interpreters of Rousseau, because it appears to contradict directly the supposedly positivist passages. This is made doubly problematic by the fact that it is retained by Rousseau in his final draft (*SC*, 66/*OC*, III:378), whereas the supposed positivistic passages are eliminated.

Melzer acknowledges the presence of this passage in the *Social Contract*

(1983, 640). He dismisses its relevance to Rousseau, however, by following the quotation further. After asserting the existence of a transcendent standard of justice, Rousseau continues, "but this justice, to be admitted among us, has to be reciprocal" (*SC, 66/OC,* III:378). Melzer notes that because there are no sanctions in the state of nature, there is no admitting justice. Therefore, although there very well may be a universal standard of justice issuing from the heavens, it is of no relevance to Rousseau.

What burdens this reading is that it does not follow Rousseau's reasoning to its conclusions. One must read even further down the paragraph. After noting that justice must be reciprocal, he argues that "conventions and laws are therefore necessary to combine rights with duties and to *bring justice back to its object*" (*SC, 66/OC,* III:378, emphasis added; *GM,* 189/OC, III:326).[23] The point of conventions and laws is not to replace the transcendent idea of justice. The point of conventions and laws is just the opposite: to provide justice with the practical backbone it needs to be a positive force in civic life.

If this is the true meaning of Rousseau's chapter, one must still reconcile it with the apparently contradictory subsequent statements. Consider the two most difficult passages in turn. What does Rousseau mean when he suggests that positive right is "different from natural right properly so called, for the latter is based on nothing but a true but very vague sentiment that is often stifled by love of ourselves"? In this context, one would do well to remember Hendel's caution that Rousseau is still feeling his way through his own system. As a draft, the *Geneva Manuscript* was subject to much revision and refinement. This particular sentence was no exception. Although dropped from the *Social Contract,* a version of it is found in the *Emile:* "*justice* and *goodness* are not merely abstract words—pure moral beings formed by the understanding—but are true affections of the soul enlightened by reason, and are hence only an ordered development of our primitive affections; that by reason alone, independent of conscience, no natural law can be established" (*Emile,* 235/ *OC,* IV:522). The refinement in Rousseau's work is easy to identify. The "vague sentiment" of the *Geneva Manuscript* is fleshed out as the conscience in the *Emile.* More significant than this, however, is his treatment of justice. Whereas in the *Geneva Manuscript* it appears divorced from conscience, in the *Emile* it is contingent upon it. Justice now grows out of natural sentiment, rather than artifice. This lends credence to Hendel's suggestion that Rousseau's draft betrays an author "uncertain of the way in which he wanted to

---

23. Similarly, Roger Masters stops his reading of Rousseau immediately before it reaches this important sentence (1968, 85).

represent his ideas." The *Emile* reads more consistently with Rousseau's assumption of a universal justice and its relevance to political life.[24]

What of the *Geneva Manuscript*'s insistence that "the law comes before justice, and not justice law"? Here again the *Emile* is of some assistance. In describing the attributes of God, the Savoyard Vicar notes an intimate relationship between justice and goodness and concludes, "the love of order which produces order is called *goodness;* and the love of order which preserves order is called *justice*" (*Emile*, 282/*OC*, IV:589).[25] Although one ought not dismiss the significant theological implications in the context of the vicar's discussion, the political implications are equally important within their own sphere. Goodness chronologically precedes justice. This means that justice comes into play only after the introduction of order. Because laws constitute the ordering of the social world, it is evident that justice is a relevant virtue in a social and legal context. Hence, Rousseau was in fact right in the *Geneva Manuscript* to assert the chronological priority of law before justice. Law is the institution of order and justice is the preservation of order, so this is perfectly logical.

To say this, however, is not to assert that justice is conventional. As has already been noted, Rousseau claims just the opposite—that its content is independent of human convention. He holds this position consistently through the *Geneva Manuscript* (*GM*, 189/*OC*, III:326), the *Social Contract* (66/*OC*, III:378), and the *Emile* (292/*OC*, IV:603).

Finally, it is important to distinguish between the savage motivations for joining the contract and the content of justice itself. Both Masters (1968, 275–76) and Melzer (1983, 639), for example, suggest that Rousseau's contract not only is based on motivations other than the natural law or transcendent norms

24. Rousseau punctuates this discussion with an intriguing footnote. In it he remarks that "Love of men derived from love of self [*l'amour de soi*] is the principle of human justice" (*Emile*, 235/*OC*, IV:522). Roger Masters has drawn attention to this passage in support of his arguments (1968, 81–82). However, as Masters himself notes, Rousseau does not mean to endorse anything like the materialist teachings of Hobbes or the philosophes: "For Rousseau such doctrines are ultimately immoral because they teach that all morality gains its effectiveness from the prior existence of a social contract concluded between purely selfish men. Although utility is indeed the first source of all contractual agreements which create mutual duties and rights, for Rousseau any contract has another basis in the *loi de la conscience*" (82). This conscience can scarcely be characterized as a principle of self-love in the modern Hobbesian sense. Consider Rousseau's passage as a whole again with an added emphasis: "*Love of men* derived from love of self is the principle of human justice." The principle of justice itself is "love of men." Self-love (*l'amour de soi*) here is not the principle of justice, as one might find in a proto-utilitarian, but is rather a tool to help one arrive at that challenging principle. Indeed, the point of the tutor in the *Emile* is to help convert these natural feelings into social feelings of justice. This theme has been treated with great skill by Laurence D. Cooper (1999, esp. 90–105).

25. The relationship of justice to order is addressed in Plato's *Republic* (443d).

of justice but also grounds a political order permanently divorced from such fancy notions. They do so in part by relying on Rousseau's argument that natural man can only be relied upon to act selfishly. Although they are right to note the importance of interest as a motivating factor in creating the social contract, they stretch the relationship too far. Rousseau never says that justice is simply the realization of self-interest. We *can* learn of justice through our self-interest. This is why he tells us in the *Emile* that "the first sentiment of justice does not come to us from the justice we owe but from that which is owed us" (97/*OC*, IV:329). This is also why he states, in the *Social Contract*, that one can get a "notion" of justice by following "one's preference for himself" (62/*OC*, III:373). The content of justice is not simply the realization of self-interest, however, as one might characterize the Hobbesian system. If that were the case, it would make no sense for Rousseau to add that in the social contract there is "an admirable agreement between justice and interest" (62/III:374). If justice were merely a matter of positive interest, this would be tautological—they would be the same thing by definition. Rousseau reflects late in life on this very point: "justice has another foundation than this life's interest" (*Dialogues*, 242/*OC*, I:972; see also 251/I:983).[26] This notion is even apparent in the *Geneva Manuscript*. Returning to the independent man or "violent interlocutor," he remarks,

> Let us enlighten his reason with new knowledge, fire his heart with new sentiments, and let him learn to increase his being and his felicity by sharing them with his fellows. If my zeal does not blind me in this enterprise, let us not doubt that if he has fortitude of soul and upright sense, this enemy of mankind will in the end abjure his hatred along with his errors, that the reason which led him astray will bring him back to humanity, that he will learn to prefer to his apparent interest his interest rightly understood; that he will become good, virtuous, sensitive, and in sum, finally, instead of the ferocious brigand he wanted to be, the most solid bulwark of a well-ordered society. (159/*OC*, III:288–89)

As Charles Hendel notes, this passage reveals "his magnificent Platonic intent" (1934, 1:133). There is a great difference between apparent interest and interest "rightly understood." The latter must conform to the idea of justice.

26. The Savoyard Vicar characterizes those motivated purely by self-interest as "cadaverous souls who have become insensitive, except where their own interest is at stake, to everything which is just and good" (*Emile*, 287/*OC*, IV:546).

Justice as a transcendent idea gives the social contract a considerably different, and more powerful, meaning from that which his positivist/materialist interpreters suggest. Yes, interest is required as a practical matter. Insofar as that is true, Rousseau is modern. But the interest must coincide with the universal idea of justice, and in this respect he is quite ancient.

Conclusions

Victor Gourevitch once remarked of Rousseau, "No one of his contemporaries is even remotely as important to his thinking as is Plato. He is certainly not a 'Platonist' in the ordinary sense of the term, but Plato—or Plato's Socrates—embodies the very idea of the philosopher for him. He does not think a thought without asking himself what Plato's position would have been on the subject" (1998, 539–40). As should be clear by now, there is much truth in this. Rousseau deeply cared about Plato and Platonic doctrines, but Gourevitch is too hasty to draw the line here. Rousseau was indeed a Platonist. His commitment to Platonism animates his entire belief system. Further, although Gourevitch is correct to emphasize the importance of Plato to Rousseau, he underestimates the significance of Rousseau's contemporaries for his thought. Though the effect of the emerging materialists on him may not have been in the form of influence, it would be incorrect to say that they did not inspire him to grab a pen and set out to write. There would be no need to revive the doctrines of Plato if it were not for their particular form of anti-Platonism. In his own words, "I admit in good faith that when my adversaries' works no longer survive, my own will be perfectly useless" (Rousseau 1994a, 45/*OC*, III:516). Rousseau's Platonism is intimately linked to his relationship with his anti-Platonist contemporaries.

In this respect, the parallels between Rousseau and Plato grow even stronger. When Plato arrived in Athens, there had already been an enduring debate between Heraclitus and Parmenides. Heraclitus argued that the ultimate substance of the universe was fire. This was because all was in flux. The world was dominated by "becoming." On the other hand, Parmenides argued that that which was "becoming" was not actually anything. Rather, true substance resided in "being." If something were to exist, it would have to be permanent and eternal.[27] Subsequently, the Sophists would emerge in Athens,

---

27. In this context, it is not surprising that Plato had Socrates describe Parmenides as the "one being whom I respect above all" (*Theaetetus*, 183e).

taking sides with Heraclitus.[28] Protagoras's assertion that man was the "measure of all things" rejected the Parmenidean claim of eternal truths. They put their convictions into practice by indiscriminately making the weaker argument the stronger and taking money to this end. Forging their own "truths," they were free to do so without the burdens of conscience.

Plato's theory of ideas was the ultimate response to the Sophists. He anchored truth in objects beyond human beings, beyond their whims, and beyond their agreement. Truth stood above convention. The Sophists represented everything he found vile about his society. The Sophists' philosophy of relative truth fostered Athenian imperialism and hubris, as illustrated in Thucydides' Melian Dialogue (see Seung 1996, 95). If Athens believed it was right to conquer its neighbors, then by definition it was right. This was not only sloppy philosophy, as Plato viewed it, but it also led to devastating defeats, particularly in Sicily. If might made right, then whoever conquered Athens would subsequently establish "right"—and one would be hard pressed to find an Athenian willing to accept the rule of "the Thirty Tyrants" as truly right. It might be added that embedded in the doctrine of might makes right is an implicit hedonistic or utilitarian philosophy. The pleasure of the powerful becomes the good.

Further, many Sophists—such as Prodicus and Critias—denied the existence of the gods altogether. In this respect, the Sophists represented the shift in Athenian normative culture from theonomy (god-derived laws) to anthroponomy (human-derived laws). Earlier Greeks had assumed the existence of the gods and had attributed to them the creation of law. Lycurgus was said to have received the law from Apollo of Delphi. Minos was likewise said to have received the Cretan law from Zeus. It was also claimed that Zaleucus received the Locrian laws from Athena. With gods as the fountain of the laws, compliance was expected to be high, because violation of the law would by necessity invoke the wrath of the gods. Sophist agnosticism or atheism, on the other hand, reversed this. In a system of sophistic anthroponomy, as long as one could evade human surveillance, one could truly be said to get away with a crime (Seung 1996, 7–11).

Plato's *Republic* is in many respects best seen as a response to the Sophists.

---

28. That Plato understood the Sophists to be drawing on a Heraclitean worldview is evident in the *Theaetetus:* "believers in a perpetually changing reality [such as Heraclitus] and in the doctrine that what seems to an individual at any time also is for him [such as Protagoras] would, in most matters, strongly insist upon their principle, and not least in the case of what is right they would maintain that any enactments a state may decide on certainly are right for that state so long as they remain in force" (177c).

He firmly rejects their relativism, atheism, and utilitarianism. The forms are the ultimate response to sophistic relativism. Plato denies that truth can vary from person to person or culture to culture. Only that which is eternal is real. Being is favored over becoming. Further, in book 10 of the *Republic* he introduces the Myth of Er, where the laws are traced back to the gods, with divine consequences established for earthly mischief. Of course, divine sanctions consequently affect earthly behavior. To the extent that we desire a pleasant afterlife, we have every incentive to act well (i.e., in accordance with the laws) in this world. Finally, Plato conceived of the Form of the Good as transcending mere pleasure, which can be base (*Gorgias,* 492a–500a).

Like Plato, Rousseau arrived at a time when the very foundations of philosophy were being challenged by powerfully seductive thinkers. And as in ancient Greece, the debates concerned the existence of eternal truths. The parallel between Heraclitus and Diderot is too striking to ignore. Echoing the Heraclitean doctrine that everything is in flux, Diderot remarked, "All nature is perpetually in flux. . . . Every animal is more or less human; every mineral is more or less vegetable; every plant is more or less animal" ([1830] 1956, 124). Rousseau very consciously understood both the nature and gravity of this challenge. A victory by the positivists/materialists would, in his eyes, open the door to all forms of despotism. This concern is explicit in his *Dialogues:*

> I don't doubt any more than you do that the new philosophers wished to prevent the remorse of dying with a doctrine that put their conscience at ease, however burdened it might be, noting especially that the impassioned preaching of this doctrine began precisely with the execution of the plot and appears to be related to other plots of which this one is only a piece. But this infatuation with Atheism is an ephemeral fanaticism, a product of fashion that will be destroyed by it too; and the enthusiasm with which the people surrender to it shows it is nothing but a mutiny against its conscience, whose murmur it feels with resentment. This convenient philosophy of the happy and rich who build their paradise in this world cannot long serve as the philosophy of the multitude who are the victims of their passions, and who—for lack of happiness in this life—need to find in it at least the hope and consolations of which that barbarous doctrine deprives them. Men nurtured from childhood by an intolerant impiety pushed to fanaticism, by fearless and shameless libertinage; youth without discipline, women without morals, peoples without faith, Kings without law, without a Superior whom they fear and free of

any kind of limit, all the duties of conscience destroyed, patriotism and attachment to the Prince extinguished in all hearts, and finally no social bond other than strength: it seems to me one can easily foresee what must soon come of all that. Europe prey to masters taught by their own teachers to have no guide than their interest nor any God besides their passions, at times secretly starved, at times openly devastated, inundated everywhere with soldiers, Actors, prostitutes, corrupting books and destructive vices, seeing races unworthy to live be born and perish in its bosom, will sooner or later feel that these calamities are the fruit of the new teachings, and judging them by their deadly effects, will view with the same horror their professors, the disciples, and all those cruel doctrines which, conferring absolute empire over man to his senses and limiting everything to the enjoyment of this brief life, make the century in which they reign as despicable as it is unhappy. (242/*OC,* I:970–72)

The despotism described here is at least twofold. There is the obvious tyranny of the doctrine of might makes right, which Rousseau views as one inevitable consequence of the materialist philosophy. That is quite bad enough on its own, but there is even more. There is also the personal despotism of the passions over reason. Once one has cast conscience to the wind, the passions run amok over the soul. Because our ability to reason and act on the basis of conscience establishes our humanity (*SD,* 140/*OC,* III:141), it is, in effect, the end of our very humanity.

Again, the Platonic parallels are too striking to go unnoticed. One of the central purposes of Plato's *Republic* is to counter the dangerous teachings of Thrasymachus, who holds that "might makes right": "I affirm that the just is nothing else than the advantage of the stronger" (*Republic,* 338c). If there is no transcendent moral and political authority, all is power. This has been understood to be the case throughout the entire history of philosophy—from the Sophists to Foucault. Foucault arrives at his analyses of the modes of power in part because he denies the existence of transcendent norms. This is why he says that the proletariat does not fight wars against the bourgeoisie for any reason having to do with justice. It does so instead because "it wants to take power" (Foucault and Chomsky [1971] 1997, 136).

The similarities between Plato and Rousseau do not stop at the level of political institutions. Rather, they extend into the analysis of the individual. Just as Rousseau describes the tyranny of the passions as the senses' "empire over man," so, too, does Plato. He in fact links the political and the personal

in books 8 and 9 of the *Republic,* just as Rousseau does above. The very definition of a tyrant is a person who responds only to pleasure. The tyrant is
unconcerned with conscience. It has either never been developed, or it has
been completely obliterated. His soul is overwhelmed with "boundless servil-
ity and illiberality, the best and most reasonable parts of it being enslaved,
while a small part, the worst and the most frenzied, plays the despot" (*Republic,* 577d).

Finally, with all this in place, one cannot help but notice the terminology
Rousseau uses to condemn his materialist opponents. They are for him nothing other than "sophists." On at least three occasions he refers to Hobbes, the
modern founder of materialism, as a "sophist" ("State of War," 165/*OC,*
III:601; "Letter to Voltaire," 244/*OC,* IV:1072; *Emile,* 458/*OC,* IV:836). This
language is not limited to describing Hobbes. It permeates all his attention to
materialist doctrines. In the *Emile,* he remarks, "I can see in him [the material-
ist] only a *sophist* speaking in bad faith who prefers to attribute sentiment to
rocks than to grant a soul to man" (279/IV:584, emphasis added). In the *Reveries,* he refers to their doctrines as "sophisms" (25/*OC,* I:1021).[29] In this light,
we can begin to appreciate how Rousseau viewed his own project. It was for
him the same battle that engaged Plato some two millennia before. The challenge was at least as formidable, and the consequences nothing less than the
perceived future of all political societies.

---

29. In an undated fragment with unidentified audience, Rousseau also wrote, "Read, Sir, the
Dialogues of Plato and you will find that you were playing the role of the prideful sophist and your
adversary that of Socrates. He crushed you modestly with fearsome arguments which you very haugh-
tily answered with insults instead of reasons" (2007, 283/*OC,* II:1329). One might easily narrow down
the intended recipient of this fragment to those he elsewhere identified as "sophists"—the philosophes. This passage also reveals that he consciously perceived there to be contemporary sophists and
a contemporary Plato, with this Plato having the better argument.

FOUR

THE GENERAL WILL:
ON THE MEANING AND PRIORITY OF JUSTICE IN
ROUSSEAU

While the Savoyard Vicar provides answers to some of the most debated issues in modern philosophy, his monologue is in some sense a preface or prolegomena to his politics. Metaphysics comes before morals. In this respect, Rousseau is following one of the great traditions of political philosophy. Before we get philosopher-rulers, Plato gives us the ideas. Before we get the Leviathan, Hobbes outlines his materialism. Before the *Doctrine of Right*, Kant writes his *Critique of Pure Reason*. Thus, it can be little surprise that to develop his most important political concept, the general will, Rousseau would likewise have to devise a metaphysics. This is one of the central functions of the Savoyard Vicar. In his Profession of Faith, the vicar establishes the existence of God, an immaterial soul, freedom of the will, and transcendent ideas—all of which are accessible through the faculty of "inner sentiment" or "conscience." While many of these would play some role in Rousseau's political philosophy,[1] the most important of these is the last: the transcendent ideas of justice and the good.

The principle of justice is nothing other than "conscience" for Rousseau (*Emile*, 289/*OC*, IV:598), and the principle of conscience is that which speaks to us from the depths of our hearts (286/IV:596). It is that which precedes the maxims of culture, convention, opinion, or the passions and eventually serves as a standard by which to judge all norms. It can serve as this standard because it is necessarily something that all of these are not—transcendent: "All of the duties of the natural law, which were almost erased from my heart by the

---

1. For example, in the *Social Contract*, Rousseau finds that "[a]ll justice comes from God" (66/ *OC*, III:378) and, further, that one purpose of the state is to establish "moral freedom, which alone makes man truly the master of himself" (54/III:365).

injustice of men, are recalled to it in the name of the *eternal justice* which imposes them on me and sees me fulfill them" (292/IV:603, emphasis added).

Of course, it is one thing to say that *justice* is transcendent for Rousseau. It is perhaps another to claim that this is of central importance to his political doctrines. This is because the general will has typically (and with good reason) been taken to be the central element of his political philosophy. As Judith Shklar famously remarked, "It conveys everything he most wanted to say" (1969, 184). The dominant way to read the general will for the past century has been as a conventional substitute for transcendent ideas. According to this reading, the general will is grounded on nothing more than consent. In other words, it has been interpreted as precisely the opposite of his principle of justice.

Although much has been said about the general will, less has been written on his understanding of justice. For that matter, Rousseau himself never gives it systematic treatment. But it, too, could be considered a primary principle. Although it would be foolish to dismiss the importance of the general will to Rousseau, it would be equally problematic to explore it independently of his idea of justice. The question in understanding his work is which of these two principles—the general will or justice—is primary or fundamental. If it is the general will, a persuasive case can be made that the positivist interpreters are right and Rousseau is a Hobbesian. If justice is prior, on the other hand, there is ground to believe that he is a Platonist.

I argue that the transcendent idea of justice is prior to Rousseau's conception of the general will. Indeed, my thesis is that he is among the greatest and most consistent Platonists of the modern era. His explicit rejections of Hobbes are not merely rhetorical. In fact, they represent the true impetus of his social contract. This contract is designed explicitly to counter Hobbesian positivism. In the same way that Plato responds to Protagoras and his claim that "man is the measure of all things" with his theory of ideas, Rousseau responds to Hobbes's brutish Leviathan with a morally grounded social contract.[2] To this extent, he is following in the footsteps of Locke, who through his theory of natural law also hoped to avoid the problems associated with Hobbes's positivism. Unlike Locke, however, he appeals to the abstract idea of justice rather than a determinate set of rules. To do this, he necessarily embraces the *ontological* and *political* dimensions of Platonism. He does the latter, I argue, by placing the idea of justice prior to the general will itself. In understanding

---

2. This analogy is given force by the fact that Rousseau himself labels Hobbes a "sophist" ("State of War," 165/*OC,* III:612).

THE GENERAL WILL ■ 95

Rousseau this way, we are able to make sense of both the standards to which the general will must conform and his frequent references to the idea of justice.[3]

In arguing for the priority of justice to the general will, this approach assumes Rousseau's metaphysics to be an essential component of his politics. That is to say, he is a *political Platonist*. Because justice is established as an eternal, noncontingent, universal, and transcendent idea, it is every bit as metaphysical as God, free will, and the immateriality of the soul are. Without this metaphysical conception of justice, there is little to distinguish the general will from the will of all. Indeed, if the general will were nothing other than convention or agreement, there would be nothing to distinguish the social contracts of the *Second Discourse* and the *Social Contract*. This claim challenges one of the great arguments of Roger Masters—that Rousseau's metaphysics, while sincere, is inessential to his politics. Masters argues that the content of the vicar's doctrines is "detachable" from his political theory (1968, 73–74). To the contrary, I find not only that Rousseau believes in a transcendent idea of justice but also that it is the very fountain of his constructive political thought.

1. The Will of All Versus the General Will

It is no mystery that the general will is central to Rousseau's program of political construction. Its appearance is ubiquitous. Its content is, by contrast, notoriously vague. One consistent feature found in his rare attempts to define it, however, is that it is distinct from what he calls the will of all. The will of all is "nothing but a sum of particular wills" (*SC*, 60/*OC*, III:371). A society governed by this principle would have to take into account everything that participating individuals desire. A pure democracy run according to majoritarian principles might be the best example of the will of all. It is purely positivistic. Its content may include anything the will of the people adds up to, whether that is respect for liberty and equality or principles of tyranny and genocide. Prior to the expressed will of the people, it is contentless. Subsequent to the expressed will of the people, its content is arbitrary. To be certain, if this were the ground upon which Rousseau meant to rest his theory, there is absolutely

3. As I hope will become clear, this theory of the ideas is the one Plato employed not in the *Republic* but in the *Laws*, and the nature of the metaphysics he employs explains much of the confusion regarding the reported influence of these seemingly two incommensurable influences. In making this distinction, I rely significantly on Seung (1996).

no doubt that he would be modern in the Straussian sense of defining justice according to convention. To be sure, however, Rousseau explicitly rejects this as a foundation. Because it is informed by private interests, it cannot possibly serve this function. It is almost by its very definition contrary to the general will: "One ought rather to presume that the particular will will often be contrary to the general will, for private interest always tends to preferences, and the public interest always tends to equality" (*Emile*, 462/*OC*, IV:842).

What then of its counterpart—the general will? The most famous description of the general will comes from the *Social Contract:* "if, from these same [particular] wills, one takes away the pluses and the minuses which cancel each other out, what is left as the sum of the differences is the general will. . . . If when an adequately informed people deliberates, the Citizens had no communication among themselves, the general will would always result from the large number of small differences, and the deliberation would always be good" (60/*OC*, III:371). Some words here require unpacking. First, there are the deliberations of "adequately informed people." This phrase itself needs to be broken down into two inquiries: (1) what does Rousseau mean by deliberation, and (2) what is a people "adequately informed"?

It is unfortunate that Rousseau does little explicitly to help us understand these terms. The idea of deliberation has recently grown in popularity. Jürgen Habermas, for example, suggests that politically legitimate decisions can be made only in public deliberations under the constraints of the ideal speech conditions. But what does Rousseau say? Rousseau briefly mentions the idea of deliberation in book 2 of the *Social Contract* but does not return to the derivation of the general will again until book 4. And Rousseau's idea of deliberation is just the opposite from the contemporary vision. Rather than having a public forum where individuals might congregate to exchange ideas about public matters, Rousseau has his citizens turn inward. We thus find that the derivation of the general will requires that citizens do not have any "communication among themselves" (*SC*, 60/*OC*, III:371). He suggests this because he tells us that the general will cannot be influenced by "partial views." If people are allowed to communicate with one another, they are tempted to succumb to their own local—and politically illegitimate—preferences.

What, next, is an adequately informed people? Or, to rephrase the question slightly, what is a proper personal deliberation? Rousseau warns us that we may well err in calculating the general will: "it does not follow . . . that the people's deliberations are always equally upright. One always wants one's good, but one does not always see it: one can never corrupt the people, but one can often cause it to be mistaken, and only when it is, does it appear to want what is bad" (*SC,* 59/*OC,* III:371). The way to avoid this dangerous problem is to will only what is the generally good. The people must remove all personal considerations in their deliberations and consider those things that promote the common good: "What these different interests have in common is what forms the social bond, and if there were not some point on which all interests agree, no society could exist. Now it is solely in terms of this common interest that society ought to be governed" (57/III:368). Rousseau hints that the best way to inform people of the common good is through education. Indeed, one of the primary ends of education, in *Emile,* is that students learn of justice and goodness (235/IV:522).

A further component of the general will, beyond deliberation, is agreement. The people have to come to a consensus on the general will. There can be no necessary dispute on whether the general will is a matter of consent. It is partially on this basis that many argue that Rousseau is a Hobbesian, and, to be sure, to the extent that he argues that the general will requires consent, he is surely a modernist. According to John A. Clark, it is "an actual agreement" (1943, 82) between citizens. The idea of consent was clearly a modern innovation on ancient politics. Following the lead of Hobbes, Locke, and Pufendorf, Rousseau likewise thought it important that his state be grounded in the agreement of his citizens.

Consent, however, can be of two types. One may consent to anything, or one may consent only to a circumscribed set of options. The first is *open consent;* the second is *constrained consent.*[4] A new country drawing up its laws has open consent. There are no limits to what its members might agree. The U.S. Congress, by contrast, is constrained. Congress might like to consent to grant a title of nobility to Mickey Rooney, for example, but it is prohibited from doing so by article I, section 9 of the Constitution. Further, constrained consent may be of two kinds. The constraint can be positive or transcendent. The constraint prohibiting Congress from passing a title of nobility is *positive constraint,* because that prohibition is recognized in the positive authority of the U.S. Constitution. *Transcendent constraint,* however, is moral and not contingent upon being written or recognized. The constraint people place on themselves not to cheat on their taxes, even with a high likelihood of not getting caught, could be considered transcendent constraint.

What, if any, constraint does Rousseau place on the formulation of his general will? It is difficult to argue that he places no constraint on its formula-

---

4. This distinction bears some resemblance to that between realist and constructivist standards in Trachtenberg (2001).

tion. As discussed above, he has minimally placed the constraints of deliberation and good information. Further, he has argued that the will itself must be general. It cannot be directed at any individual or group's private interest. Each one of these constraints is, for him, both genuine and substantial.

The next question, then, is whether his constraint is either positive or transcendent. This question is more difficult. There is a great deal of literature that suggests that constraints on the general will must be positive. John Rawls's construction of the difference principle, for example, is shaped by the positive constraints of the veil of ignorance. Likewise, there is a formidable body of Rousseau scholarship arguing that the constraints of the general will are purely positive. The most persuasive cases are made by the Straussians, including Masters, Melzer, and Strauss himself. According to Masters, "[a]lthough the just and legitimate end of civil society is defined in terms of the general will, the general will is not that just end properly speaking; rather it is a formal requirement which must be fulfilled by the laws which constitute any legitimate regime" (1968, 327–28).

The final possible understanding of the general will is that it is transcendently constrained. Transcendent constraints are inherently controversial because they presuppose the existence of universal and immutable standards. Such standards, argue many, do not exist. Contemporary liberal theorists argue that they are epistemologically indemonstrable. Others argue that, whatever we might think about them, they have been more or less dead for political philosophy since Machiavelli. In any case, central to any conception of universal principles of political morality are the ideas of justice and the good. As Strauss characterized ancient thought, "The nature of things and not convention . . . determines in each case what is just" ([1953] 1965, 102). If it is the case that justice is to Rousseau what it was for the Ancients, then one might be able to say that justice is prior to the general will. And if that is the case, we then have to rethink entirely the ontological status of the general will and its implications for his thought.

2. On Positivist Interpretations of Rousseau

Even if justice were a constraint on the general will, one could still possibly make the claim that this is a positive rather than a transcendent constraint. For Strauss, the very definition of justice, for modernity, is convention ([1953] 1965, 187), but the argument that Rousseau rejects transcendent ideas has an even longer pedigree. This section and the next both examine the hypothesis that he consciously created the general will as a positive, not a transcendent, standard. In examining some of the following significant positivist interpreters of Rousseau, I hope to demonstrate that the thesis—while sometimes tempting—is not consistent with Rousseau's writings or his intentions.

One of the earliest substantial arguments against the presence of morality of any sort in Rousseau is found in Irving Babbitt's *Rousseau and Romanticism*. According to Babbitt, there were two modern attacks on universal morality. The first was the new science, stemming largely from Francis Bacon. What advances in the natural sciences told moral philosophers, so the argument goes, was that we are biologically and mechanistically determined, rather than creatures possessing a free will: "The truths of humanism and religion, being very much bound up with certain traditional forms, have been rejected along with these forms as obsolescent prejudice, and the attempt has been made to treat man as entirely the creature of the natural law" (Babbitt 1919, 120).

The second half of the modern assault on morality, according to Babbitt, is Rousseau's moral psychology. For Rousseau, man is born with the purest of souls. His only inclination is toward goodness, specifically exhibited in his pity for others. This is *natural*. The irony in his praising our natural virtue, suggests Babbitt, is that it cannot truly be a virtue. Virtue—or true moral behavior—can be exhibited only in acts of moral struggle. One finds in Rousseau "a virtual denial of a struggle between good and evil in the breast of the individual" (Babbitt 1919, 120). We likewise find in the second half of the *Second Discourse* this lack of struggle. Individuals have become socially determined by their corrupt surroundings. Their opinions and behavior have become chained to their environment, thus denying their free will in a manner analogous to that perpetrated by natural science. In both the idyllic state of nature and the corrupt civil society, man has not consciously chosen his dispositions or behavior, and without this there can be no morality.

Babbitt's argument is forceful and has the appeal of placing Rousseau in the context of an alluringly comprehensive intellectual history. This ought not blind us, however, to the philosopher's own words on free will and morality found in the first half of the *Second Discourse*. There he tells us what he understands to be the difference that sets human beings apart from animals. This difference lies in what he calls the "metaphysical and moral aspects" (*SD,* 140/ *OC,* III:141). According to Rousseau, an animal is merely a machine, only far more sophisticated than any existing in his day: "I see in any animal nothing but an ingenious machine to which nature has given senses in order to wind itself up and, to a point, protect itself" (140/III:141). Man, by contrast, is perfectly free to deny all impulses of nature. "Nature alone does everything in the operations of the Beast, whereas man contributes to his operations in his capacity as a free agent. . . . The beast chooses or rejects on instinct, man by an act of freedom. . . . [M]an often deviates from [instinct] to his own detriment" (140/III:141). It is our ability to act against our instincts that sets us apart from the animals, according to Rousseau—even among the "natural savages."

Babbitt might respond that whereas Rousseau speaks of a man capable of acting contrary to natural impulses, he nevertheless in practice ignores all voices other than the voice of nature. This response, however, would contradict the second half of the *Second Discourse*. As Babbitt tells us, civilized man becomes a creature of his social environment and natural impulses and talents. The social context allows for our natural talents to distinguish us from the herd. This, combined with our naturally generated *amour-propre,* leads us to the radical inequalities that characterize "civil" society. Rousseau goes on to label this society "wicked" (*SD,* 171/*OC,* III:176). One cannot, however, condemn those who are incapable of being otherwise. One does not excoriate a dog for being brown—it has no choice but to be that color. Likewise, we (theoretically) do not condemn the mentally ill for whatever crimes they commit, because they lack the freedom to resist their impulses. Rousseau, though, condemns those in civil society who have exploited others to climb to the peak of the social world. In this condemnation is implicit that element of human nature he describes in the first half of the discourse—that humans can resist the temptations of social esteem and be more just in their dealings with others. This requires the assumption of freedom that Babbitt denies Rousseau. Without this assumption, he is speaking pure nonsense. This is not to make the radical claim that human beings have no social or natural influences. Of course they do. What sets them apart from all other creatures is their capacity to resist these influences, and that Rousseau makes abundantly clear.

Rousseau further tells us that one purpose of the social contract is to transform the nature of man from a creature acting largely upon instinct to a moral one.

> This transition from the state of nature to the civil state produces a most remarkable change in man by substituting justice for instinct in his conduct, and endowing his actions with the morality they previously lacked. Only then, when the voice of duty succeeds appetite, does man, who until then had looked only to himself, see himself forced to act on other principles, and to consult his reason before listening to his inclinations. (*SC,* 53/*OC,* III:364)

To read these words and come to any other conclusion than that Rousseau meant his social beings to be free for moral behavior is, in the words of Jacques Barzun, "the imaginings of ignorance" ([1943] 1961, 24).

Babbitt's attack is against the *possibility* of there being moral questions for Rousseau. Other interpreters, however, accepted that possibility without accepting its necessity. They have done so by rejecting the existence of transcendent ideas in Rousseau. The earliest significant argument to this effect is in C. E. Vaughan. According to Vaughan, Rousseau sees himself as introducing an important improvement over Locke's theory. In Locke's state of nature, the laws of nature are present and binding, even if they are violated with sufficient frequency to demand the institution of positive laws. By contrast, Vaughan tells us, Rousseau "is under no such illusion" ([1915] 1962, 16). He makes no mention of an operative set of natural laws in his state of nature. His savage men instead act according to instinct. There can be no moral laws where men have not the capacity to understand them. In this respect, Vaughan's reasoning resembles Babbitt's. As Babbitt suggests that we are unaccountable for our behavior because we are shaped completely by social and mechanistic forces, Vaughan suggests that we are unaccountable for our behavior because our minds and social conditions are incompletely developed in the state of nature so as to render moral questions irrelevant. Vaughan, however, takes his argument one step further. Because there is no capacity to discern moral principles, there are none in the state of nature or in civil society. Rousseau, he suggests, "sweeps away the idea of natural Law, root and branch" (Vaughan [1915] 1962, 16). So whereas Babbitt does not address the presence or absence of substantive ideas in Rousseau's theory, Vaughan does, and his conclusion is that there are none.[5]

Insofar as Vaughan is describing the state of nature, there can be little dispute. As George Kateb has correctly remarked, "When applied to a man without property, the principle of . . . justice is a mockery" (1961, 524; see also Shklar 1969, 178). What, however, does this suggest about the possible presence of transcendent ideas in civil society? To be sure, Vaughan's argument is subject to reasonable criticism. As Bernard Bosanquet noted in response to Vaughan, "it is a pity to convey the impression that Rousseau . . . 'refuted the idea of natural law.' What he refuted was the conception that man in a very early state could be conscious of the Law of Nature" (1916, 402). The fact that

---

5. Vaughan's challenge is taken up effectively by Robert Derathé, who at the end of a long argument concludes, "all the efforts of Rousseau tend to result in a political system which conforms with the idea of natural law" (1970, 171).

we may not be engaged in a game of chess at the moment does not necessarily mean that there is no such thing as rules for the game of chess. The instant at which we drop everything and begin a game, the rules apply.[6] No one argues that the rules of chess apply to lunch, discussion, traffic, or any other aspect of life. This does not mean, however, that they do not exist. They do, and in the appropriate context they are every bit as applicable as they were at any other chess-playing moment in history. Likewise, we may say that transcendent ideas are latent in the state of nature—existent but inoperative. The moment an individual claims property and hence founds civil society, however, the principle of justice is called out of its latency. Not coincidentally, it is immediately after this moment in the *Second Discourse* that Rousseau offers his first moral judgment of human behavior.[7]

Though useful, this analogy is not a perfect one. There is an important distinction to be made between the rules of chess and the idea of justice. On the one hand, the rules of chess do not exist before the invention of the game of chess. The idea of justice, on the other, may be said ontologically to precede civil society. Not only this, but we might also add that whereas the rules of chess are determinate, the idea of justice is relatively indeterminate. The rules of chess tell one exactly what is permitted and forbidden. The idea of justice is more of a vague impression. N. J. H. Dent tells us, "Rousseau nowhere gives . . . a general definition of justice" (1992, 138). In this respect, Rousseau's understanding of justice is very close to Plato's. As T. K. Seung notes, Plato's definition of justice in the *Republic* itself—"Justice obtains in a cooperative enterprise, when all the participants do their justly allocated parts and receive their justly distributed benefits"—already presupposes the idea of justice. Seung rightly argues that such definitions, by virtue of their inherent circularity, presuppose that "the intuition of Justice is ineliminable in any discourse about justice" (1996, 221). Rousseau, too, suggests that the idea of justice is intuitive and indefinable: "There is in the depths of souls . . . an innate principle of justice" (*Emile*, 289/*OC*, IV:598).[8] What distinguishes the chess game from the idea of justice is that we cannot intuit the rules of chess—they are

---

6. One might argue that we could begin a game of "chess" with an entirely different set of rules or perhaps no rules at all. A fair response to this, however, is that any game with significantly different rules is a different game. Hockey and soccer are not all that dissimilar by their rules, but the one rule that says that hockey must be played on ice is enough to transform it into an entirely different sport from soccer.

7. "Beware of listening to this imposter" (*SD*, 161/*OC*, III:164).

8. This description of justice is found in the vicar's Profession of Faith, which I, following Cranston (1991, 197), take to be the authentic voice of Rousseau.

conventions. The idea of justice for Rousseau, however, exists outside convention.

Vaughan further extends his argument to suggest that "the meaning of 'natural Law' necessarily varies from age to age. It stands for nothing more than the code of morality commonly accepted in a given state of civilisation" ([1915] 1962, 17). In making this case, Vaughan relies on the *Geneva Manuscript*. Unfortunately, he does not cite a specific passage, guiding us only to the vicinity of paragraphs 15–18 of book 1, chapter 2. It is true that Rousseau describes an individual who takes his cues about right from his social and cultural surroundings. It is also true, however, that he does not describe this man in flattering tones. He is describing here the "average man" and why this man's normal reasoning process cannot be an adequate source of our ideas about political right. Nowhere does Rousseau suggest that moral or political truths are contingent upon the vicissitudes of historical circumstances. To the contrary, he is warning us against this very type of reasoning. Such short-sighted visions of moral truth allowed past civilizations to think that "it was permissible to rob, pillage, mistreat foreigners, and especially barbarians, until they were reduced to slavery" (*GM*, 162/*OC*, III:288). Far from being an endorsement of positivism in regard to moral and political principles, Rousseau's discussion here is meant to be a warning against its dangers.

We still have not addressed the question of whether Rousseau believes that transcendent ideas exist in civil society. We have only so far established that his rejection of it *in the state of nature* does not tell us very much, if anything, about its presence or absence *in civil society*. John H. Noone Jr., however, has taken on this very issue in Rousseau scholarship in his "Rousseau's Theory of Natural Law as Conditional" (1972, 23–42). Noone rightly draws our attention to an important and all-too-frequently neglected passage from the *Social Contract*.

> No doubt there is a universal justice emanating from reason alone; but this justice, to be admitted among us has to be reciprocal. Considering things in human terms, the laws of justice are vain among men for want of natural sanctions; they only bring good to the wicked and evil to the just when he observes them toward everyone while no one observes them toward him. Conventions and laws are therefore necessary to combine rights with duties and to bring justice back to its object. (*SC*, 66/*OC*, III:378)

Because the idea of justice is not "self-enforcing," as Noone describes it, it is not in effect. This brings to mind the important distinction between the existence of a transcendent idea and its efficacy. Both the state of nature and civil society are questions of efficacy because they are creatures of time and history. The existence of transcendent standards, on the other hand, is never affected by historical context. The passage Noone cites reveals Rousseau's concern with both the efficacy and existence problems. Once sanctions are in place and a certain amount of compliance can be expected, the laws come into effect. Thus, we have the purpose and function of positive law—to bring substantive ideas out of their latency and into place as the source of moral and political norms for society.

Another positivist reading is found in the writings of Leo Strauss—without a doubt both the best known and most influential of all positivist interpreters of Rousseau. His most focused essay on this question is "Three Waves of Modernity." Strauss announces early in the essay what he considers to be the great crisis of modernity—the death of universal standards for right and wrong. The belief in such standards characterized the thought of the Ancients, particularly Plato. "In our time," Strauss tells us, "this faith has lost its power" (Strauss 1975, 81). The modern assault on transcendent standards came, as the title suggests, in three waves. The first wave was delivered by Machiavelli, who, through his transformation of politics from a moral to a technical problem, "completely severed the connection between politics and natural law or natural right, i.e., with justice understood as something independent of human arbitrariness" (88). Skipping for a moment, the third stage of modernity was Nietzsche, who capitalized on the historicism of the early to mid-nineteenth century. The conclusion of the early and midcentury theorists, such as Hegel, was that "all ideas are the outcome of human creative acts" (96), thus denying the notion that ideas were beyond convention. From this assumption, Nietzsche constructs a political philosophy based upon historicity in the "transvaluation of all values."

Rousseau is sandwiched between Machiavelli and Nietzsche as the second wave and is characterized as having his own mode of rejection of transcendent ideas. It is in what Strauss perceives to be the absence of nature in Rousseau's work. In moving from the state of nature to civil society, man has lost the only potential source of objective standards—nature. Artificial society does not hear its faint voice, and even if it could, according to Strauss, it would have nothing instructive to tell us. Into this void Rousseau inserts his general will: "The source of the positive law, and of nothing but the positive law, is the general will; a will inherent or immanent in properly constituted society takes the place of the transcendent natural law" (Strauss 1975, 91). Further evidence for the general will's being merely a positive artifice—independent of natural law—can be found, Strauss tells us, in Rousseau's dictum that it cannot err.

Strauss is correct to tell us that the general will becomes the appropriate standard for the positive law. The general will, however, can be conceived of in two ways. It may be either a positive or a transcendent standard. If it were a positive standard, its content should be of no interest. Nor should we ultimately be concerned with the circumstances of its formation, because all positivists recognize the arbitrariness of standards. The transcendent construction of the general will, on the other hand, presupposes that there is a nonarbitrary higher standard by which we can judge that will to be good or bad. It is not clear that Rousseau believed the general will to be purely positive. If he intended it to be so, why then should he have preferred the general will to the will of all? If they were both merely meant to be positive standards, there is no meaningful standard by which we could choose between the two. There can be no doubt, however, that he meant the general will to be the only legitimate standard for our positive law. So what makes the general will preferable to the will of all? Patrick Riley reasonably suggests that it is because the general will secures the more "ancient" (in the Straussian nomenclature) goals of the state—morality, the common good, and the lack of dangerously extreme individualism (Riley 1970, 88). These are goals that Strauss recognizes in the Ancients to be transcendent. The only significant difference between the Ancients and Rousseau, according to Riley, is that Rousseau wants to secure political obligation. By securing consent to these transcendent standards, compliance to subsequent laws becomes a far more reasonable expectation—particularly in an era when people are more prone to seek their individual goals at the expense of more universal ones.

The standard of consent, however, should not be considered a standard in itself—that would be positivism. Again, if it were the case that consent were the only standard of right—as one might plausibly say is the case in Hobbes—there would be no reason to prefer the general will to the will of all. But the fact that he rejects the latter out of hand tells us that consent alone cannot be a standard. Further, and perhaps more telling, is that if consent and artifice were Rousseau's standards, there would be no significant difference between the contract of the *Social Contract* and that of the *Second Discourse*. From Strauss's perspective, they are both agreements and therefore have equivalent ontological and political status. Such a position, however, is highly counterintuitive. Rousseau instead appears to presuppose the priority of justice to consent. Consent is merely a useful artifice for securing transcendent political ideas. As Riley aptly says, "Though 'that which is good and conformable to order is such by the nature of things, independent of human conventions,' those conventions are yet required" (1970, 91).

3. Justice, the General Will, and the Detachability Thesis

At least two scholars acknowledge the possibility that Rousseau might truly believe in the existence of something like Platonic standards. Roger Masters notes that the Profession of Faith "presents an explicit rejection of materialism" and that in the vicar's dualism is indeed Rousseau's own view. He goes on to argue, however, that although Rousseau accepts the existence of such standards, he does not find them useful in his constructive politics. For Masters, Rousseau's metaphysics is "detachable" (1968, 62, 68, 73–74). That is to say, he is a *metaphysical* Platonist, but not a *political* one. Likewise, Arthur Melzer has granted the presence of "contradictory" doctrines—that is, passages in which Rousseau explicitly embraces natural law or some version of Platonism (Melzer 1990, 146–49).[9] Also following Masters, he has argued that even if Rousseau believed what he wrote in embracing eternal values, he did not think that they were relevant to his politics. According to Melzer, Rousseau's political goal is to liberate "mankind from all transcendent guidance" (1990, 148).

Before moving forward, it is important to distinguish between natural right and natural law in interpreting Rousseau. For Masters, Rousseau retains a standard of natural right throughout his writings, though it has a limited role. This standard emerges from his discussion in the *Second Discourse,* where he acknowledges that there is great "uncertainty and obscurity on the genuine definition of natural right" (125/*OC,* III:124). This obscurity is attributable to the failure to understand human nature, according to Rousseau. Human beings possess two fundamental traits: self-preservation and compassion. It is from these that "all the rules of natural right seem to me to flow" (127/III:126), though Masters notes that self-preservation is far stronger and more important than compassion. Early in part 2 of the *Second Discourse,* Rousseau cites two natural rights derived in this way: the right of first occupant and the right of the strongest. These two rights inevitably come into conflict, because the powerful will inevitably desire the property held by first occupants. This conflict

9. He also claims that, whereas Rousseau explicitly advocates natural law, he truly "regards such moral doctrines as . . . false and pathetically ineffectual" (Melzer 1990, 148).

is only resolved by the social contract, in which the poor abandon their natural rights to almost everything in exchange for the protection of the wealthy and powerful. At this moment, natural right ceases to function in society and is replaced by positive right. Masters notes, however, that natural right remains for Rousseau a "criterion which permits criticism of political society" (1968, 161).

The content of these rights appears to be largely Hobbesian. For Hobbes, the right of nature is defined as "the liberty each man hath to use his own power as he will himself for the preservation of his own nature; that is to say, of his own life; and consequently, of doing anything which, in his own judgment and reason, he shall conceive to be the aptest means thereunto" (*Leviathan*, 14.1). This is to say that, for Hobbes, one can do absolutely anything, as long as that behavior is aimed at the agent's own preservation.[10] On Masters's reading, this is more or less Rousseau's conception of natural right. Thus, "right of the strongest might be called *the* natural right *par excellence*," because strength is the most valuable tool an individual has to promote his own preservation (Masters 1968, 164). The rich, acting on this right, lead to the social contract with the poor and the system of despotism it institutes. As Rousseau describes the resulting political system, it has brought humanity full circle— back to another kind of state of nature, this one more closely resembling the one described by Hobbes.

Thus, although the standard of natural right may exist for Rousseau, it is not particularly helpful. Indeed, it appears that if it is scrupulously followed, it inevitably results in the end of civil society and a return to a state of nature. Thus, Masters very reasonably concludes that in the end, it is "self-defeating" (1968, 165). Further, one might wonder if this standard is even particularly useful in the respect that Masters suggests it might be—that is, as a standard by which civil society may be criticized. He cites the conclusion of the *Second Discourse*, in which Rousseau appears to be citing this standard: "moral inequality, authorized by positive right alone, is contrary to Natural Right whenever it is not directly proportional to Physical inequality" (188/*OC*, III:193–94). This, however, appears to be more the exception than the rule. Rousseau frequently condemns this so-called natural right. Specifically, he unambiguously rejects the doctrine that Masters cites as the natural right *par excellence*—the right of the strongest (*SC*, 43–44/*OC*, III:354–55). This, then, can be of no use as a standard in evaluating political societies. He suggests

---

10. A. P. Martinich notes that Hobbes on occasion extends this right to even those things that do not promote self-preservation (1995, 264–65).

elsewhere that behavior is to be judged by something completely independent of natural right—the idea of justice. On several occasions, Rousseau reports a story of witnessing a wrongdoing. In each instance, he reports that his judgment is informed by an intuition of the idea of justice (*Emile*, 287–88/*OC*, IV:596–97; *Lettres morales*/*OC*, IV:1106–7; *Reveries*, 54/*OC*, I:1057; *Confessions*, 17/*OC*, I:20). This standard does not appear to be attached in any way to the natural right Masters perceives in Rousseau that would authorize "the violent theft of food from a helpless child" (Masters 1968, 163).

Beyond natural right, Masters also acknowledges in Rousseau the presence of natural law. He accepts that the views of the Savoyard Vicar are indeed the personal metaphysical views of Rousseau. Thus, in this regard, he accepts that Rousseau is a *metaphysical Platonist*. Natural law is written on the heart and takes shape through education and experience. The problem with this conception of natural law, according to Masters, is that it is "impotent in the face of any man who denies that God exists and rejects a dualist metaphysics" (1968, 85). Unlike the character of Raskolnikov in Dostoevsky's *Crime and Punishment*, for example, who through his remorse and metaphysical faith confesses his heinous murders, atheists and materialists cannot be expected to have any knowledge of the natural law. They therefore presumably have neither conscience nor any possibility of remorse. Thus, for Masters, Rousseau cannot possibly rest his state on this conception of natural law. He concludes that "as a result of the impotence of the natural law, Rousseau was forced to base virtue on a stronger foundation," namely, contract and the force of positive law (Masters 1968, 85).

Arthur Melzer shares Masters's skepticism about the role of natural law in Rousseau's politics and even extends it to argue that the threat of transcendent ideas or natural law represents a great danger to the state. His construction of the general will centers on Rousseau's treatment of equality. Contrary to received opinion, Melzer argues that Rousseau is not a great egalitarian. He is, rather, fundamentally inegalitarian. To make this argument, Melzer relies on a thin construction of equality. He says that Rousseau recognizes different talents in individuals and holds that people ought to be treated differently according to these different talents (Melzer 1990, 156–57). Melzer points to the existence of the legislator, for example. The lawgiver would need to be someone of "superior intelligence" with great aptitude for making judgments (*SC*, 69/*OC*, III:382). Melzer is right to note that this constitutes recognition of inequality, and it is also true that, by virtue of the legislator's superior tal-

THE GENERAL WILL ■ 109

ents, he should have a position of power not entrusted to inferiors. According to Melzer, this principle of inequality is Rousseau's idea of justice.

Rousseau, however, does not base his society on this supposed principle of justice. He instead grounds legitimate society in the general will. The general will, according to Melzer, is founded upon a strict principle of egalitarianism and hence injustice: "First, it requires the superior few to be ruled and led by laws made by the inferior multitude. And second, it makes the superior fit into the narrow mold of what is good for the inferior" (1990, 157). For Melzer, this is the embodiment of Rousseauean *injustice:* "If Rousseau favors the general will, then, it is most certainly *not* as the *embodiment* of justice but rather as a hardheaded and practical *replacement* for it" (157). One might reasonably ask why Rousseau, in Melzer's account, would consciously choose to replace a just principle with an unjust one. Melzer provides two answers: justice itself has no natural sanctions, and the unjust principle of the general will is more conducive to self-preservation.[11]

Melzer's understanding of the general will, however, rests upon some challengeable assumptions. First, although he is correct to say that Rousseau recognizes and approves of certain natural inequalities, this is irrelevant to the principle of equality he endorses by virtue of the general will. There are two principles of equality at work here: *equality of talents* and *equality of rights.* Melzer is concerned with the inequality of talents. The equality established in the social contract, however, is an equality of rights. These are two distinct notions of equality, and it is important not to conflate them. Rousseau himself says, "From whatever side one traces one's way back to the principle, one always reaches the same conclusion: namely, that the social pact establishes among the Citizens an equality such that all commit themselves under the same conditions and must enjoy all the same rights" (*SC,* 62–63/*OC,* III:374). Nowhere in Rousseau's writings does he suggest that we should by virtue of the social contract erase or refuse to recognize differences in natural talents.[12] The equality imposed upon citizens is mere legal equality. All are equally subject to the laws, regardless of their natural inequalities. And if their natural inequalities lead to further social differences, then so be it.[13]

---

11. This latter explanation would be the Hobbesian minimum of what is required (i.e., peace and survival).

12. Though, to be sure, he is concerned about some of their social consequences (see McLendon 2003).

13. This is, of course, only true to a certain limit, beyond which he says we must guard against inequalities of wealth for the purposes of social stability: "It is . . . one of the most important tasks of government to prevent extreme inequality of fortunes" (*Political Economy,* 19/*OC,* III:258).

Second, and even more important, it is not clear that Rousseau ever defines inequality as being equivalent to justice.[14] To the contrary, he explicitly identifies this equality of rights as a principle of justice: "The first and greatest public interest is always justice. All wish the conditions to be equal for all, and justice is nothing but this equality" (*Letters*, 301/*OC*, III:891). Not only does he strongly link justice and equality, then, but he also identifies justice as the greatest civic priority.[15]

The general will is not the antijustice principle. It is rather a principle aimed at realizing the abstract idea of justice. As George Kateb has claimed, "[T]he aim of the general will is justice" (1961, 520). In Rousseau's own words, "one need only be just in order to be sure of following the general will" (*Political Economy*, 12/*OC*, III:251). In *Letters Written from the Mountain*, he writes that it is impossible for the general will to be unjust (232/*OC*, III:807). This sentiment is also found in the *Social Contract*, when he tells us that in civil society justice is the rule of conduct (53/*OC*, III:364). Because Rousseau says elsewhere that the general will is the fundamental rule of conduct (*Emile*, 460/*OC*, IV:840; *Political Economy*, 9/*OC*, III:247; *SC*, 57/*OC*, III:368; *Poland*, 206/*OC*, III:984), there is good reason to believe that these two notions—justice and the general will—are intimately connected. Minimally, these are not the words of someone who conceives justice and the general will to be antithetical, as Melzer suggests. Justice does not merely provide an impetus for Rousseau's thoughts on politics. It plays a central role in the construction of his most fundamental political concept in the general will. Indeed, for

14. An important apparent exception may be found at the very end of the *Second Discourse*, where he remarks, "Moral inequality, authorized by positive right alone, is contrary to Natural Right whenever it is not directly proportional to Physical inequality; a distinction which sufficiently determines what one ought to think in this respect of the sort of inequality that prevails among all civilized Peoples: since it is manifestly against the Law of Nature, however defined, that a child command an old man, an imbecile lead a wise man, and a handful of people abound in superfluities while the starving multitude lacks in necessities" (188/*OC*, III:194). So Rousseau does acknowledge a kind of inequality as just. But, again, a Platonic comparison helps to clarify his position. There are two important parallels. First, Plato similarly notes that it is foolish to allow children and imbeciles to rule wise adults—and calls this "nature's own ordinance" (*Laws*, 690ac). Second, Plato distinguishes between two types of equality: absolute equality and proportional equality. Absolute equality grants equal shares of everything without individual distinctions on the basis of talent or merit. Proportional equality grants shares according to merit. Those attaining the same level of merit get the same shares; those with different merit, different shares. It is only the latter that Plato calls "a true and real equality" (*Laws*, 757d). Absolute equality, on the other hand, harkens back to democratic norms that offend Plato's political sensibilities. With regard to legal rights, Rousseau appears to endorse absolute equality. Regarding other principles, he is sympathetic to proportional equality. The upshot here is that to the extent Rousseau appears to embrace inequality, he does so with a distinctly Platonic flavor.

15. Elsewhere Rousseau states that "justice and the public good" are the first rules of the legitimate state (*Letters*, 249/*OC*, III:828).

Rousseau, the two most important prerequisites for thinking about government are a "sincere love of justice and a true respect for the truth" (*Emile*, 458/ *OC*, IV:837).[16] Given this, it seems unlikely that he wants, as some suggest, to divorce political thought from the idea of justice.

Defining justice as inequality fails to characterize accurately many of Rousseau's references to justice. Consider his discussion of the lawgiver. This individual is to create the laws and then exit society, having no further power over citizens. If the lawgiver were to have both the powers of writing the constitution and of ruling, "the laws, as ministers to his passions, would often only perpetuate his injustices, and he could never avoid having particular views vitiate the sanctity of his work" (*SC*, 69–70/*OC*, III:382). Rousseau apparently associates the idea of injustice with partiality, and, recalling his distinction between the general will and the will of all, the flaw of the will of all is that it incorporates these partial views: "One ought . . . to presume that the particular will will often be contrary to the general will, for the private interest always tends to preferences, and the public interest always tends to equality" (*Emile*, 462/*OC*, IV:842). The logic here is clear enough: partiality equals inequality equals injustice. Justice and equality have a strong relationship. To argue that they are opposites obscures Rousseau's uses of the word "justice."

Finally, Melzer suggests that one reason why the general will must replace justice is that justice has no natural sanctions. To be sure, he is right in noting Rousseau's awareness of this problem. Rousseau himself says, "Considering things in human terms, the laws of justice are vain among men for want of natural sanctions; they only bring good to the wicked and evil to the just when he observes them toward everyone while no one observes them toward him" (*SC*, 66/*OC*, III:378). If one only reads to this point, a very strong case indeed could be made for a comparison to Hobbes. Hobbes also rejects the prudence of obeying the laws of nature in the state of nature, but the paragraph, significantly, adds: "Conventions and laws are therefore necessary to combine rights with duties and to bring justice back to its object." Rousseau's purpose in placing the people under the authority of the general will is not to defeat or "replace" justice. It is rather to enable justice and make it binding on persons so that no one may violate its principles with immunity. We might further ask why Rousseau desires the sanctions. Is it at least plausible to argue that he believed the sanctions to be demanded *by* justice? Many have drawn the

---

16. Subsequently, the tutor notes the importance of the laws insofar as they "give him [the virtuous citizen] the courage to be just even among wicked men" (*Emile*, 473/*OC*, IV:857). This likewise suggests the relationship of law and justice, a relationship some would deny.

connection of Rousseau to Kant. For Kant, justice demands sanctions. Would it be unreasonable to expect Rousseau to authorize punishment on similar grounds?

In spite of the interpretive questions surrounding the positivist reading, Melzer draws our attention to an important consideration. The general will is not the same thing as justice. Justice is an idea for Rousseau. The general will, on the other hand, as Melzer properly notes, "exists as a *will:* it is not . . . a 'truth'" (1990, 160). This is clear from the very meaning of the word "will." Ideas, such as justice, are not willed. They simply exist as abstractions.[17] A will, on the other hand, belongs to an agent or agents. It is a concrete entity. In this respect, one can see both how close and how far away Jacob L. Talmon was to a correct understanding of the general will: "Ultimately the general will is to Rousseau something like a mathematical truth or a Platonic idea. It has an objective existence of its own, whether or not it is perceived" (1955, 41).[18] If he were talking about justice rather than the general will, his remarks would be perfectly accurate. This characterization, though, is not true of the general will itself, the existence of which is contingent, even if its content is not. At any rate, one would be right to connect the general will to the people. The important point, however, is that our unrefined will can converge on or diverge from an idea. Melzer cites the very passage where Rousseau makes this point absolutely clear without drawing attention to its significance in this respect.

> If, when an adequately informed people deliberates, the citizens were to have no communication among themselves, the general will would always result from the large number of small differences, and the deliberation would always be good. But when factions, partial associations at the expense of the whole, are formed, the will of each of these associations becomes general with reference to its members and particular with reference to the state. One can say, then, that there are no longer as many voters as there are associations. The differences become less numerous and produce a result that is less general.

17. This is speaking purely metaphysically, though, to be sure, arriving at them epistemologically may at first require more base appeals (e.g., *Emile,* 97–100/*OC,* IV:329–33).

18. Talmon later says that, for Rousseau, "There is such a thing as an objective general will, whether willed or not willed by anybody" (1955, 43). This characterization, however, includes an obvious self-contradiction. It is in the very nature of a will that it in fact be willed. This is one clear advantage of my interpretation of Rousseau. The general will does not have this self-contradictory independent ontological existence. It must be willed, if it is to exist. That will, however, must mirror the idea of justice if it is to exist.

Finally, when one of these associations is so big that it prevails over all the others, the result is no longer a sum of small differences, but a single difference. Then there is no general will, and the opinion that prevails is merely private opinion. (*SC,* 60/*OC,* III:371–72)

The concern here is with the presence of factions. This is as true for Rousseau as it is for Plato, Hume, or Madison. To the extent that the will of the people is less general, the more it resembles a faction. The question, however, is why Rousseau should care whether factions exist. This draws us to the very nature of partisanship. Partisanship is the enriching of some at the expense of others. This has long been received as a principle of injustice. Madison, for example, describes factions as deciding policy contrary "to the rules of justice" (Madison, Hamilton, and Jay [1789] 1961, 77). According to Rousseau, the more partial or factious people are, the further away they are from justice. We might also infer that the closer the general will is to justice, the more "enlightened" it is (*SC,* 68/*OC,* III:380).[19]

If this characterization is correct, and the general will is contingent upon the transcendent idea of justice, it is finally possible to challenge Masters's enduring thesis that Rousseau's metaphysics is "detachable" from his politics (Masters 1968, 73–74).[20] Masters argues that, whereas Rousseau might have believed the claims of the Savoyard Vicar, he was not willing to base his politics on it. The idea of justice, however, is surely a central element of the vicar's Profession of Faith. The idea of justice also informs the general will. It is again worth quoting Rousseau: "one need only be just in order to be sure of following the general will" (*Political Economy,* 12/*OC,* III:251). This is not the voice of someone with a design to separate the general will from the idea of justice. Rather, it is the voice of someone who understands that the general will finds its foundation and support in justice. Rousseau explicitly makes this link on multiple occasions. In book 2, chapter 4 of the *Social Contract,* he argues that what unites us in the general will is an "admirable agreement between interest and justice" (62/*OC,* III:374). Two chapters later, he claims that the purpose

19. It is worth noting that Rousseau marks with a vertical line and a " + " the following passage in Plato's *Laws:* "Whoever enslaves the laws by bringing them under the rule of human beings, whoever makes the city subject to faction, and does all this through violence and the stirring up of civil strife against the law, this man must be regarded as the greatest enemy of all to the whole city" (*Laws,* 856b; Rousseau, notes on Plato, V:470). The interest in the problem of faction considerably precedes modernity—and Rousseau was obviously aware of this.

20. An effective response to Masters's "detachability" thesis can be found in O'Hagan (2004). O'Hagan focuses on the importance of Rousseau's commitment to free will, whereas I am here focusing on his commitment to eternal ideas.

of the law—which issues from the general will—is to "bring justice back to its object" (66/OC, III:378).[21] Justice is not the sole criterion for the general will. Agreement is also required. But without an independent standard of justice, there is no reason to prefer one agreement over another, and agreement is clearly not the standard in Rousseau. If it were, then he truly would have as much in common with the positivist Hobbes as many suggest. This, however, simply does not square with either Rousseau's specific words or the big picture. Most obviously, there would be no basis to distinguish the legitimate contract of the *Social Contract* from the illegitimate one of the *Second Discourse*. The obvious difference between them is the former's concern with justice and the latter's hardheaded violation of justice. The centrality of the idea of justice for Rousseau is too important to ignore, and his continual barbs against Hobbes and praises of Plato suggest that this is not mere show. Rather, it fits into a larger plan to halt modernity's momentum toward positivism and return it to Platonism. Thus, Rousseau's metaphysics is not "detachable" from his politics—it is essential.

4. The Idea of Justice and Rousseau's Political Constructivism

Rousseau says little explicitly about justice. Seung correctly notes that Rousseau never gave "an ontological account of moral principles and the general will" (1994, 66).[22] Yet as we read closely, there are enough pieces of the metaphysical puzzle to allow us to put it together. The most important ontological feature of such a concept is whether it is transcendent: "What is good and conformable to order is so by the nature of things and independently of human conventions. . . . No doubt there is a universal justice emanating from reason alone" (*SC*, 66/OC, III:378).[23] Rousseau believes this to be true ratio-

---

21. This interpretation is shared with N. J. H. Dent: "Rousseau thinks that the operation of the GENERAL WILL is the means whereby justice is most comprehensively procured for all persons" (1992, 139). Dent also writes, "Fundamentally, he [Rousseau] holds that the rules of justice emanate from God and are implanted in each person's CONSCIENCE, although it may require the enactment of positive law to ensure obedience to these requirements" (138), and adds, "A criterion of good law for Rousseau is that it should procure mutual justice; and this requirement underpins the proper functioning of the general will in declaring fundamental laws" (143).

22. See also *Emile* (235/OC, IV:522): "I am reminded here that my business here is not producing treatises on metaphysics and morals or courses of study of any kind. It is sufficient for me to mark out the order and the progress of our sentiments and our knowledge relative to our constitution. Others will perhaps demonstrate what I only indicate here."

23. That justice might be written on the heart for Rousseau is clear from many passages, including his obviously passionate and heartfelt reactions to injustice—for example, "My moral being would have to be annihilated for justice to become unimportant to me. The sight of injustice and wickedness still makes my blood boil with rage" (*Reveries*, 54/OC, I:1057). Rousseau says elsewhere

nally; moreover, the universality of justice is also evident to him from casual empiricism. "Cast your eyes on all the nations of the world, go through all the histories. Among so many inhuman and bizarre cults, among this prodigious diversity of morals and character, you will find everywhere the same ideas of justice and decency, everywhere the same notions of good and bad" (*Emile*, 288/*OC*, IV:597–98). Rousseau synthesizes both metaphysical and empirical claims in his "Third Walk," if we consider justice to be one of "the eternal truths which have been accepted at all times and by all wise men, recognized by all nations, and indelibly engraved on the human heart" (*Reveries*, 25/*OC*, I:1021). This appeal to a universal and invariant standard is none other than an appeal to the metaphysical and ontological components of Platonism. The essential characteristics of Plato's theory of ideas, throughout all his dialogues, are the universal, noncontingent features. Ideas do not change from time to time or circumstance to circumstance, and there is nothing people can do to alter this condition. The idea of justice, according to Rousseau, is universal, completely beyond human alteration. People cannot make something just by willing it to be so. Rousseau can only hope that their will can somehow be brought to see the idea of justice. This is the aim of what he calls the general will. Inasmuch as the general will can be brought to see the eternal truth of justice, it will, in Rousseau's words, "always be good" (*SC*, 60/*OC*, III:371). This is what can be called the ideal construction of the general will. As Zev Trachtenberg has aptly noted, "In this regard Rousseau is very much a follower of Plato" (2001, 186).

This, however, necessarily begs a question relating back to the opening paragraph. Several have argued that Rousseau explicitly rejected Platonism. He did not see the ideas, and therefore could not have employed them. This argument, made prominently by James Miller, rests upon Rousseau's rejection of Plato's early theory of ideas. Supporting Miller's case is Rousseau's reference to Plato's *Republic* as belonging to the "land of the chimeras" (*Letters*, 234/*OC*, III:810). To appreciate this apparent rejection, however, it is important to keep in mind that Plato himself was highly critical of both his earlier metaphysics (e.g., *Parmenides*) and his politics (e.g., *Laws*). This led him to reformulate his ontology to serve the purposes of political philosophy.[24] And

---

that the principles of right and wrong are "engraved in the human heart in indelible characters" ("State of War," 166/*OC*, III:602). Consider also his remarks from the *Lettres morales:* "there is, at the bottom of all souls, an innate principle of justice and of moral truth [which is] prior to all national prejudices, to all maxims of education" (*OC*, IV:1108). It is difficult to reconcile Rousseau's remarks with Masters's interpretation of justice merely as "a mental construction" (1968, 271).

24. See Seung (1996, ix–xiv).

it is this later ontology, I argue, that Rousseau employs as if he were a proud student at the Academy himself.[25] As he said himself many times, Rousseau was no professional metaphysician, but this does not make him an anti-Platonist. Rather, it means that we must try to understand the implicit system supporting his explicit claims.

Platonism can be of two kinds: implicit and explicit. Implicit Platonists rely upon transcendent standards in making judgments, but they do not necessarily declare or elaborate ontological commitments concerning their supersensible existence. Rousseau, as indicated, clearly has such a disposition. Explicit Platonists, on the other hand, not only rely on such standards but also declare the ontological existence of the forms. Rousseau never makes such a claim.[26] He is not a metaphysician in the tradition of the explicit Platonists, such as Leibniz or Malebranche, with an interest in spelling out the principles and assumptions that support his normative claims. Nevertheless, implicit Platonists, whether they claim to or not, ultimately rely on some conception of metaphysical Platonism. In what follows, I sketch out some of the dimensions of Rousseau's implicit ontological assumptions.

In the *Republic,* Plato proposes a version of the ideal state, and it is a well-known tale to all political philosophers that this state is run by the perfectly wise and just philosopher-rulers. But it is equally well known that such a state is entirely impracticable. The philosopher-ruler is nowhere to be found in the real world. The true nature of human beings does not admit to the existence of such persons: "no human being is competent to wield an irresponsible control over mankind without becoming swollen with pride and unrighteousness" (*Laws,* 713c). It was *this* element of the *Republic* that led Rousseau to his claim that it belonged to "the land of the chimeras" (*Letters,* 234/*OC,* III:810).

A further problem associated with the *Republic* was the inflexibility of the ideas. The ideas of the *Republic* were pronouncedly determinate. If one wanted to know the idea of a bed, one only needed to consult the relevant form in Platonic heaven. Thus, when it came time for Plato to articulate his theory of the state, all he needed to do was to look up to the idea and bring the entire edifice down to the real world (*Republic,* 592b). Hobbes mocked the consequences of these metaphysics as practiced among his contemporaries. As

25. There can be no doubt that Rousseau studied Plato's *Laws* carefully. His copy is available at the British Library for examination and includes over forty markings, evidencing a studied read (Rousseau, notes on Plato, V:85–568).

26. He does say in the *Persifleur,* however, that the "most profound metaphysics" is to be found in "Plato, Locke, or Malebranche" (*OC,* IV:1111).

Charles Hendel noted, "He repudiated their ideas of 'natural laws' and 'rights' and 'fundamental laws.' Such laws were a feudal strait-lacing of the body-politic; they prevented its 'representative' from meeting the exigencies of public affairs. . . . they were a fatal restriction on the new power of sovereignty which was to save the day" (1934, 1:169). The inability to meet the exigencies of circumstance is indeed a tricky problem for a determinate theory of ideas, and it is not clear that there is anything that can be done about it within the scope of Plato's metaphysics in the *Republic*. It is for this insensitivity to context and change, Shklar argues, that Rousseau rejects Plato's treatise "utterly and completely" (1969, 9). In a similar vein, Zev Trachtenberg has suggested that Rousseau is a Platonist in many respects, but departs from his "master" when he insists that we must possess "immanent" knowledge of circumstances in order to implement the common good. According to Trachtenberg, in this respect, "Rousseau elevates immanent over transcendent knowledge" (2001, 187).

We would severely underestimate Plato's resourcefulness were we to think that Plato himself was unaware of these concerns. Plato famously criticizes himself in the *Parmenides*, for example, where Parmenides asks Socrates if there is not a form for everything as trivial as mud, hair, and dirt (*Parmenides*, 130c). The implication is that the multiplicity of ideas rendered them unwieldy. Along with the problem of eidetic overpopulation comes the problem of overdeterminacy. The ideas described in the earlier dialogues are inflexible and unable to meet the challenges of the real world. Plato's story of the physician in the *Statesman* reveals this realization. Plato tells us of a doctor who is preparing for an extended trip abroad. Before he leaves, he gives his patient a prescription. The patient is expected to follow the prescription carefully. Yet, what would happen if the physician did not leave town? Would he give precisely the same prescription? Plato suggests that a commitment to do so would be absurd (*Statesman*, 295b–f). The physician must be flexible enough to address whatever conditions might arise during the patient's convalescence. As I have suggested, Plato revised his ontology to meet these objections. The new theory of ideas shared in the transcendent ontology of the old one, but there is at the same time a significant ontological shift: the new theory no longer described determinate entities but instead described indeterminate ideas. After transcendence, this is the second most important *ontological* feature of Platonic ideas, and it had two important implications. First, the number of ideas was reduced from something perhaps infinite to just a handful. This addressed the triviality problem brought up in the *Parmenides*.

Second, because the ideas were so indeterminate, their articulation in the phenomenal world required the art of construction.[27]

The political implications of this new metaphysics are explored in the *Statesman.* Here Plato tells the myth of two ages: the age of Cronus and the age of Zeus. In the age of Cronus, divine beings governed the state where no laws were needed. Because of this, Plato says, "there were no political constitutions" (*Statesman,* 271e–272a). The gods who ruled this age would have only found laws to be restricting. This is the sort of ruler one might have expected the philosopher-ruler of the *Republic* to have been.

The age of Zeus followed the age of Cronus and ushered in the world in which we now live. In this age, mere mortals must find ways to govern themselves, and, because people lack the acumen found only among gods, they must resort to the implementation of law. With law, human beings do their best to approximate the wisdom of the gods, and it is this age in which the Athenian Stranger constructs the city of Magnesia in the *Laws.* Plato tells us, "Mankind must either give themselves a law and regulate their lives by it, or live no better than the wildest of wild beasts" (*Laws,* 874e–875a). Here he foreshadows Rousseau, who likewise said, "I assume men having reached the point where the obstacles that interfere with their preservation in the state of nature prevail by their resistance over the forces which each individual can muster to maintain himself in that state. Then that primitive state can no longer subsist, and humankind would perish if it did not change its way of being" (*SC,* 49/*OC,* III:360). Thus, Plato suggests, we embrace law as a second-best option. Although we would prefer the perfect understanding of the gods, we can still live meaningful and just lives under the conditions of human-created law. The task of political and legal construction is the task of articulating the indeterminate ideas in a manner that will promote justice to the greatest extent. Furthermore, this task is a necessary one, *because* ideas are indeterminate. Indeterminate ideas cannot, because they exist, function as a legal code.

Now it is a fact of the world that the simple articulation of any idea into rules renders it less than perfect: "The differences in human personality, the variety of men's activities, and the inevitable unsettlement attending human experience make it impossible for any art whatsoever to issue unqualified rules holding good on all questions at all times" (*Statesman,* 294b). Rousseau

27. This art is called various things in different dialogues. In the *Statesman* and *Sophist,* it is called "weaving"; in the *Philebus,* it is called "mixing."

digested this lesson as well: "The inflexibility of the laws, which keeps them from bending to events, can in some cases make them pernicious, and through them cause the ruin of a State in crisis" (*SC*, 138/*OC*, III:455). Hence no constitution could ever do the job that the gods in the age of Cronus could. It is merely the task of the lawmaker to provide laws that promote the idea of justice to the greatest extent possible.

A significant consequence of this lesson is that different lands will require different sets of laws, and, because ideas are indeterminate, they possess the requisite flexibility for the task. The ideas Plato employs in the *Laws* are unlike those found in the *Republic*. There is a multiplicity of ideas in the *Republic*, but there are considerably fewer in the *Laws*. In Plato's last major dialogue, each law is drawn from the idea of justice and then articulated with knowledge of the empirical world. This can be seen with the ages of Cronus and Zeus. In the former world, Plato suggests that laws are unnecessary because of the nature of the rulers. In the latter, laws become necessary because of the empirical fact that human beings do not possess perfect judgment. Therefore, it stands to reason that other empirical factors would equally affect the construction of political institutions and the laws. Plato, in the *Laws,* draws attention to numerous empirical considerations such as proximity in relation to the sea (704b), productivity of the land (704b), proximity to other cities (704c), topography (704d), and origins of the people (707e). Of such considerations, he says, "An intelligent lawgiver . . . will inquire about these places as closely as a human being can in such matters, in order to try to formulate laws that are appropriate" (747e). Such empirical matters are of no concern to the Plato of the *Republic,* but by the time he has arrived at the *Laws,* they become paramount. His revised ontological conception of ideas provided both the force of transcendent norms and the ability to fit them to circumstances. Thus, for Plato, transcendent and immanent knowledge coexist. The former is the standard, and the latter represents the conditions under which those standards must be articulated. Without this knowledge, the lawgiver is helpless. Transcendent ideas are necessary, but not sufficient, for wise political governance.

Rousseau understood this lesson as well as anyone else in the modern age. In this light, we might gently challenge Trachtenberg's otherwise remarkably insightful and important essay. Rousseau was not departing from Plato in his appeals to immanent knowledge. Just the opposite. He was following him even more closely than has been appreciated previously. Both Plato and Rousseau articulate transcendent knowledge with attention to the constraints derived from immanent knowledge. This should not be surprising in light of the careful readings he gave to Plato's *Laws*.[28] It is not difficult to find evidence that he came to the same conclusions as the Athenian. The first form of evidence comes in his appeals to the *contextual sensitivity* of the law. There are numerous occasions on which Rousseau suggests that regimes, laws, and institutions must take into account the circumstances under which they will be realized. Each of these suggests Rousseau's commitment to an important element of what was earlier described as ontological Platonism—the indeterminacy of the ideas themselves and hence the flexibility in their implementation.

> [The] general aims of every good institution must be adapted in each country to the relations that arise as much from local conditions as from the character of the inhabitants, and it is on the basis of these relations that each people has to be assigned a particular system of institutions which is the best, not perhaps, in itself, but for the State for which it is intended. (*SC*, 79/*OC*, III:392)

> [T]here is no unique and absolute constitution of Government, but . . . there may be as many Governments differing in nature as there are States differing in size. (*SC*, 85/*OC*, III:398)

> [S]ince a thousand events can change the relations of a people, not only can different governments be good for different people, but they can also be good for the same people at different times. (*SC*, 83–84/ *OC*, III:397)

> [T]he question, which is absolutely the best Government, does not admit to a solution because it is indeterminate: or, if you prefer, it has as many good solutions as there are possible combinations in the absolute and relative positions of peoples. (*SC*, 104–5/*OC*, III:419)

> [T]he science of government is nothing but a science of combinations, applications, and exceptions, according to times, places, circumstances. ([1767] 1997, 269)

The second place to look for Rousseau's understanding of this lesson is in his explicit calls for empirical knowledge in the construction of government

28. See Silverthorne (1973).

and law. To carry out an indeterminate idea of justice, as Plato demonstrates, one must know the circumstances in which it is to be realized.

> Just as an architect, before putting up a large building, observes and tests the ground to see whether it can support the weight, so the wise institutor does not begin by drawing up laws good in themselves, but first examines whether the people for whom he intends them is fit to bear them. (*SC*, 72/*OC*, III:384–85)

> Unless one knows the Nation for which one is working thoroughly, one's labor on its behalf, regardless of how excellent it may be in itself, will invariably fall short in application, and even more so in the case of an already fully instituted nation, whose tastes, morals, prejudices and vices are too deeply rooted to be easily stifled by new seeds. A good institution for Poland can only be the work of the Poles or of someone who has studied the Polish nation and its neighbors at first hand. (*Poland*, 177/*OC*, III:953)

> Although the form of government adopted by a people is more often the work of chance and fortune than of its own choice,[29] there are nevertheless certain qualities in the nature and soil of each country which make one government more appropriate to it than another; and each form of government has a particular force which leads people toward a particular occupation. ([1765] 1986, 284/*OC*, III:906)

> The problem is to adopt this code [of pure moral laws] to the people for which it is made and to the things about which it decrees to such an extent that its execution follows from the very conjunction of these relations; it is to impose on the people . . . less the best laws in themselves than the best of which it admits in the given situation. (*Letter to d'Alembert*, 66/*OC*, V:61)

Because the idea of justice is indeterminate, great contextual sensitivity is required of the lawgiver. This seems obvious, but its importance should not be underestimated. The ontological fact of the ideas' indeterminacy allows for

---

29. See also Plato's *Laws:* "I was about to say that no human being ever legislates anything, but that chances and accidents of every sort, occurring in all kinds of ways, legislate everything for us" (709a).

this contextual sensitivity. As Seung remarks, the articulation of Plato's idea of justice in the real world "requires empirical knowledge" (1996, 233).

If one reads only Plato's *Republic,* this point is lost. This, again, was one of Hobbes's problems with the Platonism of his contemporaries (Hendel 1934, 1:169). If the ideas are completely determinate, as he suggests them to be, they cannot meet the idiosyncratic demands of any particular state. The only two possible solutions to this are positivism or the Platonism of the *Laws.* Positivists are not held to any standards when making laws. Thus, when exigencies arise, they are free to address them. Lacking any transcendent standard, however, they have no constraints either. The consequence is that it is impossible for Hobbes's Leviathan to be unjust: "whasotever he [the sovereign] doth, can be no injury to any of his Subjects nor ought he to be by any of them accused of injustice" (*Leviathan,* 18.6).[30] The Leviathan is above the law. Legislation and legislators in Plato's *Laws* and Rousseau, however, are capable of being unjust. Thus there are limitations placed upon Rousseau's sovereign that have no place in Hobbes's philosophy (*SC,* 61–64/*OC,* III:372–75). Scholars too frequently forget this important element of Rousseau's theory of the state. While it is a well-known maxim that the general will is always rightful, what is forgotten is that it can only exist when formed according to the appropriate standards. It is not the case that any calculation of the people's will suffices. This is the difference between the will of all and the general will. The former is only an aggregation of individual desires. It does not pretend to have any higher aspirations, whereas the latter represents the people's agreement to the idea of justice.

5. Hobbes, Locke, and Rousseau: Three Modern Political Ontologies

We are finally in a position to understand Rousseau's Platonism as one of three fundamental options for political ontology in the modern period. The first option is Hobbes's materialism. He denies the existence of any immaterial substance, including an immaterial God, free will, an immaterial soul, and a transcendent idea of justice. To the extent that any of these things are to exist, they must be located in the material world. This, for instance, leads him to

---

30. Even this, however, is somewhat misleading, because positivism does not necessarily have the flexibility described here. It only has this degree of flexibility if the laws are revisable under any conditions whatsoever. To the extent that most positive systems of law circumscribe the conditions under which the law may be revised, positivism may not satisfy the conditions Hobbes thought it necessary to meet.

construct an understanding of a material God in *De Cive*.[31] Another important consequence of his materialism is his denial of transcendent ideas. As Ross Harrison has summarized Hobbes, "There are no such independently accessible standards" (2003, 101). The absence of immaterial ideas forces him to seek another ground on which to rest his principles of justice and the natural law. He finds this in the supposedly universal motivation of fear that inspires the social contract. The contract thus determines justice, which is nothing other than the performance of contract.

The great advantage of Hobbes's contract, as outlined in Chapter 1, is its capacity to be sensitive to context. There is in Hobbes, for example, no preexisting right to private property that would constrain the sovereign's use of it for important public purposes. The Leviathan is completely free to act as circumstances demand. The absence of any preexisting standards means the absence of any constraints. The great disadvantage of Hobbes's system is embedded in this very same liberty and lack of constraint. The sovereign has free rein to act for the public good but also has the liberty to act for purposes contrary to the public good. This is because there is no independent standard of justice to which the sovereign must be held accountable. The Leviathan sets all the rules—for good or ill.

John Locke's conception of natural rights can be understood as a response to fears associated with this unconstrained sovereign. The list of a series of natural rights serves, in his theory, to restrict the government's legitimate behavior. This is why Locke permits revolution and Hobbes does not. Hobbes does not permit revolution because his government is not accountable to any standards other than those of its own whim. For Locke, the government must respect the laws of nature. If it violates them in a pattern evidencing a design to do so, the people are perfectly within their rights to remove the government and replace it with one more conducive to the protection of these rights. The problem with Locke's theory, however, is that, in establishing these rights, it has constrained the government in just the ways that Hobbes found problematic. The natural rights may well get in the way of the government's acting for the public good.

Locke actually has a provision to meet this concern—his concept of executive prerogative. He defines it as *"nothing but the power of doing publick good without a Rule"* ([1690] 1988, §167). This would evidently allow the executive

31. See Hobbes ([1642] 1949, 15.14). This conception of God is also entertained by Diderot, who speaks of a "material God-part of the universe . . . subject to its processes [that] might grow old and even eventually die" ([1830] 1956, 128).

to violate apparent natural rights in order to secure the general good. Although the goal of serving the general good is difficult to argue with, it raises a tricky question—if the natural rights are his primary principles, how can anything justify their violation? This means that either Locke does not hold natural rights to be primary, or he has contradicted himself.

A further problem for both Hobbes and Locke is reconciling their metaphysics and epistemology with their politics. Hobbes's empirical materialism is perfectly consistent with his positivism. The problem is that he does not always speak like a positivist. On occasion, rather, he asserts that the principles of his natural law are "immutable and eternal" (*Leviathan*, 15.38; see also Hobbes [1640] 1994, 18.4). These claims are simply irreconcilable with his materialism. The materialist mantra—stemming back to Heraclitus—is that material substance is perpetually in flux. It is therefore dubious to argue that principles based on this doctrine can transcend the ephemeral nature of material. Matter—in all its manifestations—cannot yield necessary universals. Some of Hobbes's defenders valiantly argue that he has found a suitable replacement for transcendent immaterial ideas in the universal motivation of fear and desire for self-preservation,[32] which in turn help establish universal laws of nature (e.g., Harrison 2003, 64–69). The problem with this is that not even the fear of death is truly universal. As a material phenomenon, it is necessarily contingent. This is confirmed by the practice of terrorism. One of the defining features of terrorists is that they do not fear death. Rather, they invite it. Thus, the fear of death fails—as would all material phenomena—as a basis for universal laws of nature. If Hobbes was aware of this, he knew that he was cheating. If he was not, he simply did not think through the consequences of his materialism for his laws of nature.

Likewise, Locke is burdened by epistemic difficulties. These problems are evident both in the reconciliation of the *Second Treatise* with the *Essay Concerning Human Understanding* and with his *Essays on the Law of Nature*. In the *Essays,* he argues that the laws of nature can be derived purely from sense-experience. His argument runs into trouble, however, when he brings in rational concepts such as God and Beauty to demonstrate the existence of the natural laws ([1664] 1997, 100–106). Thus, he has assumed what he has told us he was going to prove—the existence of immaterial rational concepts. Likewise, he runs into difficulties reconciling the empirical assumptions of the *Essay*

---

32. It is worth noting that Rousseau carefully marked a passage from Plato's *Laws* where preservation is expressly rejected as the purpose of a political society: "we do not agree with the multitude that the most precious thing in life is bare preservation in existence" (*Laws,* 707c; Rousseau, notes on Plato, V:200–201).

Concerning Human Understanding with the natural laws of the *Second Treatise*. His rejection of innate ideas in the former flatly contradicts his employment of innate ideas to ground the natural law in the latter ([1690] 1988, §§11 and 136). Locke wanted the rigorous scientism attached to empiricism but could not accept its consequences. This led him to the contradictions that litter his works.

The final modern political ontology is Rousseau's, as sketched out in this chapter. Like Locke, Rousseau finds Hobbes's politics unacceptable. For him, positivism is nothing less than the rule of the strongest. He repeatedly denounces it as unacceptable (*SD*, 186/*OC*, III:191; *Julie*, 474/*OC*, II:579; *SC*, 43–44/*OC*, III:354–55; *Emile*, 459/*OC*, IV:838; *Letters*, 239/*OC*, III:815; "State of War," 162/*OC*, III:609).[33] It is difficult to find a doctrine more firmly and frequently rejected anywhere by anyone. It is in this light that one can appreciate his appeal to transcendent or eternal standards to ground his politics. Authority is not lodged in power, but in justice itself. Only with this assumption can he argue, as he does, that the positive law can have "nothing contrary to the natural Laws" (*Letters*, 231/*OC*, III:807), and it is on this basis that he both lodges his critiques of existing regimes and grounds the construction of his own political systems.

In this commitment to eternal ideas, Rousseau stands together with Locke. The ontology of these ideas, however, differs significantly from that found in Locke. Locke's eternal principles are discrete rules, whereas Rousseau's are abstract and indeterminate. Their indeterminate nature means that they are capable of being articulated differently under different circumstances. Thus, Rousseau rejects the one-size-fits-all approach to statecraft: "there is no unique and absolute constitution of Government, but . . . there may be as many Governments differing in nature as there are States differing in size" (*SC*, 85/*OC*, III:398). He would reject any attempt to impose democracy on a nation, for example, because it may be believed to be the "best" in an abstract sense. It may very well be the best for a given circumstance, but this can only be determined insofar as its realization promotes the highest degree of justice and the good. Justice and the good—not democratic institutions or any other determinate notion—are the ultimate standards. Rousseau's system thus shares with Hobbes's a high degree of flexibility and the capacity to address particular circumstances. Rousseau's ontology, then, combines the best of both worlds. He has the flexibility of the Hobbesian ontology along with the transcendent authority appealed to by Locke.

33. Rousseau also marks his copy of the *Laws* where Plato rejects the doctrine (*Laws*, 714b; "Rousseau," notes on Plato, V:212).

In performing this synthesis, he avoids the pitfalls that burdened both Hobbes and Locke. Rousseau never entertains for a moment the idea that he is either a materialist or a strict empiricist,[34] and he therefore avoids their contradictions. To be sure, he borrows from both materialism and empiricism in his treatment of the material world. He is not, after all, an idealist.[35] But his treatment of normative ideas is quite different from his philosophy of natural science. Ideas are not material and hence cannot be derived by empirical means. This is why he turns to intuitionism in the form of "inner sentiment." By doing so, he avoids the conflicts found in both Hobbes and Locke. The British theorists deeply desire eternal, transcendent norms, but their materialism and empiricism cannot accommodate it. Rousseau understands better than his predecessors that transcendent norms cannot be derived from material substance. Heraclitus was in part right—*material* is perpetually in flux.[36] Thus, any attempt to locate eternal standards must go beyond material substance. This is why he operates the way he does.

To say that Rousseau has solved the problems that burdened Hobbes and Locke is not to say that he solved all the problems of political philosophy, much less philosophy in general. His reliance on intuition is incapable of empirical demonstration, after all. The transcendent ideas of justice and the good are likewise impossible to locate in space (by definition) and are thus capable of being abused by those who would characterize vicious laws as "eter-

---

34. It has frequently been noted that Rousseau once had planned a work entitled *La materialisme du sage* [Materialism of the Sage]. Although he never wrote the book, he outlined some of its principles in the *Confessions:*

> Climates, seasons, sounds, colors, darkness, light, the elements, food, noise, silence, motion, rest, all act on our machine and consequently on our soul, all offer us a thousand almost guaranteed holds for governing in their origin the feelings by which we let ourselves be dominated. Such was the fundamental idea for the outline for which I already had on paper, and from which I hoped for an all the more certain effect on well-disposed people who, while they sincerely love virtue, mistrust their weakness, since it appeared easy to me to write a book out of it that would be as pleasant to read as it was to compose. Nevertheless, I worked very little on this work whose title was *sensitive morality,* or the *Wise Man's materialism. (Confessions,* 343–44/*OC,* I:409)

Rousseau undoubtedly admits here the operations of nature and matter on the will. But it would be a mistake to argue that this assumption is evidence that he is a materialist (Hulliung 1994, 189–200). Rather, it is one of the primary assumptions of philosophic *dualism*—that we are composed both of material and immaterial substance. The immaterial assumptions in Rousseau—the soul and free will—have already been demonstrated in Chapter 3.

35. Rousseau, in fact, dismisses the most prominent idealist of the age—George Berkeley—as a "charlatan" in the *First Discourse (FD,* 25/*OC,* I:27).

36. As Rousseau himself explicitly acknowledges (see *Reveries,* 68/*OC,* I:1046).

nal laws of nature."[37] Appeals to supersensible ideas are not likely to lure great numbers of followers in the twenty-first century. They were already, in some respects, losing credibility in the increasingly scientifically conscious eighteenth century. But Rousseau was aware of this. This is why he never attempts to make the kinds of tortured arguments for transcendent ideas such as those found in Locke's *Essays on the Law of Nature*. Rousseau's argument is always simple: consult the conscience.

> Yield to your arguments only when you feel that they agree with the dictamen of your conscience. ([1769] 1997, 283/*OC*, IV:1145)

> Are not your principles engraved in your hearts, and is it not enough in order to learn your Laws to return into oneself and to listen to the voice of one's conscience in the silence of the passions? (*FD*, 28/*OC*, III:31)

> I have already told you that I wanted not to philosophize with you but to help you consult your heart. Were all the philosophers to prove that I am wrong, if you sense that I am right, I do not wish for more. (*Emile*, 289/*OC*, IV:599)

This appeal to inner sense and conscience may not be very much—but, according to Rousseau, it is all that we can possibly have.

---

37. This possibility was particularly well understood by Marx and Engels in the *Communist Manifesto* (175).

FIVE

OF CHAINS, CAVES, AND SLAVES:
ALLEGORY AND ILLUSION IN ROUSSEAU

If the first glimmers of judgment dazzle us and at first make a blur of objects in our sight, let us wait for our weak eyes to open up again and steady themselves, and soon we shall see these same objects again in the light of reason.
—ROUSSEAU, *Emile*

[P]ower, glory, riches, and pleasures are all eclipsed and disappear like a shadow before justice and virtue.
—ROUSSEAU, "IMITATION"

Bound by a thousand chains to inanimate things, in vain you will miss the happy times when you depended only on yourself and when your home was entirely in your soul.
—ROUSSEAU, NOTES ON PLATO

It has often been said of political solutions that the cure is worse than the disease, and perhaps no work of political theory strives to illustrate this point more than Rousseau's *Discourse on the Origin and the Foundations of Inequality Among Men,* or *Second Discourse.* According to him, the disease is "the most horrible state of war" (*SD,* 172/*OC,* III:176). The "cure" is a social contract between the rich and the poor. The poor seek an end to war for obvious reasons—to put an end to bloodshed and establish civil order. The rich also seek these things, but further hope to protect their dubiously acquired extensive property holdings. Thus, having more at stake than the poor, it is the rich who devise the agreement. Their plan, however, is the very definition of deviousness. In drawing up a one-sided contract, they find the means to perpetuate their status and holdings, and through their deceit and cunning, they not only get the consent of the destitute but actually also get them to defend the norms of the new contract with great enthusiasm and vigor. The contract promises to institute laws, rules of justice, and the protection of everyone's liberty, all of which prove impossible to refuse in the context of war. The poor sign on, and thus comes the end of overt conflict.

This signing signals one of the most significant moments of political history for Rousseau: the enchaining of the people. While overt warfare has ended, a covert one has begun: "Such was, or must have been, the origins of Society and of Laws, which gave the weak new fetters and the rich new forces" (*SD*, 173/*OC*, III:178). Without realizing it, the poor have become the slaves of the rich. They become the defenders of society's laws and rules of justice—even though these very laws and rules seek to prevent them permanently from attaining the privileges of true citizens. Thus is born the age of chains.

It is in this set of chains that Rousseau's citizens find themselves bound at the opening of the *Social Contract:* "Man is born free, and everywhere he is in chains" (*SC*, 41/*OC*, III:351). Rousseau claims to be unaware of how these fetters were imposed, but the careful reader knows better. They are the chains found at the end of the *Second Discourse.*[1] As Rousseau says, the aim of the *Social Contract* is to turn these chains of slavery into legitimate chains of citizenship.

Surprisingly little, however, has been written of these chains that play such a large role in Rousseau's political theory. This chapter seeks to demonstrate exactly what they mean in the context of his larger vision of politics. Rousseau once suggested that, to understand his works properly, readers would need to "follow the *chain* of their contents" (*Dialogues*, 211/*OC*, I:933, emphasis added). It cannot be said for certain that Rousseau was providing us here the essential clue to decoding his system. It does, however, appear quite suggestive. The metaphor of the chain owes a great deal to Plato, and Rousseau's employment of it suggests deeper affinities with the Athenian than are commonly acknowledged.[2] This reading of Rousseau serves at once as a heuristic to his corpus and at the same time demonstrates the depth of his philosophic affiliations.

---

1. This has been previously noted in Strong (2002, 68).

2. Only a small handful of scholars have gone so far as to suggest that Rousseau has a theory of the cave. In discussing the chains found in the *First Discourse,* Robert Wokler says, "Here is Rousseau's myth of the cave. No postmodernist critic of the Enlightenment Project ever plumbed the depths of his deconstruction of *Homo sapiens* into *Homo deceptus* more deeply" (2001, 421). Allan Bloom proposes reading the *Emile* as a retelling of Plato's Cave ([1963] 1987, 8–9). And Laurence D. Cooper suggestively remarks that by virtue of his philosophic training, Emile "would have avoided ever being imprisoned in the *Republic*'s famous cave" (2002, 116; see also Cooper 1999, 59). I hope to vindicate these suggestions here with a more fully articulated Platonic reading of Rousseau that extends beyond the *Emile* to many of his substantial works.

1. Plato's Chains

1.1. THE ALLEGORY OF THE CAVE

Plato's cave is home to several individuals, each chained to its walls by the legs and neck, "compelled to hold their heads unmoved throughout life" (*Republic,* 515b). In front of them are shadows on a wall, projected by firelight beyond their scope of vision. The captives have no other vocation than to observe these images, and consequently they come to assume that they are themselves reality. In view of their experience, how could they believe anything else? One day, however, a captive is released from his bonds and removed. As he is pushed toward the cave's exit, he complains of the brilliant light; the closer to the external world he comes, the more acute the pain. This is not an easy journey—and it is not carried out without the use of compulsion. The freed captive would much prefer to return to the comfort of the cave, but is pressed on by an escort. Finally, he exits the cave. He is bewildered at first by the bright light. Slowly, however, he begins to make a series of life-altering observations. First, he discovers that the shadows on the wall were mere projections. Then, as his eyes grow accustomed to the brilliance of the sun, he takes in reflections in the water, objects on the earth's surface, the light of the stars and moon, and finally the sun. It is at this moment that he comes to understand that the sun is responsible for the seasons, the yearly cycle, and even everything he saw in the cave. Now that he knows what he sees is truth, he realizes that what he saw in the cave were shadows.

Upon these discoveries, the man outside the cave takes a moment to reflect upon his former fellow captives. He feels sorry for them. He knows now that they have mistaken mere shadows for reality. What would happen, Plato asks, when this individual returns to the cave? As soon as he returns to his old friends and reports what he has seen, he would be mocked, ridiculed, and scorned. They may think that his vision is skewed; they may try to kill him.

1.2. THREE INTERPRETATIONS OF THE CAVE

The allegory of the cave has been interpreted in at least three significant manners. These are the educational, epistemic/metaphysical, and political interpretations. I will focus most extensively on the last of these, but each sheds important light on Plato's intentions. It must be further kept in mind that the interpretations cross each other's boundaries and become important dimensions of one another.

1.2.1. The Educational Interpretation

No one doubts the importance of education to Plato. Rousseau remarks that the *Republic* was "the most beautiful educational treatise ever written" (*Emile*, 40/*OC*, IV:250). This is apt when one considers the role of education in Kallipolis. Plato himself says that education is "the chief safeguard" against tyranny (*Republic*, 416b), that a proper education is the "one great thing" that will guide citizens in the absence of law (423e), and that an education of approximately fifty years is necessary to become a ruler. This is why, perhaps, the educational interpretation of the cave is the most intuitive. This reading is buttressed by his very introduction to the allegory: "Next, said I, compare our nature in respect of education and its lack to such an experience as this" (514a).

On this account, the cave symbolizes the world of the ignorant, the un- or miseducated. R. G. Tanner persuasively builds a case that the allegory is consciously developed to illustrate the failings of Greek education. Dissatisfied with musical education, in particular, Plato attacks the standard practice of teaching music by imitation. Such training fails to provide the students with any genuine insight into the music or appreciation of the ideas that music represents: "Athenian education, viewed in Platonic terms, served only to feed children's minds on shadows, reflections, and echoes" (Tanner 1970, 88). Thus, the captive's ascent from the cave is symbolic for the acquisition of a genuine education. Properly trained, the pupil comes to genuine understandings of the most central lessons and enters a realm unknown and unavailable to the uneducated.

1.2.2. The Epistemic/Metaphysical Interpretation

If Plato's cave is addressed in part to a proper education, it is logical to ask, "What is the aim of this education?" This leads to the second interpretation of the allegory—the epistemic/metaphysical. It is epistemological insofar as it is concerned with *how* we know; it is metaphysical insofar as it is concerned with *what* we know. The purpose of Plato's extensive educational program is ultimately to produce rulers with knowledge of the Form of the Good, a transcendent normative idea, extending beyond all times, places, and cultures—in short, beyond all contingency. That Plato is making epistemic and metaphysical allusions here is evident from the fact that his discussion of the cave is carefully placed between the important similes of book 6, immediately prior to the allegory, and the training of philosopher-rulers immediately afterward.

The two similes of book 6 are the simile of the sun and the simile of the divided line. The latter describes the epistemic ladder from the cognition of shadows on the bottom to the eternal ideas at the top. Awareness of images represents the lowest form of cognition, resting on imperfect perceptions of perishable objects. Intelligibility of the ideas, by contrast, is the highest form of knowledge—uncorrupted understanding of unchanging objects.

The simile of the sun describes the necessity of light for visual perception. We cannot see things properly without sunshine. Likewise, Plato suggests that we cannot have true normative knowledge without the idea of the good: "This reality, then, that gives their truth to the objects of knowledge and the power of knowing to the knower, you must say is the idea of good, and you must conceive it as being the cause of knowledge and truth" (*Republic,* 508e).

On the other side of the allegory resides Plato's education of the rulers. Here he outlines a curriculum extending approximately fifty years. He emphasizes mathematics, geometry, astronomy, and dialectic. The aim of this education is the knowledge of ideas. Mathematics "tends to draw the mind to essence and reality" (523a).[3] Geometry "tends to facilitate the apprehension of the idea of good" (526e). Finally, dialectic seeks understanding of "the very essence of each thing, and does not desist till [it] apprehends by thought itself the nature of the good in itself" (532ab). Plato provides two thematic pointers useful to the reader. First, he draws our attention back to the simile of the sun, where he associates the idea of the good with the sun (532a). Second, he suggests that knowledge of eternal ideas is a "release from bonds" and an "ascent from the subterranean cave to the world above" (532b). He carefully links together here the simile of the sun, the allegory of the cave, and the education of the rulers.[4]

In this context, the cave is clearly more than an educational metaphor. It is an epistemic and metaphysical one. The captive's education raises the pupil up the ladder of the divided line simile to the realm of ideas. Once one knows the sun, the shadows and images no longer appear real. They are now known *as* shadows and nothing more. This, of course, is not to deny the importance of the world of shadows as the place where physical and political life takes place, but a proper philosophical education reveals a higher level of reality to which all transcendent appeals must go. On this dimension, according to Julia Annas, "Abstract thinking, which leads to philosophic insight, is boldly por-

3. As Darrell Dobbs notes, "The model city's mathematical curriculum is perfectly congenial to genuine philosophy" (2003, 1072).
4. The relation of the allegory of the cave, the simile of the sun, and the simile of the divided line is persuasively outlined in White (1979, 184–86).

trayed as something liberating" (1981, 253). Once we come to understand the eternal truths, we have been liberated from the shadow world of opinion.

1.2.3. The Political Interpretation

Although these interpretations shed much light on Plato's allegory, the political interpretation is perhaps the most resonant to contemporary ears. There is a great deal to suggest such a reading. The *Republic* is, after all, a political book. It offers answers to, or at least speculations about, many great political questions: Who should rule? What is justice? What kind of regime should we have? What is the role of the individual in society? Even if some argue that Plato does not have prescriptions here,[5] it would be impossible to argue that he does not address political questions. This has led more than one interpreter to pursue political readings of the allegory (e.g., Ferguson 1922; Laird 2003). Plato himself also provides suggestive evidence of the political nature of the cave. At its conclusion, he remarks on the difficulty of the philosopher's return to the cave, where he will be "compelled in courtrooms or elsewhere to contend about the shadows of justice or the images that cast the shadows" (*Republic*, 517de). Although he is surely pointing to the difficult task ahead—that of getting the philosophers to take on their difficult political role—he also reveals that the cave itself has political dimensions. The shadows are specifically political here. Not only do the shadows concern *justice* (which in isolation may be taken to refer to the justice of the soul), but the fact that Plato makes reference to courtrooms also suggests that it is particularly *political* justice that interests him.

Further, if politics is about power, the cave surely has its political dimensions. The allegory opens with two distinct parties of different powers and functions. The focus of the educational and epistemological/metaphysical interpretations is the captives. The political interpretation, however, notes an important second party—those casting the shadows. The shadows do not appear *ex nihilo*. They are, rather, the products of human intervention. There are shadow-casters, and they play a central function in Plato's story. It is their job to fascinate and distract the cave dwellers with their show on the walls. George Klosko notes, "They are of course bound and are manipulated by their unseen captors. They hold false opinions and values because they have been conditioned to do so" (1986a, 92). Annas similarly finds that the cave dwellers are "manipulated by others" (1981, 253). And A. S. Ferguson likewise infers that "all signs point to its being contrived by human minds for human

5. See, for example, Leo Strauss's *The City and Man* (1964, 127).

ends" (1922, 16). These ends are, presumably, the sustaining of their own advantage in the political system.

Relations of power are also suggested by Plato's vocabulary. As Andrew Laird says, "His diction is peppered with terms conveying force and control" (2003, 11). Glaucon notes in response to Socrates' account that the captives are "compelled" to hold their heads straight (*Republic*, 515b). Glaucon's word choices also suggest compulsion. At 515b and 515c, he employs *anagkê*, which is the noun for "compulsion." As Klosko remarks, "the prisoners' condition is *forced* on them" (1986a, 92, emphasis added).

What are the shadows in this scheme? On the political interpretation, they are the positive norms of the community. Plato tells us that they are "shadows of justice" (*Republic*, 517d). The purpose of the shadows is to mislead and distract the captives so that they have absolutely no notion that what they are seeing are shadows and that these shadows function to their detriment.

These shadows, however, can work only on a captive audience. This brings us to the crucial metaphor of the chain. Nothing of the above can happen were it not for this device. Plato tells us that the people have "their legs and necks fettered from childhood" (514a). Beyond this, the very word used to describe those in chains—*desmôtai*—literally means "enchained one." The common English translation, "prisoner," has no precise corollary in ancient Greek, because prisons themselves were not prevalent at the time. It is revealing that Plato employs this same noun later to speak of the "prison house in which the tyrant is pent, being of a nature such as we have described and filled with multitudinous and manifold terrors and appetites" (*Republic*, 579b).

Everything in the political interpretation rests on the strength of these chains. If they are weak, the captives have the capacity to step out of the cave on their own volition and assess their sham world at face value. To the extent that the captives are able to escape from the cave, the existing political system collapses. Plato assures us that no one who ascended ever desires to return (to enlighten others, or at least protect them against dangers lurking in the cave). If the chains are strong, the status quo is protected. These chains, however, are not to be taken literally on the political interpretation. The "chains" are created by those manipulating the system in the form of ideology. The captives are held in place by the belief that their cave is pleasant. As Annas remarks, the cave dwellers "are used to their state and *like* it, resisting efforts to free them from it. Their satisfaction is a kind of false consciousness about their state; they cannot even recognize and respond to the truth about their terrible condition" (1981, 253). In this respect, we can understand the political interpretation as a way in which to characterize the tyranny depicted in books

8 and 9 of the *Republic.* The tyrant spreads falsehoods about himself and his intentions (*Republic,* 566de) only to gain the consent of the multitude. These lies ultimately make the cave dwellers happy in their chains and their condition of servitude, willing to fight off those who would free them.

It is important to understand how this interpretation interacts with both the educational and epistemological/metaphysical readings. The educational dimension is crucial insofar as learning is the only means of escape. As Ferguson writes, "Rescue comes from a method of education" (1922, 23). The metaphysical dimension is just as significant. Without true ideas of justice or the good, there are no meaningful ways the escapees can label their former dwelling "bad." In this context, it is important to revisit Plato's concern about the difficulty of the escapee's returning to the darkness, where "he is compelled in courtrooms or elsewhere to contend about shadows of justice or the images that cast the shadows and to wrangle in debate about the notions of these things in the minds of those who have never seen justice itself" (*Republic,* 517d). Without "justice itself," there is nothing to distinguish the "shadows of justice" from genuine justice. It is this combination of education in accordance with intelligible ideas, according to Klosko, that provides the cave dwellers' best hope: "As the prisoners' upbringing in the cave corrupts them, so being raised and educated in a properly run state can give them true ideas and values, and set them free" (1986a, 92).

Of course, the language of liberation must be understood in proper context. Although the political reading of the allegory of the cave might conclude with the manumission of cave dwellers, this does not necessarily mean that they will be liberated in all respects. Their liberation is primarily from an outwardly imposed tyranny, such as that described in books 8 and 9 of the *Republic.* On this particular dimension, Plato relies on the talents of the scarce philosopher-rulers. Whether individuals can be liberated from the shadows of their own making—e.g., those of their passions—is a different matter. Plato is not confident that any but the most gifted of individuals can be liberated in this sense.

2. Jean-Jacques Rousseau and the Metaphor of the Chain

"Man is born free, and everywhere he is in chains" is perhaps the most famous line Rousseau ever uttered. Almost by default, every student of political philosophy is aware of his interest in chains. They are for him an obsession, appearing in all of his major works, often taking a central role. It is thus surprising that they remain largely ignored by his interpreters. This section seeks to redress this oversight and, further, to illustrate the striking parallels of his chains to Plato's.

2.1. CHAINS IN THE *FIRST DISCOURSE*

Rousseau's interest in chains stems back to the *First Discourse*. Written to address the question of whether the arts and sciences served to improve the moral life of modern Europe, the *First Discourse* offers a counterintuitive thesis: the arts and sciences contributed more to decadence than improvement. Early modern advances in science, the arts, and philosophy had been celebrated across Europe. Celestial motions now had an incontestable logic, technology was making life more comfortable than ever, and new advances in jurisprudence promised to make civil relations more just. Rousseau found, however, that these so-called improvements were instead the symptoms of pathologies: "Without men's injustices, what would be the use of Jurisprudence?[6] What would become of History if there were neither Tyrants, nor Wars, nor Conspirators?" (*FD*, 16/*OC*, III:17).

Much has been written on his stunning challenge to the Enlightenment, but placing it alongside Plato's cave puts it in relief:

> The mind has its needs, as has the body. The latter make up the foundations of society, the former make for its being agreeable. While the Government and the Laws see to the safety and the well-being of men assembled, the Sciences, Letters, and Arts, less despotic and perhaps more powerful, spread garlands of flowers over the iron chains with which they are laden, throttle in them the sentiment of original freedom for which they seemed born, make them love slavery, and fashion them into what is called civilized Peoples. Need raised up Thrones; the Sciences and Arts have made them strong. Earthly Powers love talents and protect those who cultivate them! Civilized peoples cultivate them: Happy slaves, you owe them the delicate and refined taste on which you pride yourselves; the sweet character and urbane morals which make for such engaging and easy relations among you; in a word, the appearances of all the virtues without having a single one. (*FD, 6/OC,* III:6–7)

6. Consider the similarity to Plato: "Do you not think it disgraceful and a notable mark of bad breeding to have made use of a justice imported by others, who thus become your masters and judges, from lack of such qualities yourself?" (*Republic,* 405a).

The imagery is striking. The function of the arts and sciences is in this passage something considerably different from an aid to humankind or even pleasant diversion. They are the indispensable tools of oppression. Consider Rousseau's choice of words. The "civilized peoples" are "slaves." Worse than that, they are "happy slaves" [*(h)eureux esclaves*]. As happy slaves, they have no idea just how bad their lot has become. This ignorance leaves them perfectly content and docile.

This contentment, however, is only possible through trickery. Consider other significant words in the above paragraph. One cannot easily establish a class of slaves without *chains:* "While the Government and the Laws see to the safety and the well-being of men assembled, the Sciences, Letters, and Arts . . . spread garlands of flowers over the iron chains with which they are laden." This is not bald oppression. It is rather a subtle, clever, tricky, and profoundly effective mode of enslavement. The slaves are bound, to be sure, but the chains are ornamented so as to go unnoticed. This has at least two dimensions for Rousseau. First, the arts and sciences are the bread and circus that distract citizens from the horrors of their actual condition. Second, the "urbane morals" discussed, promoted, and practiced in existing society provide the false belief that we are living in an age of enlightened morality. It is important to observe Rousseau's own word choice—society has the "*appearances* of all the virtues without having a single one" ["*les apparences* de toutes les vertus sans en avoir aucune"] (emphasis added).

Rousseau's vocabulary borrows extensively from Plato—chains, slaves, garlands, appearances. Both depict the domination of one group by another. With Plato, the shadow-casters are dominant. In Rousseau, it is not yet clear who is responsible for the condition.[7] It is also the case in each that chains are the means of oppression. With Plato, the chains hold the captives to the walls. In Rousseau, the chains hold the slaves to the existing set of norms—both moral and political. Further, the chains themselves are made comfortable by illusions that make the slaves' world appear real or even pleasant. With Plato, the cave dwellers are captivated by the shadows. Citizens living deep in the cave—in democratic society, for example—cherish what should properly be called "vices," crowning them with "garlands" (*Republic,* 560e). In Rousseau, the slaves are charmed by the "garlands of flowers over the iron chains" in the form of the arts and sciences. Finally, the slaves come to love their chains and

7. The men of letters Rousseau condemns clearly have their role, but it is not evident from his words that they are ultimately responsible for the existing condition. A responsible party is not identified until the *Second Discourse.*

the interest of the powerful is served. With Plato, the captives are so fond of their chains that they mock the returning escapee who has their best interests at heart. In Rousseau, the "happy slaves" have no interest in dropping their chains in favor of simple virtue.

The parallels between Rousseau and Plato are already compelling.[8] There remain, however, unanswered questions in Rousseau's version. Who is imposing the chains? Is there a way to cast them off? What lies outside the cave? How does one descend back to liberate others? These questions are taken up successively in the *Second Discourse,* the *Emile,* and the *Social Contract.* Indeed, the questions unanswered in the *First Discourse* lay out the structure of Rousseau's subsequent substantial moral and political works.

2.2. CHAINS IN THE *SECOND DISCOURSE*

The *Discourse on the Origin and the Foundations of Inequality Among Men* (the *Second Discourse*) is explicitly aimed at answering a question posed by the Academy of Dijon: "What is the origin of inequality among men, and is it authorized by Natural Law?" Rousseau's answer is that the natural equality existing among human beings is disturbed by the onset of civil society. Civil society, in turn, explodes into a state of war that is terminated only by a dubious social contract. This contract cements the inequalities that Rousseau claims to exist in his day.

His answer to the academy's question begins to help us understand one of the cited important questions left unanswered by the *First Discourse:* Who is responsible for the enchained condition of the majority of civilization? Rousseau's complete answer to the academy will provide the answer to our question.

The *Second Discourse* begins in the state of nature. Unlike the state of nature found in Hobbes, however, it is a peaceful and asocial condition. Individuals live alone. They move about as their needs guide them. No one has any possessions, no one has any friends, and no one has any enemies. People satisfy their physiological needs as they arise and spend their remaining time reclining against tall trees, enjoying cool breezes.

---

8. Another striking parallel is Rousseau's comment that "some excesses will be proscribed, some vices held in dishonor, but others will be emblazoned with the name of virtues" (*FD,* 8/*OC,* III:9). This immediately calls to mind Plato's description of democracy: "they euphemistically denominate insolence 'good breeding,' license 'liberty,' prodigality 'magnificence,' and shamelessness 'manly spirit'" (*Republic,* 560d–561a). Given that Rousseau's community is growing increasingly democratic (see McLendon 2003, 128–33), his remarks make Plato look prophetic.

This continues until a series of natural disasters and hardships force people to combine for survival. Once together, life begins to transform. Social life begets new necessities—the "necessities" of social life, such as song, dance, romantic love, eloquence, attractiveness, and so forth. It is at this moment when individuals come to assess their social esteem: "Everyone began to look at everyone else and wished to be looked at himself. . . . The one who sang or danced best; the handsomest, the strongest, the most skillful, the most eloquent came to be the most highly regarded, and this was the first step at once toward inequality and vice" (*SD*, 166/*OC*, III:169). Inequalities emerge from these various talents. Some will be more talented than others, and in civil society this has consequences. In the state of nature, these latent talents are of no consequence. One may be able to sing, but without an audience it has no value. Once in civil society, however, great singing ability can lead to a lucrative career in music. Great eloquence leads to lucrative careers in public speaking or politics. Skills in mathematics may lead to prominent careers in science or engineering.

The cultivation and exploitation of these talents ultimately leads to great inequalities of wealth and property. If one has the talent to accumulate wealth, one typically becomes wealthy. This results in the development of two classes—the rich and the poor. The differences between them are further exacerbated by generations of inheritance. The rich grow to love their high status and wealth, and this love soon turns into irrational passion, according to Rousseau: "The rich . . . had scarcely become acquainted with the pleasure of dominating than they disdained all other pleasures. . . . [L]ike those ravenous wolves which once they have tasted human flesh scorn all other food, and from then on want to devour only men" (*SD*, 171/*OC*, III:175–76).

This irrational passion eventually manifests itself in the bourgeois belief that everything belongs to them. They are soon engaging in outright thievery—seizing the possessions of the poor on the assumption that it is their natural right to do so. The poor naturally resist. Thus results the state of war: "Nascent society gave way to the most horrible state of war: Humankind, debased and devastated, no longer able to turn back or to renounce its wretched acquisitions, and working only to its shame by the abuse of the faculties that do it honor, brought itself to the brink of ruin" (*SD*, 172/*OC*, III:176). It is later to arrive than on Hobbes's account, but it is no less fierce.

Although the state of war is brought on by the vices of the rich, its termination is instigated by their Machiavellian *virtù*. Seeing that war could only threaten their prosperity, the rich devise a plan to escape war and thus secure their ill-gotten gains. This leads them to the fantastic proposal of a social contract:

> Let us unite . . . to protect the weak from oppression, restrain the ambitious, and secure for everyone the possession of what belongs to him: Let us institute rules of Justice and peace to which all are obliged to conform, which favor no one, and which in a way make up for the vagaries of fortune by subjecting the powerful and the weak alike to mutual duties. In a word, instead of turning our forces against one another, let us gather them into a supreme power that might govern us according to wise Laws, protect and defend all the members of the association, repulse common enemies, and preserve us in an everlasting accord. (*SD*, 173/*OC*, III:177)

This offer, in the form of a social contract, sounds too good to be true from the perspective of the long-suffering and war-weary poor—justice, law, peace. And, of course, it *is* too good to be true. It is a lie. And, like most lies, its authors issue it as a means of protecting and promoting their own interests.[9]

It is a persuasive and attractive lie, however, and consequently the poor buy it, hook, line, and sinker. This dubious contract also returns us to the metaphor of the chain: "All ran toward their chains in the belief that they were securing their freedom" (*SD*, 173/*OC*, III:177). Rousseau's discussion here helps illuminate his remark from the *First Discourse* that the chains of tyranny were covered in "garlands of flowers." We can now extend Rousseau's own reasoning to read these garlands of flowers as promises of justice, law, peace, and freedom. In reality, the weak are given "new fetters and the rich new forces" (*SD*, 173/*OC*, III:178). Attractive ornamentation indeed, but still mere decoration—like an ogre outfitted by Brooks Brothers.

Once Rousseau introduces his metaphor of the chain in the *Second Discourse,* he returns to it over and over again. His subsequent discussion empha-

---

9. One may reasonably ask, "If the tyrants are themselves in their own cave (one where pleasure and power take precedence over genuine virtue), how can they imprison others?" The answer is that tyrants need not know what lies outside the cave any more than the prison warden knows the laws. There is no need to be in touch with Plato's highest metaphysical principles in order to be a nuisance to others. Plato makes this point in the *Phaedrus:* "When a master of oratory, who is ignorant of good and evil, employs his power of persuasion on a community as ignorant as himself . . . by extolling evil as being really good, and when by studying the beliefs of the masses he persuades them to do evil instead of good, what kind of crop do you think his oratory is likely to reap from the seed thus sown?" (260cd). In fact, it is not even necessary to be another human being. As will be revealed shortly, opinion and passions are additional chains in Rousseau's cave, but they certainly have no self-awareness of their status as imprisoners.

sizes fundamental points of the *First Discourse*. The theme of the happy slave is revisited: "I know that [the poor duped in the social contract] do nothing but boast of the peace and quiet they enjoy in their chains, and that *they call the most miserable servitude peace*" (*SD*, 177/*OC*, III:181). If the slaves believe themselves to be surrounded by flowers rather than chains, it is possible to see how such tricks work. Everything depends upon the success of the illusion—the shadows on the wall. Once the tyrant can make shadows appear as reality, then all are putty in the tyrant's hands.

The illusion created is so successful that by the end of the *Second Discourse*, Rousseau remarks that it is "already past the state where they could break their chains" (*SD*, 182/*OC*, III:187). Even worse, the poor are so oblivious that they eagerly participate in the scheme themselves: they "consent to bear chains so that they might impose chains [on others] in turn" (183/III:188).[10] Thus, the chains of the *First Discourse* return with a vengeance. In retrieving the image, Rousseau addresses one of the unanswered questions of the *First Discourse*: Who imposes the chains? It is now more than obvious that the rich both cast the shadows and impose the chains. The conclusion of this work finds the overwhelming majority of citizens to be victims of an insidious despotism, and one would be tempted to believe that there is no escape. Rousseau's next two major works, however, suggest a way out.

2.3. CHAINS IN THE *EMILE*

The *Emile* is best known as a normative program of education, but tucked away between its pedagogical lessons are important social observations. These observations uphold Rousseau's earlier characterizations of civil society. He confirms here that the despotic scheme reported in the *Second Discourse* was profoundly successful. The rich and powerful have consolidated their gains and employ civil institutions at will to oppress others. Law is now an instrument of oppression by which the strong subjugate the weak. The highest aspirations of civil society have been perverted: "Those specious names, justice and order, . . . serve as instruments of violence and as arms of iniquity" (*Emile*, 236/*OC*, IV:524).

Thus, it is unsurprising to see that metaphoric chains play a significant role in the *Emile*. Everywhere he looks, Rousseau sees them fettering citizens liter-

10. This precedes by more than two centuries Foucault's observation, in *Discipline and Punish*, that delinquents will be employed by the bourgeoisie in order to keep others in line and hence serve bourgeois interests (279–82).

ally from cradle to grave: "Civil man is born, lives, and dies in slavery.[11] At birth he is sewed in swaddling clothes; at his death he is nailed in a coffin. So long as he keeps his human shape, he is enchained by our institutions" (*Emile*, 43/*OC*, IV:253). Whereas the *Second Discourse* describes the enchaining of society, the *Emile* describes the enchained society.

The fundamental function of the early chains is to stifle the child's natural inclination to exercise its freedom. Swaddling clothes restrict its free movement. Such measures are born of parental laziness, Rousseau tells us. It is easier to manage an immobile child than an unrestrained one. The consequences of these seemingly benign restrictions, however, are dire. Because the child cannot move, it finds its only freedom in crying: "Having nothing free but voice, how would they not make use of it to complain? They cry because you are hurting them. Thus garroted, you would cry harder than they do" (*Emile*, 44/*OC*, IV:254–55).

This constant crying is not without consequence. It builds deep patterns of behavior that ultimately shape the social world. Whereas crying may begin as a natural response to the child's bonds, it slowly transforms into something far more disturbing. It gives birth to "the idea of empire and dominion" (*Emile*, 66/*OC*, IV:287). This is because the child soon learns that crying is more than simply an exercise of its limited capacity for freedom. It is a *command*. The only means by which children can satisfy their desires—reasonable or otherwise—is by crying. When they see adults responding to their tears, they soon learn how to make others responsive to their whims: "Children begin by getting themselves assisted; they end by getting themselves served" (66/IV:287). Thus, the chains form a vicious cycle. The fetters placed on young children ultimately feed their desire to enchain others. And so it goes, ad infinitum. Rousseau's prescription for this malady is to grant the children more freedom from infancy forward. If children have the liberty to grasp the objects of their desire, they will not grow accustomed to making others instruments of their whims.[12]

Another chain in the *Emile* is imposed by opinion: "Even domination is servile when it is connected with opinion, for you depend on the prejudices of those you govern by prejudices. To lead them as you please, you must conduct yourself as you please. They have only to change their way of thinking,

11. It is worth noting here that he appears to contradict the opening of the *Social Contract*, where "man is born free" only to end up in chains. This apparent contradiction can be resolved by noting that Rousseau refers here to "civil" man, and the *Social Contract* alludes to natural man.

12. Rousseau's first formulation of this pattern comes in *Julie* (466–67/*OC*, II:569–70).

and you must perforce change your way of acting" (83/IV:308).[13] The chains of opinion are for Rousseau "slavery, illusion, and deception" (83/IV:308);[14] they are a "poison" (178/IV:444).[15]

The parallels with Plato are again striking.[16] "Chains," "slavery," "illusion," "deception," "opinion"—the vocabulary is remarkably reminiscent of the Platonic lexicon.[17] Opinion, of course, plays an important role in Plato's *Republic*. Its central role is as a contrast with knowledge. Knowledge is an understanding of the ideas themselves. Opinions, however, are fallible beliefs about the ideas. In this sense, the shadows on Plato's cave wall are surely opinions. The captives fervently believe them to be reality, but are deceived. Plato even says that anything would be better for the cave escapee than to "opine with them [the cave dwellers] and live that life" (*Republic*, 516d). When opinions are shared and multiplied, they become factions. In this context, it is easy to understand why Plato referred to them as the greatest enemy of the city (*Laws*, 856b).[18] Opinions function in much the same way for Rousseau. They are claims about reality, but have no necessary connection to it, and, like Plato's shadows, the opinions of society can enchant and mislead citizens into false beliefs. This is confirmed in Rousseau's recently rediscovered "Letter on Virtue, the Individual, and Society": "Swayed as we are by opinion . . . we must, when judging things, take every possible precaution to distinguish appearance from reality" ([1757] 2003, 32). Rousseau not only cites opinion as a danger but also does so in clear Platonic language.

13. This passage has also been cited by Christopher Bertram to illustrate the problem of slavery to opinion as understood by Rousseau (2004, 44).

14. Rousseau echoes this point later in the *Dialogues*: "When I published my first writings, the public was still left on its own, it hadn't yet completely adopted a sect and could hear the voice of truth and reason. But completely subjugated today, it no longer thinks, no longer reasons, it is no longer anything by itself, and no longer follows anything but the impressions given to it by its guides" (140/*OC*, I:841). It is reasserted once more in the *Reveries*, which speaks of the "tyranny [*joug*] of public opinion" (129/*OC*, I:1079).

15. His thoughts here echo those of Julie: "O opinion, opinion! How difficult it is to shake its yoke! It always leads us to injustice" (*Julie*, 514/*OC*, II:627). He also earlier cites the danger of opinion in his *Letter to d'Alembert*: "Opinion, queen of the world, is not subject to the power of kings; they are themselves her first slaves" (73–74/*OC*, V:67).

16. Similarities between Rousseau's *Emile* and Plato's *Republic* have been well outlined by Laurence D. Cooper. Cooper astutely argues that Rousseau follows Plato's model of speaking on two levels simultaneously—to both philosophic and nonphilosophic educations. In this respect, he argues, the *Emile* is "far more sympathetic [to Plato's *Republic*] than it first appears" (2002, 109).

17. Louis Millet has previously noted the close relationship of Rousseau to Plato on this dimension (1967, 3).

18. As J. M. Silverthorne has discovered, Rousseau carefully marked this passage in his personal copy of the *Laws* and would later incorporate it into the *Social Contract*, book 4, chapter 2 (1973, 245).

The big question, of course, is this: How do we break free of the chains? For Plato, the answer is education. Notably, Rousseau's prescription here is the same.[19] This is where we can cease reading the *Emile* as a descriptive account of civilization and can begin reading it as a normative program of education. What is notable about his educational program in this context is the end it promotes: freedom. The point of removing the restrictive swaddling on infants, of taking the child out of the crib to let him or her roam, of shielding the child from mind-numbing books, of letting the child choose his or her own religion—all of these aim to foster the pupil's freedom.

This freedom is particularly ancient in its conception. It is the capacity to become one's own master. This is the Platonic virtue of *sophrosune*, which plays a significant role in both the *Republic* and the *Laws*. In the *Republic*, it is one of the four fundamental virtues of both the individual and the state. Of particular interest is its role in the individual. He who has *sophrosune* is "master of himself" (*Republic*, 430e). It is the ability to master pleasure and pain in order to be guided by "reason and right opinion" (431c). For Plato, it is possible to be good only if we are able to exercise self-mastery and silence all other influences on our behavior—be they false opinion, the passions, or excessive self-love. He later begins the *Laws* with an extended examination of *sophrosune*. His long discussion of drinking is ultimately aimed at determining who possesses this virtue. Because drunkenness is "the condition in which his self-command is at its lowest" (*Laws*, 645e), the person able to exercise self-mastery in this state truly has *sophrosune*.

Rousseau's conception of freedom in this context is remarkably similar. He has the tutor tell Emile that

> all passions are good when one remains their master; all are bad when one lets oneself be subjected to them. . . . It is not within our control to have or not to have passions. But it is within our control to reign over them. All the sentiments we dominate are legitimate; all those which dominate us are criminal. A man is not guilty for loving another's wife if he keeps this unhappy passion enslaved to the law of duty. (*Emile*, 445/*OC*, IV:819)

19. Patrick Riley says, "Education (domestic and civic) is everything in Rousseau" (2001, 126). Although this might be slightly exaggerated, Riley is right to emphasize the centrality of education to Rousseau's overall program. Evidence for this can be found in his *Political Economy*: education "is the most important business of the state" (22/*OC*, III:261). It is worth noting here that Plato identified the position of supervisor of education as the most important in the city (*Laws*, 765e).

In modern terminology, this freedom is the ability to legislate for oneself.[20] Individuals are free insofar as they are dominated by nothing other than their own will, and, just as the virtue of *sophrosune* has a close relationship to Plato's conception of justice, Rousseau declares that "liberty without justice is a genuine contradiction" (*Letters*, 261/*OC*, III:842). One exercises true freedom only by acting in accordance with justice. All else is slavery. This theme is persistent throughout his career. It can be found in his *Discourse on Heroic Virtue*, where he writes, "To be great one need only assume mastery of oneself" ([1768] 1997, 315/*OC*, II:1273), as well as in *Julie:* "A rarer spectacle and one worthy of the wise man's eye, the spectacle of a sublime and pure soul overcoming its passions and reigning over itself is the one you are now enjoying" (430/*OC*, II:524). In his *Letter to Beaumont*, Rousseau argues that "It is always noble to be in command of oneself" ([1763] 2001, 54/*OC*, IV:970), and in the *Reveries*, he speaks of the necessity of "becom[ing] one's own master" (134/*OC*, I:1083) and of asserting "self-control" (135/*OC*, I:1084).

The successful completion of this education leads to the *Emile*'s stunning conclusion. Rousseau ultimately has his pupil exchange one set of chains for another. The chains of opinion, despotism, institutions, and passions are cast off in favor of others:

> the eternal laws of nature and order do exist. For the wise man, they take the place of positive law. They are written in the depth of his heart by conscience and reason. It is to these that he ought to enslave himself in order to be free. The only slave is the man who does evil, for he always does it in spite of himself. (*Emile*, 473/*OC*, IV:857)

These words (obviously reminiscent of his "forced to be free") turn the tables, in a sense. Chains themselves are not the ultimate burden for Rousseau. Chains can be good or bad. The chains of oppression, passion, and opinion are obviously bad, whereas the chains of the "eternal laws of nature" constitute the legitimate fetters that will guide the *Social Contract*. Again, we find a close parallel here to Plato's observation that in order to be a good citizen, one must be a "servant . . . of the laws" (*Laws*, 772e). Neither Rousseau nor Plato ultimately abolishes slavery per se. Rather, slavery to anything other than principles of goodness and justice finally proves noxious.

---

20. See O'Hagan (2004, 79).

2.4. CHAINS IN THE *SOCIAL CONTRACT*

Although the *Emile* has an optimistic conclusion, it is important to remember that Rousseau does not seriously hold it to be practicable. The time and effort necessary to invest in the child for this education, while noble, would be superhuman. It would require the tutor to dedicate a substantial portion of his life to the education of the pupil. Thus, it is unsurprising to see how he opens his *Social Contract:* "Man is born free, and everywhere he is in chains." Because we are doomed to live in a society that does not permit us the resources to be our own masters in the fashion of the *Emile,* we shall have to devise another. The *Social Contract* is a second attempt at this same goal, and just as he hoped to provide a means to freedom in the *Emile,* here he aims at granting men "moral freedom, which alone makes man truly the master of himself" (*SC,* 54/*OC,* III:365).

Understanding this, however, requires a closer examination of Rousseau's own words, carefully chosen to introduce the reader to his most substantial and explicitly political tract: "Man is born free, and everywhere he is in chains. One believes himself the others' master, and yet is more a slave than they. How did this change come about? I do not know. What can make it legitimate? I believe I can solve this problem" (*SC,* 41/*OC,* III:351). The first problem in reading this familiar passage is understanding what Rousseau means by "freedom." After examining the *Emile* and understanding its goal of freedom as being won only after much hard work and extensive education, it is surprising to find that he here grants its presence by the mere fact of birth. Reading the text in this way, however, would obscure the fact that he operates with two very different conceptions of freedom. One has already been addressed: *sophrosune,* or moral freedom, i.e., the liberty to make moral choices. One cannot have this type of freedom at birth, says Rousseau, because children lack knowledge of good and bad (*Emile,* 92/*OC,* IV:321). Thus, it is impossible that he meant this kind of freedom in the opening paragraph of the *Social Contract.* The second type of liberty is natural freedom—physically unrestricted movement. It is this second type to which Rousseau refers in his famous opening. Being born "free" does not mean that we are fully functioning moral beings. It simply means that our behavior is free of external constraint.

The next sentence comes in the form of a paradox: "One believes himself the others' master, and yet is more a slave than they." This reference takes us back to the *Emile.* There he cautions against setting up the child as master, by virtue of succumbing to crying and actively presenting him with all he desires.

To do so is to set the child up to be helpless as an adult. The master (by virtue of habitually issuing orders) ultimately becomes a slave (by virtue of becoming dependent on others for the satisfaction of needs and desires). This is no less true of actual slaves and masters. In this respect, Rousseau anticipates Hegel's famous master/slave story. Although the master in the beginning sets himself above the slave, he ultimately becomes a slave himself. It also takes us back to Plato, who says that "the real tyrant is really enslaved to cringings and servitude beyond compare, a flatterer of the basest men" (*Republic*, 579de). The master is ultimately a slave, and Rousseau is committed to breaking this cycle.

The next two sentences are more mysterious: "How did this change come about? I do not know." It would seem that Rousseau is being coy. Because the *Second Discourse* is dedicated to detailing our enchaining, it appears that he knows very well indeed how this change came about, but he adds that his historical speculations "ought not be taken for historical truths, but only for hypothetical and conditional reasonings; better suited to elucidate the Nature of things than to show their genuine origin" (*SD*, 132/*OC*, III:133). In light of this, we might be tempted to disagree with Tracy Strong ([1994] 2002), who suggests that the chains at the opening of the *Social Contract* are the same as those at the conclusion of the *Second Discourse*. It is unnecessary to reason this way, however; the text allows for us to agree with Strong and at the same time recognize that the *Second Discourse* is mere speculation. Although Rousseau admits the speculative status of the historical dimensions of the *Second Discourse*, he is confident of the accuracy of his conclusions. He is not ultimately concerned with the "genuine origin" of the condition as much as its current predicament. Examining the text here again makes this clear: his *Second Discourse* is "better suited to elucidate the *Nature of things* than to show their *genuine origin*" (emphasis added). He is more interested in showing *that* we are in chains than in *how* these chains were actually imposed. As F. C. Green has noted, although Rousseau is not certain of his history, "It is . . . a painfully evident fact that our primitive ancestors somehow took the wrong turn" (1955, 286). This interpretation ultimately explains why Rousseau might claim an otherwise puzzling ignorance about the origin of man's chains in the *Social Contract*.

The remaining sentences of the paragraph excerpted above are less cryptic. "What can make it [the enchained condition] legitimate? I believe I can solve this problem." This is the problem Rousseau articulated in the *Emile* (473/*OC*, IV:857). How can we replace illegitimate chains (those of tyranny, opinion, ill-guided emotion, and so forth) with legitimate ones (those of the eternal laws of nature)? The solution constitutes the bulk of the *Social Contract.* This is the function of the general will.

Once more, Rousseau's use of Platonic metaphor is notable. The chains of the *First Discourse, Second Discourse,* and *Emile* are again present here, and the fact that he chose to open with men in chains is undoubtedly intentional. Rousseau initially tucked the passage away in book 1, chapter 3, of the first draft of the *Geneva Manuscript (GM,* 163/*OC,* III:289), scarcely the first place anyone would look. His obvious fondness for it, however, led him to move it to the very front of the final draft. This is a thematic pointer to his loyal readers, who were, by now, well familiar with his chains.

Also significant in the *Social Contract* is his emphasis on slavery. He draws here on slavery both as a metaphor and as a political reality. As for the latter, volunteering for slavery as a political institution is "illegitimate and null" (*SC,* 45/*OC,* III:356). According to Rousseau, it is illegitimate because no person of sound mind would submit to it. To give oneself over to slavery is, in effect, to submit to arbitrary government or tyranny. This is a legal despotism, a notion that strikes him as "nothing but two contradictory words" (Rousseau [1767] 1997, 271). This fails because a submission to slavery and tyranny constitutes a surrender of one's freedom—all along one of Rousseau's most fundamental ends. To deprive oneself of freedom "is to deprive one's actions of all morality" (*SC,* 45/*OC,* III:356).[21] He subsequently adds that it is only in a legitimate state that we can exercise "moral freedom, which alone makes man truly the master of himself; for the impulsion of mere appetite is slavery, and obedience to the law one has prescribed oneself is freedom" (54/III:365).[22]

In this spirit, Rousseau finds fault with Aristotle's defense of slavery, saying that he has mistaken effect for cause. Aristotle defends the institution on the grounds that some people are naturally born for servitude. Rousseau agrees that some *appear* to be born for slavery, but this is because they have been conditioned to grow comfortable in their fetters: "Slaves lose everything in their chains, even the desire to be rid of them; they love their servitude" (*SC,* 43/*OC,* III:353). Rousseau repeats here his previous assertions that slaves love their chains (*FD,* 6/*OC,* III:6–7; *SD,* 177/*OC,* III:181). Once more this reminds us of Plato's admonition that returning to the cave is a dangerous task because of how much the captives have grown to love their chains (see Annas 1981, 253).

21. He later adds, "Vile slaves smile mockingly at the word freedom" (*SC,* 110/*OC,* III:425).
22. Rousseau concludes the paragraph by chiding himself: "But I have already said too much here on this topic, and the philosophic meaning of the word *freedom* is not my subject here." Presumably this is because it is a central task of the *Emile.* Notably, however, he continues to operate with this conception of freedom in the *Social Contract* (e.g., 123/*OC,* III:439).

He also looks to slavery more metaphorically in the *Social Contract*. Although it does not involve physical restraint, "the impulsion of mere appetite is slavery, and obedience to the law one has prescribed to oneself is freedom" (*SC*, 54/*OC*, III:365). In this respect, he is repeating one of his claims in the *Emile* (445/*OC*, IV:819). This also serves to emphasize one of his central dichotomies: one can be either free or enslaved.[23] Habitual submission to the appetites is merely a form of slavery. Again, Rousseau here echoes "[t]hat noble genius [who] had planned everything, foreseen everything" (*Emile*, 362/*OC*, IV:700). Plato cites appetite as a component of human nature but insists that it must be controlled by reason (*Republic*, 441ab).

Beyond the metaphor of slavery exists that of the cave itself. Rousseau makes only one reference to a grotto in his *Social Contract*, but it is potentially revealing. It is important to note that this takes place in his discussion of slavery and despotism:

> The despot, it will be said, guarantees civil tranquility for his subjects. All right; but what does it profit them if the wars his ambition brings on them, if his insatiable greed, the harassment by his administration cause them more distress than their own dissensions would have done? What does it profit them if this very tranquility is one of their miseries? Life is also tranquil in dungeons; is that enough to feel well in them? The Greeks imprisoned in the Cyclops's cave lived there tranquilly, while awaiting their turn to be devoured. (45/*OC*, III:355–56)[24]

This is Homer's cave from the *Odyssey*, and it is certainly not the same as Plato's. Rousseau's characterization of it reveals important similarities. First, he raises the cave of the cyclops in the context of a discussion of despotism. This directs us to the political interpretation of the cave. On this reading, the cave dwellers both in Plato's allegory and Rousseau's *Second Discourse* are the victims of a sinister regime. Second, Rousseau tells us that the cave is tranquil (variants of the word appear no fewer than four times in this one paragraph).

23. Rousseau also emphasizes this dichotomy in his "Fragments of the Letter to Beaumont" ([1763] 2001, 92/*OC*, IV:1019).
24. Rousseau is here repeating an earlier reference to Homer's cave made in the "State of War": "I see unfortunate peoples groaning under an iron yoke, mankind crushed by a handful of oppressors, starving masses overwhelmed by pain and hunger, whose blood and tears the rich drink in peace, and everywhere the strong armed against the weak with the frightful power of the laws. All this happens peacefully and without resistance; it is the tranquility of the companions of Ulysses shut up in the Cyclops's cave until they get devoured" (162/*OC*, III:609).

Not only does this reiterate his earlier claim that once the chains are secure, the slaves' "tranquility" has been "consolidated" (*SC*, 182/*OC*, III:187), but it also harkens back to the relative tranquility of Plato's cave. We know this of the latter because, upon release and ascent, Plato's captives "felt pain" (*Republic*, 515c), felt "pain [in] the eyes" (515e), "would turn away and flee" back to the relative security of the cave (515e), and once more "find it painful" (515e). Life outside the cave—at least at first—is anything but tranquil. This is why the initial escapee desires to flee back into the ground and why the others would kill their potential manumitters. Rousseau's depiction of Homer's cave thus points to the many features that define Plato's.

The next question to be answered concerns what lies outside Rousseau's cave. On what basis does one know one is in a cave, fettered with chains? For Plato, the answer is knowledge of the transcendent idea of the good. With this knowledge, one can see that the shadows are simply shadows. Rousseau's answer appears to be the same, and this is what completes the remarkable correspondence between the two great thinkers. Rousseau had indicated in the *Emile* that there are "eternal laws of nature" (473/*OC*, IV:857). He also speaks there of an "eternal justice" (292/IV:603). It is unsurprising, then, to find him declaring in the *Social Contract*, "What is good and conformable to order is so by the nature of things and independently of human conventions. . . . No doubt there is a universal justice emanating from reason alone" (66/*OC*, III:378). Later, in the *Reveries,* Rousseau says that the "subtle sophistries of metaphysicians . . . cannot outweigh the eternal truths which have been accepted at all times, recognized by all nations, and indelibly engraved on the human heart" (59/*OC*, I:1021). Although outlining all the dimensions of Rousseau's metaphysics, such as it is, is beyond the scope of the present chapter, a few remarks are merited. First, both Plato and Rousseau characterize their highest principles as "eternal." Second, they both eschew agreement or convention as the source of these highest principles. Third, they both deny that empirical data of any kind can be the source of these ideas. Fourth, they believe that these principles hold across cultures. And fifth, their works suggest that these principles are in some sense indeterminate—that is, they are not so concrete as to be easily definable (Seung 1996, 306; *Emile*, 108/ *OC*, IV:345).

At any rate, all of these passages suggest that there is indeed something outside Rousseau's cave. Diving back into the world of allegory, this makes perfect sense. If there are such things as "appearances" (*FD*, 6/*OC*, III:7), there must be reality. If there is such a thing as "deception" (*Emile*, 83/*OC*, IV:308), there must be truth. If there is injustice (*SD*, 173/*OC*, III:177), there must be justice. If there are shadows, there must somewhere be substance. That Rousseau's obvious admiration of Plato extends to the metaphysical level is suggested by his own words. In the *Persifleur,* he says that the "most profound metaphysics" is to be found in "Plato, Locke, or Malebranche" (*OC,* I:1111).[25] Further, one should not neglect the original subtitle chosen for the *Social Contract* found in its first draft: *Essay About the Form of the Republic.* As Roger Masters and Christopher Kelly point out, there are obvious and deep Platonic connections here—both in the words "form" and "republic" (Masters 1978, 18–20; Masters and Kelly 1994, xx–xxii). Rousseau was far too familiar with Plato to have chosen these words unaware of their strong Platonic overtones.[26]

This idea of eternal justice is essential for Rousseau's version of the allegory, both epistemologically and politically. Epistemologically speaking, without justice, we cannot even be aware that our chains are tyrannical or insidious in some other fashion. The idea of justice itself informs the captive of bondage. Without it, any escape would merely be an exchange of shadows for shadows. There is no compelling reason to leave. Politically speaking, the captive requires a reason above existing political norms to exit the cave. Without some higher idea, there may be no such reason. The positive norms of the despotism found in the *Second Discourse,* for example, would surely require habitual obedience to the unjust contract. Appealing to the higher norm, however, allows Rousseau's captives to call this contract "unjust" and then take steps to free themselves.

With these norms established, Rousseau can commence the task of the *Social Contract* and of his politics generally. As he states at its beginning, his goal is to replace the chains of slavery with legitimate chains. These are the same chains of which he speaks in the *Emile*—the fetters of the "eternal laws of nature" (473/*OC,* IV:857). These transcendent principles anchor his social contract and guide its government. They are the standards by which its actions are to be judged (*Political Economy,* 7/*OC,* III:245). The purpose of the law, as Rousseau states, is "to bring justice back to its object" (*SC, 66/*

25. The addition of Locke and Malebranche to Plato are significant here, as well, because Malebranche was well known to Rousseau as a Platonist (Hendel 1934, 1:4), and Locke has his own connections to Platonic metaphysics (Lovejoy [1936] 1963, 362). An insightful discussion of the influence of Malebranche on Rousseau can be found in Riley (1992, 91–109).

26. It is also worth observing that in Rousseau's planned larger work on politics, of which the *Social Contract* was only meant to be a part, Rousseau had intended to write his final chapter on Plato's *Republic* (Rousseau 1994a, 16/*OC,* III:473).

OC, III:378).[27] In a sense, what he hopes to achieve in his social contract is to bring the transcendent idea—or the "sun," in Platonic terms—down to earth, or down into the cave, so that it may improve the lives of its residents.

To do this, however, one more device is necessary. There must be an agent charged with the task of bringing these ideas down. This position would "require a superior intelligence who saw all of man's passions and yet experienced none of them, who had no relation to our nature yet knew it thoroughly, whose happiness was independent of us and who was nevertheless willing to care for ours; finally, one who, preparing his distant glory in the progress of times, could work in one century and enjoy the reward in another" (*SC,* 68–69/*OC,* III:381). This is Rousseau's lawgiver (*législateur*). Although the above lists some of the office's essential prerequisites, it is far from a full description of its duties. Its charge is nothing less than "changing human nature" (69/III:381), or transforming individuals into citizens—turning amoral atomistic units into a moral community. It is exchanging a natural man for a social one. And whereas Rousseau often speaks with nostalgic fondness for his savage, there is no disputing that he views this transformation as an improvement: "The more these natural forces are dead and destroyed, the *greater* and more lasting are the acquired" (69/III:382, emphasis added). The lawgiver achieves this effect through the introduction of sound law, in the spirit of Lycurgus or Solon.

In this context, it is noteworthy that Rousseau cites Plato's *Statesman* as a source of sound advice concerning the attributes of a lawgiver: "The same reasoning Caligula made as to fact, Plato made as to right in defining the civil or royal man he seeks in his book on ruling [i.e., the *Statesman*]" (*Social Contract* 69/*OC,* III:381). The authority of Plato's ruler here rests on that ruler's wisdom and reason (see Klosko 1986a, 190). This, however, is scarcely the only virtue required of the *Statesman*'s prince. The prince must possess all the Platonic virtues—not only wisdom but also courage, moderation, and justice—and, in this respect, the affinities of the *Statesman*'s prince and the philosopher-ruler of the *Republic* are evident (see Seung 1996, 257).

The office of Rousseau's lawgiver is foreign to contemporary minds. Like the functions fulfilled by Lycurgus and Solon, this office is finite—present only at the founding. It is neither magistracy nor sovereignty and has no place

27. This is likely why Melissa Schwarzberg notes that "the end [of the fundamental law in Rousseau] . . . is to bring the sovereign, as it must be by definition, in line with morality and justice" (2003, 389).

within the constitution. The reasons for this are carefully outlined. Were the lawgiver to have a permanent place in the government, "the laws, as ministers to his passions, would often only perpetuate his injustices, and he could never avoid having particular views vitiate the sanctity of his work" (*SC*, 69–70/*OC*, III:382). Thus, the Greeks were right to delegate this task to foreigners. Having no personal stake in the laws of the nation they were founding, they were free to exercise their talents for the general will, rather than their own particular interests.

The office of lawgiver suggests an important Platonic parallel. Just as Plato suggested that few would ever have the aptitude to serve as philosopher-ruler (*Republic*, 427e), so, too, does Rousseau suggest that the lawgiver's skill set is rare. "Philosophy, . . . the love of wisdom," Plato reminds us, "is impossible for the multitude" (494a). Similarly for Rousseau, the lawgiver is "an extraordinary man," distinguished by his "genius," implying that few ever possess the lofty attributes required by this station (*SC*, 69/*OC*, III:382). This individual must be extremely intelligent and divested of dangerous passions.

This leads us back to the cave. Both the philosopher-ruler and the lawgiver are charged with heady duties. In Plato's allegory, the philosopher must not only make the difficult climb out of the cave but also make the even more painful journey back in. Getting out of the cave requires decades upon decades of education in all things, culminating with an understanding of the good. In light of the difficulty of the ascent, philosophers are not eager to return to the cave. But justice and the state compel them: "Down you must go, each in his turn, to the habituation of the others and accustom yourselves to the observation of obscure things there" (*Republic*, 520c). This is required because they are the only ones who have seen true beauty, justice, and the good. As a consequence, the philosophers issue a new age of truly enlightened rule, according to Plato, as opposed to the "dark" rule exhibited in most states where men "fight one another for shadows" (520d). The necessity of philosophic rule ultimately registers with the philosophers themselves, who will approach their office "as an unavoidable necessity" (520e). So, whereas Plato speaks of the compulsion necessary to get the philosophers back in the cave, it is all in the form of persuasion.

While Rousseau's lawgiver likewise must enter the cave, as it were, his origins and motives are less clear than in Plato's account. Plato has a system of education in place to produce philosopher-rulers, but Rousseau has instituted no such system for his lawgiver. He admits that the task of finding such an individual is "difficult" and even "discouraging" (*GM*, 179/*OC*, III:313). Rather, the lawgiver must come from an external community, one with no

interests attached to the state being founded. In this respect, Rousseau is relying to some degree on chance—the chance that such a person can be discovered.[28] There is another important difference in this dimension: the lawgiver
never really needs to descend back into the cave. Because Rousseau's lawgiver
is not a ruler in any sense, he need not return to the people to dwell there. In
this respect, we can appreciate that Rousseau could write his proposals for
constitutional reforms in Poland and Corsica. He could sketch a system, in
some sense, from outside the cave. This role is undoubtedly less involved than
what is required of the philosopher-ruler, and perhaps in this respect easier to
fill.

2.5. "ON THEATRICAL IMITATION"

Although the similarities between Plato and Rousseau examined above are
deep, some might view them more as coincidental than as profound and conscious affinities. This objection is difficult to sustain, however, in the face of
Rousseau's little-known essay "On Theatrical Imitation: An Essay Drawn
from Plato's Dialogues." The title of the essay is not misleading. It is a substantially faithful meditation on Plato's *Republic,* largely with reference to his
discussion of art in book 10. It encompasses more than just Plato's theory of
art, however. It takes into account, assumes, and even advocates some of the
most important Platonic doctrines, including his account of virtue, his theory
of ideas, and his theory of the soul. That Rousseau is deeply sympathetic to
Plato's thought in these important respects lends credence to a Platonic reading of Rousseau's corpus.

Rousseau initially wrote the essay in 1758, in preparation for his *Letter to
d'Alembert.* He ultimately did not include it in the letter, because it could not
"fit into that work comfortably." The essay subsequently sat for several years
before finding its way into a publisher's hands in 1764. Rousseau does not
suggest that the publishing was of his own choosing, but he does not apologize
for the work, either, even if he characterizes it as a "bagatelle" ("Imitation,"
337/*OC,* V:1195).[29] In the *Dialogues,* Rousseau cites the essay, along with the
Letter to d'Alembert, Julie, Emile, and the *Social Contract,* as a work demonstra-
ting that no "philosopher ever meditated more profoundly" (*Dialogues,* 101/

28. Of course, even in this respect he bears similarity to Plato. Before Plato's ideal state is instituted, one can rely only on "chance" to have a philosopher-ruler (*Republic,* 499b).

29. Rousseau also refers to the Savoyard Vicar's Profession of Faith as a "bagatelle" (*Emile,* 264/
OC, IV:562).

OC, I:791). That he would include this in a list of his greatest writings is sufficient evidence to treat the work seriously.

In order to understand this "bagatelle" properly, it is important to know
the themes of his *Letter to d'Alembert*. The letter is a public response to
d'Alembert's *Encyclopédie* entry on Geneva. Amid his descriptions and prescriptions for Rousseau's hometown, d'Alembert advises that it institute a theater. Rousseau's response is that of fierce rejection. Although d'Alembert's
proposal is "seductive," Rousseau writes, it is "dangerous" (*Letter to d'Alembert,* 5/*OC,* V:5). It is, in fact, largely attributable to the theater's seductiveness
that it is dangerous. The purpose of a theater, as he describes it, is pleasure
(18/V:17). The arts, theatrical and otherwise, must thus appeal to pleasure and
the passions if they are to be successful. Given this, flattery of mass and "vulgar" opinion is the playwright's muse. Thus, the artist is hardly in a position
to change public opinion. Just the opposite: "An author who would brave the
general taste would soon write for himself alone" (19/V:18).[30] And because
public opinion is often ignorant, the artist finds himself appealing to the audience's passions, rather than its reason. This is contrary to virtue and, as we
will discover with Rousseau, the proper ordering of the soul.

The essay "On Theatrical Imitation" repeats many of these themes. It does
so, however, with an overt attention to its obvious Platonic dimensions. In
fact, Rousseau even writes it in the voice of Plato. This being said, it is
unlikely that the voice of Plato is meant to distance Rousseau from its claims,
because the essay largely repeats the themes Rousseau put in his own voice in
the *Letter to d'Alembert* and the *First Discourse*. He seems almost as much at
home speaking in Plato's voice as Plato does speaking in the voice of Socrates.

The essay begins with a faithful rendition of Plato's attack against the poets
by way of painters. These "dangerous enemies" are nothing less than "corrup-
tors of the People" ("Imitation," 337/*OC,* V:1196). To understand how this is
the case, Rousseau turns to the three types of palaces, modeled on Plato's discussion of the three types of beds in book 10 of the *Republic*. The first is that
which is "abstract, absolute, unique, and independent of the number of examples of this thing which may exist in nature" ("Imitation," 337–38/*OC,*
V:1196). This idea exists prior to its articulation in the world of artifacts. The
second palace is that created by the architect. The architect draws upon the
first palace in creating one with physical dimensions. Although it may be well

---

30. The vision of the artist indifferent to popular taste is depicted even more direly in the *First
Discourse:* "If, by chance, someone among the men of extraordinary talents were steadfast of soul and
refused to yield to the genius of his century and to debase himself by puerile productions, woe betide
him! He will die in poverty and oblivion" (20/*OC,* III:21).

executed, it is nothing more than an "image" and not the idea of a palace itself. The third palace is that of the painter. This painter refers only to the architect's palace in creating his work.[31] Thus, his palace is at two removes from the idea of a palace. The proper term for such creations is "imitation"— the very subject of the essay itself. And, like the message lost in multiple translations, the idea of the palace is similarly perverted in moving from its initial idea to the imitation of the painter.

The painter's spectators, however, do not judge according to how much the painting meets this idea. Rather, their standard is pleasure. To the extent that the spectator is pleased by the work, it is a success, regardless of the lack of any relation to the idea of the subject. Thus, repeating an important theme from the *Letter to d'Alembert,* Rousseau says that the aim of the painter is to flatter the people and the ignorant. He paints at two removes from reality, completely oblivious to it. In fact, the idea of the object is completely irrelevant to the task, because the real purpose is to please. It is in this way that the painter, "deprived of all reality, produce[s] even this appearance only with the help of some vain shadows and of some flimsy simulacra that he causes to be taken for the thing itself" ("Imitation," 339/*OC,* V:1198). The Platonic language here is hardly coincidental. The references to "shadows" and "reality" point to Plato's cave. At any rate, the task Rousseau describes is not so different from the job of the portraitist. It is not so important to render the subject accurately as it is to flatter the person paying for it.

Not only is the audience ignorant on this account but so, too, is the painter. According to Rousseau, "the compass of his art is founded only on his ignorance" ("Imitation," 340/*OC,* V:1199). Painters have no notion of a real palace. They offer mere imitation, from one perspective, without any necessary connection to reality. Despite this ignorance—and perhaps even assisted by it—the people accept the painter's imitations as reality: "the illusion will be such that simpletons and children will be taken in by it, they will believe they are seeing the objects which the Painter himself did not know and workers in arts about which he understands nothing" (340/V:1999– 2000). Employing language that evokes the sinister social contract of the *Second Discourse,* Rousseau refers to the painter's audience as the "dupe of the magic tricks of a charlatan" (340/V:1200).

Of course, the main purpose of the essay is to address the theater, and the lessons drawn from the world of painting are found to apply here. The poets

---

31. I employ masculine pronouns here because Rousseau uses them in his own work. To neutralize language here would give him credit that perhaps he does not deserve in this respect.

claim to know virtues, vices, politics, morality, divine and human laws, and all the sciences. This would seem necessary, because their works touch on all these matters. But just as was the case with the painters, all they truly need command are "vain phantoms, shadows" (340–41/V:1200)—Rousseau's second reference to shadows. And, as in the realm of painting, the true standard is not fidelity to an idea (e.g., to justice, virtue, and the like), but rather the pleasure of the audience: "Thus, the names and the words cause an illusion for those who, sensitive to rhythm and harmony, allow themselves to be charmed by the enchanting art of the Poet and yield to the seduction by the attraction of the pleasure" (343/V:1203).

Pleasure is, in fact, one of the most important components of Rousseau's argument. The poet succeeds only by appealing to the audience's pleasure. It is the author's most crucial tool. Nothing is as important to the audience as its own pleasure. In this respect, we should recollect that society Plato characterizes as dominated by pleasure: it is tyranny (*Republic,* 573d). This is true of both the tyrannical individual and the tyrannical city. The tyrannical individual or soul has only pleasures for motivation. All that feels good is given top priority. Anything involving deprivation of or hindrance to pleasure is to be avoided. Likewise, Plato's tyrannical city is one where the lowest elements rule. Just the opposite of his ideal regime, there is no wisdom or understanding of ideas among those with political power. The highest standard of Plato's tyranny thus becomes the highest standard of the playwright, on Rousseau's reading. The pleasure seeking of the audience necessitates the composition of pleasure-producing works. This association of pleasure with tyranny calls to mind the "happy slaves" of Rousseau's other works. Pleasure is a chain imposed from within—but it is one to be exploited by enterprising tyrants, who in turn pursue their own pleasure.

For this reason Rousseau gives special attention to the virtues and components of the soul. He addresses this in the context of explaining error. The errors we make are always, according to Rousseau, errors in judgment.[32] These errors are themselves attributable to acting on the basis of false or insufficient information and making judgments on the basis of "appearances alone." These false inductions are consequently the source of "a thousand illusions" ("Imitation," 344, 345/OC, V:1205). Rousseau's example is that of a stick placed in water. It appears crooked, even when it is actually straight. The

---

32. This discussion anticipates a very similar account in the *Emile* (206/OC, IV:486). It is worth noting that attributing error to judgment rather than to sensory flaws is Malebranchean. Because Malebranche himself was an avowed Platonist, this is not entirely surprising.

appearance of crookedness, however, misleads those unwilling to employ their reason to discover the truth, and, as a result, the illusion succeeds. The part of the soul described here is that which is "deprived of prudence and reason and incapable of knowing by itself anything of prudence and truth" and is "low by its nature" (345/V:1205).

We escape error and illusion only by employing the reasoning portion of the soul—the "most noble of our faculties" (345/V:1205). Reason guides us to look further and deeper to see what the truth is and prevents us from succumbing to illusion. Of course, the exercise of reason in the assistance of judgment is not easy and immediately available to all. On the contrary, it involves work and refinement. Developing this theme in the *Emile,* Rousseau cautions us in Platonic language, "If the first glimmers of judgment dazzle [*éblouissent*] us and at first make a blur of objects in our sight, let us wait for our weak eyes to open up again and steady themselves, and soon we shall see these same objects again in the light of reason" (*Emile,* 290/*OC,* IV:600). The resemblance here to the cave is strong. Plato refers to the "dazzle and glitter of the light" that must be overcome in order to see "more truly" (*Republic,* 515cd). Nonetheless, this noble faculty of reason fights against the lower ones in keeping the individual from falling into error.

The virtue characterized by the triumph of reason over pleasure seeking is moderation. We are frequently, if not always, engaged in a battle within ourselves between the parts of the soul.[33] Passion pulls in one direction, reason another. The struggle for moderation is witnessed in the theater, particularly in tragedy: "What troubles him [the virtuous man] and agitates him is grief and passion; what stops and contains him is reason and law; and in these opposed movements his will always declares for the latter" ("Imitation," 346/*OC,* V:1206). Of course, as has already been mentioned, moderation (*sophrosune*) is one of the principal virtues for both Plato and Rousseau. For Plato, the moderate individual places reason above the passions. For Rousseau, the

---

33. Rousseau adds the following important footnote: "This word *part* [of the soul] here must not be taken in the precise sense, as if Plato supposed the soul to be really divisible or composed. The division he assumes and which makes him use the word *part* regards only the various kinds of operations by which the soul is modified, and which are otherwise called faculties" ("Imitation," 345/ *OC,* V:1206). If Rousseau is sincere here—and there is no reason to believe he is not—this offers a powerful objection to Arthur Melzer's hypothesis that Rousseau was consciously attacking Plato in his works by attributing multiple divisions to Plato's theory of the soul and then refuting it (1990, 20). This footnote suggests that Rousseau thought that he and Plato were on the same page with regard to the soul. Whether Rousseau is correct in interpreting Plato this way is perhaps a matter best left to others, but what is clear is that Rousseau is in no way targeting Plato or Platonism *as he understood it.* He rather appears to be endorsing the Platonic account of the soul. Further evidence against the unitary soul thesis can be found in Cooper (1999, 118) and Marks (2005, 54–88).

virtuous person uses reason to control the passions. This virtue of moderation is at the core of both accounts.

The failure of moderation results when "the most noble faculty of the soul [reason], thus losing power and empire over itself, grows accustomed to be under the passions" ("Imitation," 348/*OC*, V:1209). This is exactly what the playwright encourages, according to Rousseau. Knowing the priority of plea-sure in his audience, the author must necessarily flatter its passions. Thus, the art and its means of thriving depend on violating the virtue of moderation.

> In addition, the skillful Poet, the Poet who knows the art of succeed-ing, seeking to please the People and vulgar men, is quite wary of offering them the sublime image of a heart that is master of itself, that hears only the voice of wisdom; but he charms the spectators by characters who are always in contradiction, who want and do not want, who make the Theaters ring with cries and moans, who force us to pity the virtuous, even when they do their duty, and to think virtue is a sad thing, since it makes its friends so miserable. It is by this means that, with easier and more diverse imitation, the Poet moves and further flatters the spectators. (346–47/V:1207)

The playwright only reinforces the prejudices existing among the people, scorning reason and moderation in favor of unrestrained passion and pleasure.

What, then, is left? Something akin to the worst societies described by Plato. In its privileging of pleasure, it resembles Plato's account of tyranny. In other respects, it resembles his account of democracy, only one shade away from tyranny: "equality, force, constancy, the love of justice, the empire of reason imperceptibly become detestable qualities, vices that are decried; men are honored for everything that makes them worthy of scorn, and this inver-sion of healthy opinions is the infallible effect of the lessons one goes to receive at the Theater" ("Imitation," 347/*OC*, V:1207; see *Republic*, 560d–561a). In a different sense from Nietzsche's, this is a transvaluation of values. What was once good is bad; what was once bad is good. And, contrary to Kantian opti-mism, this represents a downward spiral in the march of moral history.

It would be difficult to argue that Plato's voice here is not Rousseau's. This is because Rousseau virtually repeats the idea in the *First Discourse*. According to this text, society is progressing to the point where soon "some excesses will be proscribed, some vices held in dishonor, but others will be emblazoned with the name of virtues" (*FD*, 8/*OC*, III:9). And it is significant that in both the *First Discourse* and the essay "On Theatrical Imitation," Rousseau places part of this blame on the arts.

This is scarcely the only overlap between the essay and the rest of Rousseau's oeuvre. The emphasis on the dangers of pleasure is held in common with the *Letter to d'Alembert*. The danger of the passions is found in the *Emile*. The importance of reason is shared with the *Emile* and the *Social Contract*. The existence and importance of ideas is also shared by the *Emile* and the *Social Contract*. The virtue of moderation or self-control is spread throughout many of his works. It is, in fact, difficult to find any significant points of disagreement between the voice of Plato in the essay and Rousseau's voice in his other works. The reason for this is that Plato's own dialogues assert the same principles. Plato warns against the dangers of pleasure (*Philebus*, 65d; *Republic*, 561bc, 571bc); the passions are likewise to be discouraged from gaining ascendancy within the soul (*Laws*, 863a; *Republic*, 550ab, 581); the faculty of reason is one of the most central elements of Platonic philosophy (*Republic*, 582e, 587a); and the virtue of *sophrosune* is one of his most esteemed values (*Laws*, books 1 and 2; *Republic*, 430e; *Phaedrus*, 237de; *Charmides*, 157ab). As if this were not enough, Rousseau marks several passages of his personal copy of Plato's dialogues with respect to these very same principles. He marks the *Laws* where the Athenian Stranger warns of the danger of the passions to reason (*Laws*, 835d–837a; Rousseau, notes on Plato, V:429–31). He likewise marks the *Phaedrus* when Socrates speaks of the importance of *sophrosune* (*Phaedrus*, 68e; notes on Plato, I:189). All evidence suggests a great interest in and correlation to Platonic principles.

Rousseau concludes the essay with a caution to would-be playwrights and a final allusion to Plato's cave: "It is, I admit, a sweet thing to yield to the charms of an enchanting talent, to acquire by means of it goods, honors, power, glory. But power, glory, riches, and pleasures are all eclipsed and disappear like a shadow before justice and virtue" ("Imitation," 350/*OC*, V:1211). Placing this in the context of the cave is not difficult to do. In fact, the entire essay fits extremely well into the narrative of the allegory. Again, Rousseau makes multiple references to "appearances," "shadows," "reality," and "ideas." And more explicitly here than anywhere else, Rousseau ties reality to the world of ideas and appearances and shadows to the false world of the cave. The playwrights are indeed the shadow-casters in this account. They entertain and deceive the cave dwellers with comedies and tragedies, shadows on the walls. The "virtues" they celebrate are passions and pleasures, while the real virtues of reason and moderation remain hidden outside the cave.

Recalling the *Social Contract*, of course, the picture is more complex. As

Rousseau says there, "One believes himself the others' master, and yet is more a slave than they" (*SC,* 41/*OC,* III:351). This is certainly true of the playwright. Whereas he is indeed manipulating the shadows on the wall, he is at the same time a puppet of the multitude of cave dwellers. Their demand for passion-laden dramas and comedies making light of serious moral flaws is the poet's muse. If he fails to follow this master, he is no longer able to practice his craft for a living. This cave is not only a place where the blind are leading the blind, but is also one from which there is no obvious escape. One wonders if Rousseau's account offers any hope of escape when circumstances have gotten this bad. His remark that the theater is permissible for the corrupt city of Paris (though not for the republic of Geneva) suggests a level of resignation that might support this speculation. Again, we might turn to the *Social Contract* for an answer. Political solutions to problems of societies like those in Paris may ultimately be futile: "peoples, like men, are docile only in their youth, with age they grow incorrigible; once customs are established and prejudices rooted, it is a dangerous and futile undertaking to try to reform them; the people cannot tolerate having their evils touched even if only to destroy them, like those stupid and cowardly patients who tremble at the sight of a doctor" (72/III:385). This cynical view, however, is immediately tempered by optimistic speculation. Even if this task is difficult, memories of the past can be erased in a state by moments of great turmoil and violence, allowing a state to recover "the vigor of youth as it escapes death's embrace." Such opportunities, however, are rare and not to be repeated within one state.

2.6. THE *DIALOGUES* AND *REVERIES*

The last stop of this Platonic tour of Rousseau's corpus ends with his final two autobiographical works, the *Dialogues* and *Reveries*. In at least one respect, this may seem the least appropriate place to punctuate an argument for Rousseau's Platonism. This is because the portrait emerging thus far is of a vigorous champion of reason and self-mastery, whereas the final works portray his own character as positively lethargic and incapable of either of these Platonic traits. This is not a mere impression. It is his own explicit description. In the *Dialogues,* the character of "Rousseau" portrays Jean-Jacques as having a "laziness about thinking" (115/*OC,* I:809); he is "indolent, lazy, without vigor" (122/ I:817). In the *Reveries,* he paints himself as practically incapable of virtue, insofar as he cannot muster the necessary effort to resist his inclinations, even when commanded to do so by duty (51/*OC,* I:1053). The late self-portrait of Rousseau, in many respects, is of someone far too languorous to carry out the necessary reflection to derive the principles of morals and politics, much less act on them.

That Rousseau would characterize himself as lazy should be no surprise. This is because he aspired to be natural in certain respects, and his account of *l'homme sauvage* in the *Second Discourse* is that of the profoundly lazy individual—someone who does no more than eat, drink, and sleep for the entirety of nearly every day. He repeats this description in the *Dialogues:* "All men are naturally lazy, even their interest doesn't animate them, and the most pressing needs make them act only in spurts" (144/*OC,* I:846). Rousseau certainly means to be describing himself, but this discussion takes on complex dimensions as it evolves, because he also admits to being "active, ardent, laborious, and indefatigable" on occasion (122/I:817).

There are at least three distinct levels of philosophic thought for Rousseau, and the last two autobiographical works are our best guides. I will call these *active mediation, lazy mediation,* and *the application of mediations.* Whether the meditations of Rousseau are either active or lazy, they have the same goal: to escape from the "[c]ompetitions, preferences, jealousies, rivalries, offenses, revenges, discontents of all sorts, ambition, desires, projects, means, obstacles" that tend to overwhelm most social individuals. The individual who succeeds in casting these off breaks

> out of the narrow prison of personal interest and petty earthly passions, rises on the wings of imagination above the vapors of our atmosphere, one who, without exhausting his strength and his faculties fighting against chance and destiny, knows how to soar to the ethereal regions, hover and sustain himself there by sublime contemplations, can brave from there the blows of fate and the senseless judgments of men. He is beyond their reach; he does not need their suffrage to be wise or their favor to be happy. (*Dialogues,* 120/*OC,* I:815)

Whether he is active or lazy, his purpose in thought is to remove himself from all of the distractions of social life and transcend them from the metaphorical heights.

One has the option of achieving this state either actively or lazily. Rousseau, however, explains that he has particular difficulty in active meditation.

> An active heart and a lazy nature must inspire the taste for reverie. The taste emerges and becomes a very lively passion if it is helped in

the slightest by the imagination. This is what very often happens to the Orientals. This is what happened to J.J., who resembles them in many respects. Being too subjected to his senses to throw off their yoke as his imagination plays its games, he would not easily rise to purely abstract meditations, and he would not maintain himself there for very long. (*Dialogues,* 120/*OC,* 1:816)

Although the senses might be distracting in some respects, Rousseau also finds an advantage in his weakness. By surrendering to his senses, he can enter a kind of meditative state. This is *lazy meditation* and is best exemplified in his botanizing. In giving himself over to the pure pleasures of nature, he is able to release himself from the harmful effects of opinion, *amour-propre,* and all the ills of the social world. This is not a complete release from the senses, as Socrates desires in the *Phaedo,* but it is a kind of release nevertheless. It even frees him from many of the burdens that Plato cites as getting in the way of epistemic access to the truth. As just mentioned, Rousseau is released from all social concerns while botanizing. He is also freed from the damaging passions that accompany social life. Indeed, in reflecting on his botanical wanderings through St. Peter's Island, he writes: "Delivered from all the earthly passions the tumult of social life engenders, my soul would frequently soar above this atmosphere and commune in advance with the celestial intelligences whose number it hopes to augment in a short while" (*Reveries,* 48/*OC,* 1:1048–49). This is certainly the "lazy" Rousseau, as he describes himself, who gives in to his senses. At the same time, however, he resembles the character of Socrates in the *Phaedo,* who is abandoning thoughts of sexual pleasure, fashion, and so forth to commune with the ideas.

To be sure, Plato explicitly encourages his philosopher to leave behind the senses altogether. In this kind of reverie, Rousseau retains the senses, but in a paradoxical manner: an obsession with the sensual world is a means of escape from that very world. This is an *epistemic* departure from Plato. The goal here is the same—to contemplate the eternal truths—but the mode of access is different. For Plato, the senses are to be eliminated as much as possible.[34] For Rousseau, the distractions of the sensual world are also to be eliminated, but one can do so with meditative attention to nature. Consider his description of the consequences of such reveries: "Intoxicated by his contemplation of nature's charms, his imagination [is] filled with the types of virtue, beauty,

---

34. The notable exception here is the appeal to *eros* in the *Symposium* as a means of ascent up the "ladder of love."

and perfection of all sorts" (*Dialogues*, 125/*OC*, I:821).[35] Thus, Rousseau's "laziness" is his unique *epistemic* approach for accessing the higher ideas.

Yet even nature-inspired reveries have their limits for Rousseau. He makes this clear in the *Reveries*: "[There are] eternal truths admitted at all times by all wise men, recognized by all nations, and engraved on the human heart in indelible characters. While meditating about these matters, I knew that human understanding, circumscribed by the senses, could not embrace them in their full extent" (*Reveries*, 25/*OC*, I:1021–22). Thus, although *lazy meditation* is an effective mode of philosophizing, Rousseau suspects that his best access to the "eternal truths" might be done in the complete absence of the senses. This would be *active meditation*. The problem is that Rousseau reports his soul to be too weak to endure this kind of abstraction: he "would not easily rise to purely abstract meditations, and he would not maintain himself there for very long."

There is one great exception in Rousseau's experience. This is his infamous collision with the Great Dane, as recorded in the second walk of the *Reveries*.

> I was on the road . . . when some people walking ahead of me suddenly swerved aside and I saw a huge Great Dane rushing down upon me. Racing before a carriage, the dog had no time to check its pace or turn aside when it noticed me. I judged that the only means I had to avoid being knocked to the ground was to make a great leap, so well-timed that the dog would pass under me while I was still in the air. This idea, quicker than a flash and which I had the time neither to think through nor carry out, was my last before the accident. I did not feel the blow, nor the fall, nor anything of what followed until the moment I came to. (*Reveries*, 11/*OC*, I:1004–5)

The accident was severe enough to have knocked Rousseau unconscious until nightfall. According to witnesses, the dog had run directly into him, knocking him in the air, his head landing first on the hard pavement. From his own account, he bled profusely after the collision. Far more significant than his injuries, however, was his experience in slowly regaining consciousness:

> Night was coming on. I perceived the sky, some stars, and a little greenery. This first sensation was a delicious moment. I still had no

---

35. It is worth observing that the idea of perfection was commonly viewed as a Platonic notion in the eighteenth century. Kant remarks, "The *maximum of perfection* is nowadays called the ideal, while for Plato it was called the idea (as in the case of his Idea of the state)" ([1770] 1992, 388/*KGS*, 2:396).

feeling of myself except being "over there." I was born into life at that instant, and it seemed to me that I filled all the objects I perceived with my frail existence. Entirely absorbed in the present moment, I remembered nothing; I had no distinct notion of my person nor the least idea of what had just happened to me; I knew neither who I was nor where I was; I felt neither injury, fear, nor worry. I watched my blood flow as I would have watched a brook flow, without even suspecting that this blood belonged to me in any way. I felt a rapturous calm in my whole being; and each time I remember it, I find nothing comparable to it in all the activity of known pleasures. (11–12/I:1005)

The collision with the Great Dane made possible something Rousseau found impossible on his own—complete abstraction from his senses. In many respects, it resembles the condition that Socrates anticipates in his death. He no longer cares about his squabbles with others. He is not agitated by his passions. He is released from the concerns of his worldly obligations. His senses are, in part, disabled. He feels no physical sensations. He does not think of himself as himself. He is rather detached and part of something presumably larger. It is in such a condition that Plato says we are prepared to acquire "pure knowledge" (*Phaedo,* 66e). This is as close as Rousseau would come to the Platonic goal of being completely released from the senses in order to contemplate.

There is yet a third mode of philosophic activity in Rousseau's account of the workings of his mind: the application of meditations. Recall that Rousseau described himself as part lazy and part active. It has been established now that his meditation was overwhelmingly "lazy." To understand the sense in which he considered himself "active," it is important to consult his remarks in the *Dialogues,* where he contrasts natural and social individuals. Whereas natural individuals are lazy, social ones are those for whom, "as amour-propre is progressively aroused, it excites them, pushes them, keeps them going constantly breathless because it is the only passion that speaks to them" (*Dialogues,* 144/ *OC,* I:846). Rousseau's characterization of himself lies at the crossroads of both the natural and social man in these respects. He aspires to be natural, yet he cannot help but be moved on occasion by his *amour-propre.* Thus, although he is always ready to describe himself as "lazy," he also admits that he is "active, ardent, laborious, and indefatigable" (122/I:817). This is not necessarily a bad thing, of course, even by his own account. As Laurence Cooper has correctly argued, whereas *amour-propre* has a tendency to lead to socially destructive behavior, it can also be shaped into a force for good. Indeed, Cooper has gone so far as to say that "the passion for justice"—one of the great forces of Rousseau's conscience, a theme repeated over and again in his works—"is born . . . of *amour-propre*" (Cooper 1999, 128).[36]

Thus, the *application* phase of philosophy for Rousseau is to bring the objects of his meditation down to the world of the senses. His reveries could not be sustained forever. The material world always pulls us back. The greatest example of this is his own account of the origin of his *First Discourse*. Prior to his literary career, Rousseau describes his youth as being consumed by his "continual intoxication" of contemplation. It was also in this condition of youthful reverie that he arrived at the conclusion that human beings were made to be "good, wise, and happy" (*Dialogues*, 130/*OC*, I:828), but his abstract thoughts were shaken considerably when the Academy of Dijon announced its essay contest question: "Whether the restoration of the Sciences and Arts have contributed to the purification of morals." This question brought him back down from his abstract contemplation and forced him to confront the question of why the *ideal* human beings of his reveries were not the same as those who surrounded him in Paris. As Rousseau describes it, "Enflamed by the contemplation of these great objects, they were always present in [my] thought, and comparing them to the real state of things, [I] saw them each day in relationships that were totally new." This contrast between the ideas of his reveries and reality ignited his *amour-propre* with the "ridiculous hope of making reason and truth triumph at last over prejudices and lies, and of making men wise by showing them their true interest" (*Dialogues*, 131/ *OC*, I:829). He would thus combine his meditations with application to produce his first great work, and it would set the pattern for many of his subsequent works—abstract reflection punctuated by great passion. By removing himself from his contemporaries, his passions, and his senses, he could locate the first principles engraved in his heart. Descending from these lofty heights, his *amour-propre* would inspire him to employ these ideas with the hope of benefiting humankind.

This is Rousseau's method, but in this, too, resides a Platonic parallel. Consider the opening words of Plato's *Republic:* "I went down" (*Republic,* 327a). Plato's characterizations of philosophizing are typically upward. The simile of the divided line takes the philosopher up. Likewise with the similes

---

36. Matthew W. Maguire, in his discussion of Rousseau's *Fiction, ou Morceau allégorique sur la Révélation,* includes an instructive case study of how pride "makes him [the philosopher] want to help others rather than turn away" (2006, 78).

of the sun and the allegory of the cave. This is just as Rousseau's contemplation takes him up to heights where he "soar[s] to the ethereal regions" (*Dialogues*, 120/*OC*, I:815). To do Platonic *political* philosophy, however, one must bring these high ideas down and give them practical application. There is also in Plato the same positive interpretation of *amour-propre*, which he calls "spirit": "what happens when a man believes himself to be wronged? Does not his spirit in that case seethe and grow fierce . . . and make itself the ally of what he judges just?" (*Republic*, 440cd). In this respect, Plato says that spirit becomes reason's ally, aiding it in its application in the material world. Thus, for Plato, as well as Rousseau, there is a common tie between abstract contemplation and a spirited application of its reflections in the world down below. Indeed, this constitutes the essence of political Platonism.

3. Differences and Conclusion

Although the parallels between Plato and Rousseau should now appear obvious, one should be careful not to overstate them. There are significant differences. As will become evident, these divergences stem largely from one extremely important empirical dimension of epistemic Platonism: the percentage of the population that has the capacity to know the ideas. Plato is unambiguous on this matter. Philosophic enlightenment is available only to the exceptionally rare individual, who merits the distinguished title of "philosopher" (*Republic*, 491ab). Among the traits required to achieve this status are age, intelligence (412c), an eagerness to pursue the good (412e), a love of the truth (475e), abandonment of the pleasures of the flesh (485d), disinterest in money (485e), courage (486a), quick learning, remarkable memory, and even some musical ability (486cd). In sum, Plato asks, "Is there any fault, then, that you can find with a pursuit which a man could not properly practice unless he were by nature of good memory, quick apprehension, magnificent, gracious, friendly, and akin to the truth, justice, bravery, and sobriety?" (487a). If this were not enough, on top of all the innate talents required of aspiring philosophers, they must also undergo an education that extends from precious youth to the ripe age of fifty. In contrast with this portrait, the multitude will always be contending with shadows of one type or another, even after the philosopher-rulers come to their assistance. It becomes the rulers' task to bring the shadows in line with justice and the good. For the vast majority, however, it is unlikely that they will ever know the eternal ideas and the benefits that can be derived from an acquaintance with them. They can only hope that others might know what is best for them, and this knowledge will be employed to improve their lives.

Rousseau, on the other hand, suggests at least on occasion a far more extensive enlightenment. Whereas Plato's ideas are accessible only to philosophers, Rousseau's eternal ideas are apparently available to any- and everyone. Eternal ideas are "engraved in the human heart" ("State of War," 166/*OC*, III:602). Rousseau never suggests that one must be a philosopher to have access to the eternal ideas.[37] In fact, those who carried the title of "philosopher" in eighteenth-century Europe were more likely to go astray than those who were not, because Rousseau most often associated the word with the worst elements of the philosophes.[38] But even then, "the subtle sophistries of metaphysicians . . . cannot outweigh the eternal truths which have been accepted at all times and by all wise men, recognized by all nations, and indelibly engraved on the human heart" (*Reveries,* 59/*OC,* I:1021).

37. This is disputed by Melzer, who argues that for Rousseau, "*Genuine philosophy* will always remain the preserve of the few" (1990, 137, emphasis added). In support of this claim, he cites the "Preface to Narcissus": "I acknowledge that there are a few sublime geniuses capable of piercing the veils in which the truth wraps itself, a few privileged souls able to resist the folly of vanity, base jealousy, and other passions aroused by a taste for letters" ([1752–53] 1997, 102/*OC,* II:970). If Rousseau were referring in this passage to "genuine philosophy," this would indeed be troubling both for Rousseau and for my interpretation of Rousseau. It would be a problem for Rousseau insofar as it would contradict his many statements to the contrary. It would be a problem for my interpretation insofar as it would offer strong evidence against it. This passage, however, calls for more context. One must bear in mind that the theme of the preface is thematically linked to the *First Discourse*—the dangers of the arts and sciences. Rousseau is concerned about the natural sciences as practiced by amateurs and popularizers. He does, however, carefully carve out room for practitioners of great genius, such as Descartes and Newton: "Let learned men of the first rank find honorable asylum" (*FD,* 27/*OC,* III:30). But, whereas Newton and Descartes soar above the masses with regard to their scientific skills and insight, this is not what Rousseau means by *genuine philosophy*. At the conclusion of the *First Discourse,* he makes this perfectly clear: "O virtue! Sublime science of simple souls, are so many efforts and so much equipment really required to know you? Are not your principles engraved in all hearts, and is it not enough in order to learn your Laws to return into oneself and to listen to the voice of one's conscience in the silence of the passions? *That is genuine Philosophy,* let us know how to rest content with it" (28/*OC,* III:30, emphasis added). Genuine philosophy thus is not scientific knowledge—it is the simple knowledge of the basic principles of virtue, and it is available to all. This distinction between genuine philosophy and scientific works of genius explains the passage from the "Preface to Narcissus," which was written in the midst of the continuing controversy surrounding the *First Discourse* and represents in large part its defense. In the paragraph previous to the one cited by Melzer, Rousseau notes that "science is not suited to man in general" ([1752–53] 1997, 102/*OC,* II:970). He elaborates in some detail on how the practice of natural science is taxing for the average individual. The paragraph that Melzer cites continues these very same themes. It is not Rousseau's claim here that "genuine philosophy" lies outside the grasp of the average individual. He is merely making a claim about the natural sciences—that *they* are best left to the gifted. Indeed, to the extent that average individuals try their hand at natural science, they would lose touch with those principles that are already "engraved" in their hearts—that is, the genuine philosophy already available to them.

38. "How sweet it would be . . . if genuine Philosophy were inseparable from the title of Philosopher!" (*FD,* 7/*OC,* III:7).

The best case in point in this regard is none other than Emile. There is nothing exceptional in the nature of this child, according to Rousseau. He is of average intelligence and has no pretensions of being a professional philosopher. In fact, his vocation is to be carpentry, yet Rousseau makes claims about his genuine philosophic abilities that Plato might have found stunning. Consider that young Emile is found "all alone philosophizing in the corner" (*Emile*, 190/*OC*, IV:463; he is known to have "the taste for reflection and meditation" (202/IV:480). Later Rousseau observes Emile is a burgeoning "contemplative, a philosopher, a veritable theologian" (315/IV:637). These passages are not superficial, merely suggesting that Emile has a contemplative disposition. They indicate that he—a child of very ordinary capacities—is capable of achieving something like genuine philosophic knowledge. The following passage captures this most succinctly: "The true principles of the just, the true models of the beautiful, all the moral relations of beings, all the ideas of order are imprinted on his [Emile's] understanding. He sees the place of each thing and the cause which removes it from its place; he sees what can do good and what stands in its way. Without having experienced the human passions, he knows their illusions and their effects" (253/IV:548).[39] This is striking for both its similarities to and departures from Platonic doctrines. It relies significantly on metaphysical Platonism, insofar as Rousseau conceives justice and beauty to be eternal ideas (259/IV:556, 446/IV:820). It also shares a component of epistemic Platonism, insofar as Rousseau shares with Plato the fear that the passions form significant obstacles to understanding these ideas, but it departs from Plato in that the individual possessing this knowledge is an adolescent of decidedly average abilities. The lofty heights of philosophic wisdom—defined by knowledge of the ideas—is far more widely accessible in Rousseau's account than in Plato's.[40]

39. This and the previous citations in this paragraph have been employed for similar purposes in Cooper (2002, 117, 121).

40. There is some ambiguity on this point in Rousseau, however. Although he does point to the universal accessibility of these ideas as they reside in the conscience, he also expresses skepticism that all will make use of this reservoir of knowledge. Perhaps nowhere is this more evident than in his discussion of the lawgiver, who must make special appeals to the "vulgar," because they are not likely to have acquired the wisdom necessary to understand what is in their best interests (*SC*, 70/*OC*, III:383). It is not clear, however, that Rousseau's meaning of "vulgar" in this context is equivalent to Plato's category of those unable to access the ideas. Plato's category is defined primarily by those lacking in intelligence. A lack of innate intelligence is less concerning to Rousseau. Emile, after all, is hardly a philosopher or anything like it. Indeed, Rousseau himself claimed not to be a philosopher (*Emile*, 110/*OC*, IV:348). The best teacher of wisdom for Rousseau is simply the conscience: "conscience is the most enlightened of philosophers" (*Emile*, 408/*OC*, IV:767). This is not to say that everyone exercises and attains this kind of wisdom. Far from it. Emile must be educated with the greatest care only so that he can know what is already in this conscience. There are innumerable

From this first *epistemic* difference between Plato and Rousseau follow three significant divergences at the *institutional* level: the roles of liberty, equality, and sovereignty in their respective theories. In regard to liberty and equality, these are not trivial differences, because they ought to be "the end of every system of legislation," as Rousseau argues (*SC, 78/OC,* III:391). For Plato, political freedom is a danger to be guarded against, rather than a possession to be prized and promoted. His most famous discussion of political freedom is in his account of democracy in book 8 of the *Republic.* For him, it is the preeminent value in democracies, and in this context it is nothing other than license. Democratic citizens employ this liberty to pursue all pleasures equally—be they appetites for food, for sex, for power, for money, for glory. It is thus no surprise that on Plato's account such a society is among the worst possible. Liberty is more or less license.

Political liberty, however, is an important virtue in Rousseau. The acquisition of "civil freedom" is one of the great gains of his social contract. Indeed, Matthew Simpson has persuasively argued that Rousseau has created a "fairly robust kind of civil liberty" (2006b, 52).[41] Participants in his social contract exchange their natural liberty (the precarious Hobbesian right to acquire whatever they desire) for their mutual security. Whatever is not subsequently regulated by the general will is returned to them with the guarantee by the government that this liberty will be protected. In Rousseau's own words, "they have only made an advantageous exchange of an uncertain and precarious way of being in favor of a more secure and better one, of natural independence in favor of freedom, of the power to harm others in favor of their own security" (*SC, 63/OC,* III:375). Such considerations are far from Plato's mind.

George Klosko has argued that Plato's lack of concern for individual freedoms is a consequence of his metaphysics (1986a, 152). This argument has a certain appeal. Because Plato tended to emphasize the immaterial realm over the material, material interests, such as individual liberties, would interest him little. There are, however, two problems with this explanation. First, Plato on occasion did express great concern with material political matters. This is most evident in the *Laws.* Second, if a belief in immaterial ideas were sufficient to explain disinterest in individual liberties, Rousseau would likewise follow suit, and this is obviously not the case.

---

obstacles in the way against which the tutor must guard. Nevertheless, Rousseau does not seem to exclude anyone from this kind of knowledge by virtue of his nature, as Plato does. Indeed, as Laurence Cooper notes, "a kind of philosophic life may be possible, even if only in principle, for an ordinary man" (2002, 109). The eternal principles appear at least theoretically available to all, and this remains a significant difference between Rousseau and Plato.

41. This view is shared by Daniel Cullen (1993).

Klosko suggests another reason that might be more promising: that Plato's view of human nature is decidedly dim (1986a, 152). If human beings are corrupt by nature, it would seem to follow that they cannot be trusted with a great deal of individual liberty. The more liberty they are granted, the more opportunities they have to abuse that liberty. On the other hand, Rousseau is far more sanguine about human nature.[42] There has been much written on the subject of Rousseau's understanding of human nature, and this subject is not the focus of this book, but I do want to draw attention to a slightly unorthodox element of my interpretation. My argument for the difference between Plato and Rousseau on this account assumes that Rousseau's socialized individual has a relatively good nature, at least by the modest standards of a comparison with Plato's social individual. One must keep in mind that Rousseau's state is in large part a normative conception. The social individual—the one entitled to a healthy serving of civil liberties—is part of this normative conception. In contrast with the hapless slave in part 2 of the *Second Discourse,* the citizen of the *Social Contract* is a relatively wise and good individual. Upon entering society, Rousseau reminds the reader that "a most remarkable change [takes place] in man." Part of this change is that his citizens gain *epistemic* access to the idea of justice. Indeed, if such a thing were possible, it would almost allow the manufacturing of an instant philosopher: "his ideas [are] enlarged, his sentiments ennobled, his entire soul is elevated" (*SC,* 53/*OC,* III:364). Thus, in this normative conception of citizenship, it is perfectly plausible to grant citizens more space in which to act. Of course, one should not get carried away and assume that Rousseau would tolerate the license that disquiets Plato. Civil liberty is good, to be sure, but it is not without limits. Indeed, it is the duty of the sovereign to circumscribe civil liberty carefully by legislating according to the general will.

As with political liberty, Rousseau places a greater value on equality than Plato does. There is an obvious way in which the Plato of the *Republic* is hostile to contemporary notions of equality. People are distinguished according to their epistemic talents. Some are capable of being philosophers, and others are not. This determines virtually everything that follows, as a matter of distributive justice. The philosophers get an extensive training in a multitude of subjects. The nonphilosophers get considerably less education. The

---

42. This is the fundamental thesis of Melzer's *Natural Goodness of Man.* It requires a couple of caveats, however. First, one must admit that it is no longer "natural" man entering the social contract, but someone who has felt some of the degenerative effects of socialization. Second, Jonathan Marks has offered a significant challenge to Melzer's thesis in this respect, pointing out the ways in which human nature is less benign than as is described in Melzer's book (Marks 2005, 33–38).

philosophers go on to become rulers. The nonphilosophers go on to fill all of the subsidiary roles. Plato makes further distinctions among the nonphilosophers. Those who are spirited become auxiliaries; those who lack spirit become merchants and farmers. Platonic society is largely defined by its divisions, and these divisions are largely determined by epistemic differences among citizens.

Rousseau, on the other hand, places a premium on equality. The origins of inequality are indeed the defining problem of one of his most important essays. In the *Second Discourse,* Rousseau, like Plato, acknowledges that natural inequalities exist among human beings: "it is established by Nature, and . . . consists in the differences in age, health, strengths of Body, and qualities of Mind, or of Soul" (131/*OC,* III:131). Unlike Plato, however, Rousseau is uncomfortable with where these natural inequalities lead in political society. Whereas for Plato these inequalities lead to just divisions of vocation and power, in Rousseau they combine with artifice to promote unjust divisions of wealth and power. What is the difference? It lies primarily in how this power is used. In Plato's *Republic,* the power is used to promote the good of the entire community. In Rousseau's narrative, the power is employed to advance only the interests of the powerful.[43]

Rousseau's normative accounts of the state in the *Social Contract, Political Economy, Considerations on the Government of Poland,* and *Constitutional Project for Corsica* are quite concerned with promoting equality of many types. First among these is an equality of rights. Regardless of station, all citizens receive the same legal rights. For Rousseau, the social contract "establishes among the Citizens an equality such that all commit themselves under the same conditions and must all enjoy the same rights" (*SC, 63/OC,* III:374). No one is entitled to special legal treatment on the basis of having been born with different attributes or parents. Although Rousseau admires the *Republic* as "the most beautiful educational treatise ever written" (*Emile,* 40/*OC,* IV:250), he never seriously proposes a tracked educational system to parallel Plato's. The education of Emile is not proposed as something for the elite— intellectual, financial, or otherwise. In fact, he elsewhere specifically notes, "I do not at all like the distinctions between schools and academies which result in the rich nobility being educated differently and separately from the poor nobility. Because all are equal by the constitution of the state, all ought to be educated together and in the same fashion" (*Poland,* 190/*OC,* III:967). Sig-

43. There is an irony here, in that Plato and Rousseau appear to reverse their understandings of human nature. This is resolved easily, however, with the realization that Plato's *Republic* is a normative account of the state and Rousseau's is a quasi-descriptive account.

nificantly, Rousseau notes the equality of citizens by virtue of the "constitution of the state," but it is worth observing that this equality might further be tied to the *epistemic* access to the ideas that all modestly mature individuals possess. If almost everyone has access to philosophic knowledge, it would indeed be logical to open up equal opportunities to all to assist in this process.[44]

Rousseau is also careful to promote equality of wealth, because radical inequality of wealth tends toward injustice and instability. In the *Social Contract*, he asks, "Do you . . . want to give the state stability? Bring the extremes as close together as possible; tolerate neither very rich people nor beggars. These two states, which are naturally inseparable, are equally fatal to the common good" (78/*OC*, III:392). Rousseau was deeply concerned to prevent inequality of fortunes, because it would lead to factions and hence obfuscate public wisdom concerning the general will. He consequently advocated bringing the classes together as much as possible by virtue of progressive and luxury taxes. Although it may seem obvious to some readers why Rousseau might have desired to promote social order, it is important to make this perfectly clear. The idea of justice is *about* order. As the Savoyard Vicar remarks, "the love of order which preserves order is called *justice*" (*Emile*, 282/*OC*, IV:589). Thus, the social order stemming from keeping the classes together is specifically a matter of justice—one of the great ideas of metaphysical Platonism.

There is a further dimension of economic equality that worries Rousseau. Great wealth becomes a virtually insurmountable barrier to epistemic access to the ideas. The wealthier one is, the easier it is to be seduced by shadows. Luxuries only weigh down potential philosophers, persuading them that all good is purely sensual or earthly. Rousseau sees this already being a sadly foregone conclusion among his contemporaries: "Let our politicians . . . learn once and for all that with money one has everything except morals and Citizens" (*FD*, 19/*OC*, III:20). Indeed, this is scarcely an isolated comment. Rousseau repeatedly suggests that money and luxury are great threats to knowledge of the moral and political ideas (e.g., *Poland*, 188/*OC*, III:964, 227/III:1006; *Political Economy*, 27/*OC*, III:267; *Emile*, 190/*OC*, IV:463, 228/IV:513). At the end of the *First Discourse*, after explaining the epistemically corrupting effects of money and luxury, he makes a specific appeal back to his fundamental point concerning epistemic access to the ideas: "O virtue! Sublime science of simple souls, are so many efforts and so much equipment really required to

44. Plato makes a similar argument from epistemic equality that suggests that opportunities should be available to women.

know you? Are not your principles engraved in all hearts, and is it not enough in order to learn your Laws to return into oneself and to listen to the voice of one's conscience in the silence of the passions? That is genuine Philosophy, let us know how to rest content with it" (28/*OC*, III:30). Of course, as already noted in this chapter, luxury is far from being the only obstacle to this kind of knowledge. Fame, the passions, and susceptibility to flattery are among many other causes, but wealth and its attendant luxury indeed pose serious threats to the state at its most foundational epistemic level.

On this dimension of equality, of course, Rousseau is very much in step with Plato.[45] Plato, too, is concerned with the politically destabilizing effects of radical inequality of wealth as well as the epistemic effects of wealth and luxury on those who might otherwise have a chance to know the ideas. Plato was well aware of history and the fact that both Athens and Sparta had to reestablish their laws as a consequence of their profound inequalities. As Lycurgus would later report, Sparta was overwhelmed by "extreme inequality" that had brought the state to a troubling impasse (Plutarch 2001, 29). Athens suffered from the same problem to such a disturbing degree that people sold themselves and their children into slavery. To restore order, both Lycurgus and Solon would make wealth equality a top priority in refounding their respective states. Plato clearly learned from this experience, as he called wealth stratification to be "the most fatal of disorders" (*Laws,* 744d). The Athenian Stranger from the *Laws* proposes radical measures to prevent Magnesia from ever descending to the depths of Sparta and Athens before their lawgivers. First, citizens are given equal plots of land at the founding of the state. Second, these plots cannot be bought or sold, hence preventing the accumulation of property in any one set of hands. Third, for similar reasons, there can be no private possession of gold or silver. Fourth, money cannot be lent with interest. Fifth, no citizen can accumulate wealth of any kind beyond four times the original allotment. Any surplus income is automatically returned to the state for redistribution (741–44).

Moreover, Plato (like Rousseau) sees wealth and luxury as a threat to epistemic access to the ideas. This is precisely why philosopher-rulers must be prohibited from owning property. To the extent that they concern themselves with personal property and wealth, they cannot be expected to have consistent access to the ideas necessary for sound rule. In a similar respect, the Athenian Stranger from the *Laws* warns that the "furious thirst for gold and silver"

---

45. This is addressed in Sharon Vaughan's forthcoming *Poverty, Justice, and Western Political Thought.*

threatens to reduce an otherwise admirable citizen to "some brute beast, with a perfect glut of eating, drinking, and sexual sport" (*Laws,* 831de). Indeed, for the Stranger, it is generally impossible for a citizen to be wealthy and good at the same time: "that one who is exceptionally good should be exceptionally wealthy too is a mere impossibility" (743a).

A third striking *institutional* difference between Rousseau and Plato also stems, in part, from the question of epistemic access: popular sovereignty. Rousseau firmly holds to the principle of popular sovereignty. He never offers a systematic account of why sovereignty resides with the people. There are a few potential reasons, however, that might lend themselves to this conclusion. First, the individuals chronologically precede the state. Therefore, one might conclude that by creating the state, the people themselves must retain political authority. The problem with this explanation for popular sovereignty is that the same is true of Hobbes's theory, and yet for him the people surrender their sovereignty to the Leviathan. Thus, it is not logically necessary to conclude from the temporal precedence of individuals to the state that the people must be sovereign. Second, it is possible that Rousseau assumes that people have a natural right to order their lives in any way they might see fit. People have a natural liberty in the state of nature to act as they please, so perhaps this means that they necessarily become sovereign. The problem with this explanation is that the people *do not* have the right to do whatever they like as a sovereign body. As discussed in Chapter 4, there are prescribed limits on what the people may do, even while acting in their legislative capacity. For Rousseau, the people must do "nothing contrary to the natural Laws," because these laws ultimately give the necessary moral force to the social contract (*Letters,* 231/ *OC,* III:807).

A third explanation for Rousseau's commitment to popular sovereignty— and probably the most persuasive—is explained by his conviction that epistemic access to ideas is far broader than on Plato's account. For Rousseau, virtually everyone possesses the ability to know the simple moral truths required of a sovereign. Recall again that even the modestly intelligent Emile has access to knowledge of the ideas. If it is the case that even a child could know the highest moral and political principles, popular sovereignty seems far more plausible than Plato ever thought.

One might argue that this explanation is suspect because Emile is the exception rather than the rule by virtue of his own unique education. That is, although Emile might come to know justice and beauty, it is only because he has had the benefit of a tutor to prepare him to think in this fashion. The people populating Rousseau's *Social Contract,* meanwhile, have not had this benefit. Nevertheless, there are reasons to think that he accounts for this to some degree. First, by no means does he suggest that the people of *any* state can exercise sovereignty in the fashion he imagines. In fact, he notes that "peoples, like men, are docile only in their youth, with age they grow incorrigible" (*SC*, 72/*OC*, III:385). After societies settle in with corrupt laws, the people themselves will be irredeemable. That is, they will have lost touch with the simple principles that come so naturally to Emile. Docile peoples are hence rare for Rousseau, which means that legitimate states are also rare. This may be problematic for Rousseau as a practical philosopher, but it certainly does not make him any more utopian than Plato. Second, even the behavior of a potentially sovereign people is carefully circumscribed. The people cannot do whatever they wish. Their laws must be general. They must be directed to the common good. They must aim toward justice; if they fail to do so, the people are no longer sovereign. They are merely a vast chorus of private wills. Indeed, for Rousseau it is not so much the people who are sovereign, but rather the general will: "sovereignty . . . is nothing but the exercise of the general will" (*SC*, 57/*OC*, III:368; see also 114/III:429).

Another difference between Rousseau and Plato is implied in their consideration of political liberty: the social contract. Here again they differ on the dimension of institutional Platonism. The notion of civic agreement is important enough for Rousseau that he would use it for the title of his most significant political essay. Legitimate government requires nothing less: "following the soundest portion of those who have discussed these matters, I posited as a foundation of the body politic [in the *Social Contract*] the convention of its members" (*Letters*, 231/*OC*, III:806). This is built into the very notion of the general will—the people must give their assent to the state in order for its proclamations to hold legitimacy.

Plato, by contrast, scarcely considers the social contract as a means to found his regime. Whether the people agree to a state has no bearing on its legitimacy. Legitimacy is only found by reference to its correspondence to the ideas of justice and the good. To Plato's credit, he is actually aware of something like a social contract, and he is the first Western philosopher to contemplate its meaning and potential purpose. In the *Republic*, Glaucon proposes that the origin of justice was an agreement among the people to prevent what is worst—to suffer wrong and be impotent to exact revenge (359ab). On this interpretation, justice is valued not as a good in itself, but only because individuals are too weak to perform injustice and get away with it. Those who are powerful have no incentive to be just. It is worth observing that Socrates provides no direct response to Glaucon's argument but sits patiently as he develops his argument with the Ring of Gyges. Socrates' ultimate response comes later, when he suggests that political societies have a more organic origin in their mutual needs. This is to say that political societies are natural for Plato, whereas they are in an important respect artificial for Rousseau.

The difference between Plato and Rousseau in this regard is very much a product of the times in which they wrote. For Plato and Aristotle, nothing is more obvious than that states are natural. There is no such thing as individuals existing prior to or independent of the polis. On the other hand, modern political theory typically begins in a state of nature—of individuals existing prior to politics. This changes a good deal, and, for all of Rousseau's ancient affinities, in this respect he is truly modern. His state of nature, no less than Hobbes's, assumes that people exist as individuals prior to a state. Consequently, the move from the state of nature to political society has to be explained in a way that Plato never seriously entertained. Absent a social contract, the only other option would appear to reside in force, something Rousseau adamantly opposes. Thus, the contract is the one remaining option. It is worth observing that the contract provides Rousseau with at least one advantage that might have escaped Plato's consideration. Consenting citizens are more likely to be compliant than those who are simply assumed as part of the polity. Thus, a regime founded in consent has a greater likelihood to be stable.[46]

The last three differences between Rousseau and Plato treated here correspond to what is frequently identified as the "three waves" of book 5 from the *Republic*.[47] All three of these differences are on the institutional level. The first is Plato's recommendation that political offices (especially the position of ruler) be open to women. This was a stunning recommendation in the context of a culture that did not make a practice of including women in the affairs of the state. For Plato, however, it was practically mandated by reason. If the primary qualification to rule is wisdom, and women have access to that wisdom, they must be granted access to the office of ruler. Rousseau, however, is infamously skeptical about the mental capacities of women: "as regards the works of genius, they are out of the reach of women" (*Emile*, 386/*OC*,

---

46. It is possible that Plato did consider this issue in his discussion of the physician in the *Laws*. The Athenian Stranger notes that when a doctor gives a prescription to a free patient, he cannot do so "in the brusque fashion of a dictator" but must rather win the "patient's support" (*Laws*, 720b–e). That is, the doctor must persuade the patient to agree to take the medicine. Plato uses this as a metaphor for legislation. In order to persuade citizens to obey the laws—that is, to promote compliance—legislators must promulgate the laws with an explanation of their purpose. This is not precisely consent theory, but it is at least suggestive. For a discussion, see Klosko (1986a, 227–29).

47. In this discussion, I largely follow the arguments in Cooper (2002).

IV:737). In *Julie,* he goes so far as to note, in the voice of Julie, his disagreement with Plato on this point: "Do you remember that once while reading your Plato's *Republic* we disputed this point of the moral difference between the sexes? I persist in the opinion I then held, and am unable to imagine a common model of perfection for two beings so different" (104/*OC,* II:128). In this respect, he frequently recommends what appears to be a subordinate role of women to men.[48]

Plato claims that the second wave is even more radical than the first (*Republic,* 457d): that the traditional family should be abolished for all guardians. He makes this recommendation because the attachments to family provoke individuals to place their own families above the good of their broader community. This is unacceptable, because a ruler rules for the benefit of the whole, not for the good of a particular family. Eliminating filial ties to the rulers, according to Cooper, "would seem to express the necessity of generalizing and elevating one's eros" (2002, 113). Although Rousseau does not deny that the good of the community is the proper goal of the laws, he steadfastly defends the institution of the family. This is one of the primary reasons he is a strong advocate for mothers nursing their children. It tightens family bonds, which in turn only fosters generally better morals (*Emile,* 46/*OC,* IV:258). To remove these family bonds, then, would only manage to loosen the morals that constitute much of the fabric of social life.

Plato characterizes the third wave as the greatest of the three: that philosophers should be kings. "Unless," Plato remarks, "either philosophers become kings in our states or those whom we now call our kings and rulers take to the pursuit of philosophy seriously and adequately . . . there can be no cessation of troubles" (*Republic,* 473de). This is perhaps the most famous institutional doctrine associated with all of Plato's works, and it might be the most obvious area in which Rousseau parts company with Plato, because his conception of sovereignty and the lawmaking authority resides squarely with the people. There are no philosopher-rulers in Rousseau's polity.

Cooper argues that, despite these apparent differences, there is an underlying substratum of assumptions that brings them surprisingly close. I want to emphasize this theme and perhaps push it a bit further. These differences—while real at the *institutional* level—reveal underlying *metaphysical* similarities. Regarding the first wave, Cooper notes that there is a "bisexuality" in Rous-

48. According to Helena Rosenblatt (2002), Rousseau's reputation as a misogynist has been grossly exaggerated. Rousseau was not considerably more advanced than his peers, she argues, but even so, the majority of his most conspicuous passages are directed at the more frivolous bourgeois women, rather than at women as a whole.

seau's approach to reason. That is to say, Rousseau's conception of a moral person includes both masculine and feminine components. The masculine component is that which is most comfortable with philosophy. As Cooper notes, however, this is not necessarily high praise. Rousseau repeatedly condemns philosophy as it is practiced in his day, and this must be borne in mind when he remarks that "men will philosophize about the human heart better than she [the woman] does." The passage revealingly continues, "but she will read in men's hearts better than they [men] do. It is for women to discover experimental morality, so to speak, and for us to reduce it to a system." Through the conjunction of these two faculties, he reasons, humanity can "tend to the perfection of the instrument given by nature" (*Emile*, 38/*OC*, IV:737). Cooper goes on to argue that, despite his limitations, Emile embraces both of these faculties. By the end of the book, he knows the nature of humankind and the principles of political justice. Further, he has learned to block out the distorting influences of the senses, the passions, flattery, and public opinion. As Cooper reminds us, these are the domains of Platonic philosophic knowledge. Thus, although Rousseau does not propose that women should become rulers, as Plato did, he does suggest a necessary role for the feminine in philosophic thought. Indeed, it is the feminine element of the mind that is most in touch with our fundamental intuitions of the metaphysical ideas. Without this component, reason can only construct castles in the air. And, indeed, this is precisely what the philosophes do for Rousseau. Although they employ great masculine talents of reasoning, they lack the fundamental feminine intuitions of what is just and good. This can only lead to bad philosophy and moral corrosion.

Regarding the second wave, although their positions on the family represent a significant difference on the institutional level, Cooper observes that Plato's true intention in abolishing the family is to divert affection from the immanent to the transcendent—clearly a metaphysical move. In the spirit of Socrates' speech from the *Symposium,* where the love of individual bodies is ultimately redirected to the idea of beauty, the love of the family in the *Republic* is to be redirected to the love of the greater community, as suggested by the ideas of justice and the good. In this respect, Cooper finds Rousseau on the same page as Plato. As discussed earlier in this section, Emile is in an important respect a philosopher, interested in truths that transcend the material world. To this effect, Cooper draws attention to the fact that the adolescent pupil is instructed to contemplate a *Symposium*-like idea of beauty that transcends earthly experience (e.g., *Emile*, 446/*OC*, IV:820). This converts an *institutional* difference into a *metaphysical* similarity.

The third wave appears to set the greatest distance between Rousseau and Plato, because Rousseau never seriously contemplates rule by philosophers. To some extent, however, Cooper notes that this divergence is mitigated when Plato's principles are applied to the soul. That is, although there may not be philosopher-rulers in Rousseau, there is a philosophic component of the mind. The passages cited above already suggest that there is in Rousseau a strong philosophic component of wise soul. Through the feminine faculty of intuition or sentiment, everyone theoretically has access to these ideas. Thus, although his state may not be ruled by philosophes, both the state and the soul are ruled by philosophic ideas.

The upshot of this discussion of the differences between Rousseau and Plato comes down to a few points. First, Rousseau's most significant departure from Plato is epistemic in nature. It specifically concerns epistemic access to the ideas. Whereas for Plato the ideas are knowable only by a few elite philosophers, for Rousseau this access is potentially much broader. I say "potentially" only because, like Plato, Rousseau is deeply aware that many barriers remain between a person and the contents of his or her conscience. But it is present in everyone, and one need not be a genius in order to have this kind of knowledge. As the *Emile* reveals, it is even available to adolescents of modest intelligence.

This epistemic assumption necessarily leads to different institutional conclusions. If everyone by nature (as opposed to artifice) has access to these ideas, they can be considered equal in this important respect and are hence entitled to equal rights. Further, if everyone is acting according to these ideas, one could expect everyone to act responsibly with considerably more freedom. And finally, if everyone has knowledge of these ideas, it is not unreasonable to place sovereignty in the people's hands. In fact, it seems to be the most logical conclusion. This does not explain all the differences between Plato and Rousseau, to be sure, but it does go a considerable distance in understanding the heart of what separates them.

It is important to note that the epistemic assumption is empirical. This is significant insofar as it brings us back to what Plato and Rousseau have in common. Recall that both embrace the *metaphysical* and *ontological* components of Platonism. That is, they both insist on the existence of immaterial ideas and, further, they sketch them as indeterminate. The indeterminacy of the ideas requires construction in the real or material world. This construction, in turn, requires empirical knowledge of that world. Thus, the empirical knowledge assumed in the construction determine a great deal of resulting decisions. Consider an example. Imagine two composers writing violin concertos. One is writing before Paganini; another, after. The knowledge that a string player is physically capable of certain techniques is almost inevitably going to influence what goes into the composition. Thus, although both composers perhaps aim at what is beautiful, empirical conditions to a large extent determine the realization of that idea of beauty in the real world.

The same is true of Plato and Rousseau. They both assume an idea of justice and have a plan to articulate it in the material world. They are operating, however, with different empirical assumptions about that world. Plato assumes that knowledge of justice is limited to a few gifted individuals. Rousseau believes that it is at least latent in the heart of every human individual. This is a significant difference, and this empirical divergence, in turn, leads them to place political power and authority in different hands. If their empirical assumptions had been reversed, perhaps Plato would have looked to place power in the hands of the many, whereas Rousseau might have sought something like philosopher-rulers. The *institutional* question of where power should reside is contingent on the *epistemic* question of who is wise, and wisdom itself is contingent upon the *metaphysical* question of the ideas, such as justice and the good. All are tied together. Thus, it is perfectly possible for them to share metaphysical and ontological assumptions, while differing at the epistemic and institutional levels. In fact, it is their shared commitment to the metaphysical and ontological principles of Platonism that almost makes necessary the distinctions at the institutional level. Their differences only reveal that both were highly sophisticated thinkers who understood the extraordinary complexities involved in the political project.

SIX

ROUSSEAU'S SYSTEM OF CHECKS AND BALANCES: THE NEGATIVE FUNCTION OF JUSTICE

Chains can come in many forms. They can be passions, public opinion, the arts and sciences, or perhaps even willful ignorance, but perhaps no chains are as formidable as those imposed by a government on its people. With sufficient fortitude, one can overcome the fetters of one's passions. It takes a significant act of the will, but at least it is theoretically in one's own hands. The same can be said of public opinion. One can choose to recognize it for the illusion it is and opt to be freed from its grip. The same cannot be said, however, of the tyranny of a government. It is the most explicit and confining chain conceivable. Whereas freeing oneself from the chain of the passions is possible by an act of will, the will itself is impotent against a mighty tyrant. It is therefore among the most important tasks of any political philosopher to find some way of dealing with tyranny's ever-looming possibility.

Of course, some philosophers have been labeled as enablers of political despotism, rather than as protectors against it. Competition is fierce for the title of the "Greatest Muse of the Tyrants." Plato, Hobbes, Hegel, Marx, and Nietzsche have all had their moments of infamy. Perhaps no one, however, has so consistently been despised for the supposed consequences of his philosophy and its tendency toward tyranny than Jean-Jacques Rousseau. From Benjamin Constant, who labeled him a "support[er] of all kinds of despotism" ([1815] 1988, 177), to Isaiah Berlin, who suggested that he was "the most sinister and most formidable enemy of liberty in the whole history of modern thought" (2002, 49), Rousseau has scarcely enjoyed a universally favorable reception by the intellectual community.[1] This reputation as an advocate of

---

1. The amount of ink spilled on this question without decisive resolution is substantial. A good sample would include not only Constant ([1814, 1815] 1988) and Berlin (2002), but also Talmon (1951), d'Entrèves ([1951] 1994), Heine ([1834] 1961), Russell (1945), Nisbet (1943), Crocker (1968), Chapman ([1956] 1968), and Starobinski (1973).

tyranny stems from numerous facets of his politics—too many to enumerate and address here.[2] Instead, I focus on one particular charge: that Rousseau nourishes the tyrannical state by failing to check power adequately (Talmon 1955; Crocker 1968). Although this line of criticism is not recent in origin, it has never been refuted. The continued inattention to this accusation thus contributes to the overall assumption by many that Rousseau was a great patron and even advocate of tyranny. I argue, to the contrary, that in both theory and practical recommendations he was profoundly concerned with the problem of tyranny and the concentration of power.

This position is not in itself unique. Others have argued persuasively that Rousseau's political doctrines add up to something less than despotism.[3] My reconstruction of Rousseau as something other than an enabler of despotism, however, distinguishes itself from other approaches by focusing on an element largely ignored in Rousseau scholarship: his theory of checks and balances. It is perhaps symptomatic of this condition that N. J. H. Dent's otherwise excellent *Rousseau Dictionary* lacks an entry for either "checks and balances" or "separation of powers."[4] The importance of such mechanisms to Rousseau is evident in his extremely careful plan, laid out in the *Government of Poland,* to create a state wherein power is checked at virtually every possible stage of intervention. These checks include senatorial oversight of the king, legislative appointment of the Senate, frequent sessions of the Diet, frequent elections of the Diet, and deputy oversight of the Diet. This chapter traces his theory of checks and balances and, more significantly, the motives behind it— specifically, the desire to prevent a concentration of powers essential for the construction of tyrannical regimes. These motives also include a deep commitment to universal—but not necessarily tyrannical—political values and his desire to serve them. There is no doubt that Rousseau aimed at designing a political system that would realize universal ideals and, moreover, one that would involve nearly unanimous affirmation of the same ideals by the people. Perhaps this fact alone is enough to raise the specter of totalitarianism for the twenty-first-century reader, but the fact remains that, at the very least, Rousseau takes great pains to disallow the means by which our great totalitarian regimes attempted to realize their supposed ideals. Further, Rousseau's characterization of the ideals to be realized should make us even more skeptical of identifying his thought with the fantasies that have enthralled so many in

2. This includes, among other things, Rousseau's civil religion and vigorous support of nationalism.

3. An excellent, relatively recent example of this is Hampsher-Monk (1995).

4. André Charrak's *Le vocabulaire de Rousseau* (2002) likewise lacks equivalent entries.

modern history. He obviously feared tyrannical power precisely on the grounds that its exercise would lead to the sorts of disasters to which we have all become accustomed.

1. Defining Tyranny

Perhaps the greatest obstacle to addressing the charge that Rousseau is a friend of tyranny is defining the term "tyranny" itself. Like many words, its meaning has varied in certain respects from time to time, and even from person to person. The slippery nature of this word makes it difficult to pin down Rousseau's thoughts on tyranny. The problem is compounded further by the fact that "tyranny" appears in multiple contexts—in Rousseau's influences, in his condemnations of others, and in the condemnation by others of Rousseau. In gathering these disparate references and allusions to tyranny, we can gain greater insight into what he means when he employs the term.

1.1. ANCIENT DEFINITIONS

Because I have argued that Rousseau's most profound influences are ancient, it is particularly important to investigate the ancient understandings of tyranny. The Greek word for tyranny is *turannis,* itself derived from *turannos,* originally meaning "absolute ruler." Many Greeks used *turannos* interchangeably with "king," though, as Rousseau himself notes, it was most commonly used to describe rulers (such as Pisistratus) who usurped political power illegitimately, regardless of whether they used that power for the common benefit of all or their own personal profit. This specific and morally neutral meaning of "tyranny" is not a common one in the subsequent literature, though, and this may be partly attributable to the earliest substantial discussions of tyranny found in Plato and Aristotle.

For Plato, tyranny represents the worst of all possible forms of government, ranking beneath even democracy. His discussion of tyranny occurs amid his treatment of regime types and political change in books 8 and 9 of the *Republic.* His normative ranking of regime types corresponds to their chronological order. The first state, ruled by philosophers, rates the highest by virtue of its rule by wisdom. This is followed by timocracy, which esteems honor and courage. Next comes oligarchy, or the dominance of money interests. The penultimate stop is democracy, which prizes freedom. The last regime is tyranny. Tyranny arises, according to Plato, from a division and eventual conflict of classes in the dying days of a democracy. Tired from the excesses and tumult concomitant with a democracy, the people are ready to accept a dictator, who can secure the order they crave. What the tyrant himself evidently values most, however, is not order but his own power and the ability to exercise it arbitrarily. Power, however, is merely one manifestation of a larger malady inflicting the constitution of the dictator—pleasure seeking.[5] The tyrant has lost the ability to distinguish between the necessary pleasures, such as eating to sustain health, and the unnecessary pleasures. In short, the tyrant leads a life of unbridled selfishness. Plato informs us that "there is a dangerous, wild, and lawless form of desire in everyone" (*Republic,* 572b). The difference between the just individual and the tyrant is that the former can control these desires. Having lost this ability, the immoderate tyrant pursues an unobstructed path (at least by his own conscience) of satisfying any need, natural or otherwise, that might arise. Such a personal constitution frees the dictator from any concern with the needs of the people, justice, or the good. Such figures might kill or exile all opponents, impoverish their people, and discover that perpetual warfare is the best way by which to sustain power.

Likewise, Aristotle regards tyranny as the worst possible regime type, ranking it behind monarchy, aristocracy, polity, democracy, and oligarchy. Tyranny represents for Aristotle a perversion of monarchy. Instead of a king ruling for the common good, we have a single dictator who looks only to his own happiness. With Plato, Aristotle finds that a tyrant "never looks to the common benefit" and instead "aims at what is [privately] pleasant" (*Politics,* 1311a). This pleasure seeking most typically manifests itself in wealth augmentation, according to Aristotle. To maintain the power necessary to satisfy his desires, the tyrant engages in myriad behaviors associated with more contemporary despots. These include eliminating the intelligentsia, limiting the education of the subjects, surveillance of the citizens, impoverishing the people, extravagant taxation, and the like.[6] For Aristotle, tyrannies have neither any regard for justice nor much chance to endure for a significant period of time.

I.2. ROUSSEAU'S OBJECTION TO TYRANNY

It is indeed the rare philosopher who consciously advocates tyranny, and Rousseau is no exception. He makes many references to tyranny, none of

---

5. That this is the case is confirmed by the fact that Plato likens tyrants to pastry chefs in the *Gorgias.*

6. It is worth noting that all these techniques belong to what Aristotle describes as the most traditional and typical way by which to maintain tyrannies. He also describes a second possibility,

them remotely flattering: "despotism, instead of governing subjects in order to make them happy, makes them miserable in order to govern them" (*SC*, 101/*OC*, III:415). From this observation alone, it is reasonable to conclude that, whatever implications might be pregnant in his work, we should not assume that he *intended* to lay the foundations of tyranny. To the contrary, it is fair to say that he was deeply concerned with the problem of tyranny and that this concern represents the impetus behind much of his political thought. In his *Constitutional Project for Corsica*, Rousseau holds tyranny accountable for the end of enlightened rule and the perpetuation of unnecessary poverty ([1765] 1986, 281/*OC*, III:903, 301/III:918). In his *Political Economy*, he describes tyrants as "enemies of the people" (29/*OC*, III:269). In light of this, it is not surprising that Rousseau rejects Grotius, Pufendorf, and Hobbes as the "friends of despotism," as James MacAdam (1963) suggests.

Grotius, Pufendorf, and Hobbes hold something else in common, however, that helps complete this picture. The reason that they are so vulnerable to the charge of despotism is that they are all, to varying degrees, normative positivists. The argument for Hobbes has already been well established. As a materialist, Hobbes has only material phenomena on which to ground his politics. This foundation of material phenomena is, by definition, always changing and subject to whim. This is precisely the reason why, according to Rousseau, arguments from force are always doomed to fail as a principle of political right. Force is a material phenomenon and, as such, is always subject to change. It is far from the eternality required of genuine political principles. Rousseau asks, in the *Social Contract*, "[W]hat is a right that perishes when force ceases? If one has to obey by force, one is no longer obliged to do so. Clearly, then, this word 'right' adds nothing to force; it means nothing at all" (44/*OC*, III:354).

Without an eternal principle of right, "right" itself would be fluctuating and potentially arbitrary. It becomes the perfect tool of the aspiring tyrant. A despot would struggle with a fixed notion of right, because it would constrain his ability to achieve his aims. Consider Machiavelli's advice in the *Prince*. He stresses that an effective ruler must be open to changing circumstances and, above all, must not be constrained by what were considered the eternal moral rules. In fact, for Machiavelli, such allegiances were virtually guaranteed to be fatal. Rousseau understood such arguments and likely understood their con-

---

wherein the dictator takes on characteristics of a monarch or true statesman (1314a–1315b). I leave this from consideration for two reasons: first, Aristotle acknowledges this to be rare, and second, if a tyrant acts as a statesman, it may not be fair to call him a "tyrant."

nection, at least subconsciously, to positivism. This is why he is so comfortable in linking Hobbes and Grotius as part of the same tradition. For him, "their principles are exactly alike. They differ only in manner of expression. They also differ in method. Hobbes bases himself on sophisms, and Grotius on poets. They have everything else in common" (*Emile*, 458/*OC*, IV:836).[7] As for Pufendorf, Rousseau was likewise concerned with positivistic tendencies (*SD*, 179/*OC*, III:183–84).

MacAdam's point on this matter, however, is different. He has argued that Rousseau held more in common with Hobbes, Grotius, and Pufendorf than I suggest. In fact, the only significant point of contention is on the matter of popular sovereignty (MacAdam 1963, 40). Rousseau upholds it; Hobbes, Grotius, and Pufendorf reject it. On this interpretation, "tyranny" is defined as a denial of popular sovereignty, but this neglects the higher-order difference central to this book. In fact, for Rousseau, even popular sovereignty itself is contingent on Rousseau's appeal to the eternal political principles. This is evident in his distinction between the will of all and the general will. The people themselves are not sovereign. They are only sovereign when they embody the general will—that is to say, when their will reflects what is right. Their sovereignty is contingent and is not itself the first principle of Rousseau's politics.

This brings us to Arthur Melzer's chapter on the separation of powers and checks and balances in Rousseau—perhaps the closest thing to a definitive work on the subject (1990, 204–31). Melzer carefully and effectively deconstructs several old arguments suggesting that Rousseau was inattentive to these matters by drawing attention to long-ignored passages where he "openly and repeatedly declares his interest" in them (211). In this chapter, I do not take issue with Melzer's interpretations in this regard. I merely mean to suggest that greater light can be shed on Rousseau's impetus against tyranny if we understand his deeper metaphysical commitments. Rousseau needs checks and balances because they put the brakes on tyranny—one of the greatest possible threats to the eternal idea of justice.[8] The idea of justice, as will be demonstrated shortly, operates both in positive and negative fashions. Positively, it sets the primary condition and terms of the formation of the general will.

7. Of course, as is more than evident from the *First Discourse, Letter to d'Alembert,* and the essay "On Theatrical Imitation," the distinction between sophists and poets is practically a matter of semantics.

8. In this light, it is interesting that Melzer draws attention in a footnote to the fact that checks and balances were first formulated by Plato in the *Laws* (Melzer 1990, 206). One need only push a bit further to see that this is not necessarily coincidence—both Plato and Rousseau are motivated by similar commitments and ancillary concerns.

Negatively, it serves as a means by which to critique those regimes that one might call "tyrannical" or "despotic." And this, in turn, fuels more positive developments in the form of institution formation. In contemplating regime design, Rousseau asks what conditions might lead to tyranny (a negative function) and how this might be avoided through smart institutional construction (a positive function). As is often the case, deconstruction is followed by construction, but in both instances they are performed with reference to an idea of justice (see Balkin 1994).

1.3. ROUSSEAU'S DEFINITION OF TYRANNY

That Rousseau objects to tyranny is not difficult to establish. This, however, raises an extremely important and surprisingly neglected question in Rousseau scholarship: What is tyranny, according to Rousseau? His chapter "The Abuse of Government and of Its Tendency to Degenerate" in the *Social Contract* (III.10) represents his only direct and systematic attempt to address this question. He begins by reporting that tyranny (*tyrannie*) emerges when the prince, or government more generally, puts itself above the laws: "So that the moment the Government usurps the sovereignty, the social pact is broken, and all ordinary Citizens, restored to their natural freedom, are forced to obey, but are not obligated to do so" (*SC*, 108/*OC*, III:422–23). This definition is soon expanded to distinguish the "vulgar" from the "precise" sense of tyranny:

> In the vulgar sense of the term, a Tyrant is a King who governs with violence and without regard for justice and the laws. In the precise sense of the term, a Tyrant is an individual who arrogates the royal authority to himself without having any right to it. That is how the Greeks understood the word Tyrant: They gave it indiscriminately to good and to bad Princes whose authority was not legitimate. Thus *Tyrant* and *usurper* are two perfectly synonymous words. (108/III:423)

Rousseau attaches a footnote to this discussion in order to elaborate on Aristotle's definition of a tyrant. He notes here that Aristotle does not fit the typical Greek model by distinguishing a tyrant from a king insofar as the king rules solely for his subjects' advantage, and the tyrant rules purely for his own advantage. As noted above, Aristotle's definition of tyranny ignores the question of the rise to power, focusing instead on the exercise of that power. Thus, whereas the early Greeks follow Rousseau's "precise" definition of tyranny by linking the term to the origin of the dictator's power, Aristotle (as well as Plato) conforms to the "vulgar" definition by focusing on the manner in which the power is employed.

Although Rousseau is correct to point out that the Greeks often employed *turannis* in the precise sense of an "usurper" of political power, it is fair to ask whether he himself actually uses the terms as meticulously as he has defined them. In other words, does Rousseau employ "tyranny" in the precise or vulgar sense? There is sound evidence to believe that he makes use of both. As for his employment of the vulgar definition, this is evident insofar as Rousseau associates tyranny with the authoritative exercise of violence. In his *Government of Poland,* Rousseau finds in the Polish people a spirit that "the *force* of tyranny cannot subjugate" (178/*OC,* III:954, emphasis added). Similarly, Rousseau describes the killing of innocent citizens for a pretended "good" to be "one of the most execrable maxims that tyranny ever invented" (*Political Economy,* 17/*OC,* III:256). For perhaps this reason, Berlin is comfortable in speaking of Rousseau's famous "chains" as being "the chains of the tyrant" (2002, 44).

Related to violence, the vulgar conception of tyranny includes the violation of the idea of justice. Judith Shklar tacitly understood this when she wrote that, for Rousseau, "the *just* society is evidently a society without subjection" (1969, 182, emphasis added). "[A] Tyrant," he writes, "is a King who governs . . . without regard for justice" (*SC,* 108/*OC,* III:423). Justice and tyranny are practically incompatible, every bit as much as they are logically so. Toward the end of the *Second Discourse,* Rousseau suspects that the despot will "gradually [rear] its hideous head and [devour] everything good and wholesome it may have seen anywhere in the State." In this condition "the Subjects have no other Law left than the will of the Master, and the Master no other rule than his passions, [and consequently] the notions of the good and the principles of justice again vanish" (*SD,* 185/*OC,* III:191). Where there is tyranny, there can be no justice. It thus seems that the vulgar definition of tyranny is frequently in mind when he writes freely on political subjects.

There are other occasions, however, on which Rousseau appears to prefer the precise understanding of tyranny—that is, where the *source* of exercised power is of preeminent concern. From this perspective, tyranny is political power disassociated from legitimate sovereign authority. To this effect, Rousseau cites the 1667 declaration of Louis XIV as being the very antithesis of tyranny:

> *Let it therefore not be said that the Sovereign is not subject to the Laws of his State, since the contrary proposition is a truth of the Right of*

> *Nations, which flattery has sometimes challenged, but which good Princes have always defended as a tutelary divinity of their State. How much more legitimate it is to say with the Wise Plato that the perfect felicity of a Kingdom is that a Prince be obeyed by his Subjects, that the Prince obey the Law, and that the Law be right and always directed to the public good. (SD, 178/OC, III:183; emphasis in original)*

Anything else, according to Rousseau, would result in the "voluntary establishment of Tyranny" (*SD*, 178/*OC*, III:182), because the ruler would establish himself contrary to the sovereign will. In a similar spirit, Rousseau describes "tyrannical political economy" as that which is contrary to the sovereign will (*Political Economy*, 9/*OC*, III:247). Likewise, in the *Social Contract*, tyrants are presented as synonymous with "usurpers" of the sovereign authority (77/*OC*, III:390). He repeats this claim later in the *Social Contract*, referring to tyrants as those who "usurp from the Sovereign" (104/*OC*, III:418).

Although the vulgar and precise definitions of tyranny seem disparate, there are grounds for viewing them as two sides of the same coin. This is because sovereignty itself is, for Rousseau, "nothing but the exercise of the general will" (*SC*, 57/*OC*, III:368), and I have already made the case that the general will is an agreement to the idea of justice. As Rousseau himself remarked, "one need only be just in order to be sure of following the general will" (*Political Economy*, 12/*OC*, III:251). Thus one head of the coin is justice; the other is sovereignty. They are almost coextensive. Sovereignty cannot exist without the general will, which is itself a popular declaration of the idea of justice.

Rousseau's distinctions on the nature of tyranny, however, are not limited to that between the precise and the vulgar. He further distinguishes "tyranny" from "despotism": "In order to give different things different names, I call *Tyrant* the usurper of the royal authority, and *Despot* the usurper of the Sovereign power. The tyrant is one who insinuates himself contrary to the laws and governs according to the laws; the Despot is one who puts himself above the laws themselves. Thus a Tyrant may not be a Despot, but a Despot is always a Tyrant" (*SC*, 108/*OC*, III:423). This passage is somewhat perplexing. As written, it includes a contradiction: (1) A tyrant governs according to the law. (2) A despot places himself above the law. (3) A despot is necessarily a tyrant. It is obviously the case that (3) cannot be reconciled with both premises (1) and (2), because the defining features of (1) and (2) are mutually exclusive. The supposed distinction Rousseau means to introduce here is further complicated by his earlier implication that tyranny occurs "when the Prince no longer administers the state according to the laws" (107/III:422).

Rousseau further blurs the supposed distinction between tyranny and despotism in the *Second Discourse* in his discussion of the final days of the failed regime, where he announces the arrival of "[d]espotism, gradually rearing its hideous head and devouring everything good and wholesome it may have seen anywhere in the State [and] would finally succeed in trampling Laws and People underfoot" (185/*OC*, III:190–91). So far, so good, because his declared understanding of despotism was a fundamental disrespect for the law. He continues, however, and in the process obscures his distinction between despotism and tyranny: "and Peoples would not longer have Chiefs or Law, but only Tyrants" (185/III:191). This use of "tyrant" violates the distinction insofar as the tyrant, as defined in *Social Contract*, III.10, respects the law. Rousseau's supposed differentiation between tyranny and despotism is thus either purely technical or simply forgotten in his own discussion of more concrete political circumstances. In either case, it appears that outside this one paragraph of the *Social Contract*, he employs both "tyranny" and "despotism" synonymously.

The upshot is that Rousseau is highly flexible in both in his terminology and the meaning of these terms. In light of this, I treat "tyranny" and "despotism" to mean the usurping of the sovereign authority of the people to make their own just laws, as well as general acts of violence and injustice. Again, however, because Rousseau understood sovereignty and justice to be closely related, it is defensible for him to speak in such apparently loose terms and for us to treat his works accordingly.

To make sense of what follows, we must bear in mind that Rousseau's constructive political program is carried out on two levels. As must be the case with all substantial programs of this nature, Rousseau is concerned with knowledge and power. Whereas knowledge is necessary for the creation of wise and good laws, power is necessary for their implementation. The problem with power, however, is in its inherent nature to diverge from the demands of knowledge and wisdom. This has been true ever since Plato came to realize his own flawed proposals of the *Republic*: "no human being is competent to wield an irresponsible control over mankind without becoming swollen with pride and unrighteousness" (*Laws*, 713c). In light of the almost universal assumption that human beings are either naturally flawed, or inevitably are socialized to become such (as is the case with Rousseau), the question becomes: How can power be used in such a way as to serve its intended ends?

2. Checks and Balances

Rousseau's obvious concern about the problem of tyranny fuels the development of his sophisticated system of separation of powers. That he has a theory of checks and balances is difficult to dispute, even if it has infrequently been the subject of extended attention. His essay on the *Government of Poland* represents one of the most elaborate programs in the application of modern separation of powers theory. Rousseau offers multiple checks that, as some have noted (Kendall 1985, xxxvii–xxxix), resemble or perhaps even rival those found in the U.S. Constitution. Included are the king's reeligibility, division of the executive power, senatorial checks on the executive, splitting of the Senate, deputy oversight of the Diet, and prohibition of life terms. What motives, however, inspire their construction? To understand Rousseau's motives, it would first be instructive to examine the motives behind the Ancients who often serve as his models.

2.1. ANCIENT MODELS

As with tyranny, the tradition of checks and balances is a long one, traceable back to Plato and Aristotle. Whereas Plato's Kallipolis of the *Republic* reads for some as "fundamentally identical with [totalitarianism]" (Popper 1962, 87), others read Plato's *Laws* as the foundation of limited government. Glenn Morrow, for example, argues that "Plato not only conceived the idea of mixed state, but also anticipated some of the checks and balances necessary to maintain it" (1971, 158). T. K. Seung concurs: "The system of checks and balances that is introduced into the political structure of Magnesia is Plato's ingenious invention" (1996, 260). Plato's innovations in the *Laws* include popular juries, courts of arbitration, a program of official liability, and the Nocturnal Council.[9] George Klosko argues that Plato introduces these structures fundamentally because of his belief that "human beings cannot be entrusted with unaccountable power" (1986a, 225).[10] And given that constructive political philosophy is concerned with two problems—legislating wisely and control-

9. It is only fair to note that many of Plato's "innovations" were, in fact, already part of standard practice in the Greek world by his time. This does not detract, however, from Plato's achievement of being the first to theorize about them and advocate them to wide audiences.

10. E. P. Panagopoulos echoes the idea: "[Plato] felt the only way to avoid disaster was to distribute power among opposite interests, then to devise a well-protected system of checks to keep the power diffused" (1985, 8).

ling power—we can see that Plato's theory of checks and balances is aimed at the latter. His obsession with controlling power can be found, for example, in his relating the history of Persia, where the concentration of powers into few hands led to a vicious "despotism" (*despoitikon*) (*Laws,* 697d).

Although Aristotle is not as systematic as his teacher in this regard, it would be, in the words of Fred Miller, "an exaggeration to deny that Aristotle has any idea of checks and balances" (1995, 259). In the *Politics,* Aristotle is careful to separate power in matters such as the declaration of war, the auditing of public officials, and the forming of alliances, in addition to normal legislation. This is particularly the case in his discussion of mixed regimes, where he describes "techniques for partitioning political rights among different groups of the polis and of instituting limits upon the exercise of political power so as to prevent the excesses characteristic of tyranny" (Miller 1995, 259).

2.2. CHECKS AND BALANCES AND CHARGES OF TYRANNY

One species of argument offered as evidence for Rousseau's tyrannical tendencies has been the lack of what Plato and Aristotle offer above—a system of checks and balances. This position is found in the work of Jacob Talmon (1955) and Lester Crocker (1968). It takes roughly the following syllogistic form:

1. Rousseau argues that sovereignty is indivisible (*SC,* 57–58/*OC,* III:368–69).
2. He also insists that sovereignty is absolute (*SC,* 63/*OC,* III:375).
3. The separation of powers constitutes a division of sovereignty.
4. Therefore, Rousseau must condemn the separation of powers.

Although the argument itself is valid, it is not sound, because one of its premises represents a fundamental misunderstanding of Rousseau's notion of sovereignty. Premise (3) conflates two distinct concepts in Rousseau's lexicon: the sovereign and the government. The "sovereign," for Rousseau, is the united people acting in their public capacity (*SC,* 50–51/*OC,* III:361).[11] This definition is not unlike that suggested in *Federalist* 49 ("the people are the only legitimate fountain of power" [281]). Rousseau's critics are right to suggest that this sovereignty cannot be divided. The sovereign, however, must be dis-

11. He elaborates on the importance of this distinction in *Letters Written from the Mountain* (257/*OC,* III:837).

tinguished from the government. "Government," for Rousseau, is "[a]n intermediate body established between subjects and Sovereign so that they might conform to one another, and charged with the execution of the laws and the maintenance of freedom, both civil and political" (*SC*, 83/*OC*, III:396). The fact that he meant for government and sovereign to be distinct is evident in the very definition of this term—that it lies between subjects and sovereign. This distinction is important because it allows Rousseau to separate the *powers* of the government, not those of the sovereign. This is all that any system of checks and balances does. The Federalists, for example, do not argue for a division of the sovereign people. They argue, rather, for the separation of the branches the sovereign appoints. When Crocker and Talmon make their charges that Rousseau fails to provide the fundamental safeguard against tyranny—checks and balances between separate branches of government—they fail to understand that sovereignty and government are for him two distinct things.

That Rousseau's critics misunderstand his terms is clear in the types of evidence offered for support. Neither Talmon nor Crocker provides any passages from Rousseau that suggest antipathy toward checks and balances. Rather, they seek to associate Rousseau with others who have condemned such measures. Crocker moves from Rousseau's idea of absolute sovereignty to Robespierre's condemnation of the separation of powers within a matter of a few sentences (1968, 120). Likewise, Talmon offers no textual support for his insinuations, but rather relies on an unsubstantiated association with the Physiocrats. After discussing Rousseau's notion of sovereignty, he moves to the Physiocrats, for whom "parliamentary institutions, the separation and balance of powers, were . . . impossible as roads to social harmony" (1955, 45). He continues afterward to note that they refused to admit the possibility that the government might abuse its power. This may well be true of the Physiocrats. It has nothing to do, however, with Rousseau, as will be demonstrated in section 2.3. This is the elementary fallacy of guilt by association.[12]

2.2.1. On Using *Poland* to Defend the Charge of Tyranny

The following defense of Rousseau against the charge of tyranny relies extensively on the *Government of Poland*. Because most of the charges that Rousseau

---

12. One person for whom these charges would be true is Jean Bodin. Like Rousseau, he argues that sovereignty is indivisible ([1576] 1992, 49–50). Beyond this, however, he argues that as a consequence, the power of the government must be both concentrated and absolute. The false charges of J. L. Talmon and Lester Crocker against Rousseau are fair of Bodin, insofar as he makes the sovereign and the government one and the same body.

is a friend of tyranny stem from elements in his *Social Contract,* this requires some justification. There are at least five reasons why this is a defensible strategy. First, although one may pick and choose elements of his philosophy for the purpose of attacking his doctrines, Rousseau himself insisted that all his works formed a coherent whole—best understood when read together. He remarked in his *Dialogues* that in his work, "everything fit together" if one could only "follow the chain of their [his writings'] contents" (211/*OC,* I:932–33). Thus, to read the *Social Contract* in isolation from *Poland* is, in effect, to take his work out of context.

Second, Rousseau leaves plenty of evidence to suggest thematic connections between the *Social Contract* and *Poland.* The former famously begins, "Man is born free, and everywhere he is in chains" (*SC,* 41/*OC,* III:351); the first chapter of the latter declares that Poland "is in chains, and debates the ways to remain free" (*Poland,* 178/*OC,* III:954). The theme of chains continues throughout his essay on Poland. In chapter 6, he counsels strong fidelity to the principle of popular sovereignty, lest "you keep your brothers in chains" (196/III:974). A bit later he refers to the threat of excessive fortification, lest these strongholds "become nests of tyrants. . . . A sudden invasion is a great misfortune, no doubt, but permanent chains are a far greater one" (238/III:1018). Beyond the references to chains, Rousseau is comfortable in setting aside pertinent discussions, remarking that he has already covered these issues in the *Social Contract* (e.g., *Poland,* 181/*OC,* III:958, 200/III:978, 210/III:988, 255/III:1036), which suggests that he saw *Poland* in many respects as an elaboration or articulation of principles originally outlined in the *Social Contract.*

Third, Rousseau expresses in the *Social Contract* that he is not advocating one particular form of government: "There has always been much argument about the best form of Government, without considering that each one of them is the best in some cases, and the worst in others" (90/*OC,* III:403). He is extremely flexible on the realization of his principles. This is why he recognizes conditions under which democracy, aristocracy, and monarchy might flourish. Given this, it is not unreasonable to suggest that his proposal in the *Government of Poland* might also be consistent with the general principles of the *Social Contract.*

That this might be the case is further suggested by the fourth reason for employing the later text to defend the earlier: the fundamental principle of both political works is essentially the same, namely, that the general will is the principle of sovereignty. In the *Social Contract,* Rousseau repeatedly defends the proposition that legitimate law must be grounded in the general will. Further, he intimates there that the general will must be present in each institution as its animating principle. It is the anchor of the legislature, because "law is nothing but the declaration of the general will" (*SC,* 115/*OC,* III:430). Likewise, it informs the executive: "the Prince's dominant will is or should be nothing but the general will" (85/III:399). Rousseau echoes this point faithfully in *Poland.* The job of the legislature is to express the general will (*Poland,* 206/*OC,* III:984). Meanwhile, the executive is likewise expected to hold the just laws of the state above its own private will (252/III:1033).

Fifth and finally, it is worth noting that the checks and balances that would eventually characterize *Poland* could not have been far from Rousseau's mind while he was writing the *Social Contract,* because Rousseau advocates them in his most explicit defense of it—his *Letters Written from the Mountain.* He speaks freely here of the need for the legislature "to have inspection over the executive" (247/*OC,* III:826). And later he explicitly links references to his discussion of Roman institutions as a defense of the principle of checking executive power (*Letters,* 292/*OC,* III:880). Further, it is notable that the referenced discussion in the *Social Contract* speaks of preventing the dangers of tyranny when the tribunate seeks to usurp executive authority. This suggests not only checking power but also balancing it. For these reasons, it seems quite plausible to link Rousseau's constructive political works together as a relatively large, coherent whole.

2.3. THE *GOVERNMENT OF POLAND* AND THE "BALANCE AND EQUIPOISE OF THE POWERS"

The distinction between government and sovereign is not only crucial in directly responding to the charges of Talmon and Crocker but is also central to understanding the nature of Rousseau's complex system of government as articulated in the *Government of Poland.* A government is, for him, only contingently just and legitimate. Governments issuing just laws from the people can be said to respect and preserve the sovereign. On the other hand, governments issuing laws contrary to the general will can be said to usurp the sovereign. It is thus the highest priority for the designer of a Rousseauean constitution to ensure that all institutions are faithful to the general will.

As has been established, Rousseau is deeply concerned with the problem of tyranny, and, just as Plato and Aristotle saw checks and balances as a means by which to impede human nature's natural inclination to abuse power and commit injustice, so, too, has Rousseau developed a "balance and equipoise of the powers" ("l'équilibre et la ponderation des pouvoirs"; *Poland,* 215/*OC,*

III:993) to the same end.[13] To this, we need add only that these checks, for Rousseau, also protect the sovereign authority against any form of government contrary to the general will.

In the *Second Discourse*, Rousseau describes his modern secular version of the fall of humankind from an original state of bliss. The state of nature is, for him, a condition of abundance, peace, and compassion. Human beings are without sin and naturally feel empathy for fellow species members. This peace is disturbed, however, when someone encloses a plot of land and declares, "This is mine" (*SD*, 161/*OC*, III:164). From this development follows a series of follies through which human nature descends from its idyllic natural condition to the selfish nastiness Rousseau attributes to his contemporaries. Contemporary political institutions, in turn, are run by these corrupt souls. Instead of governing with compassion or justice, rulers seek to enhance their own property and further their selfish interests. In the *Second Discourse*, Rousseau thus says that in a tyranny there is no rule other than that of the despot's passions (185/*OC*, III:191). Similarly, he warns in his essay on Poland that modern nations must contend with the fact that their rulers will necessarily be fueled by "passions of petty self-interest" (180/*OC*, III:956). In light of the intractability of this socialized human nature, checks and balances make perfect sense. Just as Plato saw his separation of powers necessitated by the failings of human nature, so, too, does Rousseau.

His linking of the control of tyranny and the separation of powers is clear even in his most abstract work, the *Social Contract*: "If the Sovereign wants to govern, or the magistrate to give laws, or the subjects refuse to obey, disorder replaces rule, force and will no longer act in concert, and the dissolved State thus falls into Despotism" (83/*OC*, III:397). In this respect, Rousseau is not dissimilar to James Madison, who in *Federalist* 47 associates tyranny with the concentration of all governmental powers into a small group of people: "The accumulation of all powers, legislative, executive, and judiciary, in the same hands . . . may justly be pronounced the very definition of tyranny" (Madison, Hamilton, and Jay [1789] 1999, 269). As Robert Dahl has correctly pointed out, Madison does not literally mean to define tyranny as the concentration of all governmental powers in one set of hands (1956, 6–7). Rather, he suggests that this concentration of power inevitably *leads* to tyranny. What Dahl ignores, however, is *how* the concentration of powers would lead to tyranny.

---

13. Although it is indeed the case that human nature is not initially inclined to acquire power and harm others, according to Rousseau, social circumstances have evolved to make us so inclined. See McLendon (2003).

The answer is obvious, knowing that Madison held there to be a "degree of depravity in mankind which requires a certain degree of circumspection and distrust" (Madison, Hamilton, and Jay [1789] 1999, 314). Rousseau's similar fear of manifest human nature guides him to the same conclusion—that power must be divided for it to be limited.

Because Rousseau offers few concrete plans for government in the *Social Contract*, it is in his most practical work, the *Government of Poland*, that we find how he articulates this principle. This work offers several mechanisms by which he means to slow the encroachments of power and hinder its natural tendency toward tyranny. We can divide these devices into executive and legislative checks in addition to a system of graduated promotions designed to limit the encroachments of potential despots.

2.3.1. The Legislature

The fundamental task of the legislature, according to Rousseau, is to realize the general will—"law is nothing but the declaration of the general will" (*SC,* 115/*OC,* III:430).[14] And, because the general will itself is nothing less than an expression of sovereignty, any deviation from it is necessarily tyrannical. It is therefore the task of the lawgiver or constitutional author to construct a legislature as faithful to that will as the limits of human nature will allow. Doing so helps protect against the usurpation of sovereignty and consequently offers a shield against tyranny.

Rousseau famously abhors representation. In the *Social Contract,* he argues that sovereignty cannot be represented, because a will can be neither transferred nor articulated by deputies (114/*OC,* III:429–30). Yet this uncompromising position, perhaps informed by the ideal of the Greek city-state and the Swiss cantons, gives way in *Poland* to the reality of the nation-state: "One of the greatest inconveniences of large States . . . is that in them the legislative power cannot show itself as such, and can act only by delegation" (200–201/*OC,* III:978). Rousseau is clearly uncomfortable with its necessity and argues that without great care, corruption is virtually coextensive with its existence. Nevertheless, he proceeds with the assumption that, although its dangers are obvious and significant, it is necessary under the circumstances. To attenuate the danger of corruption, Rousseau suggests two methods of prevention. The

---

14. Rousseau repeats this point in his *Political Economy* and in *Poland.* The general will "is the source of the laws," "the first duty of the lawgiver is to conform the laws to the general will," and "the general will [is] the source and supplement of all the laws" (*Political Economy,* 12, 11/*OC,* III:245, 250). Moreover, "the law . . . is but the expression of the general will" (*Poland,* 206/*OC,* III:984).

first is frequent elections of the Diet, which "makes it more costly and more difficult to seduce [the representatives]" (201/III:979).

The second is to make the representatives follow the general will with precision by means of an oversight committee (201–2/III:979–80). This committee would be composed of citizens elected by the majority and headed by the marshal of the Dietine. It would have the task of writing precise instructions for the Diet to keep it faithful to the people's will. If in the judgment of this committee any representative has not been faithful, then it would rule this deputy ineligible for future elections. Rousseau envisions this as an extraordinarily intense, but necessary, scrutiny: "The Deputy must, with every word he speaks in the Diet, with every action he takes, anticipate himself under the scrutiny of his constituents, and sense the influence their judgment will have on his projects for advancement as well as on the esteem of his fellow citizens, which is indispensable for the realization of these projects of his: for after all the Nation sends Deputies to the Diet not in order to have them state their private sentiment but to declare the wills of the Nation" (202/III:980). As with frequent elections, Rousseau's purpose is to keep the representatives faithful to the general will. This in turn keeps private wills out of the government, which itself protects against the usurpation of the sovereign authority. Thus, the legislative measures are apparently aimed at mitigating the problem of tyranny.

2.3.2. Executive

Just as the task of the legislature should be to turn the general will into law, "the Prince's dominant will is or should be nothing but the general will" (*SC*, 85/*OC*, III:399). Rousseau here again reminds us of the fundamental purpose of his forthcoming measures: they are to protect against the intrusion of private wills—by definition contrary to the sovereign—into the government, and hence to guard against the possibility of tyranny.[15] He acknowledges, however, that such a task is far more easily said than done when it comes to the executive. He warns that, although the executive is required to carry out the laws, it also necessarily carries with it the danger of usurpation and tyranny. Monarchs are particularly susceptible to the temptations of power, because it is in individuals that "the particular will has greater sway and more easily dominates the other wills" (95/III:409). This concern, in turn, informs his multiple checks on the king in *Poland:* "It is a great evil for the Chief of a

---

15. Matthew Simpson (2006a) argues effectively that Rousseau's attempts to control the executive in the *Social Contract* result in an insoluble paradox.

nation to be the born enemy of the freedom whose defender he should be. This evil is not, in my view, so intrinsic to the office that it cannot be separated from it, or at least considerably reduced" (211/III:989). Rousseau advises to make the king so incapable of tyranny that he would not even dream of it. In this spirit, he praises the previous Polish constitution for slowing the natural progress of this office down "the habitual slope toward despotism" (198/III:976). This includes the division of the executive power by virtue of delegating executive tasks to trustees, ministers, and high officials and passing the top office to different hands.

The advantages of sharing the executive power with these delegates, according to Rousseau, are obvious. First, the offices operate with relative independence, thus keeping power from being too concentrated. Second, because these offices were not perpetually filled by the same families, power was not able to accumulate: "all power, even when usurped, always returned to its source" (198/III:976). Without separating power in this manner, the executive "would probably sooner or later have oppressed the legislative power and thus placed the Poles under the yoke which all nations bear" (198/III:976).

This very mechanism, however, carries seeds for future abuse, according to Rousseau. The problem with the division of executive power in this manner is twofold. First, whenever power is thus divided, harmony is lost. With independence comes disorganization and even conflict. Second, the multiplication of officials diminishes accountability. This is particularly problematic when the Diet is out of session: "It is true that he [the executive] recognizes the authority of the Diet; but since it is the only authority he recognizes, when the Diet is dissolved he no longer recognizes any authority at all" (*Poland*, 198/*OC*, III:976). Thus, although the delegation of executive tasks comes with great benefits, it is simultaneously fraught with great dangers. The executive's tendency to ignore the dictates of the absent Diet amounts to a fundamental disregard for the law—one of the key elements of Rousseau's definition of tyranny. It is thus little surprise that Rousseau characterizes executive officials as "so many petty despots who, without exactly usurping the sovereign authority, nevertheless oppress the Citizens piecemeal" (198–99/III:976).[16]

To reduce the chance of this prospect, Rousseau charges the Senate with

---

16. Here, Rousseau consciously echoes the *Social Contract:* "Dissolution of the State also comes about when the members of the Government severally usurp the power they ought to exercise only as a body; which is no less serious an infraction of the laws, and produces even greater disorder. Then there are, so to speak, as many Princes are there are Magistrates, and the State, no less divided than the Government, either perishes or changes its form" (108/*OC*, III:423).

the task of "hold[ing] to their duty Magnates tempted to stray from it" (199/ III:977). The Senate itself, though, is likewise fraught with danger. For this reason he considers Abbé de Mably's proposal of further dividing the Senate into multiple councils.[17] Each would be in charge of a particular department, have rotating offices, and serve terms of a fixed period. For obvious reasons, Rousseau insists that the king may not appoint the senators himself. They are rather to be appointed by the Diet, not having anything directly at stake. He is pleased that these devices would hinder some of the tendencies of the executive toward tyranny, but he is not convinced that it is a perfect solution. Just as the numerous magistrates of the executive open the possibility for further usurpations, so, too, do multiple councils of the Senate. In particular, he is concerned that one of these might rise above the others and dominate. It is for this reason among others, he says, that, even if it were to be adopted, other checks would be required.

Perhaps a no less important check on the king—and the one on which Rousseau spends the most effort—is the recommendation against hereditary monarchs. As with virtually all his checks, Rousseau's suggestion is informed by his fear of usurpation and despotism:

> It has been suggested that the Crown be made hereditary. Be assured that the moment this law is enacted, Poland can bid farewell forever to its freedom. They think that freedom can be sufficiently provided for by limiting the royal power. They fail to see that in the course of time these bounds set by the laws will be transgressed by gradual usurpations, and that a system adopted and uninterruptedly followed by a royal family is bound in the long run to win out over a law which by its nature constantly tends to slacken. If a King cannot corrupt the Great by favors, he can always corrupt them with promises to be redeemed by his successors, and since the plans formed by the royal family are perpetuated together with the family itself, people will trust its commitments and count on their being fulfilled much more than when the elective crown plainly shows that a monarch's plans end with his life. (*Poland,* 213/*OC,* III:991)

These fears are not new with Rousseau in his essay on Poland. The *Social Contract* likewise warns against the dangers of hereditary monarchy. This mode of

17. Both Rousseau and Mably were asked by Count Wielhorski to offer suggestions for revising the Polish constitution.

transferring power virtually guarantees, in his estimation, the rise to power of "monsters" and "imbeciles" (*SC,* 97/*OC,* III:411). The very art of raising a prince is destined to fail: "Everything conspires to deprive of justice and reason a man brought up to command others" (97/III:411). To this effect, Rousseau goes one step further in *Poland* than recommending against a hereditary monarch—he considers actively banning sons from following their fathers as kings. This proposal, however, is not ultimately adopted, because he holds that other measures sufficiently prevent this succession-related fear. What those measures might be are not exactly clear. What is clear is his purpose: "depriving Kings of all hope of usurping arbitrary power and passing it on to their children" (*Poland,* 214/*OC,* III:993). Thus, once again, Rousseau demonstrates that his checks are primarily aimed at forestalling the danger of tyranny by virtue of preventing private wills from usurping the sovereign authority.

"[B]ut it is not enough that these hands change," Rousseau warns us. "[I]f possible they should act only under the eyes of the Lawgiver . . . This is the true secret of keeping them from usurping his authority" (*Poland,* 200/*OC,* III:978). Given that power is of an encroaching nature, it will be necessary to have eyes on the executive authority with regularity. This can be carried out, he suggests, by the Diet. Elsewhere he tells us that it is an essential function of the legislature "to have inspection over the executive power" (*Letters,* 247/*OC,* III:826). Rousseau is struck by the fact that kings have not usurped legislative authority more often than they have by suspending or generally preventing legislative sessions, and he speculates that the absence of such usurpations is likely a sign of even more sinister corruption (*Poland,* 200/*OC,* III:978). With no Diet in session to watch over the king, he anticipates that the executive will assume legislative authority, pulling the state back into "despotism or anarchy" (*SC,* 83/*OC,* III:397). It therefore becomes absolutely essential to Rousseau's system of checks and balances to hold regular and frequent sessions of the Diet, "for then the Prince could not prevent them without openly declaring itself a violator of the laws and an enemy of the State" (119/III:435). He thus offers oversight of the executive on two levels. At the administrative, the Senate stands guard, and, at the legislative, the Diet maintains a watchful eye.

2.3.3. Graduated Promotions

Rousseau not only sees structural checks and balances as necessary to prevent tyranny but also conceives a system of "graduated promotions" (*marche graduelle*), designed to inhibit all but the most civic, virtuous, and competent people from attaining high offices in Poland. He designates three classes of honor that a citizen can attain, and each promotion opens the door to more important and honored positions. The first class has the title of "Servants of the State." To qualify for this distinction, one must be tested in public affairs, by virtue of service in any one of many capacities, including as a lawyer, assessor, judge, or manager of public funds, for a minimum of three years. After this time, a citizen may then apply to the local Dietine for recognition as a "Servant of the State." If the citizen secures the approval of the Dietine, he is then eligible to become a member of the Diet.

If a Servant of the State subsequently serves three two-year terms in the Diet, each time receiving the approval of the constituents at the report session of the local Dietine, he then becomes a "Citizen Elect." This position grants a series of new opportunities for the civic minded, including becoming a principal of secondary schools, inspector of the primary schools, or a candidate for the Senate. If the Citizen Elect then serves three terms in the Senate and receives a "certificate of approbation" from the Diet each time, he enters the highest rank, becoming one of the "Guardians of the Laws." Only people of this status are eligible to be elected king.[18]

Rousseau estimates that the time needed to rise from the status of ordinary citizen to Guardian of the Laws is minimally fifteen years. And, in this respect, it represents one of the most substantial checks built into his system. This substantial period of public scrutiny assures Rousseau of the competence and integrity of any person who will become king: "since they themselves will have been drawn from the order of *Guardians of the laws,* and will have passed with honor through all the grades of the Republic, their having been tested their whole life long an earned public approbation in all the positions they will have filled will be sufficient guarantee of the merit and the virtues of each one of them" (*Poland,* 249/*OC,* III:1030).

The purpose of graduated promotions is perfectly consistent with that of the checks on legislative and executive authority generally. By subjecting all potential delegates of the sovereign will to extended scrutiny by the sovereign itself, Rousseau aims to keep these delegates faithful to that sovereign will. Should some public officials be revealed to prioritize private wills over the sovereign or general will, they would be removed. To the extent that their public wills are consistent with that of the sovereign, they may continue along the path of promotion. This is yet another mode by which Rousseau aims to prevent the usurpation of sovereignty by private and hence illegitimate wills—or, in other words, tyranny.

It is perhaps fair to say that many years of public service do not always

18. They are also eligible to become life members of the Senate, in addition to Palatines.

guarantee the highest level of political performance and upright intentions. It is also fairly obvious that the measure required to advance in the ranks (the approval of other politicians) is dubious. Is it not possible that someone may rise to power in Rousseau's Poland by either buying members of the Diet or by simply being in alliance with other corrupt politicians? Rousseau is aware of this criticism. He tells us that he has one reply: "I believed myself to be speaking to a people which, while not free of vices, still had some resilience and virtues, and on that assumption my project is a good one. But if Poland is already at the point where everything is venal and rotten to the core, then it is in vain that it seeks to reform its laws and to preserve its freedom" (*Poland*, 242/*OC*, III:1023). Rousseau's response is a fascinating one. He clearly believes that some degree of virtue is necessary for carrying out his program of reforms (and indeed perhaps for any). Ultimately, the checks and balances must be carried out by human beings. We know, however, from the *Second Discourse* that Rousseau is far from persuaded that his contemporaries were virtuous. Should we read him to mean that the Poles are more virtuous than those inhabitants of part 2 of the *Second Discourse*? Does he mean to be mitigating his earlier views? Whether Rousseau's assumptions about the relative virtue of peoples can be reconciled is a question for another occasion.

Conclusions

Of all the checks in Rousseau's *Government of Poland*, it will undoubtedly be noticed that far more checks are present on the executive than on the legislative branch. There is a good reason for this, one consistent with both Rousseau's general principles and the outline of this chapter. It returns us once again to the distinction between the sovereign and the government that permeates his political works generally. For him, the legislative power is that which is more closely linked with the sovereign itself, whereas the executive power is that of the government. The legislature is closer to the people and is meant to reflect the people's refined interest, i.e., the general will. The executive is charged with the task of carrying out this will. Thus, assuming that the legislature is legitimately concerned with realizing the general will, it is not in need of checking. Most of its checking comes before its members even enter office, by virtue of graduated promotions. By contrast, the executive—as government—is further from the people and therefore more likely to superimpose a private will over the general will. This is why the executive is subjected to checks at every turn.

Regardless of whether Rousseau's system might have ever effectually combated tyranny is a matter of speculation. Arthur Melzer speculates that it would not (1990, 204–13). He might very well be correct. After all, Rousseau's checks do appear lopsided, favoring more checks on the executive than the legislature. The point here is that Rousseau recognized the concentration of power and its attendant tyranny as a serious problem, and he spent considerable effort to obviate it. To this extent, we would do well to revisit his reputation as a friend of despotism.

What is perhaps most important, however, in considering Rousseau's system of checks and balances in this context is the motivation that informs his reflections on these matters. His concern with the problem of tyranny stems from his conception of justice. The denial of any kind of transcendent norms is the denial of any effective restraints on a government in the Platonic perspective. This is less of an explicit concern in Plato's *Republic,* because the government it describes makes unrealistic assumptions about human nature— even for the best of us. The constraint on the philosopher-rulers is the idea of justice itself. To know what is just is to do what is just. Thus, once philosophers were located, they could be trusted to do what is right. This is the fundamental check of the *Republic,* and it has been reasonably criticized ever since for its sanguine approach to the nature of political power. Of course, as is often the case, Plato was his own greatest critic. By the time he wrote the *Laws,* he was keenly aware that no one could be trusted with the kind of power that Kallipolis invested in its rulers. This is why the city of Magnesia in the *Laws* is ruled by a radically different government. The essential function of the idea of justice remains the same. It warns against tyranny in both the *Republic* and the *Laws.* In the *Republic,* it warns against the dangers of concentrating power in the *wrong* hands. In the *Laws,* it warns against the dangers of concentrating power in *any* hands.

Rousseau is similarly motivated. For him, a tyrant is a ruler who governs "without regard for justice" (*SC,* 108/*OC,* III:423). The idea of justice is the most significant factor in evaluating whether tyranny exists. And, because socialized human beings inevitably have moral failings, it would be the height of foolishness to grant them unchecked power. Even the celebrated legislator, whom Rousseau singles out for his vast genius, is not capable of handling such authority, because ultimately he would create laws that would serve "as ministers to his passions . . . often only perpetuat[ing] his injustices" (70/ III:382). It is thus the Platonic idea of justice, ironically, that leads Rousseau away from the Platonic philosopher-rulers—though again, in doing so, he is following Plato's path set forth in the *Laws.*

SEVEN

KANT'S CONCEPTIONS OF THE GENERAL WILL:
THE FORMALIST INTERPRETATION

Jean-Jacques Rousseau has never been known as an especially abstract philosopher. In the *Emile*, he wrote, "The jargon of metaphysics has never led us to a single truth, and it has filled philosophy with absurdities of which one is ashamed as soon as one has stripped them of their big words" (274/*OC*, IV:577). Rousseau professed to be a simple man interested in nothing but simple virtue. Though this claim may strike some as false modesty, it is true in one respect: he rarely engaged in the extended discourses on epistemology and metaphysics that occupied so many of his contemporaries. More often, he ridiculed those who found such matters to be an obsession (*FD*, 4/*OC*, III:3). Nevertheless, in spite of himself, he on occasion expressed high esteem for metaphysicians. In praising Cato, Rousseau chose to call him "among . . . the most profound metaphysicians of his age" (*Emile*, 107/*OC*, IV:343).[1] Beyond this, he even acknowledged that his own system presupposed a metaphysics, even if he did not have the patience or training to sketch it out in any detail: "my business here is not producing treatises on metaphysics and morals or any course of study of any kind. It is sufficient for me to mark out the order and the progress of our sentiments and our knowledge relative to our constitution. Others will perhaps demonstrate what I only indicate here" (235/IV:522).

One individual would accept Rousseau's invitation to elaborate the metaphysical principles of his normative system: Immanuel Kant. That it was he should not be surprising. No less an authority than John Rawls says, "Kant sought to give a philosophic foundation to Rousseau's idea of the general will" (1971, 264).[2] Where Rousseau found reason to avoid discourses on metaphys-

---

1. Rousseau repeats this compliment when speaking of Plato, Malebranche, and Locke in the *Persifleur* (*OC*, IV:1111).

2. As George Armstrong Kelley states, "He [Kant] is, in effect, attributing to Rousseau . . . a 'metaphysics'" (1969, 100).

ics, Kant found reason to engage them. Indeed, he found metaphysics an indispensable part of normative philosophy. In the *Metaphysics of Morals,* he argued that "no moral principle is based, as people sometimes suppose, on any *feeling* whatsoever. Any such principle is really an obscurely thought *metaphysics* that is inherent in every man because of his rational disposition. . . . *thought* must go all the way back to the elements of metaphysics, without which no certitude or purity can be expected in the doctrine of virtue, nor indeed in any moving force" (510/*KGS,* 6:376). It would indeed be difficult to find a thinker more different from Rousseau in disposition. For Kant, morals and politics were impossible without metaphysics.

In spite of this obvious difference in philosophic temperament, the figures are nevertheless commonly linked (e.g., Schilpp [1938] 1960; Cassirer [1945] 1963, [1954] 1963; Rawls 1971; Riley 1982, 1983; Levine 1976; Velkley 1989; Seung 1993, 1994). The links drawn between Rousseau and Kant typically include their shared commitment to autonomy, virtue, and the rule of law. But perhaps the most significant tie is their shared employment of the general will. Although the general will was not Rousseau's own invention,[3] it is most closely associated with him. The entirety of his constructive political program is structured around it, and, in the words of Judith Shklar, "It conveys everything he most wanted to say" (1969, 184). Further, in the hands of Immanuel Kant, while the general will may be less spectacular, paradoxical, and dynamic, it also plays a highly significant role. It is a key element of Kant's politics and ethics, and he undoubtedly inherited much of his conception of it from Rousseau. We must thus push to understand Rawls's provocative but undeveloped claim that Kant sought to develop a philosophic foundation for Rousseau's general will.

This chapter aims to demonstrate not only that Kant's general will is an essential component of his thought but also that it is so important as to be given two independent lives. Early in his development, Kant borrows the general will from Rousseau, reinvents it for his critical thought, and eventually employs it in his mature work. The first, substantive version is reasonably faithful to Rousseau's conception; the second, formal, is largely Kant's own invention. The difficulties associated with Kant's invention, however, suggest that he never fully abandons the substantive account. Rather, it continues to lurk, sometimes posing as a formal principle. This chapter traces the life of the general will in Kant's thought, its relation to Rousseau, and its impact on the development of subsequent political philosophy.

3. See Riley (1986).

The lessons to be drawn from Kant's experiments with the general will are of particular interest to contemporary political thought. Variants of his formal account continue to play a large role in thinking about politics. Jürgen Habermas, for example, consciously models his program of discourse ethics on the formal understanding of Kant's general will. He even says that he is reformulating the categorical imperative (Habermas 1990, 67). In doing so, he specifies that his principles are formal, rather than substantive (1990, 93; 1993, 152). Habermas is hardly alone in his appeal to form and procedure (e.g., Cohen 1989; Fishkin 1992; Gregg 2003). As increasingly heterogeneous societies demand political cooperation, the apparent neutrality of formalism gains greater appeal.

The problem with this approach, however, may be apparent in the work of its very founder. Through a largely chronological examination of Kant's texts, we will explore the development of his theory of the general will. It begins as a reasonably straightforward appropriation of the substantive politics of Rousseau and Plato. In his next stage, he rejects the substantive account of the general will because of epistemological concerns: How can pure reason admit of intellectual intuition? This period culminates in the first formulation of the categorical imperative. Kant, however, subsequently has problems with this approach. What he gains in pure reason, he loses in substance. Without some version of intellectual intuition or substantive ideas, he cannot speak to moral and political matters in a meaningful way. This leads to his extended period of indecision—where he draws on both substantive and formal accounts of the general will without any coherent justification for the seemingly incompatible assumptions. If it is demonstrated here that the very founder of the formalist school expressed serious doubts about its probable success—and even in his most optimistic moments continued to make substantive appeals within a supposedly formalist program—it may be cause to reconsider the program itself. In this respect, we may do well to return to Kant's earlier Rousseauean formulation of the general will.

1. Preliminary Remarks on Substantive Versus Formalist Programs

Although the distinction between substantive and formalist programs is common in some literature, it does not always receive the attention it merits. This is unfortunate, because the distinction underlies so much contemporary political discourse. The fundamental difference between the two is that formalists aspire to present contentless principles, whereas the substantive theorists provide content by definition. Some examples should help clarify. In describing a law, we may do so either substantively or formally. Substantively, we may say that a law raised (or lowered) benefits for welfare recipients by x amount. Formally, we may say that the law was passed with a majority vote from both houses of Congress and the signature of the president. The first perspective describes the content of the law; the second, the procedure.

In political theory, one must choose between formal or substantive foundations. Plato, for example, has a substantive conception of justice. His definition from the *Republic* cannot be rendered formally and has material content (i.e., all ought to perform their tasks without interfering with those of others). Habermas, by contrast, suggests that justice is the consequence of following a set of procedures. On this view, justice itself has no a priori content. It is form. If we follow that form, we produce justice.

As a consequence, formal and substantive theorists speak in different ways. On the one hand, formal theorists emphasize procedure: What are the outlines of the procedure? How can we make sure that people follow the procedure? What happens if the procedure generates conflicting outcomes? Substantive theorists, on the other hand, emphasize material issues: What is right or wrong about tax reform? What is right or wrong about health care reform? What is right or wrong about welfare benefits? We can see differences of approach perhaps most clearly in constitutional issues. A formal theorist may say that racial segregation was illegitimate because it violated democratic procedures (see, for example, Ely 1980). A substantive theorist may say that racial discrimination was illegitimate because it was an insult to the dignity of human beings. Although the verdict may be the same in both cases, the reasoning is noticeably different. There are good reasons to turn to either mode of thinking, and, because of this, we find Kant indeed appealing to both.

2. The Birth of Kant's General Will: The Early Substantive Account

It is universally acknowledged that Kant held enormous respect for Rousseau as a moral philosopher. Kant—not a man given to ostentation—had only one adornment on the walls of his home: a portrait of Rousseau (Kuehn 2001, 272). People have long believed the perhaps apocryphal story (Kuehn 2001, 458 n. 153) that the only thing that could disturb Kant's remarkably regular daily constitutional was the arrival of Rousseau's *Emile,* for which he set everything aside until he had read and digested its central teachings. Beyond such anecdotes, Kant's own words suggest that his debt to the Genevan philosopher was profound.

> I am myself by inclination a seeker after truth. I feel a consuming thirst for knowledge and a restless passion to advance in it, as well as a satisfaction in every forward step. There was a time when I thought that this alone could constitute the honor of mankind, and I despised the rabble who know nothing. Rousseau set me right. This blind prejudice vanishes; I learned to respect human nature, and I should consider myself far more useless than the common laborer if I did not believe that this view could give worth to all others to establish the rights of man. (*Bemerkungen/KGS* 20:44)

This is scarcely the only tribute he paid to Rousseau. On another occasion, Kant placed him alongside Newton. Just as Newton was able to find order in the apparently chaotic natural universe, so Rousseau found it in the moral: "Rousseau was the first to discover beneath the varying forms human nature assumes, the deeply concealed essence of man and the hidden law in accordance with which Providence is justified by his observations" (Kant, *Fragments/KGS*, 8:630). In light of how central ethics became both to Kant's critical philosophy and to his personal life, it is difficult to underestimate the significance of his encounter with Rousseau.

2.1. KANT, MORAL SENSIBILITY, AND ROUSSEAU

Because Kant is primarily known today for his critical philosophy, it is sometimes forgotten that he had an extended flirtation with moral sense theory in his precritical career. Understanding this period of Kant's career helps contextualize his earliest formulations of the general will. In his *Prize Essay* (*Untersuchung über die Deutlichkeit der Grundsätze der natürlichen Theologie und der Moral* [1762]), he argues that moral obligation consists of both formal and substantive principles. The formal principles ("Realize the greatest perfection possible" and "Do not do that which can hinder the greatest possible perfection"), however, are empty by Kant's own admission. He writes, "just as nothing flowed from the first formal principle of our judgment of the true, where no material first grounds are given, so no particularly definite obligation flows from these two rules of the good, where no unprovable material principles of practical knowledge are bound with them" ([1762] 1968, 32–33/*KGS*, 2:299). To give the formal rules content, one must appeal to substantive principles.

These substantive principles, in turn, are supplied by moral sense, largely drawn from contemporary British moralists.

Although Kant was satisfied at this early stage of his career that these moral principles should be substantive, he did not long defend the notion that this substance should be derived from moral sense. This rejection came two years later in his *Observations on the Feeling of the Beautiful and the Sublime* (1764). As has been noted by T. K. Seung, in this period between the *Prize Essay* and the *Beautiful and Sublime,* "Rousseau's *Emile* and *Social Contract* arrived in Königsberg and gripped Kant's attention much more intensely than moral sense ever did" (Seung 1993, 145).[4] It is thus not surprising to see Genevan footprints here for the first time in the work of the Prussian.

Kant's early reflections on aesthetics are governed by two concepts: the beautiful and the sublime. The beautiful is that which evokes pleasure and enjoyment, such as beholding the pleasures of flower-strewn meadows, valleys with winding brooks, and the like. He saves his most reverent remarks, though, for the sublime. The sublime is accompanied by a sense of awe. This includes the feelings inspired by the sight of snow-capped mountains, raging storms, and tall oak trees casting long, lonely shadows. Most awe-inspiring of all is true virtue, according to Kant.

To demonstrate the failure of moral sense theory, he focuses on two supposed virtues of the moral sense theorists: complaisance and sympathy. Complaisance—the desire to get along well with others—certainly has its role in the social world. It is a generally beneficent inclination that leads to cooperation, good will, and good cheer. The problem, however, is that it also has the capacity to foster idleness, drunkenness, and dishonesty (Kant [1764] 1968, 59). It fails as a moral principle, because we are prepared to employ vice in misguided quests of camaraderie or friendship.

Even more significant is the treatment of sympathy. That sympathy should have been on his mind in 1764 is no surprise to Kant's biographers, in light of the arrival of Rousseau's works in his library. Sympathy first appears in Rousseau's *Discourse on Inequality,* where it—along with an inclination toward self-preservation—regulates the behavior of human beings in the state of nature. There, sympathy functions in the place of laws, mores, and virtue to regulate interaction with others, speaking to all in its irresistible "sweet voice." Rousseau is careful to specify, however, that whatever beneficent effects may follow from this inclination, we should not confuse it with morality itself. It is, in essence, premoral. In the *Emile,* Rousseau attempts to harness

4. Kant's first known reference to Rousseau is in a notice written February 10, 1764.

the positive force of sympathy or compassion (*pitié*) to foster the common good. It cannot, however, do so on its own. It is a natural passion in need of guidance: "To prevent pity from degenerating into a weakness, it must . . . be generalized and extended to the whole of mankind. Then one yields to it only insofar as it accords with justice" (*Emile*, 253/*OC*, IV:548).[5] The task of Emile's tutor is to effect just this disposition.[6]

We find a remarkably similar discussion in Kant's treatment of sympathy. As was the case with Rousseau, it is for him a "good-natured passion." Nevertheless, as is the case with all such sentiments, it is also "weak and always blind."[7] Though well-intentioned, our sympathy can lead to unfortunate results. This inclination can lead us to sympathize with scoundrels, promote incompetents, or marry badly. This is why, according to Kant's *Beautiful and Sublime*, it must be supplemented with and checked by principle, specifically, justice:

> [W]hen universal affection toward the human species has become a principle within you to which you always subordinate your actions, then love toward the needy one still remains, but now, from a higher standpoint, it has been placed in its true relation to your total duty. Universal affection is a ground of your interest in his plight, but also of the justice by whose rule you must now forbear this action. Now as soon as this feeling has arisen to its proper universality, it has become sublime. ([1764] 1968, 58)

One must take the innate feeling within, universalize it, and regard it not as sentiment but as principle. Again, the comparison with Rousseau shows remarkable similarity: "*justice* and *goodness* are not merely abstract words . . . but are true affections of the soul enlightened by reason, and are hence only an ordered development of our primitive affections" (*Emile*, 235/*OC*, IV:522).[8]

---

5. An excellent discussion of the potential dangers of pity in the social sphere can be found in Boyd (2004).

6. This theme is elaborated in Marks (2006).

7. The dangers of such approaches were first diagnosed by Plato: "A system of morality which is based on relative emotional values is a mere illusion, a thoroughly vulgar conception which has nothing sound in it and nothing true" (*Phaedo*, 69b).

8. The similarity between Kant here and Rousseau has been previously noted in Seung (1994). There is one important respect, however, in which Kant and Rousseau diverge. Whereas Rousseau suggests that justice is refined sympathy, Kant asserts complete ontological independence of sympathy and justice, even if they work together very closely in practice. Rousseau's ontology is complicated by a contradicting remark in the *Social Contract:* that justice emanates "from reason alone" (II.6/*OC*, III:378). So Rousseau actually provides two accounts: in the *Emile*, justice is simply an outgrowth of sympathy, and in the *Social Contract*, justice is ontologically independent of sympathy and serves as a measure by which one can direct sympathy in civil society. The latter is ultimately more consistent

Thus, for both Rousseau and Kant, although we have moral sentiments, they cannot be the source of a genuinely principled morality. Sentiments incline us toward some action, but they cannot serve as moral imperatives. Rather, we must instead make appeals to the substantive idea of justice, which in turn serves as the reference point for the shaping and ordering of the moral sentiments.

2.2. EARLIEST APPEARANCE OF THE GENERAL WILL IN KANT'S WORK

Although the *Prize Essay* and the *Beautiful and Sublime* offer important reflections on the nature of Kant's normative principles, it is not until his *Dreams of a Spirit-Seer* (1766) that he explicitly connects these concepts to the general will. A discussion of Emanuel Swedenborg and his alleged ability to communicate with the spirit world seems an unlikely place in which to refine the central tenets of one's moral and political philosophy, but this is precisely what Kant did. While the primary task of his *Dreams of a Spirit-Seer* is indeed to ridicule Swedenborg's claims and to develop a workable theory of the soul, he also develops a moral psychology. Kant identifies two forces capable of moving the human soul. These are self-love and altruism ([1766] 1992, 321/ *KGS,* 2:334).[9] These two forces are at war with one another in an endless contest for control over our will.

The force of egoism requires no elaboration for Kant. It lies within our hearts and is extraordinarily compelling. What is more significant is his discussion of altruism. He locates the origins of this force "outside the heart. . . . they [the feelings of altruism] rather cause the tendencies of our impulses to shift the focal point of their union *outside ourselves* and to locate it in other rational beings" ([1766] 1992, 321/*KGS,* 2:334). At first he appears to be referring to the need we have for approval from others, the same desire condemned as *amour-propre* by Rousseau. Following Rousseau, though, Kant dismisses the mere desire for approval from others as "wrong-headed and misguided" (321/ 2:334). Altruism is, for him, far more robust:

> When we relate external things to our need, we cannot do so without at the same time feeling ourselves bound and limited by a certain

---

with Kant's view. It is also more logically sound. The specific view advocated in the *Emile* is moderately troubling, because an outgrowth of an object cannot, strictly speaking, inform the object itself. It needs an external reference point. Further, Rousseau says elsewhere in the *Emile* that justice *is* this reference point (235). It is unlikely that Rousseau was aware of this problem, especially given his admitted impatience with metaphysical matters.

9. Notably, these two forces are reminiscent of Rousseau's two elements of human nature in the state of nature.

sensation; this sensation draws our attention to the fact that an alien will, so to speak, is operative within ourselves, and that our own inclination needs external assent as its condition. A secret power forces us to direct our will towards the well-being of others or regulate it in accordance with the will of another, although this often happens contrary to our will and in strong opposition to our selfish inclination. The focal point at which the lines which indicate the direction of our drives converge, is therefore not merely to be found within us; there are, in addition, other forces which move us and which are to be found in the will of others outside ourselves. This is the source from which the moral impulses take their rise. These impulses often incline us to act against the dictates of self-interest. I refer to the strong law of obligation and the weaker law of benevolence. Each of these laws extort from us many a sacrifice, and although self-interested inclinations from time to time overrule them both, these two laws, nonetheless, never fail to assert reality in human nature. As a result, we recognize that, in our most secret motives, we are dependent upon the *rule of the general will* [*des allgemeinen Willens*]. It is this rule which confers upon the world of all thinking beings its *moral unity* and invests it with a systematic constitution, drawn up in accordance with purely spiritual laws. We sense within ourselves a constraining of our will to harmonize with the general will. (322/2:334–35)

Although Kant describes the general will as a "feeling," he emphasizes that it is not a feeling, strictly speaking. While we do "feel" the general will pressing on us, it is not itself merely a feeling. The feeling is rather a manifestation of the will that has its own existence independent of our selfish interests.

The presence of the general will in Kant's theory is now beyond question. Its ontology and origins, however, remain mysterious. What is the general will? How do we acquire knowledge of it? Kant admitted that he could not answer these questions and began pushing his work in a direction that he hoped would provide an answer (Seung 1994, 24–28).

2.3. THE *INAUGURAL DISSERTATION, FIRST CRITIQUE,* AND SUBSTANTIVE PRINCIPLES

The next fifteen years saw Kant take up several of the most important questions concerning the foundations of his ethics and politics. In this period, he came to embrace Platonic ideas as the substance of his foundational principles, and he gives little hint of the formalist period to follow. And, although his main task in the *Inaugural Dissertation* (1770) is the affirmation of a dualistic metaphysics, he is also concerned with ethics, specifically the principle of ethical perfection. He had originally addressed perfection in his *Prize Essay* of 1762. There he claimed that the principle of perfection was formal, and thus by itself necessarily empty of content. The formal principle of perfection therefore had to appeal to a higher principle. At the time he located this in moral sense theory. By 1770, however, he had already rejected moral sense theory in his *Beautiful and Sublime.* He reemphasizes this rejection in the *Inaugural Dissertation:* "Epicurus, who reduced its criteria to the sense of pleasure or pain, is very rightly blamed, together with certain moderns, who have followed him to a certain extent afar, such as Shaftesbury and his supporters" (Kant [1770] 1992, 388/*KGS,* 2:396). He therefore had to find another place to rest the substantive principle of moral perfection. He finds it in substantive Platonic ideas: "The *maximum of perfection* is nowadays called the ideal, while for Plato it was called the idea (as in the case of his Idea of the state)" (388/ 2:396). A possible source of Kant's principle of perfectionism is none other than Rousseau, who in the *Second Discourse* characterizes the capacity for perfection as a uniquely human attribute.[10]

T. K. Seung suggests that this is a relocation of the founding principles of Kant's normative philosophy—that Kant moved them from the general will in the *Dreams of a Spirit-Seer* to Platonic ideas in the *Inaugural Dissertation* (1994, 30). If we assume that Rousseau's conception of the general will is itself an articulation of the Platonic idea of justice, however, this transition need not appear abrupt. We can read Kant as linking the two substantive notions together at the foundation of his normative thought. Rousseau's general will becomes the medium through which substantive ideas are transmitted.

Although he does not offer an elaboration of substantive ideas in the *Inaugural Dissertation* beyond noting that they are Platonic ideas, he does so later in the *Critique of Pure Reason,* or *First Critique.* He argues that Plato's substantive normative ontology is correct in almost all respects. What draws him to Plato is his grasp of the rational nature of morals and politics. Reasserting his rejection of moral sense theory, which is subject to contingency, he says that Plato properly abstracts ideas from all experience, without which virtue

---

10. It must be noted, however, that Rousseau does not view perfectionism as always producing positive results. Perfection may be either moral (which is good) or of particular talents (which may be bad).

would be "something that changes according to time and circumstance, an ambiguous monstrosity not admitting of the formation of any rule." Appeals to experience in such contexts now strike him as "vulgar," "the mother of illusion" (Kant, *FC,* A315/B371, A316/B373, A318–19/B375), strongly echoing Plato's rejection of sense as a source of knowledge (*Phaedo,* 65b, 83ab), as well as Rousseau's claim that foundational principles are acquired without the benefit of sensory input (*Reveries,* 59/*OC,* I:1021). Rather, the only stable, transcendent, and true foundations of normative thought lie abstracted from all experience. Kant emphasizes, however, that this does not render them mystical or chimerical apparitions. Although they originate elsewhere from the senses, they "are by no means mere fictions of the brain" (*FC,* A314/B371).

Kant defends Platonic ideas against Johann Jakob Brucker, who ridiculed Plato for his assertion of the relevance of the ideas to politics (political Platonism). Had Plato been alive to defend himself against such attacks, Kant suggests, he might have articulated the following principle: "A constitution allowing *the greatest possible human freedom* in accordance with laws by which *the freedom of each is made to be consistent with that of all others*—I do not speak of the greatest happiness, for this will follow of itself—is at any rate a necessary idea, which must be taken as fundamental not only in first projecting a constitution but in all its laws" (*FC,* A316/B373). This idea of a constitution is the clearest statement yet of Kant's commitment to a substantive foundation for his politics. And in doing so, he clearly attaches himself to both Plato and Rousseau. As Dieter Henrich has remarked, Rousseau was likely the vehicle through which Kant arrived at Plato: "Kant owes to Rousseau the correct understanding of the word which he will use in the future to denote the projection of a maxim: the Platonic word 'Idea'" (1963, 431). That this attribution is correct is confirmed by Kant himself: "Rousseau's Emile and the education to be given him is a true *Idea* of reason" (Kant, quoted in Heinrich 1963, 431).[11]

It would thus seem that Kant is—at least in the normative realm—a Platonist with a strong Rousseauean edge. He agrees with Plato that substantive ideas are necessary for grounding ethics and politics; he elaborates in a Rousseauean vein that this idea includes a commitment to the greatest freedom possible; and he declares Plato an "illustrious philosopher," one whose priority of substantive ideas "calls for respect and imitation" (*FC,* A314/B370, A318/B375). Before one declares Kant an unabashed Platonist, however, one must confront certain complicating factors.

---

11. Velkley (1989, 196 n. 13) has already observed this connection.

First, although Kant speaks enthusiastically of his Platonism in the normative realm, he strongly cautions against applying these lessons in speculative reason. Platonism as applied to mathematics and science is mysticism (*FC*, A316/B372; Kant [1796] 1993, 63/*KGS*, 8:398). This position is consistently held throughout Kant's critical period and beyond.

Second is the mysterious origin of these ideas in Kant. For Plato, the ideas are accessed as intellectual intuitions (Seung 1996, 232). Rousseau similarly suggests that the ideas are written on the heart ("State of War," 166/*OC*, III:602; *Emile*, 66/*OC*, IV:286, 289/IV:598; *Reveries*, 25/*OC*, I:1021; *Dialogues*, 242/*OC*, I:971). Kant, however, rules out this possibility in his *Inaugural Dissertation:* "No intuition of things intellectual . . . is given to man" (§10). He repeats this assertion in the *Critique of Pure Reason:* "intellectual intuition is not [a faculty] that . . . we possess, and of which we cannot comprehend even the possibility" (*FC*, A250/B307). The only intuitions he acknowledges are sensible ones from the phenomenal world, but these have no relevance for morals and politics.

It is easy to understand Kant's discomfort with intellectual intuitions. As he says of the acquisition of the intellectual intuition of speculative ideas, they appear "mystical"—hardly the label one wants in an age dominated by the marvelous new discoveries in science. The problem for Kant both in the *Inaugural Dissertation* and the *First Critique* is epistemic—uncovering the access to the ideas he clearly believes to exist. If substantive ideas are "by no means mere fictions of the brain," then where do they come from? Kant's struggle in answering this question dictates the subsequent development of his normative thought. As will be demonstrated, he derives two conceptions of the general will—each of which provides a unique answer to this question. The fact that he could never decisively choose, however, suggests the difficulties inherent in each. The problem he had in reconciling his epistemic foundations (i.e., his desire to exclude intellectual intuitions) with its substantive content (i.e., his desire to have an agreeable set of moral and political propositions) would prove to be one of the greatest tensions in his corpus.

3. Two Versions of the General Will

One problem with intuitionism is its lack of determinacy (Seung 1993, 5–8). It is easy enough to advocate political equality, for example. It is less easy to articulate the precise reasons why we should have equality under some circumstances (e.g., the application of rules in a game of chess) and not others (e.g., criminal laws discriminating against people on the basis of their tendency to harm others). The intuitionist might simply explain, "Because that's obvious—can't everyone see that?" This, however, is an unsatisfying answer. Because intuitions are by their very nature indeterminate, according to John Rawls, "[t]he only way . . . to dispute intuitionism is to set forth the recognizably ethical criteria that account for the weights which . . . we think appropriate to give to the plurality of principles" (1971, 39). Rawls, of course, is one of the giant Kantians of the twentieth century, and it is in this respect, perhaps, that he is closest to his model. Nearly two hundred years before Rawls, Kant decided that given the epistemic problem with intellectual intuitions, he would provide an alternative foundation for his normative principles. This led to the invention of his program of *normative formalism.* The problem, however, was that his reservations from the *Prize Essay*—that formal principles were empty and in need of supplementation in the form of substantive principles—never fully dissipated. This meant that he simultaneously developed and employed two conceptions of the general will. The first one is formal and is best represented in the *Groundwork of the Metaphysics of Morals* (1785). The second one is substantive and had its birth in the *Inaugural Dissertation* and *First Critique.* It is best represented in his later work by the *Rechtslehre* [*Doctrine of Right*]. This division, however, is slightly artificial. Because Kant never decisively chooses one conception over another, they are both employed in most of his writings on ethics and politics. This accounts for the wide variance in interpretation of the categorical imperative and his political principles. Some (e.g., O'Neill 1975; Korsgaard 1985; Galvin 1999) view his program as largely or even purely formalistic. Others (e.g., Seung 1993, 1994; Riley 1993) find pervasive substantive elements. Segments of his writings confirm both interpretations. Reading across his oeuvre, we can see how this can be the case: Kant operates with two conceptions of the general will, never ultimately choosing one over another.

3.1. THE FORMALISTIC ACCOUNT OF THE GENERAL WILL

As already noted, Kant expressed great suspicion concerning intellectual intuitions. This line of thought reaches its fruition in the *Groundwork* of 1785. Access to such intuitions is here labeled "heteronomous" (*Groundwork,* 89–90/*KGS,* 4:441). Understanding heteronomy requires its contrast with autonomy. Rather than grounding access to moral principles in ideas, Kant instead appeals to legislative autonomy. As was so often the case in his work, he draws this notion from Rousseau (Cassirer [1945] 1963, 31–32; Beck 1960,

200; Rawls 1971, 264). Rousseau was frequently given to insisting on the autonomy of our acts in order to regard them as moral. One of the most valuable achievements of the social contract, according to Rousseau, is the guaranteeing of this freedom: it "makes man truly the master of himself; for the impulsion of mere appetite is slavery, and obedience to the law one has prescribed to oneself is freedom" (*SC*, 54/*OC*, III:365).[12] This autonomy is not merely a happy consequence of civic institutions. It is rather a necessary prerequisite to the very formation of the general will. There can be no general will unless we are free from the constraints of passions, impulses, inclinations, factions, servitude, and tyranny. In this sense, Rousseau's understanding of freedom is significantly different from that of Hobbes, who views freedom only as the absence of external restraint.[13]

Autonomy would take center stage in Kant's *Groundwork* and is essential in forming his supreme principle of morality. The principle of autonomy "must be viewed as . . . giving a law to itself" (*Groundwork*, 81/*KGS*, 4:431). As is the case with Rousseau, this act of self-legislation makes the law binding. No one (or thing) can legislate for us—this is at the very core of his notion of autonomy. Each individual can be understood as sovereign, because he is the author of his own laws: "He cannot, however, hold the position of sovereign merely by the maxims of his will but only in case he is a completely independent being, without needs and unlimited resources adequate to his will" (83/4:434).

Kant explicitly understands the autonomous will's role as formal, thus reversing his earlier claims that formal principles are empty: "since it must . . . be determined by something, it must be determined by the formal principle of volition as such when an action is done from duty, where every material principle has been withdrawn from it" (*Groundwork*, 55/*KGS*, 4:400). As Roger Sullivan points out, for Kant "the ultimate criterion must be completely formal" (1989, 151). This formal principle is the categorical imperative, which makes its first appearance in the *Groundwork*: "*I ought never to act except in such a way that I could also will that my maxim should become a universal law*" (57/4:402). Applying this imperative, Kant claims we can generate answers to all moral questions, including his famous examples of suicide, false promises, failing to cultivate one's talents, and assisting others in need (73–75/4:421–23).

---

12. This passage is cited in Rawls (1971, 264); see also Rousseau (*Emile*, 445/*OC*, IV:818; *Reveries*, 51/*OC*, I:1053).

13. The distinction of these two freedoms is famously characterized in Isaiah Berlin's "Two Concepts of Liberty" (1969).

In this first formulation, he presents a purely formal principle. Its purported essence lies not in substance, but rather in the principle of noncontradiction. As long as a maxim can be willed or conceived universally without contradiction, according to Kant, it is morally acceptable.

This formulation is generally consistent with the formulation found in the *Critique of Practical Reason* (*Second Critique*): "So act that the maxim of your will could always hold at the same time as a principle in a giving of universal law" (Kant [1788] 1996, 164/*KGS*, 5:30). There is only one significant difference between this formulation and the first one of the *Groundwork*. In the *Groundwork*, the word "will" is employed as a verb. In the *Second Critique*, it is used as a noun [*des Willens*]. What remains common to both, however, is the employment of two words. The first, as has just been mentioned, is a form of the word "will." The second is the word *allgemeine*, which can be translated as either "universal" or "general." In both the *Groundwork* and the *Second Critique*, Kant insists that the will must be consistent with the *allgemeine Gesetzgebung*. The most common mode of translating this term has been "universal law." It is equally valid, however, to translate it as "general law."

The same word (*allgemeine*) is employed for the general will (*allgemeine Wille*). These facts help clarify a point only previously hinted at in the literature (e.g., Beck 1960; Rawls 1971). This is the relationship between the categorical imperative and the general will. Both are indeed wills, and further, both are wills with reference to the *allgemeine*, or the general. In this context, we can now appreciate Rawls's remark that "Kant sought to give a philosophical foundation to Rousseau's idea of the general will" (1971, 264). This is, at least, Kant's appropriation of Rousseau's general will in the context of his formalism.

The formal principle, in turn, is contrasted with what Kant calls "material principles." Material principles are everything not formal. The most obvious material principle Kant rejects is happiness, because it is obviously contingent and incapable of being captured in a law. But material principles extend also to those based on God, perfection, utility, ideas, and indeed anything not generated by a purely formal and autonomous will. The employment of all material principles constitutes a heteronomy of the will. Thus, we see that Kant's ethics have turned 180 degrees, insofar as he relied on ideas (now classified as "heteronomous") as the foundation of his ethics and politics in the *Inaugural Dissertation* and *First Critique*. Of course, one could also claim that the turn was far less than 180 degrees, because he had long expressed skepticism of intellectual intuitions, the source of these ideas. Such is the interpretive liberty granted by Kant's indecision.

This indecisiveness remains present in the *Groundwork*. One sees a hint of it in his discussion of the rational principles of heteronomy. In his discussion of the "Division of All Possible Principles of Morality Taken from Heteronomy Assumed as the Basic Concept," Kant separates heteronomous principles into empirical and rational categories. Empirical principles include moralities grounded in happiness, a particularly popular theory among Enlightenment thinkers such as Helvétius, d'Holbach, and Diderot. As he had done many times before, Kant quickly dismisses the approach as "most objectionable because it bases morality on incentives that undermine it and destroy its sublimity, . . . obliter[ating] the specific difference between virtue and vice" (*Groundwork*, 90–91/*KGS*, 4:442).

Rational heteronomous principles, on the other hand, are further divided into theological conceptions and those of perfection. Kant quickly dismissed the former as "dreadful representations of power and vengefulness . . . directly opposed to morality" (*Groundwork*, 91/*KGS*, 4:443).[14] Principles of perfection, however, are treated with far more care and respect. Even though he ultimately rejects this approach, "it at least withdraws the decision of the question from sensibility and brings it to the court of pure reason" (91[4:443]). Part of his rejection of rational principles of heteronomy (which he did in fact embrace in the *Inaugural Dissertation* and the *First Critique*) was based on their indeterminacy. This perhaps provides us with yet another clue to why he here favored the first formulation of the categorical imperative. It is nothing if not determinate, and in this particular sense we can appreciate the formal categorical imperative's advance over Rousseau's general will. Rousseau never presents his ultimate political principle as having determinate content (e.g., *SC*, 62/*OC*, III:374), and the attempts he makes to clarify it (e.g., *SC*, 60/*OC*, III:371) tend to obfuscate more than enlighten.

Kant's improvements, however, do not come without a cost. While he supplies practical philosophy with determinacy, he simultaneously threatens its relevance. He was aware of this danger as early as his *Prize Essay*, as already noted. Given this, it is highly unlikely that Kant was oblivious to the type of critique on which Hegel would subsequently build his reputation. The formality of the first formulation of the categorical imperative leads to some tricky problems. In particular, the formal test provides no way of distinguishing moral maxims from morally trivial or irrelevant ones, such as Onora

---

14. It is worth noting that Kant appears, in this respect, to be following Rousseau's Savoyard Vicar, who also rejected the negative sanctions of God as inconsistent with the principles of morality (*Emile*, 282/*OC*, IV:588–89).

O'Neill's example: "I will sell lettuce to others but not buy it" (1975, 68). This clearly fails the test of universalization, but would scarcely strike anyone as immoral. The only way in which one can vindicate the maxim of selling lettuce but not buying (and perhaps more relevantly to the rest of the world, the opposite and equally failing maxim of buying lettuce but not selling it) is to appeal to a substantive moral intuition (Seung 1994, 102).

That Kant might have been aware of the need for substantive norms even in his *Groundwork* is made apparent by his second and third formulations of the categorical imperative. The second formulation reads, *"So act that you use humanity, whether in your own person or in the person of any other, always at the same time as an end, never merely as a means"* (*Groundwork*, 80/*KGS*, 4:429). The third formulation of the categorical imperative instructs us to "act in accordance with the maxims of a member giving universal laws for a merely possible kingdom of ends" (88/4:439). As has been noted elsewhere (Seung 1994, 111, 113), neither of these formulations—which, Kant asserts, are essentially the same as the first—is remotely formal. Rather, they are strikingly substantive. Thus, contrary to his own professions, Kant's advances in ethics are accompanied by immediate reversions to his previous substantive commitments. His most significant students of the twentieth century face the same problem. Both Rawls and Habermas provide formal procedures, which generate political principles. Rawls operates within the original position, a procedure, to be certain. But this procedure itself is informed by a substantive commitment to the values of his own political community. Habermas likewise offers a procedure to generate political principles—the ideal speech situation. And, as with Rawls, his procedure cannot remain purely formal but must rest on substantive political values—specifically those of liberty and equality (Williams 1999).

3.2. THE SUBSTANTIVE ACCOUNT OF THE GENERAL WILL

Although we can read the first formulation of the categorical imperative as a version of the general will, it is fair to say that Kant does not himself refer to it as such. He goes nearly twenty years between references to an *allgemeine Wille* after his brief discussion of it in the *Dreams of a Spirit-Seer*. Its return comes in his essay "On the Common Saying: That May Be Correct in Theory, But It Is of No Use in Practice" (1793). This time, however, the concept is here to stay, as it recurs over and over from this point forward in his writings. It is also notable that "Theory and Practice," as well as his subsequent political thought, comes several years after his formalistic revolution of the

1780s. This perhaps gave him time to reconsider the foundations of practical philosophy in addition to the meaning of the general will.

Its reemergence comes specifically in section 2 of "Theory and Practice" in his discussion of what constitutes legitimate law. If a law is to be rightful, according to Kant, it must be the will of the "entire people [*gesammten Volks*]" ([1793] 1996, 295/*KGS*, 8:294). This is because no person could do himself wrong.[15] Similarly, no people would do themselves wrong. It is at this juncture that he returns to his Rousseauean language. Just as Rousseau eliminates the particular wills of individuals from having a role in legitimate sovereign laws, so, too, does Kant: "hence no particular will [*besondere Wille*] can be legislative for a commonwealth" (295/8:295).[16] Rousseau's original contract is likewise dependent on the general will (see *SC*, 52, 57, 95, 106, 121, 124/*OC*, III:363, 368, 409, 421, 437, 441). Legitimate law can come only from what Kant explicitly calls, in "Theory and Practice," the "general (united) will [*allgemeinen (vereinigten) Volkswillen*]" ([1793] 1996, 295/*KGS*, 8:295). The first law formed by this general will is what Kant terms the *original contract.*

As has been noted by Patrick Riley and others (Riley 1982, 125; Williams 1983, 183), Kant's social contract is unique. His original contract, derived from the general will,[17] is an idea (*Idee*) (Kant [1793] 1996, 296, 298, 301/*KGS*, 8:297, 299, 302; [1795] 1996, 318/*KGS*, 8:344; *MM*, 459/*KGS*, 6:316).[18] The consent in the contract is therefore hypothetical rather than real. Riley notes some of the benefits of conceiving the social contract in this way. Whereas others must rely on coercion, trickery, or deceit to realize their actual empirical consent, Kant's understanding of the contract as an idea allows him to avoid these difficulties. As Riley suggests, people can actually consent to anything. Political history is full of consent to the most noxious doctrines conceivable. Ideal consent, on the other hand, frees people from the abuses both of tyrants and of their own misguided temptations. Thus, Riley concludes, "this hypotheti-

15. I employ the masculine pronoun here because Kant explicitly excludes women from the rank of full citizen.

16. Kant repeats this idea in "Toward a Perpetual Peace" ([1795] 1996, 324 *KGS*, [8:352]).

17. From this point through the end of the chapter, I will group Kant's phrases "general will" (*allgemeine Wille*) and "united will" (*vereinigte Wille*) together, because Kant appears to use them synonymously. One piece of evidence suggesting this interpretation is that Kant says, in "Theory and Practice," that the original contract is derived from the general will ([1793] 1996, *KGS*, 8:295) and from the united will of the people (8:297). One should not confuse Kant's united will (the general will) with Rousseau's will of all (the will of the people without regard to ideas).

18. Seung notes that the idea of the original contract is merely one of many ideas Kant employs throughout his mature work (1994, 131).

cal consent . . . can restrict abuses in a way that actual consent might not" (1982, 127).[19]

The general will has four primary functions in Kant's mature work: (1) shaping the original contract and the constitution ([1793] 1996, 295/KGS, 8:295); (2) informing the legislative authority (MM, 457/KGS, 6:314); (3) informing the executive authority (470/6:328); and (4) serving as sovereign (479/6:339). It is obvious that these closely parallel those outlined by Rousseau. Rousseau likewise argues that the general will must shape the constitution (SC, 50/OC, III:361), inform the legislature (115/III:430), inform the executive (85/III:399), and serve as sovereign (57/III:368). These are the primary functions of the general will for Rousseau. Thus, when we read elsewhere that the general will is "central" (Dent 1992, 123) to Rousseau's teachings, it does not seem unreasonable to conclude that this is also the case with respect to Kant's political doctrines. After all, especially in a pre-Weberian era prior to the consciousness of an extensive bureaucracy, where would political power reside other than in the areas specified by Rousseau and Kant? In both thinkers, law and government are unthinkable without the general will. Laws are, for Kant, mere articulations of the general will. Ruling must subsequently be guided and policed by the general will: "For the head of state can never make a decision . . . which the united will of the people would not make" (MM, 470/ KGS, 6:328). If rulers exceed their limits, it is the general will that informs us of the transgression. In these respects, the general will is indisputably a central element of Kant's political theory.

Understanding the ontological nature of Kant's general will, however, is far trickier than adumbrating its functions. Or, I should say, it is tricky as long as one is committed to reconciling it with his formalism. Of all the virtues Riley rightly attributes to Kant's employment of ideas, consistency should not be one of them. That the general will is an idea seems easy enough to

19. Although Riley's point is extremely important and insightful in understanding Kant, there is a sense in which it might be considered slightly uncharitable to Rousseau, who also crucially relies on ideas. Whereas Rousseau does in fact require actual consent, as Riley suggests, it is not true that the people can consent to *anything*. They can only consent to those doctrines that are consistent with the idea of justice (SC, 62/OC, III:374). Thus, Rousseau has anticipated the problem that Kant's original contract purports to resolve. In fact, one might even argue that requiring actual consent in addition to the employment of ideas gives the people a double protection against the abuses that concern both Rousseau and Kant. The difference between Rousseau and Kant in this respect is substantially the difference between John Rawls and Jürgen Habermas. Following Kant, Rawls asserts that the original position is not necessarily a real circumstance or historical event. Habermas, in making the case for his ideal speech situation, dismisses Rawls's theory as resorting to the "fictitious" (Habermas [1983] 1990, 198).

establish, even though Kant never expressly identifies it as such. First, the general will is the source of the original contract, itself an idea. Second, Kant tells us that the general will is given a priori ([1795] 1996, 345/*KGS,* 8:378). Third, it is unlikely that it originates from the expressed will of the people (such as Rousseau's "will of all"), because Kant is decidedly opposed to raw democratic rule, which he calls "despotic" and is in fact "a contradiction of the general will with itself" ([1795] 1996, 324/*KGS,* 8:352).[20] Fourth, Kant tells us that the commonwealth, which requires the general will for its formation, is based on the "idea of a constitution" (Kant [1798] 1991, 187). The idea of a constitution and the general will appear here synonymous.

The general will, then, is evidently a substantive idea. Beyond this, it appears to be a Platonic idea:

> All forms of state are based on the idea of a constitution which is compatible with the natural rights of man, so that those who obey the law should also act as a unified body of legislators. And if we accordingly think of the commonwealth in terms of the concepts of pure reason, it may be called a Platonic *ideal* (*respublica noumenon*), which is not an empty figment of the imagination, but the eternal norm for all civil constitutions whatsoever, and a means of ending all wars. (Kant [1798] 1991, 187)[21]

This, however, raises the difficulty noted above. How can the idea of the general will be reconciled with Kant's earlier work? The answer is that it both can and cannot. It depends on which Kant one is reading. If one is reading the *Inaugural Dissertation* and the *First Critique,* it appears consistent. In both these works, he cites the existence of substantive ideas and their necessity for practical philosophy, in addition to their Platonic origins. If, on the other hand, one is reading the *Groundwork* or *Second Critique,* it appears irreconcilable. This is because ideas are substantive, as opposed to formal, entities (Seung 1994, 135). Further, he gives no indication of the source of his ideas. The obvious source of ideas would seem to be intellectual intuition, but he closed off this route early in his career and never expressly recanted this view.

Many Kant scholars hold that his foundational principles remain largely coherent and consistent throughout his work. This view is sensible to the extent that Kant appears to believe this himself on occasion. In spite of his

20. Kant also calls democracy despotic in the *Rechtslehre* (*MM,* 479/*KGS,* 6:339).
21. The theme of Kant's Platonism is most extensively developed in Riley (1993), Seung (1994), and Fistioc (2002).

many references to substantive ideas in his later work, he suggests on occasion that his system is perfectly formalistic. Consider his argument against rebellion. He rejects revolution as a political option in the *Rechtslehre* on the grounds that it is "self-contradictory" by virtue of a nonruler's attempt to exercise ruler functions. This is indeed a formal criterion of right.[22] Lewis White Beck, however, dismisses the argument as trivial because it merely boils down to a "point of boring obviousness" that there can be no legal right to revolution (1974, 414). Perhaps, following Beck's cue, there is then another reason that Kant might have objected to revolution. He provides this in "Theory and Practice." Here he notes that revolution is occasioned not merely by self-contradiction, but also by "anarchy . . . with all the horrors [*Greueln*] that are at least possible by means of it" ([1793] 1996, 300/*KGS*, 8:302). This passage is suggestive. Although rebellion may violate the principle of noncontradiction, it also introduces the substantive ideas of "anarchy" and "horror," appealing to our intuition that we have a moral obligation to avoid them. All this is to suggest that, even where Kant appears to be formalistic, he is pulled at the same time by substance.

His employment of substantive ideas generates certain interpretive difficulties, but one can also see what drew him to them in the first place. Tracing his thought back to the *Prize Essay*, Kant was clearly of the opinion that formal mechanisms were in themselves insufficient to generate the powerful doctrines necessary for normative philosophy. This view, of course, was by no means unique to Kant. It was later articulated by Hegel and continues to be held by many to this day (e.g., Seung 1993; Taylor 1993; Williams 1999). Restating what Kant said in 1762, Charles Taylor claims, "Procedural [formal] theories seem to me to be incoherent, or, better put, that to be made coherent, they require restatement in substantive form" (1993, 349). Kant's endless flirtation with substantive formulations of his general will suggests that this lesson was never very far from his mind. Indeed, his last work suggests that he may have been ready to accept intellectual intuitions with, perhaps, an eye to grounding ideas.[23] Of this, however, we cannot be certain, because it is unclear whether Kant was elaborating a new approach consciously opposed to his crit-

22. Kant employs similarly formal arguments in the cases of courts of equity (*MM*, 391/*KGS*, 6:234–35) and violations of the separation of powers (460/6:316–17).

23. "The understanding begins with self-perception (*apperceptio*) and with this an outer and inner intuition are joined, and the subject transforms itself into an object by an endless sequence. This intuition, however, is not empirical . . . but rather determines the object a priori through an act of the subject that creates and possesses its own inner representations" (Kant [1796–98] 1938/*KGS*, 22:82).

ical work (which this would certainly be) or whether he was simply exploring Fichte's new contributions (with which such a claim would be consistent) for the purpose of his own understanding.

3.3. RELATIVE PRIORITY OF THE GENERAL WILL IN KANT

Before proceeding to analyze how Kant employed both formal and substantive versions of the general will, there remains one last important metaphysical issue: its derivation and relation to the universal law. Which comes first, the general will or the universal law? Once again, this brings us back to Rousseau. He faced a similar choice. Although he did not have a specifically "universal law" to work with, he did have a principle of justice. If the general will precedes justice, then, as some have claimed, Rousseau might be a positivist. If a transcendent principle of justice precedes the general will, then Rousseau is a Platonist. And, as I have already argued, Rousseau chooses the latter order of prioritization. The general will is agreement with the idea of justice. Thus, the principle of justice is ontologically *independent* of the general will; the general will is ontologically *dependent* on the idea of justice. If the general will were permitted to take a shape contrary to justice, then, according to Rousseau, it would cease to be the general will (*SC,* 124/*OC,* III:441).

To understand the ontology and relative priority of the general will in Kant, it is necessary to examine it in both its formal and substantive manifestations. In the substantive account, it is important to examine Kant's discussion of Platonic principles, described multiple times as the locus of his normative program. Platonic ideas are completely abstracted from experience. This is what lends them their particular charm, from Kant's perspective: "Plato made use of the expression *'idea'* in such a way as quite evidently to have meant by it something which not only can never be borrowed from the senses but far surpasses even the concepts of understanding" (*FC,* A313/B370). In light of their abstraction from the sensible world, they are peculiarly immune to corruption and contingency and stand as eternal norms for all times and circumstances. The Platonic idea of "a perfect state may never, indeed, come into being; nonetheless this does not affect the rightfulness of the idea" (*FC,* A317/B373). Thus, Platonic ideas become for Kant the source of legislation and government. As such, they must precede the general will. The general will involves willing—a feature of the empirical world. This is not to say that we cannot construct an idea of it, a priori. We can imagine a general will—a united will of the people consistent with Platonic ideas. It is to suggest, however, that it is not the primary or first principle of his politics.

The substantive account of the general will is dependent upon Kant's theory of Platonic ideas.

Because Kant occasionally abandons Platonic ideas, it is likewise important to understand the relative priority of the general will in its formal manifestations as well. To do so, we must examine the text carefully. Consider the first formulation of the categorical imperative in the *Groundwork* and that in the *Second Critique:*

> *I ought never to act except in such a way that I could also will that my maxim should become a universal law.* (Kant, *Groundwork*, 57/*KGS*, 4:402)

> So act that the maxim of your will could always hold at the same time as a principle in a giving of universal law. (Kant [1788] 1996, 164/*KGS*, 5:30)

In both instances, Kant indicates that the will to be generalized must be consistent with the universal law. If the will were to deviate from the universal law, it would no longer be a general will. Employing Rousseauean language, it would be a particular will. Thus, the formal version of the general will is ontologically dependent upon the universal law. The general will is, in this respect, ontologically the same in both the substantive and the formal accounts. Its content is determined by Platonic ideas in the former, and the universal law in the latter. In both cases, however, its content is circumscribed by a prior law or idea. Therefore, Kant follows Rousseau in both the substantive and formal versions of the general will by making it ontologically dependent on an idea or universal law.

3.4. TWO GENERAL WILLS

Kant never firmly chose one version of the general will over the other. When he seems most committed to a formal program—such as in the *Groundwork*—he still inserts substance. When he seems most committed to a substantive program, he nevertheless expresses epistemic skepticism regarding the source of these ideas, such as in the *Inaugural Dissertation*. In fact, a close reading of his oeuvre reveals that both conceptions of the general will lurk in virtually all of his works. Perhaps the best example of this is in the *Groundwork*. Kant clearly presents the first formula of the categorical imperative as a formal principle because, as he claims, only a formal practical principle can

230 ROUSSEAU'S PLATONIC ENLIGHTENMENT

guarantee an autonomous will. Therefore, logical self-contradiction must be the standard by which the morality of acts is judged.

Kant offers four examples to illustrate the workings of his formal principle. These include the maxims of (1) suicide, (2) false promises, (3) failing to develop one's talents, and (4) helping others in need. In the case of suicide, Kant asks whether the maxim could pass the test of universality. He notes that suicide is motivated by self-love, a prioritization of oneself over the needs of others. This principle of self-love, however, is the very same feeling that impels the furtherance of life. Therefore, inherent in the maxim of suicide is a contradiction, and it fails the formal test (*Groundwork*, 74/*KGS*, 4:422).

In his second example, a man is desperate to secure a loan, even as he knows that he will not be able to repay it. If he were to go ahead with this plan, the maxim would read, "When I believe myself to be in need of money I shall borrow money and promise to repay it, even though I know that this will never happen." Kant then subjects this to the formal test of universalization and finds that it fails. Thus, like the first example, it "must necessarily contradict itself" because even though such a maxim may work for an individual, it cannot work for a society of liars (*Groundwork*, 74/*KGS*, 4:422). If everyone were to lie, no money would ever be loaned. Because no money would be loaned when the maxim is universalized, the maxim itself (presupposing the loaning of money under false pretenses) is self-contradictory, so Kant has successfully defended the formal principle now in his two first illustrations.

The third example, however, becomes more complex. In this case, a man in comfortable circumstances decides to give himself up to pleasure instead of deliberately cultivating his talents. Kant elaborates the example by suggesting that we imagine this man residing comfortably in the South Sea islands, where there is no physical necessity to give up the hedonistic life. Does the maxim of not cultivating one's talents fail the formal test of universalization? Kant says that the South Sea islander "cannot possibly WILL that this become a universal law," but, unlike the first two examples, he does not suggest that this conclusion is mandated by a formal principle of reason. In the case of both suicide and lying, Kant specifies that a contradiction sank the maxim, though he makes no such claim here.

The fourth example similarly avoids the appeal to a formal principle of noncontradiction. In this illustration, Kant takes up the maxim of helping others in need. He presents a man "for whom things are going well while he sees that others (whom he could very well help) have to contend with great hardships, thinks: what is it to me? Let each be happy as heaven wills or as he can make himself; I shall take nothing from him nor even envy him; only I do not care to contribute anything to his welfare or to his assistance in need!" (*Groundwork*, 75/*KGS*, 4:423). Kant admits that this maxim is perfectly capable of surviving the formal test of universality. The human race will not perish should the misanthrope's maxim become universal law. Nevertheless, as with the third example, he still insists that it cannot be willed.

If neither the third nor fourth example can be willed but both nevertheless fail the formal test, one is left wondering what prevents them from being willed. To help answer this, Kant introduces two different types of contradiction: (1) contradiction in conception and (2) contradiction in willing. A contradiction in conception inhibits the very notion of a maxim from forming in the rational mind, and it appears clear enough that the maxims of suicide and false promises fail this test. The contradiction in conception is purely formal.

The contradiction in willing, however, is less straightforward. He describes it in the following way: in some cases the "inner impossibility is indeed not to be found, but it is still impossible to *will* that their maxim be raised to the universality of a law of nature because such a will would contradict itself" (*Groundwork*, 75/*KGS*, 4:424). The reference to contradiction indicates to his readers that he is still operating with a formal principle, but it is not clear how it would operate in a formal manner. With the notable exception of Sullivan (1989, 152), most Kant scholars tend to agree that he is going beyond a purely formal principle of logical contradiction in the examples of failure to cultivate talent and unwillingness to help others in need. Christine Korsgaard, for example, locates three forms of contradiction: (1) logical contradiction, (2) teleological contradiction, and (3) practical contradiction (1985, 25). She admits that (1) alone will not cover all Kant's examples. Therefore, there must be an appeal to either (2) or (3). The problem for Kant, however, is that both of these contradictions are substantive, not formal. Likewise, Thomas Hill argues that Kant is appealing to the standards of rational willing. It is unclear, however, where these standards are located. There is every possibility that they are located in the second and third formulas of the categorical imperative. Again, though, these are substantive principles (Hill 2002, 72). Thus, even where Kant most firmly commits himself to a formal version of the general will, he has smuggled in the substantive version.

One finds much of the same in his later political works. In these he freely moves from formal to substantive grounds for his constructive program without any suggestion that he is doing so. When Kant explains the foundations of his political theory in "Toward a Perpetual Peace," he explicitly labels them "formalist." One must begin from either a material or a formal principle, and "the latter principle must undoubtedly take precedence; for, as a principle of right, it has unconditional necessity, whereas the former necessitates only if the empirical conditions of the proposed end, namely of its being realized, are presupposed; and even if this end (e.g., perpetual peace) were also a duty, it would still have to be derived from the formal principle of maxims for acting externally" ([1795] 1996, 344/*KGS*, :377). Published just two years before the *Metaphysics of Morals*, Kant here gives the clearest indication of his intentions. Associating substantive principles with contingency, Kant asserts the necessity of grounding his system in formal principles. With regard to welfare, for example, Kant says that the general will mandates that society be able to maintain itself. There is no reason necessarily, however, to believe that this is subjected to a formal test. However displeasing a thought it might be, it is logically possible for a state to continue while allowing the poor to go hungry. Similarly, he claims that the general will mandates life terms for all members of the bureaucracy (*MM*, 470/*KGS*, 6:328), but it is impossible to see how such a principle can be derived from a formal conception.

Conclusions

For all the difficulty associated with a purely formal conception of justice, one can understand its appeal. It is possible to argue that Kant's formalism is actually derived from Rousseau and is hence part of the Rousseauean legacy in Kant. This is implied in an argument by Arthur Melzer that Rousseau's ultimate principle is a formal principle of unity in the soul. According to Melzer, "Rousseau is the first thinker . . . to complete man's liberation from God and nature: to abandon all substantive standards, natural or divine, and to replace them with the formal standard of psychic unity or noncontradiction" (1990, 90),[24] but this is merely a question of influence rather than of the value of Kant's choice. The value of formalism is its apparent liberation from the most controversial assumptions of Platonism: its steadfast adherence to the existence of substantive objects beyond the senses. To be sure, the claims of Rousseau go beyond the most famous claims of natural science in modernity. Kant's formalism, on the other hand, has a resemblance to natural science. Specifically, by virtue of its reliance on the principle of noncontradiction, it has the feel of mathematics—the discipline that many modern philosophers

24. Interestingly, Melzer does not draw the connection to Kant, and even on occasion points to the great dissimilarities between the two, though Rousseau's alleged formalism would appear to make them engaged in almost precisely the same project.

ultimately equated with proper method. Something cannot be both p and not p at the same time, just as something cannot be both 5 and 6 at the same time. The element of certainty in Kant's formalism gives it a special appeal over the metaphysical claims of Rousseau, which transcend the realms of both mathematics and natural science. From the perspective of natural science and mathematics, whereas Rousseau appears to be grasping at straws, Kant provides a desirable determinacy.

In this light, one can appreciate Kant's great influence over the ethical and political theory of the next two centuries. Without him, the general will would not have developed in the fashion it has. His formalist program—indeed, his own invention—continues to exercise deep influence. His two greatest students of the twentieth century readily acknowledge their debts. John Rawls said that his "original position may be viewed . . . as a procedural interpretation of Kant's conception of autonomy and the categorical imperative" (1971, 256). Jürgen Habermas likewise refers to his discourse ethics as a reformulation of Kant's formalist program ([1983] 1990, 195). The reasons for their attraction to Kant's formalist conception of the general will likely follow those of Kant himself. It is almost inevitably the case, however, that they are burdened by the same problems that weighed down their teacher.

Early in his career, Rawls specified seven criteria to determine principles of justice. These include (1) "Each claim in a set of conflicting claims shall be evaluated by the same principles," (2) "Every claim shall be considered, on first sight, as meriting satisfaction," (3) "One claim shall not be denied, or modified, for the sake of another," (4) "Given a group of competing claims, as many as possible shall be satisfied, so far as the satisfaction of them is consistent with other principles," (5) "If means of any kind are used for the purpose of securing an interest, it shall be reasonably demonstrable that they are designed to secure it," (6) "Claims shall be ordered according to their strength," and (7) "Given a set of equal claims, as determined by their strength, all shall be satisfied equally" (Rawls [1951] 1999, 14–15). Following his Kantian inclinations, all of these conditions are formal. The problem with this set of criteria, however, is that it does not by itself resolve the issues it claims. After all, how does one determine the "strength" of a claim? Further, as T. K. Seung argues, these criteria "are useless for settling controversial issues because the controversy over these issues arises mostly from their substantive content rather than from their formal framework" (1993, 49). This is likely the reason that Rawls, like Kant before him, retreats from the purely formalist account and instead appeals to substantive ideas. Unlike Kant, however, who appeals to Platonic ideas, Rawls turns "to the public culture itself as the share fund of implicitly recognized basic ideas" (Rawls 1993, 8). He locates here the principles of liberty and equality central to his project. This solves the epistemic problem of intellectual intuition that concerned Kant, although it, in turn, subjects the theory to the accusation that it is culturally relativistic. A culture that embraces inequality and obedience to theistic authority may very well demand other principles from those Rawls ultimately promotes.

Habermas likewise makes the Kantian appeal to formal procedures. The principle of discourse ethics—"Only those norms may claim to be valid that could meet with the consent of all affected in their role as participants in a practical discourse"—is explicitly formal ([1983] 1990, 197). The problem for Habermas is that the rules governing the discourse make appeals to substantive ideas, such as liberty, equality, and consensus (Williams 1999). In this regard, he is committing the same error of purely formalist theories of which a young Kant was aware—that they must ultimately appeal to higher, substantive principles. Of course, this was an admonition that not even Kant himself could heed. Substantive principles, for all the controversy and problems that come with them (epistemic questions, ontological questions), nevertheless assert themselves in even the most dedicated of formalist programs. In reading Kant this way, we can begin to appreciate his struggles and at the same time appreciate why Rousseau was so hesitant to engage with these questions in the first place.

In light of the lessons drawn from Kant's failure to produce a purely formal conception of the general will, we can draw a great lesson for practical politics. The danger of the pretense of pure formalism is the confidence it instills in its advocates and followers to talk about politics without actually addressing the issues. As William B. Rubenstein (2004) has pointed out, the recent debate over gay marriage has taken the formalist turn with this particular consequence. Eager to avoid the question of what kind of society we want, politicians have been quick to turn a substantive debate into a formal one. They have done so by suggesting that the formal principle of federalism demands that each state take on the issue for itself. There are obvious political reasons for making this suggestion. Doing so alienates the fewest voters. It is an old trick of politicians to avoid embracing substantive political issues. As Rubenstein suggests, this trick was likewise employed to avoid substantive discussions on slavery and the subjugation of women for more than a hundred years in the United States. By saying that slavery was "up to the states," politicians were able to avoid the substantive issue of the unjust institution itself. Although this trick may be tolerated of politicians, it should not be tolerated of political theorists. What Kant's continual appeal to a substantive conception of the general will tells us is that substance is an inextricable part of politics. Taking it off the table fosters the forgetfulness of our most cherished values. That slavery was constitutionally tolerated for nearly a century on this basis is a testament to this fact. We would be well served by reminding ourselves of Kant's great struggle over the structure of the general will.

EIGHT

THE FOUCAULDIAN LEGACY:
CRITIQUES WITHOUT JUSTICE?

Everyone is familiar with the story about the unwitting dupe who volunteers at the magic show to be hypnotized and is convinced, under a "spell," that he is a chicken. He immediately wanders across the stage, flaps his arms up and down, and howls, "cock-a-doodle-dooo!" The audience has a good laugh, and the magician then relieves the ersatz rooster of the spell. The man has no memory of the incident, and everyone has had a grand time. What, however, if the spell caster were not a magician, but instead were the state? And what if the victim were not a volunteer looking for entertainment, but a citizen of that state? This scenario is familiar to us in twentieth-century literature. In *1984*, George Orwell describes just such an image. But Winston Smith is no volunteer looking for a good time—and the state is no benevolent magician. In tying young Winston down and refusing to let him go until he believes that "$2 + 2 = 5$," the state is actively seeking to change his most fundamental intuitions about what is true. Similarly, in *A Clockwork Orange*, Anthony Burgess graphically describes the state's tying a young man down and forcing him to watch violent images while listening to his previously beloved Ninth Symphony of Beethoven. The state considers the proceedings a success when the individual can no longer listen to the work without experiencing anguish, pain, and grief. When this is accomplished, he is free to go.

In both literary examples, the authors describe violent forms of individualized brainwashing, but we can imagine something even more sinister than this. What if the brainwashing were so subtle that the individual was not even aware of the altering of his consciousness? And what if the brainwashing worked not on one individual at a time, but on the entire populace? Such a prospect is even more sinister for two reasons. First, because the brainwashing is performed subtly, the individual has no opportunity to recognize the danger and resist. It is over before one knows that it has ever taken place. And second, because it is performed on everyone simultaneously, there are no outsiders who can observe the changes and foment revolution.

This is, however, no science-fiction scenario, according to Jean-Jacques Rousseau. It is the sad story of the development of Western politics, as described in part 2 of his *Discourse on Inequality.* Through the employment of a diabolical genius, a coalition of the rich and powerful seized control of the government, gained the consent of the less fortunate, and established rules of justice that only served to further their personal interests. It was a masterstroke of the most insidious kind—fit for science fiction, but part of a sad reality.

While Rousseau was the first to articulate this story in any detail, he was by no means the last. In broad outline, it is familiar to most contemporary intellectuals simply as Marxism. Karl Marx repeats a number of Rousseau's observations of contemporary society. History evolves as a series of class conflicts. The rich, having the most to lose, establish institutions and norms to protect their wealth and status. The poor are scarcely aware of this turn of events in each stage of history and are thus easily kept at bay. In all these respects, Marx is an intellectual descendant of Rousseau.

Likewise, echoes of Rousseau are found in the twentieth-century figure Michel Foucault. In *Discipline and Punish,* he argues that political power has been employed—especially since the Enlightenment—to create normative standards for the purpose of protecting the wealthy (76, 274). Foucault adds to the narrative by suggesting that power almost has a mind of its own—that it can be exercised for the benefit of the bourgeoisie, even if they are unaware of its machinations. He shares with Rousseau, however, the belief that power has the capacity to mold a "truth" that the poor eventually and unwittingly enforce on themselves, leaving the rich free to enjoy their lives of privilege.

With acknowledged differences, Marx and Foucault both roughly follow Rousseau's narrative. So far, so good. This, however, is only half of the story: the critique. The second half of the story is the normative foundation informing the critique. On what grounds does Rousseau refer to this state of affairs as "wicked" (*SD,* 171/*OC,* III:176)? The answer lies in his commitment to transcendent normative principles—those principles inscribed "in reason . . . [and] engraved in the human heart in indelible characters" ("State of War," 166/*OC,* III:602). This foundation, I argue, allows him to level the critique as persuasively as he does. Rousseau's commitment to transcendent ideas is as essential to his philosophy as his critique. Indeed, it constitutes the foundation and basis of his critique.

It is less clear that Marx and Foucault ground their critiques in similar principles. Although Marx employs the Rousseauean critique of society, and finds his surroundings to be likewise "odious" (*Capital,* 928), he seems to deny the standard on which this judgment is based. Only through careful examination do we ultimately find that Marx and Engels have something like a theory of justice. Foucault employs the Rousseauean critique and judges historical developments to be "insidious" (*DP,* 308), but he rejects the transcendent standard of justice entirely, turning the Rousseauean critique in on itself. This comes at great cost to the normative relevance of his observations. His account of history may very well be accurate, but he has undercut his own ability to judge its developments. We are thus left wondering why he leveled his critique in the first place.

1. Rousseau: History, Power, and Politics

1.1. ROUSSEAU'S CRITIQUE OF SOCIETY

"Everything is good as it leaves the hands of the Author of things; everything degenerates in the hands of man." The famous opening of Rousseau's *Emile* is as concise a review of his *Discourse on Inequality* (the *Second Discourse*) as any one sentence could be. The form of the sentence strengthens it in this function; divided by a semicolon, its two halves mirror the two halves of the *Second Discourse*. Part 1 depicts human beings in their natural state; part 2 traces their social development. In their natural state they are solitary and benign creatures, full of sentiment and pity for the suffering of others. Because of their relative isolation, they are remarkably simple beings. They have neither language nor social intercourse. They seek only what is necessary—food, drink, shelter, and procreative activity—and otherwise content themselves to sit back and enjoy their relatively peaceful existences. The only social virtue that all people possess is pity, and this disposition leads Rousseau to characterize the state of nature as one of natural goodness: "It is pity that carries us without reflection to the assistance of those we see suffer; pity that, in the state of Nature, takes the place of Laws, morals, and virtue, with the advantage that no one is tempted to disobey its gentle voice; pity that will keep any sturdy Savage from robbing a weak child or an infirm man of his hard-won subsistence" (*SD,* 154/ *OC,* III:156).

This natural sentiment persists as long as society itself remains natural, according to Rousseau. Yet the state of nature, like all good things, is fated to end. Human beings emerge from this state in part 2 of the *Second Discourse.*

Rousseau—a true master of compelling openings—commences part 2 by placing the blame for the fall squarely on the shoulders of one metaphoric individual: "The first man who, having enclosed a piece of ground, to whom it occurred to say *this is mine*, and found people sufficiently simple to believe him, was the true founder of civil society" (*SD*, 161/*OC*, III:164). Rousseau's opening, however, jumps the gun a bit by beginning with a conclusion. The rest of part 2 is dedicated to explaining how property came into being and how its protection, by those who had the most of it, became the central structuring principle of civilization.

According to Rousseau, human beings are coaxed out of a solitary lifestyle by a combination of environmental hardships—drought, extreme temperatures, and inhospitable terrain (*SD*, 162/*OC*, III:165) in addition to floods, volcanic eruptions, earthquakes, and fires (Rousseau 1997, 274/*OC*, V:402). These adversities forced the cooperation necessary to form the earliest societies. In itself, of course, this cooperation was no blameworthy act. The earliest stirrings of civilization were mandated by circumstances beyond the control of human beings. What followed shortly thereafter was less benign.

Because people came together by virtue of extraordinary circumstances, it was not surprising that extraordinary skills came to be valued. It was thus the case, according to Rousseau, that individuals sought to excel in these and, eventually, most measurable skills: "Everyone began to look at everyone else and to wish to be looked at himself, and public esteem acquired a price. The one who sang or danced best, the handsomest, the strongest, the most skillful, or the most eloquent came to be the most highly regarded, and this was the first step at once toward inequality and vice" (*SD*, 166/*OC*, III:169). For Rousseau, this is the instant at which human nature is transformed.[1] The competition engendered by wanting to be the best rapidly erodes the natural pity that helped make the state of nature a secular Garden of Eden. Now, instead of feeling an innate sense of sympathy for their fellow creatures, humans developed an artificial desire to dominate others and even rejoice in their suffering, if that would help elevate their own status.

From this desire to distinguish themselves against others arose another desire: to accumulate wealth. Money served as a simple means by which the talented could distinguish themselves from the less talented. The more property one had, the more esteem one had from others, and, finally, the more pride one had. At first, property was acquired from the vast spaces of the state of nature. Soon, however, one could only acquire property at the expense of

---

1. See McLendon (2003) for a thorough exposition of the importance of this transformation.

others. Thus, the skill of acquiring property transformed from the ability to build things to the ability to swindle others. This latter ability had a double reinforcement. First, the simple acquisition of property helped buttress the status of the wealthy. Second, because the property of the wealthy came with others' proportionate loss (wealth at this point being a zero-sum game), the status of the wealthy would increase with the impoverishment of their fellow citizens. Rousseau's description of those at the top of the food chain is none too flattering: "The rich, for their part, had scarcely become acquainted with the pleasure of dominating than they disdained all other pleasures, and using their old Slaves to subject new ones, they thought only of subjugating and enslaving their neighbors; like those ravenous wolves which once they have tasted human flesh scorn all other food, and from then on want to devour only men" (SD, 171/OC, III:175).

With such a menace on the prowl, it is not surprising that an outright state of war would emerge. Tasting blood, the rich seize all they can. It is a war, as Rousseau describes it, to be decided by the right of the stronger: "Nascent Society gave way to the most horrible state of war: Humankind, debased and devastated, no longer able to turn back, or denounce its wretched acquisitions, and working only to its shame by the abuse of the faculties that do it honor, brought itself to the brink of ruin" (SD, 172/OC, III:176).

The state of war, while chronologically different from that of Thomas Hobbes, is no less brutal. And, although the poor suffer, the rich have even more to lose, according to Rousseau. They stand to lose all their ill-gained property. Because their property is largely acquired through brute force, they fear its loss by precisely the same means in war. Further, because they base none of their holdings on any genuine principles of natural right, they have absolutely no basis on which to protest a like seizure of their own property. The worry that they could lose all they had worked to acquire ultimately leads them to "one of the most well-considered projects ever to enter the human mind" (SD, 172/OC, III:177).

This ingenious "project" is not "well-considered" in the sense that Rousseau holds it to be up to the highest moral standards. Quite the contrary: it is dastardly. It is "well-considered" in the instrumental sense, insofar as nothing could be more effective in achieving its desired ends. It is, for Rousseau, a diabolical genius. He is so impressed that he reproduces a transcript of the likely pronouncement by the wealthy, meant expressly to end the state of war:

> Let us unite . . . to protect the weak from oppression, restrain the ambitious, and secure for everyone the possession of what belongs to

him: Let us institute rules of Justice and peace to which all are obliged to conform, which favor no one, and which in a way make up for the vagaries of fortune by subjecting the powerful and the weak alike to mutual duties. In a word, instead of turning our forces against one another, let us gather them into a supreme power that might govern us according to wise Laws, protect and defend all the members of the association, repulse common enemies, and preserve us in everlasting concord. (*SD,* 173/*OC,* III:177)

If this proposal sounds persuasive, that is because it is meant to be. For the rich, everything rides on it. War has endangered their property, and this is their one effort to stop the bleeding and secure what is theirs. And, according to Rousseau, it works masterfully.

Just as the wealthy have their reasons to offer this proposal, the poor have their reasons to accept. First, the poor are dying, as happens in any war. The treaty offer promises to end this. Second, the proposal guarantees their possessions, however meager they may be. Third, it promises—through the institution of justice and laws—a long-lasting peace, giving the poor the stability they might need to move forward with their life plans. Thus, says Rousseau, they not only accepted the offer but also "ran toward their chains in the belief that they were securing their freedom" (*SD,* 173/*OC,* III:177).

It is obvious what the wealthy gain in the short term. They, like the poor, have an interest in ending the state of war. But what they gain in the long term is far more substantial. In this social contract, they are able to establish the law and conceptions of justice and freedom. Through these mechanisms, the rich not only secure the peace necessary to end the state of war and protect their private property but also ensure that these possessions and all the perks that accompany them (such as status) are never again threatened. Each one of these notions (law, justice, and freedom) is clearly false by Rousseau's understanding. Let us explore why this is the case.

As has been argued throughout, justice, for Rousseau, is normally transcendent. "Justice" in the social contract of the *Second Discourse* is precisely the opposite. It is specifically a human convention, neither natural nor transcendent. "Justice" is created by the wealthy as an ideology. Rousseau revisits the theme subsequently in the "State of War": "Justice and trust have to be bent to the interest of the most powerful" (162/*OC,* III:609). Further, for Rousseau, "everywhere the vain name of justice only serves as a shield for violence" (163/III:610). He returns to the theme once again in the *Emile:* "Those specious names, justice and order, will always serve as instruments of violence and as arms of iniquity" (236/*OC,* IV:524). Returning to the thread of the *Second Discourse,* Rousseau writes that if the poor are told that their conditions are "just," they will soon believe it to be true. Further, they agreed to the establishment of the social contract, so why should they not assume that the terms are genuinely just? The fact that the contract was forced by desperate circumstances is soon forgotten.[2]

"Freedom," in the social contract of the *Second Discourse,* also takes a different meaning from its standard use in the Rousseauean lexicon. His normal conception of freedom is outlined in part 1 of this very work. In comparing human beings with animals, Rousseau says that the former distinguish themselves by virtue of their capacity to will action contrary to instinct. It is this notion of will attached to freedom that leads Patrick Riley (1995) to label it "freedom of a particular kind." Rousseau carries this conception of liberty throughout his career (*Emile,* 104/*OC,* IV:339; *Reveries,* 68–69/*OC,* I:1028–29). The "freedom" of the social contract described in the *Second Discourse,* however, has nothing to do with the will. In fact, it too is the opposite of its real definition in Rousseau—it is the surrender of the will. Rather than being willing agents, the poor in fact become "enchained" (*SD,* 173, 177, 183/*OC,* III:177, 181, 188). Without realizing it, they surrender their will. It feels like freedom, however, because they actually consent to their chains. This is precisely contrary to the way in which contract should operate. For this reason, Rousseau abhors Pufendorf's argument that a social contract is the divestment of freedom in favor of another.[3] To renounce one's freedom in this regard is to "debase one's being . . . as no temporal good can compensate for life or freedom, it would be an offense against both Nature and reason to renounce them at any price whatsoever" (*SD,* 179/*OC,* III:184). As Rousseau suggests later, "To renounce one's freedom is to renounce one's quality as a man, the rights of humanity, and even its duties" (*SC,* 45/*OC,* III:356). He continues by suggesting that such contracts are in their nature contradictory. Indeed, contracts divesting subjects of their freedom eliminates all obligation, because everything the subjects have, in essence, belongs to the ruler: "For what right can my slave have against me, since everything he has belongs to me, and his right being mine, this right of mine against myself is an utterly meaningless expression?" (46/III:356). Further, he might have argued, all moral obligation to the state ceases when the citizens are deprived of freedom. This is because

2. More will be said about this later in the chapter.

3. While Rousseau attributes this argument to Pufendorf, it is equally attributable to Hobbes and many other modern social contractarians.

freedom is a necessary prerequisite for moral acts, according to Rousseauean moral theory. Once the citizens have been converted to slaves, they are no longer free. Once they become determined creatures, they, like the animals, are no longer moral subjects, and, like animals, they cannot be held morally responsible to the state (or anyone else, for that matter). They are simply Hobbesian matter in motion—the very opposite of what Rousseau takes to be the proper aim of politics.

The "law" proposed in the social contract of the *Second Discourse* does no better. It likewise contradicts its genuine definition. Laws, for Rousseau, are simply official proclamations of the general will (*SC,* 67/*OC,* III:379), itself a notion closely related to justice (Kateb 1961, 524). The "law" Rousseau speaks of in the *Second Discourse,* however, is nothing other than the wealthy using their position of power to protect their ill-gained holdings from the less fortunate. As he remarks in his "Political Fragments," "Laws and the practice of justice among us are only the art of sheltering the Nobles and the rich from the just reprisals of the poor" (Rousseau 1994a, 32/*OC,* III:496). It is, in fact, the law of the strongest. The wealthy have all the power in society and use it to convert their will into law. This doctrine of the rule of the strongest is repeatedly rejected in Rousseau's works (*SD,* 186/*OC,* III:191; *Julie,* 474/*OC,* II:579; *SC,* 43–44/*OC,* III:354–55; *Emile,* 459/*OC,* IV:838; *Letters,* 239/*OC,* III:815).[4] Use of the law to safeguard tyranny is, for him, "more fatal than Tyranny itself" (*Letters,* 262/*OC,* III:843).

I.2. ROUSSEAU, POWER POLITICS, AND JUDGMENT

Rousseau's judgment of this state of affairs, found in part 2 of the *Second Discourse,* is harsh. This is not unexpected, because all three elements of the social contract pushed by the wealthy—justice, freedom, and law—contradict his definitions of these concepts elsewhere. Nor is it surprising that Rousseau tells us early in the discussion that the emergence of classes in society has made men "wicked" (*SD,* 171/*OC,* III:176). This language leaves the reader no room to think anything other than that Rousseau disapproves of the event he is describing. This, however, is just a warm-up to the parade of judgments he offers throughout part 2 of the *Second Discourse.*

Cataloging Rousseau's judgments could easily be a full-time job. The following list is by no means exhaustive, but it gives the reader a sense of Rousseau's disposition.

---

4. Louis Millet has noted that Rousseau's arguments against this doctrine correspond closely to those of Plato's *Gorgias* (Millet 1967, 3).

1. Men are "greedy" and "wicked" [*méchans*] (*SD*, 171/*OC*, III:176).
2. The rich behave like "ravenous wolves" (171/III:175).
3. The acquisitions of the wealthy are "wretched" [*malheureuses*] (172/III:176).
4. These possessions are further acquired by "abusive" rights (172/III:176).
5. Again, these possessions are described as "plunder" [*pillage*] (172/III:177).
6. The reasoning of the rich is "specious" (173/III:177).

Elsewhere in Rousseau's writings, one finds a similar forthrightness in describing the perceived failings of his contemporaries.

1. The source of "moral evil" [*la mal moral*] is to be found in man alone ("Letter to Voltaire," 234/*OC*, IV:1061). This is repeated in the *Emile*: "Moral evil is incontestably our own work" (281/*OC*, IV:587).
2. "[T]he laws of justice are vain among men for want of natural sanctions; they only bring good to the wicked [*méchant*] and evil to the just when he observes them toward everyone while no one observes them toward him" (*SC*, 66/*OC*, III:378).
3. If a man has once committed an act with the intention of doing harm, then he has become "wicked" beyond salvation (*Emile*, 93/*OC*, IV:322).

In each instance, Rousseau does nothing to hide his contempt. He genuinely believes the phenomena described to be morally reprehensible. This should be obvious to even the most casual readers of Rousseau. His lack of reservation is a large part of his charm, and even perhaps a large part of the anger some feel toward him to this day. Observing his writings side by side with contemporary philosophy, one is particularly struck by the role of judgment in his work. As Joseph R. Reisert notes, "Rousseau is certainly more strident [in his moral judgments] than today's canons of academic propriety would allow" (2003, 9). On what basis does Rousseau offer moral judgment?

1.3. ROUSSEAU AND THE FOUNDATION OF POLITICAL JUDGMENT

We know thus far that Rousseau describes a considerable downfall from the state of nature to civil society.[5] The rich, inspired by motives of self-aggran-

---

5. It should be noted that the trajectory of this downfall is not linear. As Jonathan Marks astutely notes, there is a considerable upswing in overall circumstances between the state of nature and the slavery of the poor (2005, 60–65).

dizement, seek to take all they can from the poor and then brainwash them into believing that the protection of the goods now in their hands is a foundational principle of society. Further, we know that Rousseau is livid at this arrangement. What remains to be determined is the basis of his anger. He provides us with what might be a clue in the *Emile*. He recounts an incident of child abuse he once observed. The child's beating caused Rousseau to reflect:

> The unfortunate [child] was suffocating with anger; he had lost his breath; I saw him become violet. A moment after came sharp screams; all the signs of resentment, fury, and despair of this age were his accents. I feared he would expire in this agitation. If I had doubted that the sentiment of the just and the unjust were innate in the heart of man, this example alone would have convinced me. I am sure that a live ember fallen by chance on this child's hand would have made less of an impression than this blow, rather light but given in the manifest intention of offending him. (*Emile*, 66/*OC*, IV:286–87)

Rousseau's heartfelt example is profound. It is not the pain of the blow that hurt the child. Rather, it was the intention to harm. The child's sense of injustice—informed by the fact that someone would consciously choose to cause pain for no other purpose than delivering that pain—causes the anger and resentment. Rousseau returns to this theme later in the Savoyard Vicar: "One sees some act of violence and injustice in the street or on the road. Instantly an emotion of anger and indignation is aroused in the depths of the heart, and it leads us to take up the defense of the oppressed" (*Emile*, 287–88/*OC*, IV:596–97).[6] Even more explicitly, he now tells us that the injustice is related to oppression—just as he illustrated in the *Second Discourse*.[7] Rousseau returns to this theme at least twice more. In the *Confessions*, he reveals, "my heart is inflamed at the spectacle or narrative of all unjust actions" (17/*OC*, I:20). This is echoed in remarkably similar terms in his *Reveries:* "My moral being would

6. This is merely a restatement of the *Lettres morales:* "If one sees in the street some act of violence and injustice, at that instant an impulse of anger and indignation arises in the heart" (*OC*, IV:1106–7). An excellent discussion of Rousseau's theory of the development of conscience can be found in Marks (2000).

7. In fact, Rousseau describes the first wrongs in civilization as being attached to this notion of intent: "here arose the first duties of civility even among Savages, and from it any intentional wrong became an affront because, together with the harm resulting from the injury, the offended party saw in it contempt for his person, often more unbearable than the harm itself" (*SD*, 166/*OC*, III:170).

have to be annihilated for justice to become unimportant to me. The sight of injustice and wickedness still makes my blood boil with rage" (54/*OC*, I:1057).

All of the above excerpts suggest the same thing: that indignation and anger are, for him and others, informed by a sense of justice. Rousseau's examples could be multiplied hundreds of times in the lives of all people. Our sense of justice more often reveals itself when we witness not justices but rather injustices—being passed over for a promotion by someone less competent, being rejected by a school that clearly accepts less able students, watching the umpire miss a call, seeing our children being ignored by teachers in favor of other students, watching our siblings getting gifts from our parents that we deserved but never received, and so forth. Everyone has experienced these moments, and the most typical response, according to Rousseau, is anger. This anger is the consequence of observing the violation of justice. It is a natural sentiment, as Rousseau suggests above, both written on the heart and essential to our identity as moral beings.

Of course, it is one thing to suffer wrong and then be cognizant of it as a violation of justice. It is still another thing to observe it when not a party to its effects. The latter is relatively easy to inculcate, Rousseau believes, because it is essentially innate. This is why the tutor's first lesson to Emile about justice, involving Robert the gardener, concerns a perceived injustice aimed at Emile himself: "the first sentiment of justice does not come to us from the justice that we owe but from that which is owed us" (*Emile*, 97/*OC*, IV:329). When wronged, it is relatively easy to access the idea of justice. For Rousseau, this is because it has been "graven in our hearts by the Author of all justice" (100/IV:334). The function of education is to broaden this preexisting sentiment. Thus, "[t]he more one generalizes this interest, the more it becomes equitable, and the love of mankind is nothing other than the love of justice" (252/IV:547). It is this developed sense of justice that allows us objectively to judge the actions not involving ourselves immediately as a party.

It is worth pointing out that this represents an important apparent difference between Rousseau and Plato. Whereas Plato appears concerned to eliminate the passions entirely from the development of the sense of justice through dialectic, Rousseau endorses a cautious plan to develop the sense of justice through the passions. "Let us extend *amour-propre* to other beings," he says in the *Emile* (252/IV:547).[8] It seems that the initial sense of justice is an inward manifestation of self-love for Rousseau. He appears to make a similar point with regard to the natural sense of pity, which can also be "generalized and

---

8. This argument has been developed in Cooper (1999, 125–36). See also Shklar (1969, 19).

extended to the whole of mankind" (253/IV:548). The passions thus play an important role in developing the sense of justice.

It is important to note, however, that this point is more epistemic than metaphysical or ontological, for even as Rousseau suggests that self-love and pity can be generalized to help Emile come to know and even love justice, it is not the principle of justice itself. With regard to pity, for example, Rousseau says that "one yields to it only insofar as it accords with justice" (*Emile*, 253/ *OC*, IV:548). Pity can yield to justice only if they are distinct and separable concepts. Using justice to check pity in this fashion prevents pity from being misemployed, such as is the case with pity for the wicked. Likewise with *amour-propre*. Although it can be cultivated and generalized to help acquire a better sense of justice, it is by no means the metaphysical foundation for the idea of justice itself. Unchecked, *amour-propre* leads to vanity and pleasure in domination.

This is why Rousseau frequently cautions against the passions—especially in his embrace of the virtue of self-mastery, or *sophrosune*. Managing the passions, for Rousseau, is much like early human beings' managing fire. Properly managed and directed, the passions can do much good—both for individuals and the larger community—but proper management is not easy. Many lack this talent or never receive adequate instruction. Handing fire over to such people is akin to asking them to burn down the village. Likewise, telling people to act on their passions is akin to asking them to establish a tyranny. One thus finds far more caution in Rousseau about the management of the passions than encouragement to act on them, and in this respect, again, he begins more closely to resemble Plato.[9]

Regardless of how he gets there, it is clear that his rejection of the social contract of the *Second Discourse* appears motivated by its violation of the principles of justice. As Jean Starobinski writes, "History has no moral legitimacy, and Rousseau does not hesitate to condemn, in the name of eternal values, the historical mechanism whose necessity he has proven and whose effects he has extended to the moral functions themselves" ([1971] 1988, 24). One can now follow the train of Rousseau's thought reasonably clearly.

9. It should be noted that Plato is not without his own enthusiasm for the passions. The spirit, after all, is an important element of the soul that, rightly directed, can do much good. In words that bear a striking resemblance to Rousseau's, Plato asks, "Isn't the spirit within him boiling and angry, fighting for what he believes to be just? Won't it endure hunger, cold, and the like on till it is victorious, not ceasing from noble actions until it either wins, dies, or calms down, called to heel by the reason within him, like a dog or a shepherd?" (*Republic*, 440cd). Likewise, in the *Symposium*, Plato appears to endorse a cautious ride of the passion of *eros* to arrive at philosophic wisdom. As Seung observes, Plato's goal in the *Symposium* is not to slay the beast of the passions, as was the case in the *Phaedo*, but to ride it (1996, 59).

1. He observes the practice of the rich oppressing and manipulating the poor.
2. He judges this practice to be reprehensible.
3. This judgment is informed by anger, which itself is inspired by witnessing a violation of the principle of justice.
4. Finally, the sentiment of justice—the foundation of his judgment—is an eternal norm.

Rousseau's confidence in the existence and ontology of this norm provides the confidence he has in his judgments.

2. Marx: History, Power, and Politics

2.1. MARX'S CRITIQUE OF SOCIETY

With the possible exception of Kant, no philosopher is more associated with the notion of critique than Karl Marx. Critique is the essence of his work. From his early writings on alienated labor to his nuanced analyses in *Capital*, his approach was almost always that of critique. As Robert C. Tucker has noted, "The idea of *Kritik* is . . . a great unifying theme running through the writings of classical Marxism, and a key to the continuity of the thought of Marx and Engels from their youthful philosophical writings to the productions of their mature years" (1978, xxix). Marx's youthful claim that he would critique everything ([1843] 1978, 13) was not merely the boasting of a young and quixotic intellectual. His subsequent writings confirm that this ambition was indeed sincere.

Of course, all critique must begin somewhere, and Marx begins exactly where we would expect him to: in the real world. He makes this clear in declaring his opposition to Hegelian idealism.

> My dialectical method is, in its foundations, not only different from the Hegelian, but exactly the opposite to it. For Hegel, the process of thinking, which he even transforms into an independent subject, under the name of "the Idea," is the creator of the real world, and the real world is only the external appearance of the idea. With me the reverse is true: the ideal is nothing but the material world reflected in the mind of man, and translated into forms of thought. (*Capital*, 102)

Marx found it unhelpful and even silly to begin with ideas when it was clear to him that individuals existed in particular circumstances. To reach true conclusions, one must begin with the most obviously true assumptions—those residing in the material world.

Marx's examination of the material world begins with the most material of assumptions: that "life involves before everything else eating and drinking, housing, clothing, and various other things" ([1845] 1998, 47). The first historical act, then, is the fulfillment of these particular needs. Shortly after this is the second historical act—the production of new needs. Sometime after this comes the development of consciousness. Remaining faithful to his historical materialism, Marx says in *The German Ideology* that this consciousness is not "pure" in the Hegelian sense. Rather, "consciousness is . . . from the very beginning a social product, and remains so as long as men exist" ([1845] 1998, 49–50). Insofar as we think, Marx suggests, we think in terms derived from our social context and inculcation.

Once human beings have developed a consciousness and have new needs that require fulfilling, they begin to engage in labor, and, from this point forward, Marx suggests that history is best understood according to the means of the division of labor or ownership. The first stage is that of "tribal property" ([1845] 1998, 38). This society is characterized by rudimentary social structures, and divisions of labor are generally allocated within familial structures. Production is limited mostly to simple hunting and gathering. The second stage is "ancient and communal state property" (39). This system is characterized by communal ownership of the land, existing side by side with some private property. There is a more highly developed division of labor and a significant slave population, on whom rests the most burdensome tasks. The third stage is "feudal or state property" (39). This system is characterized by varying elaborate hierarchies. In the Middle Ages, Marx locates "feudal lords, vassals, guild-masters, journeymen, apprentices, [and] serfs" (*Communist Manifesto,* 159). The serfs emerge in this system as the producing class.

From the ruins of this feudal system emerges the era that most interests Marx: industrial capitalism. By the time that capitalism hits its stride, two classes have emerged as dominant—the bourgeoisie and the proletariat. The former controls property and the means of production. The latter populates the workplaces (specifically, the factories). This parallels Rousseau's characterization of modern society being broken up into two classes, rich and poor, and, like Rousseau's modern society, the relation between the two is one of violence, domination, manipulation, exploitation, and devastation.

The bourgeoisie is naturally dominant in industrial capitalism. It wrested

power away from the nobles by taking advantage of the growth of new mar-
kets, especially the world market. As this market expanded, so did the wealth
of the bourgeoisie. Further, given the natural relationship between money and
power, as the wealth of the bourgeoisie increased, so did its power. This power
ultimately became so saturated, according to Marx, that "the executive of the
modern State is but a committee for managing the common affairs of the
whole bourgeoisie" (*Communist Manifesto*, 161).

Though the consolidation of power suggests the possibility of tyranny and
abuse, it does not necessitate it. Yet Marx's description of the bourgeoisie's
behavior confirms the fears one associates with unchecked power:

> The bourgeoisie, wherever it has got the upper hand, has put an end
> to all feudal, patriarchal, idyllic relations. It has pitilessly torn asun-
> der the motley feudal ties that bound man to his "natural superiors,"
> and has left remaining no other nexus between man and man than
> naked self-interest, than callous "cash payment." It has drowned the
> most heavenly ecstasies of religious fervour, of chivalrous enthusiasm,
> of philistine sentimentalism, in the icy water of egotistical calcula-
> tion. It has resolved personal worth into exchange value, and in place
> of the numberless indefeasible chartered freedoms, has set up that
> single, unconscionable freedom—Free Trade. In one word, for
> exploitation, veiled by religious and political illusions, it has substi-
> tuted naked, shameless, direct, brutal exploitation. (*Communist Man-
> ifesto*, 161)

By virtue of its single-minded drive for profit, the bourgeoisie has removed all
humanitarian considerations. Marx's vision of the capitalist morality is precisely the opposite of Kant's Kingdom of Ends. For the bourgeoisie, everyone
must be treated as a means to the ends of profit and self-interest.

The bourgeoisie especially wreaks havoc on the proletariat, who represents
the means to the capitalist's ends. In working for wages, he alienates himself
from his labor, the most important mechanism of identity that human beings
possess. When he hands over the fruits of his labor to the bourgeoisie, he
becomes a commodity, no different from the tools he uses or the roof under
which he works: "the worker sinks to the level of a commodity" (Marx [1844]
1994, 58). The process of wage labor, according to Marx, is explicitly a process
of dehumanization: "The result, therefore, is that man (the worker) feels that
he is acting freely only in his animal functions—eating, drinking, and procre-
ating, or at most in his shelter and finery—while in his human functions

[labor] he feels only like an animal. The animalistic becomes human, and the human becomes animal" (62).

One might wonder how such a scandalous state of affairs is tolerated. Following Rousseau, Marx suggests that it is tolerated cheerfully by the oppressed by virtue of an elaborately constructed ideology. This ideology represents the key to the bourgeoisie's successful reign. By carefully creating and maintaining a belief system, the capitalist is able to control almost every aspect of the proletariat's life:

> The ideas of the ruling class are in every epoch the ruling ideas: i.e., the class which is the ruling *material* force of society is at the same time its ruling *intellectual* force. The class which has the means of material production at its disposal, consequently also controls the means of mental production, so that the ideas of those who lack the means of mental production are on the whole subject to it. The ruling ideas are nothing more than the ideal expression of the dominant material relations, the dominant material relations grasped as ideas; hence of the relations which make the one class the ruling one, therefore, the ideas of its dominance. ([1845] 1998, 67)[10]

This is perfectly consistent with Marx's historical materialism. If the material world is the origin of all inquiry, the material world can explain the origin of our ideas. They are given to us by those who can most profit from them. And, also following Rousseau, they are accepted "voluntarily" (*Capital*, 899) by all those who suffer the most.

The parallels in Marx's and Rousseau's descriptions of society are too striking to go unnoticed.[11] The wealthy use their power to create an ideology that

10. This important element of Marxian epistemology can be found in many places in his writings. Not only does it constitute a substantial theme in the *German Ideology*, but it is also a significant part of the *Communist Manifesto* (172–74) and the preface to his *Contribution to the Critique of Political Economy* ([1844] 1987, 263).

11. This connection, while not emphasized to a great extent in the literature, has been noted by Colletti (1972), Lecercle (1982), Wokler (1982), Horowitz (1987), and Dannhauser (1997). Interestingly, the one who seems least aware of this connection with Rousseau is Marx himself. Marx makes at least a dozen references to Rousseau in his writings, and almost every one of them is to his *Social Contract*. Further, none of these references resembles homage. In fact, they are more often than not proscriptions. It is noteworthy, however, that Engels was aware of the connection and drew attention to this in his *Anti-Dühring*: "Already in Rousseau . . . we find not only a sequence of ideas which corresponds exactly with the sequence developed in Marx's *Capital*, but that the correspondence extends also to details, Rousseau using a whole series of the same dialectical developments as Marx used: processes which in their nature are antagonistic, contain a contradiction, are the transformation of one extreme into its opposite" ([1878] 1939, 153–54).

effectively persuades the people that they are happy. Rousseau reports that this ideology includes the ideas of justice, law, and freedom. Marx tells us that it encompasses "freedom" (*Communist Manifesto,* 171), "justice" (175), and "jurisprudence" (172). For Marx, freedom is particularly potent as ideology, insofar as it is the bourgeoisie's greatest tool of profit enhancement. As long as the people demand their "freedom," Marxian philosophy suggests, the bourgeoisie is free to plunder in the open market. Of course, consistent with Marx's desire to critique everything, he does not stop at Rousseau's categories of ideology. In *The German Ideology,* he extends it to include the "language of politics, . . . morality, religion, metaphysics, etc." ([1845] 1998, 42).

2.2. MARX AND JUDGMENT

"The philosophers have only *interpreted* the world in various ways; the point is, to *change* it." Marx's famous dictum from "Theses on Feuerbach" suggests that his characterization of modern industrial capitalism is not an end in itself. The critique is, rather, a call to action. It can only be interpreted as such, however, if we first understand it as an indictment of the existing regime. And there is plenty of evidence in Marx of just that. His texts are full of judgmental language. Consider the following passages:

1. "It [the bourgeoisie] has resolved personal worth into exchange value, and in place of the numberless indefeasible chartered freedoms, has set up that single, *unconscionable* freedom—Free Trade. In one word, for exploitation, veiled by religious and political illusions, it has substituted naked, *shameless,* direct, *brutal* exploitation" (*Communist Manifesto,* 161, emphases added).
2. "The more openly this *despotism* proclaims gain to be its end and aim, the more *petty,* the more *hateful,* and the more *embittering* it is" (*Communist Manifesto,* 165, emphases added).
3. "All we want to do away with is the *miserable* character of this appropriation" (*Communist Manifesto,* 171, emphasis added).
4. "France . . . seems to have escaped the *despotism* of a class only to fall back beneath the *despotism* of an individual" ([1852] 1994, 198, emphases added).
5. "The bourgeois order . . . has become a vampire that sucks the blood and brains and throws them into the alchemist's cauldron of capital" ([1852] 1994, 203).
6. "There have been in Asia, generally, from immemorial times, but

three departments of Government: that of Finance, or the *plunder* of the interior; that of War, or the *plunder* of the exterior; and, finally, the department of Public Works" ([1853] 1978, 655, emphases added).

7. "That *monstrosity,* the disposable working population held in reserve, in misery, for the changing requirements of capitalist exploitation, must be replaced by the individual man who is absolutely available for different kinds of labour required of him" (*Capital,* 618, emphasis added).

8. "The expropriation of the direct producers was accomplished by means of the most *merciless barbarism,* and under the stimulus of the most *infamous,* the most *sordid,* the most *petty* and the most *odious* of passions" (*Capital,* 928, emphases added).

9. "The *theft of alien labor time, on which the present wealth is based,* appears a miserable foundation in face of this new one, created by large-scale industry itself" ([1857–58] 1973, 705).

Expanding the scope to include Engels, one finds even more direct moral condemnations of capitalist society:

1. "Modern economics . . . reveals itself to be that same *hypocrisy, inconsistency* and *immorality* which now confront free humanity in every sphere" (Engels [1844] 1975, 420, emphases added).

2. The liberal economic system has transformed people into "ravenous beasts" ([1844] 1975, 423).[12]

3. "The *immorality* of lending at interest, of receiving without working, merely for making a load, though already implied in private property, is only too obvious, and has long ago been recognized for what it is by unprejudiced popular consciousness, which in such matters is usually *right*" ([1844] 1975, 430, emphasis added).

4. "The perpetual fluctuation of prices such as is created by the condition of competition completely deprives trade of its last vestige of *morality*" ([1844] 1975, 434, emphasis added).

5. "*[I]mmorality's* culminating point is the speculation on the Stock Exchange" ([1844] 1975, 434, emphasis added).

6. "Am I to go on any longer elaborating this *vile,* infamous theory, this *hideous blasphemy against nature and mankind?*" ([1844] 1975, 437, emphasis added).

12. This is a clear echo of Rousseau's wealthy "ravenous wolves" (*SD,* 171/*OC,* III:175).

7. "Class warfare is so open and *shameless* that it has to be seen to be believed. The observer of such an *appalling* state of affairs must shudder at the consequences of such feverish activity and can only marvel that so crazy a social and economic structure should survive at all" ([1844] 1958, 31, emphasis added).

8. The women in factories are persistently exposed to the *"moral evils"* of their employers ([1844] 1958, 166, emphasis added).

There is little room for doubt here. As was the case with Rousseau, judgment is indeed a substantial component of Marx's and Engels's thought. By whatever standard they may be employing, they genuinely find the circumstances they describe to be troubling. On what foundation do they offer such judgments?

2.3. THE FOUNDATIONS OF MARXIAN JUDGMENT

The vast literature on Marx reveals two truths. First, Marx clearly disapproves of the conditions of modern industrial capitalism (Tucker 1969, 34–36; Tucker 1978, xxxi; Wood 1980b, 106; Husami 1980, 43–44; Lukes 1985, 3; Seung 1994, 221; Torrance 1995, 281). Second, he never elaborates a moral or political theory to support these judgments (Tucker 1978, 725; Wood 1980a, 3). On the one hand, this is not surprising, given his general antipathy for idealism. The world of judgment is necessarily entangled with the realm of ideas. On the other hand, the lack of an obvious theoretical underpinning is frustrating for his readers, because his overt moral language begs for development at the metaethical level. His interpreters are thus left to attempt this development themselves. My task here is not to elaborate a full theory of Marxian justice, as others have done, but to get to the foundations of his judgments.

On the matter of foundations, the Marx literature is divided. One camp (Husami 1980; Torrance 1995), relying on much of the evidence provided above, argues that Marx has a theory of justice. After all, how can Marx and Engels make the judgments they do without having something to back up their claims? To lack at least an implicit theory of justice would appear irrational. The other camp (Tucker 1969; Wood 1980ab) suggests that Marx has no theory of justice. On this view, there abounds too much textual evidence explicitly denying the existence of anything like transcendent moral norms to accommodate a transhistorical conception of justice.

The existence of the two opposed camps can be partly explained by the fact that Marx himself employs moral vocabulary in two different contexts

(Husami 1980, 47; Torrance 1995, 287). There is, according to Husami, a difference between the "Marxian Sociology of Morals" and the "Marxian Moral Theory." The sociology of morals refers to Marx's understanding of moral vocabulary in particular contexts. This helps to explain some otherwise perplexing passages. When Marx refers to the "beauty of capitalist production" (*Capital,* 935), for example, he appears to be speaking contrary to all his judgments that condemn the system. He is, however, clearly speaking in such contexts not to some external, transcendent conception of justice, but rather to a localized, relative norm. Capitalism has its own rules of "justice" and "beauty," which are codified in laws and culture. As addressed above, they were created by the bourgeoisie to help maintain control over the masses. They vary from place to place and time to time. Therefore, "justice" and "beauty" (and it is important here to read these words with the quotation marks) can take virtually any form whatsoever. It is contingent on the will of the ruling class, as Marx often says. This understanding of Marx's "sociology of morals" can therefore explain the many instances of "justice" as a relative concept in his writings.

"Marxian Moral Theory," on the other hand, refers to the judgments Marx and Engels make outside these particular contexts—judgments made either of a system as a whole, judgments within a particular system but contrary to its positive norms, or comparisons of entire systems. The examples provided in section 2.2 represent such judgments. Judgments of entire cultures or the employment of norms not embraced by the particular culture being judged can be considered transcendent. We might here be tempted to conclude that Marx has a "transhistorical" (Torrance 1995, 297) or "transcendent" (Seung 1994, 221) conception of justice on the occasions when he speaks of justice and morality outside the context of particular systems. This interpretation, however, is complicated by Marx's and Engels's apparent claims to the contrary. Those who argue that Marx and Engels critique the very notion of justice itself cite passages such as the following:

> Proudhon creates his ideal of justice, or *"justice éternelle,"* from the juridical relations that correspond to the production of commodities: he thereby proves, to the consolation of all good petty bourgeois, that the production of commodities is a form as eternal as justice. Then he turns round and seeks to reform the actual production of commodities, and the corresponding legal system, in accordance with this ideal. What would one think of a chemist who, instead of studying the actual laws governing molecular interactions, and on that basis

solving definite problems, claimed to regulate those interactions by means of "eternal ideas" of *"naturalité"* and *"affinité"*? Do we really know any more about "usury," when we say it contradicts *"justice éternelle,"* *"mutualité éternelle,"* and other *"vérités éternelles"* than the fathers of the church did when they said it was incompatible with *"grâce éternelle,"* *"foi éternelle,"* and *"la volunté éternelle de Dieu"*? (*Capital,* 178–79)

Engels provides an apparently franker statement of the same position in his *Anti-Dühring:*

> We . . . reject every attempt to impose on us any moral dogma what-soever as an eternal, ultimate and forever immutable moral law on the pretext that the moral world too has its permanent principles which transcend history and the differences between nations. What we maintain on the contrary is that all former moral theories are the product, in the last analysis, of the economic stage which society had reached at that particular epoch. And as society has hitherto moved in class antagonisms, morality was always a class morality; it has either justified the domination and the interests of the ruling class, or, as soon as the oppressed class has become powerful enough, it has represented the revolt against this domination and the future inter-ests of the oppressed.[13] That in this process there has on the whole been progress in morality, as in all other branches of human knowl-edge, cannot be doubted. But we have not yet passed beyond class morality. A really human morality which transcends class antago-nisms and their legacies in thought becomes possible only at a stage of society which has not only overcome class contradictions but has even forgotten them in practical life. ([1878] 1939, 104–5)

Tucker says that such passages reveal that "the principle of . . . justice is alien to the mental world of Marxism" (1969, 41). At first glace, this is certainly persuasive. More apparently emphatic dismissals of transcendent norms of jus-tice and morality would be difficult to find. At this juncture, Marx and Engels seem to depart from Rousseau's model.[14] Whereas Rousseau criticizes the existing system by virtue of its violation of a transcendent standard of justice,

---

13. One cannot help but note Engels's resemblance to Nietzsche here.

14. I speak here, of course, only of the dimensions of epistemology and metaphysics and not of the specific details of the critiques.

Marx and Engels explicitly deny this very standard itself. Or this, at least, is what some argue.

The excerpts, however, require closer examination. Although it is true that Engels "reject[s] every attempt to impose . . . any moral dogma whatsoever as eternal," it is also true that he is speaking specifically of historically bound theories of justice and morality. He adds that he is speaking of "former moral theories," suggesting that some contemporary understandings may not be subject to his critique. Further, he notes that there has been progress in morals. In this respect, he begins to sound like Kant. " 'Progress' is not a neutral term," noted the great twentieth-century Marxist Herbert Marcuse: "it moves toward specific ends, and these ends are defined by the possibilities of ameliorating the human condition" (1964, 16). Engels suggests these ends himself, saying that we are working toward a "really human morality which transcends class antagonisms."

In fact, what Engels appears to be pointing toward is the final stage of history, when class conflict is only a memory rather than a fact of life. It is at this stage that Engels suggests we can begin to speak of morality. Of course, he already has this standard in mind when he observes his contemporary surroundings. This standard apparently informs his myriad judgments, for example, in the *Conditions of the Working Class in England.* There he speaks of "repulsive and disgraceful" living conditions, the "cheating" of the bourgeoisie, "the poor state of health of the working class," "workers who are treated like beasts," the lack of heat in workers' homes, the "high mortality among the children of the workers," and so forth ([1844] 1958, 31, 82, 117, 129, 145, 169). These are all empirical claims, to be certain. One may subsequently be tempted to say that his judgment that these features of modern industrial capitalism are also "immoral" is also an empirical judgment, but this cannot be so. Empirical observation only provides the data on which one can make a judgment. It does not provide judgment itself. It is logically possible to view the conditions Engels describes and not say that they are immoral or unjust. It is even possible that in a perverse world, someone could observe the same phenomena and judge that these circumstances are just. Engels does not see "immorality"; rather, he sees empirical circumstances that compel his judgment of immorality. It is observations such as those above that lead him to call the conditions of the working class "truly deplorable . . . [and] an affront to human dignity" (37). Nor is Engels averse to relying on the idea of justice: "The just claim of the workers . . . will one day be realized" (141). Engels is not opposed to justice—but he is opposed to bourgeois justice, and in this sense he appears faithful to the legacy of Rousseau. It is not clear that Marx or Engels ever explicitly embraces anything like a Platonic idea of justice. It is evident, however, that they have a standard of justice that transcends particular cultures or moments in history, and this itself is part of the ontological claims of Platonism. This is extremely important in reading them, because a failure to do so renders their many judgments nonsensical. It is worth adding, however, that this is likely as far in the direction of Plato as they will go. Unlike Rousseau, they do not make any statements of faith in metaphysical or epistemic Platonism or in the tenets of modern European Platonism.

3. Michel Foucault: Power, Justice, and Epistemology

3.1. FOUCAULT AND THE CRITIQUE OF MODERNITY

In the spirit of Rousseau, Michel Foucault opens his *Discipline and Punish* with great flair (perhaps too much so for the weak of stomach). He graphically describes an episode of drawing and quartering as recorded by an eyewitness in 1757. His point in portraying this act is not to argue against such violence; rather, he means to illustrate the dying gasp of an outmoded and inefficient "technology of power." The practice of public torture had its place in the history of Western law and politics, to be sure, according to Foucault. It had the effect of asserting the king's sovereignty, and no doubt discouraged some from carrying through with illicit plans in fear of suffering such torment themselves. Public torture, however, came at a cost to the king. It could, for example, have the effect of making the condemned an object of pity and even admiration (*DP*, 9). This was precisely the opposite of the intended effect, which was to make him the object of hatred and ridicule. Rulers were thus compelled to look for other, more effective ways in which to achieve their goals. This quest ultimately led to the development of not only the modern prison but also an elaborate system of pervasive surveillance and measurement in the modern state.

The modern state marks an important transition for Foucault—from the body to the soul as the locus of the state's operation on the individual (*DP*, 101). Punishment is no longer seen as a physical means to beat down the opponents of the state. Instead, it is a technique to remake their minds. Prison slowly began to fulfill this function, according to Foucault. The incarcerated were no longer subject to excessive and public physical abuse (in fact, the less public, the better). They were, however, subject to a rigid regulation of every element of their lives. This included a strict timetable, forced religious readings, and constant supervision. By controlling the prisoner's every move, the prison itself became "a machine for altering minds" (125). Just as Rousseau describes it, the state assumes the function of a brainwashing institution. This process of soul transformation could only be carried off with extensive surveillance and measurement. Thus, the warden needed access to large amounts of data. The greater the data, the more refined the treatment. The obvious irony, in Foucault's eyes, is that prison reform was not effected with the humane goal of creating decent citizens, but rather for the more sinister goal of creating docile subjects: "ultimately, what one is trying to restore in this technique of correction is not so much the juridical subject, who is caught up in the fundamental interests of the social pact, but the obedient subject, the individual subjected to habits, rules, orders, an authority that is exercised continually around him and upon him, and which he must allow to function automatically on him" (128–29).

This process was not limited to the arena of the prison, according to Foucault. Rather, it became the model for an entire society. Subjects were not valued for their intellect, achievements, moral virtue, or any other dimension than that of their ability to obey commands. In this respect, the prison became a model for society. The schoolhouse, with its constant supervision and measurement, was an exceptionally natural and useful place in which to implement this model. That children were young and had malleable minds made it all the more efficacious. All of these processes had the effect of "transform[ing] the confused, useless or dangerous multitudes into ordered multiplicities" (*DP*, 148). Whether in the prison or the school, the goal was the same: to create subjects easily controlled by the state.

Foucault describes a similar history in *Madness and Civilization.* The resident of the asylum was taught "virtue by force" ([1961] 1988, 61). The staff would work to inculcate not just a set of ethical rules but also an actual conscience, so the patient would eventually become self-regulating. Any time the patient would commit an act contrary to the norms of the dominant power (and its accompanying morality), he would feel an acute sense of guilt. "In other words," Foucault writes, "by this guilt the madman became an object of punishment always vulnerable to himself and to the Other; and, from the acknowledgement of his status as object, from the awareness of his guilt, the madman was to return to his awareness of himself as a free and responsible subject, and consequently to reason" (247).[15] The establishment of "reason"

15. The formation of conscience, particularly a bad one, is a Nietzschean concept Foucault undoubtedly got from Nietzsche himself. See Nietzsche ([1888] 1994, 52–53). Although Foucault's Nietzschean elements do not form the substance of this essay, it would be irresponsible not to acknowledge them. As Foucault himself says, "I am simply a Nietzschean, and I try as far as possible,

was in fact the establishment of the dominant power's preferences. As soon as prisoners exhibited the capacity to regulate their own behavior along these lines, they were free to go.

Without knowing who the authors of this radical plan are, however, we lack a significant element of Foucault's narrative. His own words suggest that locating a responsible party is exceptionally tricky. More than once he tells us that the power exercised is diffuse and "cannot be localized in a particular type of institution or state apparatus" (*DP*, 26, 138). In this respect, Foucault appears to diverge from both Marx and Rousseau, who place blame squarely on particular classes. And Foucault is undoubtedly sincere in suggesting that power cannot be attached to any particular institution or class. On at least a few occasions, however, he appears to place blame on the bourgeoisie (*DP*, 76, 274; [1961] 1988, 58, 259; [1978] 1990, 1:124–25). In *Madness and Civilization*, for example, he suggests that the purpose of at least one form of treatment was to "guarantee bourgeois morality a universality of fact and permit it to be imposed as a law upon all forms of insanity" ([1961] 1988, 259). This bourgeois morality associated madness with "indigence, laziness, and vice" (259) and was able to exercise social control over those disinclined to take their role in the new economy. To be "reasonable" was to accept its moral norms (59–60). Yet although this is a bourgeois morality, it is not clear that the bourgeoisie is consciously applying it—and, in this respect, Foucault distinguishes himself from the specifics of Rousseau and Marx while remaining faithful to the spirit of their critique.

We are now in a position to understand Foucault's famous knowledge/power epistemology. Those who have power have the capacity to reshape the consciences of their subjects:

> We should admit . . . that power produces knowledge (and not simply by encouraging it because it serves power or by applying it because it is useful); that power and knowledge directly imply one another; that there is no power relation without the correlative field of knowledge, nor any knowledge that does not presuppose and constitute at the same time power relations. These "power-knowledge relations" are to be analyzed, therefore, not on the basis of a subject of knowledge who is or is not free in relation to the power system, but, on the contrary, the subject who knows, the objects to be known

on a certain number of issues, to see with the help of Nietzsche's texts . . . what can be done in this or that domain" (1991, 327). Nietzsche himself follows some of Rousseau's argumentation as laid out in the *Second Discourse*, but to discuss this here would be to embark upon another essay.

and the modalities of knowledge must be regarded as so many effects of these fundamental implications of power-knowledge and their historical transformations. In short, it is not the activity of the subject of knowledge that produces a corpus of knowledge, the processes and struggles that traverse it and of which it is made up, that determines the forms and possible domains of knowledge. (*DP*, 27–28)

On this critical dimension, Foucault is following closely in the footsteps of both Rousseau and Marx. Knowledge of things such as "justice," "law," and "freedom," for Rousseau, entails the content of whatever ideology the rich are feeding the poor. The same goes for Marx as well as Foucault. Whoever holds power has the capacity to remake the minds of the citizens.

In what fashion does the bourgeoisie reshape the poor and unwitting? It does so partly in secret, and partly very much in the open. Foucault writes that "power is only tolerable on condition that it mask a substantial part of itself" ([1978] 1990, 1:86). Ironically, this secretive part can be executed in the full view of the citizens. This public portion is the social contract. Following Rousseau yet once more, Foucault says that the social contract is the sugar that helps this bitter pill (the norms that serve to support the bourgeoisie) go down easily:

> By operating at every level of the social body and by mingling ceaselessly the art of rectifying and the right to punish, the universality of the carceral lowers the level from which it becomes natural and acceptable to be punished. The question is often posed as to how, before and after the Revolution, a new foundation was given to the right to punish. And no doubt the answer is to be found in the theory of the contract. But it is perhaps more important to ask the reverse question: how were people made to accept the power to punish, or quite simply, when punished, tolerate being so. The theory of the contract can only answer this question by the fiction of a juridical subject giving to the other the power to exercise over him the right that he himself possesses over them. It is highly probable that the great carceral continuum, which provides a communication between the power of discipline and the power of the law, and extends without interruption from the smallest coercions to the longest penal detention, constituted the technical and real material counterpart of that chimerical granting of the right to punish. (*DP*, 303)

As in Rousseau's account, here the consent of the oppressed is a prerequisite to the functioning of the system. The genius of the social contract for Foucault is that it operates both clandestinely and out in the open simultaneously. It is open insofar as the citizens are, generally speaking, aware of their consent to the laws and norms of society. It is secretive insofar as they have no true idea of what these laws and norms are doing to them. It is this secretive component that is the most normatively disconcerting. That Foucault does not take this contract to be legitimate is obvious from his vocabulary. He speaks above of the "fiction of the juridical subject" and the "chimerical granting of the right to punish." Both comments suggest that there is something awry with this "contract." If the citizens are not aware of the terms to which they are agreeing, in what sense can one consider the agreement legitimate?

3.2. FOUCAULT AND JUDGMENT

Finding explicit judgments in Foucault can be difficult. His tone of speech is decidedly different from that found in Rousseau or Marx. Rather than finding outright condemnations of the bourgeoisie, we find what appears to be a carefully sketched, morally neutral history. This is perhaps one reason Foucault preferred not to be called a "philosopher" ([1981] 1991, 29) but was more comfortable with the label of "historian" (1989a, 12).[16] Historians are not required to offer judgment on the phenomena they describe. Rather, they can present a value-free recounting of past events. Or at least this is the theory. Foucault himself suggests that exceptions abound. The practice of historians, on his account, "was the simplest way of reconciling their political conscience and their activity as researchers or writers. Under the sign of the cross of history, every discourse became a prayer to the God of just causes" (1989a, 12).

Although Foucault speaks here of "uninformed and traditionalist" historians, his remarks could be applied with equal justice to his own work. This is because, in spite of his obvious attempts to purge his writings of normative content, judgment rears its head on a few occasions.[17] Nancy Fraser finds the Foucauldian vocabulary rife with "ominous overtones" in the employment of such words as "domination," "subjugation," and "subjection" (Fraser 1981, 282). It is possible, however, to use some of these terms in morally neutral ways. One can say that "Serena Williams *dominates* her competition" without

16. It is worth noting that Foucault considers the terms "Marxist" and "historian" potentially synonymous: "One might wonder what difference there could ultimately be between being a historian and being a Marxist" (1980, 53).

17. Balkin argues persuasively that this is the fate of all "neutral" critiques (1998, 124).

suggesting that this phenomenon is either good or bad. There are other words, however, hidden in the depths of Foucault's texts that suggest he is not as neutral as he would like the reader to believe.

1. "There was the great 'confinement' of vagabonds and paupers; there were other more discreet, but *insidious* and effective ones" (*DP*, 141, emphasis added).

2. "Hierarchized, continuous and functional surveillance may not be one of the great technical 'inventions' of the eighteenth century, but its *insidious* extension owed its importance to the mechanisms of power that it brought with it" (*DP*, 176, emphasis added).

3. "[T]he development and generalization of disciplinary mechanisms constituted the other, *dark side* [*obscur*] of these processes [of equal protection under the law]" (*DP*, 222, emphasis added).

4. "[T]he notions of institutions of repression, rejection, exclusion, marginalization, are not adequate to describe, at the very centre of the carceral city, the formation of the *insidious* leniencies, unavowable petty cruelties, small acts of cunning, calculated methods, techniques, 'sciences' that permit the fabrication of the disciplinary individual" (*DP*, 308, emphasis added).

5. "Nothing is more *inconsistent* than a political regime that is indifferent to the truth; but nothing is more *dangerous* than a political system that claims to prescribe the truth" (Foucault 1989b, 308, emphasis added).

Although none of these statements represents a moral imperative, they all retain the tone of moral judgment. Further, they are more decisive than words such as "dominate." "Insidious" is never a word someone employs in order to praise a person or a practice. Likewise with "dark side" or "dangerous." These are terms of warning that something is wrong and requires attention.

3.3. FOUCAULT AND JUSTICE

If it is true that Foucault offers judgment when employing such words and phrases as "insidious," "dangerous," or "dark side," on what grounds is he basing these evaluations? By what standard is something "insidious"? This was an easy question for Rousseau to answer, because he presumed the existence of transcendent norms. It was more difficult for Marx and Engels, because they appeared to deny the existence of such norms. Foucault, as we shall see, goes a step further than this: he denies transcendent norms without qualification.

Because Foucault's writings frequently have more the character of history than they do philosophy, they rarely address philosophic questions directly. On one occasion, however, he took up the ontological nature of justice—in his 1971 interview on Dutch television with Noam Chomsky. Chomsky's reflections years later suggest that the meeting made a deep impression: "I'd never met anyone who was so totally amoral" ([1990] 1993, 201).

The interview began with an exchange on the fixity of human nature but slowly evolved into one on the question of justice, when Chomsky suggested that it was morally proper to disobey unjust laws. Foucault responded by asking whether he meant to justify his civil disobedience on the basis of a "superior legality" (Foucault and Chomsky [1971] 1997, 134) or as a tool in class struggle. After further exchange, Foucault repeated his question: "Are you committing this act [of civil disobedience] in virtue of an ideal justice, or because the class struggle makes it useful and necessary? Do you refer to ideal justice, that's my problem." Chomsky responds that there is a justice higher than that of the positive law. This provoked Foucault to elaborate his theory of "justice":

> There is an important question for us here. It is true that in all social struggles, there is a question of "justice." To put it more precisely, the fight against class justice, against its injustice, is always part of the social struggle: to dismiss judges, to change the tribunals, to amnesty the condemned, to open prisons, has always been part of social transformations as soon as they become slightly violent. . . . But if justice is a stake in a struggle, then it is an instrument of power; it is not in the hope that finally one day, in this or another society, people will be rewarded according to their merits, or punished according to their faults. Rather than thinking of the social struggle in terms of "justice," one has to emphasize justice in terms of the social struggle. (135–36)

Foucault's answer distinguishes his view from Chomsky's. "Justice" is not an idea but is rather a tool employed in the promotion of social conflicts. More than this, it is a tool *fabricated* for this purpose: "it seems to me that the idea of justice in itself is an idea which in effect has been invented and put to work in different types of societies as an instrument of a certain political and economic power or as a weapon against that power. But it seems to me that, in any case, the notion of justice itself functions within a society of classes as a claim made by the oppressed class and as justification for it" (139).[18] It is difficult to be any more explicit on the ontological nature of justice than this. There is no higher conception of justice beyond that which we invent for ourselves. Anything perceived to exist in this place is a fiction, likely created for the purpose of fooling us into accepting the bourgeoisie-serving status quo. This is the classic antithesis of metaphysical and ontological Platonism.

In some sense Foucault has taken the Rousseauean critique to its logical limits: it has turned the critique against itself. Rousseau suggested that the wealthy created norms of "justice" to manipulate and dominate the poor, but he based his critique and judgment on a higher standard of justice. Foucault says that this *higher notion of justice is itself a bourgeois invention* created for the same purpose.[19] We cannot trust appeals to higher justice, because they only reinforce the existing structural domination.

There is a sense in which Foucault's stance is highly understandable. For all of the claims of Plato and Rousseau, there is precious little empirical evidence that immaterial ideas play a role in politics, at least when contrasted with simple brute power. Power—for all its diffuseness—has empirical manifestations. Power makes things happen. It shapes the actions of both individuals and states. In Foucault's own youth, this was particularly evident. Power overtook Poland and the Sudetenland. Power forced the *Anschluß*. Power brought the Nazis to France, and power made some French officials welcoming of this presence. There is no questioning the empirical evidence of force.

His critique of justice, however, is subject to scrutiny. If there is only "justice" without justice, on what basis can he normatively evaluate the system of bourgeois domination? As Nancy Fraser has asked, "Foucault calls for resistance to domination. But why? Why is the struggle preferable to submission? Why ought domination to be resisted? Only with the introduction of normative notions of some kind could Foucault begin to answer such questions" (1981, 283).

The answer, alas, appears to be that Foucault implicitly betrays his own work. In section 3.2 we examined a few passages revealing *negative* judgment, but a little more digging through his corpus reveals also some *positive* judgment.

18. One consequence of this fact, according to Foucault, is that people do not engage in war because they perceive the violation of some right. Rather, people create "rights" in order to support their wars ([1976] 2003, 16–17).

19. This should not be a surprise, because, as Thomas R. Flynn has remarked, "Foucault's anti-Platonism is well known," and his specific problem with Plato was "the metaphysical notion of truth" (1985, 531).

1. "If governments make *human rights* the structure and the very framework of their political actions, that is well and good. But *human rights* are, above all, that which one confronts governments with. They are the *limits* that one places on all possible governments" ([1982] 2000, 471, emphases added).

2. "There exists an international citizenship that has its *rights and its duties,* and that obliges one to speak out against every *abuse of power,* whoever its author, whoever its victims" ([1984] 2000, 474, emphases added).

3. "It is a *duty* of this international citizenship to always bring the testimony of people's suffering to the eyes and ears of governments, sufferings for which it's untrue that they are not *responsible.* The suffering of men must never be a silent residue of policy. It grounds an *absolute right* to stand up and speak to those who hold power" ([1984] 2000, 474–75, emphases added).

In some sense, in quoting from these sources, I have caught Foucault off guard. Each of these writings was written for popular audiences and for specific political ends. They were not carefully crafted academic works. Nevertheless, they give us perhaps the best clue to the inner workings of Foucault's normative system. He clearly evokes rights, responsibilities, and duties—absolute ones, no less.[20] The result of this is even more judgment. With the acceptance of such standards, Foucault can make even stronger *negative* judgments than those we found earlier:

1. "A punishment that goes unaccounted for may well be justified; it will still be an injustice" ([1979] 2000, 441).

2. Europe presently hosts "[t]wo political forms that are not only incompatible but one of which is utterly intolerable. There are hundreds of millions of Europeans separated from us by a line that is both arbitrary in its reason for being and uncrossable in its reality: they are living in a regime of totally restricted freedoms, in a state of

20. It is possible that Foucault's conception of human rights here is a positivistic conception, grounded in some kind of international compact. But this has its own problems. First, Foucault condemns the social contract in *Discipline and Punish* as being a tool of the bourgeoisie. Second, if this potential international compact were somehow impervious to this critique, Foucault would need some kind of account of which contracts were legitimate and which ones were illegitimate. This would require a theory of political legitimacy, which suggests an appeal to higher norms than his theory would permit.

subright. This historical fracture of Europe is something that we must not resign ourselves to" ([1982] 2000, 469).

These passages clearly contradict Foucault's suggestions of neutrality. One cannot speak of injustice without implicitly relying on a standard of justice.

Foucault's employment of normative vocabulary may be explicable in terms of his discussion of a similar vocabulary employed by others. People create "justice" to support or advance particular political interests or claims.[21] On this interpretation, Foucault is doing what he accuses others of doing—he is inventing the terms "justice" and "rights" to bolster the social movements in Poland and Iran. This interpretation has one clear advantage: it is perfectly consistent with many of his explicit claims. The problem, however, is that on this interpretation, the concepts of "justice" and "rights" lack normative force. If "justice" is Foucault's invention in these instances, on what grounds could his reader prefer his "justice" to that of the critiqued regimes?[22] This reading of Foucault leaves one with no reason to choose his version of justice over the state's. Alternatively, he might be relying on a personal taste shared with the reader. Yet given that one of the above examples comes in the form of a letter to an opponent, this cannot be a reasonable expectation. An opponent, by definition, is presumed to have an alternative opinion. The entire problem is that his correspondent does not share his understanding of justice. Further, people do not argue about taste in any meaningful sense. No public official, to my knowledge, has ever been written to correct his taste in, for example, ice cream. Foucault thus appears to be engaged in an act of persuasion—that his own conception of justice is *better* than that of his correspondent. This, however, takes him to the next level of ontological abstraction. A claim that one conception of justice is better than another implies a higher standard than a localized fabrication. It requires a standard external to both him and his correspondent—the Rousseauean standard—the existence of which he explicitly denies.

Moreover, if Foucault is employing claims of rights and justice as a rhetorical form of power, he runs into another difficulty. He is relying on a presupposed shared sense of justice with his audience. Shared norms, however, are difficult to presuppose when one denies transcendent norms and at the same

21. This is the interpretation recommended in at least one instance by James Miller (1993, 452).

22. In this respect, Charles Taylor finds Foucault's work to be paradoxical, "because Foucault's analyses seem to bring evils to light; and yet he wants to distance himself from the suggestion that would seem inescapably to follow, that the negation or overcoming of these evils promotes a good" (1984, 152).

time challenges existing conventions. If the dominant conventions are truly dominant, and there are no transcendent norms, then it is difficult to imagine where Foucault expects to find a sympathetic audience. Such arguments are more successful—not only in their ontological consistency, but also in their rhetorical power—when they appeal to a shared set of norms lying underneath the dominant ideology.

What is particularly frustrating in Foucault's writings is his willingness to contradict himself on this matter—sometimes within the same work. In "The Moral and Social Experience of the Poles Can No Longer Be Obliterated," Foucault reports that the Polish people are "living in a regime of totally restricted freedoms, in a state of subright," only to assert a few pages later, "One must guard against the reintroduction of a hegemonic thought on the pretext of presenting a human rights theory or policy. After all, Leninism was presented as a human rights policy" ([1982] 2000, 472). Ignoring the guilt by association fallacy, we can read his use of "right" in a few different ways. First, we could read "subright" as an emotive claim with no universal significance and "human rights theory" as an ontologically similar claim by the state. If Foucault's claim is merely emotive, however, he has given us no reason to prefer his conception of "subright" over the state's "human rights theory." Second, we could read his "subright" as a transcendent claim and the state's "human rights theory" as a positive one. This, however, directly contradicts his statements that there are no transcendent claims of justice. Further, if he believed that there was such a thing as transcendent rights, it would be difficult to imagine that he would proscribe the state's protection of them. Third, we could read his "subright" as emotive and the state's "human rights theory" as transcendent. Again, however, if Foucault's claim is emotive or positive, he can offer his reader no reason to prefer his conception of right over that of the state. Finally, we could read both "subright" and "human rights theory" as transcendent. This, however, would lead to contradiction, because the two rights claims conflict with one another, according to Foucault. Thus, his ontology cannot protect him against apparent contradiction, on the one hand, or normative triviality, on the other.

The best possible construction of Foucault draws on J. M. Balkin's distinction between "transcendence" and "imperialist universalism" (1998, 150–55). "Transcendence" is the concept on which Rousseau has been demonstrated to rely for his critique of modernity. "Imperialist universalism" involves making "truth" claims for underhanded purposes without any necessary relation to actual or transcendent conceptions of truth or justice. Imperialist universalism can be imposed by any dominant group on its inferiors, often with disastrous consequences. When white southern slave owners justified their treatment of African descendants as property on the basis of its "rightness," they relied on just such a technique. Of course, to take the next step and judge such instances of imperialist universalism unjust requires a standard external to the white slave-owning justificatory scheme: "one needs to presuppose transcendent standards to make the case against imperialist universalism" (Balkin 1998, 151). To make Foucault both coherent and normatively viable, in other words, one must return to Rousseau.

Conclusions

Karl Marx is most frequently characterized as both a scientist and historian. His impulses in both directions helped inform his metaphysical choices. As a historian, he was keenly aware of Hobbes and the philosophes and of their peculiar role in the development of philosophical, moral, and political thought in modern Europe. As a scientist, he was eager to employ their advances in order to promote what he perceived to be a more humane politics.

For Marx, the central figure in modern European intellectual development was René Descartes. This is because he would give birth to two trends. On the one hand, his commitment to speculative metaphysics would continue the old traditions of Plato, Aristotle, and the Scholastics and further inspire the modern European Platonists, such as Leibniz and Malebranche. On the other hand, his deep interest in physics and mechanics fueled the exploration of the French materialists, such as Helvétius and d'Holbach. Descartes's dual influence in two wildly different directions is made possible by his own dualism—his belief in two distinct metaphysical planes, and hence two distinct realms of intellectual inquiry.

The metaphysical dimension of Descartes would offend the scientific Marx. For him, this was "tempered with *positive,* profane content. . . . The whole metaphysical realm was reduced to thought-entities and heavenly things when real entities and earthly things began to be the center of all interest. Metaphysics had become stale. In the very year that Malebranche and Arnaud, the last of the great French seventeenth-century metaphysicians, died, *Helvétius* and *Condillac* were born" (Marx and Engels [1844] 1967, 389–90). The way out of this perceived Cartesian rut was the other, mechanical Descartes, who, in his *Treatise of Man,* outlined the mechanical operations of human behavior. The intellectual father of this movement in England, according to Marx, was none other than Francis Bacon. By focusing on that which could only be perceived by the senses, he had set forth a mode of inquiry that could dispense with the old and tired fashions associated with medieval science. After this, Marx observes, Hobbes would synthesize Baconian materialism into a grand and largely coherent, empirical, and scientifically justifiable system.

The laws of the natural world outlined by the mechanical Descartes, Bacon, Hobbes, and the philosophes would be the model for Marx's mode of social inquiry. Eschewing the vestigial Platonism and Scholasticism found in Hegel's idealism, Marx insisted that the laws of the social world must necessarily be empirical. History does not begin with an abstract notion of ideas or "mind" for Marx. It begins in the real world with real human beings and real-world problems—such as the lack of food, shelter, and clothing. From these empirical presuppositions would follow his laws of history and economics and, presumably, the ultimate goals of history. Marx understood all of this to fit together relatively neatly. The assumptions of materialism and determinism would naturally lead the thoughtful scholar to his prescriptions for social structure: "No great acumen is required to see the necessary connection of materialism with communism and socialism" (Marx and Engels [1844] 1967, 394). If we begin with the material suffering of human beings, it seems obvious that the purpose of history would be to alleviate it on a sound, permanent basis.

Perhaps the great failing of the Enlightenment, from Foucault's perspective, might have been its inability to follow through on its assumptions with more conviction and consistency. To be sure, the philosophes questioned and even rejected the intermingling of religion or immaterial ideas with politics. They argued that these were the great obstacle to human progress. But human progress itself, as Foucault would view it, was likewise a concept burdened by deep metaphysical assumptions. They had thought that they were replacing an ineffective and unsustainable metaphysics with one that would propel humankind into an unimaginable age of bliss. But in fact, for Foucault, they were simply replacing one set of biases for another. And each bias, in turn, would help support the power of a particular party.

Growing up in Nazi-occupied France, Foucault had firsthand experience of the effects of political power. When the Nazis marched into France, did the local governments comply as a matter of principle or because they wanted to keep their hands on what power they might plausibly retain? For Foucault, there is an easy answer to such questions. It is power, not principles, that motivates action. To the extent that principles are used, they are tools—the intellectual equivalent of tanks and bombs. Paraphrasing Clausewitz, Foucault might say that philosophical argument is war carried out by other means, because both war and argument with reference to ideas are simply two means by which one hopes to acquire power over others. To be sure, one has at least to ask the question of what might have happened in the West had Nazi Germany won its war. Would not millions of people confess allegiance to a decidedly different set of principles from those we found as a result of an Allied victory? In a world that seems more obviously dictated by power than ideas, Foucault's analysis appears to have great currency.

In this context, it is not difficult to deduce a Foucauldian interpretation of the philosophes. In their quest to catalogue and systematize all of human knowledge in the *Encyclopédie,* they were promoting the cause of their own power. Knowledge is indeed power, to cite Bacon. But it is a particular partisan power, according to a Foucauldian reading, in the context of the Enlightenment. This obsession with knowledge was ultimately aimed at promoting their own interests. The class of people most associated with this movement—La Mettrie, Helvétius, d'Holbach, and so on—were those people who stood to benefit the most from the accumulation and celebration of the growth of knowledge. Thus, it can be no surprise that their political theories would inevitably celebrate those who most resembled themselves and those who shared their interests. Political theory for Foucault is not about principles. It is about power.

In this respect, we might understand both Marx and Foucault as the outcome of the two opposing forces of the Enlightenment: Rousseau and the philosophes. From Rousseau they inherit a vast suspicion of power and the understanding that power can operate in diffuse, almost imperceptible ways. Yet while they accept the general outlines of Rousseau's critique, they are uncomfortable with its normative foundations. In this respect, they are influenced by the philosophes. From them they inherit a vast suspicion of anything metaphysical. Thus, Marx and Foucault are in a very real sense the ultimate modern philosophers—combining the assumptions of the two competing forces of the Enlightenment.

This takes us back to Rousseau. Of course, Rousseau understood the role of power in political theory. And in this respect, again, he establishes a trajectory that goes through Marx and on to Foucault. Indeed, the history of the Rousseauean critique is the history of an epistemology. Rousseau establishes what would become a major theme of modernity—that individuals can form ideas of "justice" based on what is being fed to them. Prior to Rousseau's *Second Discourse,* one finds "justice" coming from an "inner sense," as John Ponet suggests; from willfully constructed contracts, as Hobbes says; or from

God, as one finds in Locke. Rousseau opens modernity's eyes to the possibility that not all of our ideas are authentic. This is an extraordinary achievement in modern epistemology—that we may harbor and even on occasion defend to the death ideas that are not only illusions but also actively work against our well-being.

This advance in epistemic understanding is further developed and refined by Marx and Foucault. Marx takes the framework of Rousseau's work and expands the categories of critique to include not only "justice," "freedom," and "law" but also religion and morals generally. He also refines Rousseau's critique by explaining the mechanics of ideology and exploitation in industrial capitalism. Foucault further develops the critique by elucidating the role of power in "knowledge." He explores the "micro-physics of power" (*DP*, 29), showing how "knowledge" can be imposed in the least perceptible manner, even perhaps without the conscious awareness of its beneficiaries.

Foucault's refinements and developments, however, fail to take account of the most important element in Rousseau's epistemology—that there are two distinct levels of knowledge.[23] For Rousseau, there is the *knowledge of appearances* and *genuine knowledge*. Rousseau's essay "On Theatrical Imitation" states, "Not only does the imitator or the author of the simulacrum know only the appearance of the thing imitated, but the genuine knowledge [*véritable intelligence*] of that thing does not belong even to the one who has made it" (343/*OC*, V:1203). The artist, according to Rousseau, has access only to the knowledge of appearances, not of ideas themselves. This is made clear with regard to justice in his "Fragment on Freedom": "They [tyrants] enforce justice, they say, yet all their behavior is nothing but injustice, violence, and cruelty" (1994b, 12). Rousseau obviously means two very different things in this sentence by "justice" and "injustice"—and not simply that one is the negation of the other. For him, the "justice" of the tyrants is obviously a sham. He condemns this sham "justice" with a distinct alternative notion of justice, one independent of that society—one transcending agreement. Such judgments, however, are unavailable to Foucault, because he does not distinguish the two epistemic levels. So, whereas Foucault speaks in his most carefully crafted works only of "justice" (appearance or ideology), Rousseau distinguishes between "justice" (appearance or ideology) and justice (genuine knowledge). For all three thinkers, "justice" is in essence the same. It is an ideology created by the wealthy in order to establish or maintain their own power. One acquires knowledge of "justice" by either force or, even more

---

23. This is *precisely* what Herbert Marcuse means by "two-dimensional thought" (1964, 134–35).

effectively, through the cunning of the bourgeois. Justice, on the other hand, is not an ideology. It is an intuition, contingent on nothing in this world—especially the cunning or the power of the wealthy. It is, in fact, the individual's unadulterated access to knowledge of justice that represents the best chance against despotic regimes. As long as somewhere in our depths we have access to this knowledge, we can stand up against the injustices perpetrated every day.

In this respect, the epistemic transgressions of Foucault are of particular interest. Even though he carefully eliminates consideration of a genuine knowledge, he still appeals to it. Foucault admits as much in the introduction of volume 2 of the *History of Sexuality:* "The object was to learn to what extent the effort to think one's own history can free thought from what it silently thinks, and so enable it to think differently" ([1984] 1990, 9). His program is designed to break the pattern of thinking in terms of the dominant ideology or appearances. In other words, he subtly advocates that we think genuinely. This is, of course, even more apparent in the ground covered above, when he himself relies on the principles of this genuine knowledge to make his claims of right, duty, and justice. Similarly, Marx and Engels also appeal to genuine knowledge, insofar as they want us to condemn capitalism along with them. They do not want us to condemn it on the ground of some alternative ideology. They want us to condemn it because it is simply wrong.

This exercise reveals what can be called the "gravitational force of transcendent ideas." No matter how far we may get from transcendent norms in our carefully measured thought, we cannot help but appeal to them when we need them. Even the great skeptic Bertrand Russell once admitted, "When I am compelled, as happens very frequently in the modern world, to contemplate acts of cruelty which make me shudder with horror, I find myself constantly impelled towards an ethical outlook which I cannot justify intellectually. I find myself thinking, 'These men are wicked and what they do is bad in some absolute sense for which my theory has not provided'" (1954, 128). Kant conceived of the pull of transcendent standards in similar terms. We cannot help "feeling ourselves bound and limited by a certain feeling that draws our attention to the fact that an alien will, as it were, is at work in us and that our own choice requires the condition of an external decree. A secret power requires us to adjust our intentions to the welfare of others." He goes on to describe this "secret power" as being akin to Newton's principle of gravity (Kant [1766] 2002, 322/*KGS*, 2:335). There are, of course, plenty of reasons why many, along with Foucault, hesitate to defend such abstractions. Unlike accounts of the knowledge of appearances or ideology, which can be traced and measured empirically, genuine knowledge of ideas remains elusive. Informed by this epistemic unease, modernity—and especially postmodernity—has found it easiest to dismiss simply Platonism. Marx and Foucault provide further reasons to be suspicious of anyone claiming access to genuine knowledge. We would do well to heed these warnings, as so many claiming authority on such a basis have been societal nemeses. But this very concern is ultimately informed by that which Rousseau says we cannot dispense with—our intuitions of transcendent norms. Their gravitational force inevitably pulls us back to a reliance on them, regardless of the elaborate dismissals we may construct.

Annas, Julia. 1981. *An Introduction to Plato's Republic*. Oxford: Oxford University Press.

Aquinas, St. Thomas. 1988. *Summa Theologicae*. In *On Law, Morality, and Politics*, ed. William P. Baumgarth and Richard Regan, S.J. Indianapolis: Hackett.

Aristotle. 1984. *The Complete Works of Aristotle: The Revised Oxford Translation*. Princeton: Princeton University Press.

Babbitt, Irving. 1919. *Rousseau and Romanticism*. Boston: Houghton Mifflin.

Bacon, Francis. [1605] 2002. *The Advancement of Learning*. In *Francis Bacon: The Major Works*, ed. Brian Vickers. Oxford: Oxford University Press.

Balkin, J. M. 1994. "Transcendental Deconstruction, Transcendent Justice." *Michigan Law Review* 92 (5): 1131–86.

———. 1998. *Cultural Software: A Theory of Ideology*. New Haven: Yale University Press.

Barber, Benjamin. 1984. *Strong Democracy: Participatory Politics for a New Age*. Berkeley and Los Angeles: University of California Press.

Barker, Ernst. 1964. *Greek Political Theory: Plato and His Predecessors*. London: University Paperbacks.

Barzun, Jacques. [1943] 1961. "Rousseau and Modern Tyranny." In *Classic, Romantic, and Modern*. Garden City, N.Y.: Anchor Books.

Beck, Lewis White. 1960. *A Commentary on Kant's "Critique of Practical Reason."* Chicago: University of Chicago Press.

———. 1974. "Kant and the Right to Revolution." *Journal of the History of Ideas* 32 (July–September): 411–22.

Berlin, Isaiah. 1969. "Two Concepts of Liberty." In *Four Essays on Liberty*. Oxford: Oxford University Press.

———. 1991. *The Crooked Timber of Humanity: Chapters in the History of Ideas*. Princeton: Princeton University Press.

———. 2002. *Freedom and Its Betrayal: Six Enemies of Human Liberty*. Ed. Henry Hardy. Princeton: Princeton University Press.

Bertram, Christopher. 2004. *Routledge Philosophy Guidebook to Rousseau and the "Social Contract."* London: Routledge.

Bloom, Allan. [1963] 1987. "Jean-Jacques Rousseau." In *The History of Political Philosophy*, ed. Leo Strauss and Joseph Cropsey. 3rd ed. Chicago: University of Chicago Press.

———. [1969] 1991. Introduction to *The Republic of Plato*. New York: Basic Books.

———. 1979. Introduction to *Emile*, by Jean-Jacques Rousseau, trans. Allan Bloom. New York: Basic Books.

Bobbio, Noberto. 1994. *Thomas Hobbes and the Natural Law Tradition*. Trans. Daniela Gobetti. Chicago: University of Chicago Press.

Bodin, Jean. [1576] 1992. *On Sovereignty.* Ed. Julian Franklin. Cambridge: Cambridge University Press.

Bosanquet, Bernard. 1916. "The Political Writings of Jean-Jacques Rousseau." *Mind* 25 (99): 399–404.

Boyd, Richard. 2004. "Pity's Pathologies Portrayed: Rousseau and the Limits of Democratic Compassion." *Political Theory* 32 (4): 519–46.

Bradley, James E., and Dale K. Van Kley. 2001. *Religion and Politics in Enlightenment Europe.* South Bend, Ind.: University of Notre Dame Press.

Braybrooke, David. 2001. *Natural Law Modernized.* Toronto: University of Toronto Press.

Brooke, Christopher. 2001. "Rousseau's Political Philosophy: Stoic and Augustinian Origins." In *The Cambridge Companion to Rousseau,* ed. Patrick Riley. Cambridge: Cambridge University Press.

Buchanan, Allen. 1982. *Marx and Justice.* Totowa, N.J.: Rowman and Allanheld.

Budziszewski, J. 1997. *Written on the Heart: The Case for Natural Law.* Downers Grove, Ill.: Intervarsity Press.

Bull, Headley. 1983. "Hobbes and the International Anarchy." *Social Research* 48 (4): 717–38.

Butterworth, Charles E., Alexandra Cook, and Terence E. Marshall. 2000. Annotated notes to *The Reveries of the Solitary Walker, Botanical Writings, and Letter to Franquières,* ed. Christopher Kelly. Vol. 8 of *The Collected Writings of Rousseau.* Hanover, N.H.: University Press of New England.

Cairns, Huntington. 1949. *Legal Philosophy from Plato to Hegel.* Baltimore: Johns Hopkins University Press.

Cassirer, Ernst. [1945] 1963. *Rousseau, Kant, and Goethe: Two Essays by Ernst Cassirer.* New York: Harper and Row.

———. [1954] 1963. *The Question of Jean-Jacques Rousseau.* Trans. Peter Gay. Bloomington: Indiana University Press.

Chapman, John W. 1956. *Rousseau: Totalitarian or Liberal?* New York: Columbia University Press.

Charrak, André. 2002. *Le vocabulaire de Rousseau.* Paris: Ellipses.

Chomsky, Noam. [1990] 1993. Interview. Quoted in James Miller, *The Passion of Michel Foucault.* New York: Simon and Schuster.

Clark, John A. 1943. "A Definition of the General Will." *Ethics* 53 (2): 79–88.

Cobban, Alfred. 1951. "New Light on the Political Thought of Rousseau." *Political Science Quarterly* 66 (2): 272–84.

Cohen, G. A. 1983. "Book Review: *Karl Marx* by Allen Wood." *Mind* 92 (367): 440–45.

Cohen, Joshua. 1989. "Deliberation and Democratic Legitimacy." In *The Good Polity,* ed. Alan Hamlin and Philip Pettite. Oxford: Blackwell.

Colletti, Lucio. 1972. *From Rousseau to Lenin: Studies in Ideology and Society.* London: New Left Books.

Constant, Benjamin. [1814] 1988. *The Spirit of Conquest and Usurpation and Their Relation to European Civilization.* In *Political Writings,* ed. Biancamaria Fontana. Cambridge: Cambridge University Press.

———. [1815] 1988. *Principles of Politics Applicable to All Representative Governments.* In *Political Writings,* ed. Biancamaria Fontana. Cambridge: Cambridge University Press.

Cooper, Laurence D. 1999. *Rousseau, Nature, and the Problem of the Good Life.* University Park: The Pennsylvania State University Press.

———. 2002. "Human Nature and the Love of Wisdom: Rousseau's Hidden (and Modified) Platonism." *Journal of Politics* 64 (1): 108–25.

Coppleston, Frederick. [1960] 1994. *Modern Philosophy: From the French Enlightenment to Kant.* Vol. 6 of *A History of Philosophy.* New York: Image Books.

Cranston, Maurice. 1957. *John Locke: A Biography.* New York: Macmillan.

———. [1982] 1991. *Jean-Jacques: The Early Life and Work of Jean-Jacques Rousseau, 1712–1754.* Chicago: University of Chicago Press.

———. 1991. *The Noble Savage: Jean-Jacques Rousseau, 1754–1762.* Chicago: University of Chicago Press.

Crocker, Lester G. 1968. *Rousseau's Social Contract: An Interpretive Essay.* Cleveland: Press of Case Western Reserve University.

Cudworth, Ralph. [1731] 1996. *A Treatise Concerning Eternal and Immutable Morality with a Treatise of Freewill.* Ed. Sarah Hutton. Cambridge: Cambridge University Press.

Cullen, Daniel E. 1993. *Freedom in Rousseau's Political Philosophy.* DeKalb: Northern Illinois University.

Dahl, Robert A. 1956. *A Preface to Democratic Theory.* Chicago: University of Chicago Press.

Damrosch, Leo. 2005. *Jean-Jacques Rousseau: Restless Genius.* Boston: Houghton Mifflin.

Dannhauser, Werner J. 1997. "The Problem of the Bourgeois." In *The Legacy of Rousseau,* ed. Clifford Orwin and Nathan Tarcov. Chicago: University of Chicago Press.

Darwall, Stephen. 1995. *The British Moralists and the Internal "Ought": 1640–1740.* Cambridge: Cambridge University Press.

Dent, N. J. H. 1992. *A Rousseau Dictionary.* Oxford: Blackwell.

Derathé, Robert. 1970. *Rousseau et la science politique de son temps.* 2nd ed. Paris: Librairie Philosophique J. Vrin.

Descartes, René. [1637] 1968. *Discourse on Method.* In *Discourse on Method and the Meditations,* ed. F. E. Sutcliffe. London: Penguin Books.

———. [1641] 1968. *Meditations.* In *Discourse on Method and the Meditations,* ed. F. E. Sutcliffe. London: Penguin Books.

———. [1649] 1989. *The Passions of the Soul.* Trans. Stephen Voss. Indianapolis: Hackett.

Diderot, Denis. [1755] 1992. *Droit naturel.* In *Diderot: Political Writings,* ed. John Hope Mason and Robert Wokler. Cambridge: Cambridge University Press.

———. [1765] 1992. *Hobbisme.* In *Diderot: Political Writings,* ed. John Hope Mason and Robert Wokler. Cambridge: Cambridge University Press.

———. [1830] 1956. *D'Alembert's Dream.* In *Rameau's Nephew and Other Works,* trans. Jacques Barzun and Ralph H. Bowen. Indianapolis: Hackett.

Dobbs, Darrell. 2003. "Plato's Paragon of Human Excellence: Socratic Philosopher and Civic Guardian." *Journal of Politics* 65 (4): 1062–82.

Dunn, John. 1968. "Justice and the Interpretation of Locke's Political Theory." *Political Studies* 16 (1): 68–87.

Ely, John Hart. 1980. *Democracy and Distrust.* Cambridge, Mass.: Harvard University Press.

Engels, Friedrich. [1844] 1958. *Conditions of the Working Class in England.* Stanford, Calif.: Stanford University Press.

———. [1844] 1975. *Outlines of a Critique of Political Economy.* Vol. 3 of *Karl Marx and Friedrich Engels: Collected Works.* New York: International Publishers.

———. [1878] 1939. *Herr Eugen Dühring's Revolution in Science (Anti-Dühring).* New York: International Publishers.

Engeman, Thomas S., Edward J. Erler, and Thomas B. Hofeller, eds. 1988. *The Federalist Concordance.* Chicago: University of Chicago Press.

d'Entrèves, Alexander Passerin. [1951] 1994. *Natural Law: An Introduction to Legal Philosophy.* New Brunswick, N.J.: Transaction Publishers.

Fénelon, François de. [1699] 1994. *Telemachus.* Ed. Patrick Riley. Cambridge: Cambridge University Press.

———. [1714] 1970. *Lettre à l'Académie.* Ed. Ernesta Caldarini. Geneva: Librarie Droz.

Ferguson, A. S. 1922. "Plato's Simile of Light: Part II: The Allegory of the Cave (Continued)." *Classical Quarterly* 16 (1): 15–22.

Ficino, Marsilio. [1469–73] 2001. *Platonic Theology.* Vol. 1. Trans. Michael J. B. Allen with John Warden. Cambridge, Mass.: Harvard University Press.

Finnis, John. 1980. *Natural Law and Natural Rights.* Oxford: Oxford University Press.

Fishkin, James S. 1992. *The Dialogue of Justice.* New Haven: Yale University Press.

Fistioc, Mihaela C. 2002. *The Beautiful Shape of the Good: Platonic and Pythagorean Themes in Kant's "Critique of the Power of Judgment."* London: Routledge.

Flynn, Thomas R. 1985. "Truth and Subjectivation in the Later Foucault." *Journal of Philosophy* 82 (10): 531–40.

Foucault, Michel. [1961] 1988. *Madness and Civilization: A History of Insanity in the Age of Reason.* New York: Vintage Books.

———. [1975] 1977. *Discipline and Punish: The Birth of the Prison.* New York: Vintage Books.

———. [1976] 2003. *Society Must Be Defended.* New York: Picador.

———. [1978] 1990. *The History of Sexuality: An Introduction.* Vol. 1. New York: Vintage Books.

———. [1979] 2000. "Open Letter to Mehdi Bazargan." In *Michel Foucault: Power,* ed. James D. Faubion. New York: The New Press.

———. 1980. *Power/Knowledge: Selected Interviews and Other Writings, 1972–1977.* Ed. Colin Gordon. New York: Pantheon Books.

———. [1981] 1991. "How an 'Experience Book' Is Born." Interview in *Remarks on Marx: Conversations with Duccio Trombardori,* trans. R. James Goldstein and James Cascaito. New York: Semiotext(e).

———. [1982] 2000. "The Moral and Social Experience of the Poles Can No Longer Be Obliterated." In *Michel Foucault: Power,* ed. James D. Faubion. New York: The New Press.

———. [1984] 1990. *The Use of Pleasure: The History of Sexuality, Vol. 2.* Trans. Robert Hurley. New York: Vintage.

———. [1984] 2000. "Confronting Governments: Human Rights." In *Michel Foucault: Power,* ed. James D. Faubion. New York: New Press.

———. 1989a. "The Discourse of History." Interview in *Foucault Live: Collected Interviews, 1964–84,* ed. Sylvère Lotringer. New York: Semiotext(e).

———. 1989b. "The Concern for Truth." Interview in *Foucault Live: Collected Interviews, 1964–84,* ed. Sylvère Lotringer. New York: Semiotext(e).

———. 1991. *Remarks on Marx: Conversations with Duccio Trombardori.* Trans. R. James Goldstein and James Cascaito. New York: Semiotext(e).

Foucault, Michel, and Noam Chomsky. [1971] 1997. *Human Nature: Justice Versus Power.* Chicago: University of Chicago Press.

Fraser, Nancy. 1981. "Foucault on Modern Power: Empirical Insights and Normative Confusions." *Praxis International* 1 (1): 272–87.

Furet, François. 1997. "Rousseau and the French Revolution." In *The Legacy of Rousseau,* ed. Clifford Orwin and Nathan Tarcov. Chicago: University of Chicago Press.

Galvin, Richard. 1999. "Slavery and Universalizability." *Kant-Studien* 90 (2): 191–203.

Glenn, Gary D. 1984. "Inalienable Rights and Locke's Argument for Limited Government: Political Implications of a Right to Suicide." *Journal of Politics* 46 (1): 80–105.

Goldie, Mark. 1997. Introduction and notes to *Locke: Political Essays,* ed. Mark Goldie. Cambridge: Cambridge University Press.

Gray, John. 1995. *Liberalism.* 2nd ed. Minneapolis: University of Minnesota Press.

Green, F. C. 1955. *Jean-Jacques Rousseau: A Critical Study of His Life and Writings.* Cambridge: Cambridge University Press.

Gregg, Benjamin. 2003. *Coping in Politics with Indeterminate Norms: A Theory of Enlightened Localism.* Albany: State University of New York Press.

Grimsley, Ronald. 1972. Introduction and notes to *Du contrat social,* by Jean-Jacques Rousseau, ed. Ronald Grimsley. Oxford: Oxford University Press.

Gourevitch, Victor. 1994. "Rousseau and Lying." *Berkshire Review* 15:93–107.

———. 1997. Introduction and notes to *The Discourses and Other Early Political Writings,* by Jean-Jacques Rousseau, ed. Victor Gourevitch. Cambridge: Cambridge University Press.

———. 1998. "Recent Work on Rousseau." *Political Theory* 26 (4): 536–56.

Guttman, Amy, and Dennis Thompson. 1996. *Democracy and Disagreement.* Cambridge, Mass.: Belknap Press of Harvard University Press.

Habermas, Jürgen. [1983] 1990. *Moral Consciousness and Communicative Action.* Trans. Christian Lenhardt and Shierry Weber Nicholsen. Cambridge, Mass.: MIT Press.

———. [1991] 1993. *Justification and Application: Remarks on Discourse Ethics.* Trans. Ciaran Cronin. Cambridge, Mass.: MIT Press.

———. [1992] 1996. *Between Facts and Norms.* Trans. William Rehg. Cambridge, Mass.: MIT Press.

Hampsher-Monk, Iain. 1995. "Rousseau and Totalitarianism—with Hindsight?" In *Rousseau and Liberty,* ed. Robert Wokler. Manchester: Manchester University Press.

Harrison, Ross. 2003. *Hobbes, Locke, and Confusion's Masterpiece: An Examination of Seventeenth-Century Political Philosophy.* Cambridge: Cambridge University Press.

Heine, Heinrich. [1834] 1961. *Zur Geschichte der Religion und Philosophie in Deutschland.* Ed. Hans Kaufmann. Vol. 5 of *Werke und Briefe.* Berlin: Aufbau-Verlag.

Helvétius, Claude A. [1758] 1809. *De l'esprit, or, Essays on the Mind and Its Several Faculties.* London: J. M. Richardson.

Hendel, Charles. 1934. *Jean-Jacques Rousseau: Moralist.* London: Oxford University Press.

Henrich, Dieter. 1963. "Über Kants früheste Ethik: Versuch enier Rekonstruktion." *Kant-Studien* 54:404–31.

Hill, Thomas E. 2002. *Human Welfare and Moral Worth: Kantian Perspectives.* Oxford: Oxford University Press.

Hobbes, Thomas. [1640] 1994. *The Elements of Law: Human Nature and De Corpore Politico.* Ed. J. C. A. Gaskin. Oxford: Oxford University Press.

———. [1642] 1949. *De Cive; or, The Citizen.* Ed. Sterling P. Lamprecht. New York: Appleton-Century-Crofts.

———. [1651] 2002. *Leviathan.* Ed. A. P. Martinich. Peterborough, Ont.: Broadview Press.

———. [1681] 1971. *A Dialogue Between a Philosopher and a Student of the Common Laws of England.* Ed. Joseph Cropsey. Chicago: University of Chicago Press.

d'Holbach, Paul-Henry Dietrich von (Baron). [1770] 1999. *The System of Nature.* Trans. H. D. Robinson. Manchester: Clinamen Press.

Horowitz, Asher. 1987. *Rousseau, Nature, and History.* Toronto: University of Toronto Press.

Horwitz, Robert. 1990. Introduction to *Questions Concerning the Law of Nature,* by John Locke, trans. Robert Horwitz, Jenny Strauss Clay, and Diskin Clay. Ithaca, N.Y.: Cornell University Press.

Hulliung, Mark. 1994. *Autocritique of the Enlightenment: Rousseau and the Philosophes.* Cambridge, Mass.: Harvard University Press.

Husami, Ziyad I. 1980. "Marx on Distributive Justice." In *Marx, Justice, and History,* ed. Marshall Cohen, Thomas Nagel, and Thomas Scanlon. Princeton: Princeton University Press.

Hutton, Sarah. 2002. "The Cambridge Platonists." In *A Companion to Early Modern Philosophy,* ed. Steven Nadler. Oxford: Blackwell.

Jessup, Bertram E. 1948. "Relation of Hobbes's Metaphysics to His Theory of Value." *Ethics* 58 (3, pt. 1): 209–17.

Kant, Immanuel. [1762] 1968. *Enquiry Concerning the Clarity of the Principles of Natural Theology and Ethics (The Prize Essay).* Manchester: Manchester University Press.

———. [1764] 1968. *Observations on the Feeling of the Beautiful and the Sublime.* Berkeley and Los Angeles: University of California Press.

———. [1766] 1992. *Dreams of a Spirit-Seer Elucidated by Dreams of Metaphysics.* In *Theoretical Philosophy: 1755–1770.* Cambridge: Cambridge University Press.

———. [1770] 1992. *Inaugural Dissertation,* or *On the Form and Principles of the Sensible and the Intelligible Word.* In *Theoretical Philosophy: 1755–1770.* Cambridge: Cambridge University Press.

———. [1781] 1965. *The Critique of Pure Reason.* Trans. Norman Kemp Smith. New York: St. Martin's Press.

———. [1785] 1996. *Groundwork of the Metaphysics of Morals.* In *Practical Philosophy,* trans. Mary Gregor. Cambridge: Cambridge University Press.

———. [1788] 1996. *Critique of Practical Reason.* In *Practical Philosophy,* trans. Mary Gregor. Cambridge: Cambridge University Press.

———. [1793] 1996. "On the Common Saying: That May Be Correct in Theory, But It Is of No Use in Practice." In *Practical Philosophy,* trans. Mary Gregor. Cambridge: Cambridge University Press.

———. [1795] 1996. "Toward a Perpetual Peace." In *Practical Philosophy,* trans. Mary Gregor. Cambridge: Cambridge University Press.

———. [1796] 1993. "On a Newly Arisen Superior Tone in Philosophy." In *Raising the Tone of Philosophy: Late Essays by Immanuel Kant, Transformative Critique by Jacques Derrida,* ed. Peter Fenves. Baltimore: Johns Hopkins University Press.

———. [1796–98] 1938. *Opus Postumum.* In *Kants gesammelte Schriften.* Berlin: Walter de Gruyter.

———. [1797] 1996. *The Metaphysics of Morals.* In *Practical Philosophy,* trans. Mary Gregor. Cambridge: Cambridge University Press.

———. [1798] 1991. "The Contest of Faculties." In *Kant's Political Writings,* ed. Hans Reiss. Cambridge: Cambridge University Press.

———. 1817. *Vorlesungen über die philosophische Religionslehre.* Ed. K. H. L. Pölitz. Leipzig: Carl Friedrich Franz.

———. 1902–. *Kants gesammelte Schriften.* Berlin: Prussian Academy.

Kateb, George. 1961. "Aspects of Rousseau's Political Thought." *Political Science Quarterly* 76 (4): 519–43.

Kelley, George Armstrong. 1969. *Idealism, Politics, and History: Sources of Hegelian Thought.* Cambridge: Cambridge University Press.

Kelly, Christopher. 2003. *Rousseau as Author: Consecrating One's Life to the Truth.* Chicago: University of Chicago Press.

Kendall, Willmoore. 1965. *John Locke and the Doctrine of Majority Rule.* Urbana: University of Illinois Press.

———. 1985. "Introduction: How to Read Rousseau's *Government of Poland.*" In *The Government of Poland,* by Jean-Jacques Rousseau, ed. and trans. Willmoore Kendall. Indianapolis: Hackett.

Klosko, George. 1986a. *The Development of Plato's Political Theory.* New York: Methuen.

———. 1986b. "On the Straussian Interpretation of Plato's *Republic.*" *History of Political Thought* 7:275–93.

Kors, Alan. 1976. *D'Holbach's Coterie: An Enlightenment in Paris.* Princeton: Princeton University Press.

Korsgaard, Christine. 1985. "Kant's Formula of a Universal Law." *Pacific Philosophical Quarterly* 66:24–47.

Kristeller, Paul. 1964. *Eight Philosophers of the Italian Renaissance.* Stanford, Calif.: Stanford University Press.

Kuehn, Manfred. 2001. *Kant: A Biography.* Cambridge: Cambridge University Press.

Laird, Andrew. 2003. "Death, Politics, Vision, and Fiction in Plato's Cave (After Saramago)." *Arion* 10 (3): 1–30.

La Mettrie, Julien de. [1748] 1994. *Man a Machine.* Ed. Justin Leiber. Indianapolis: Hackett.

Lamy, Bernard. [1683] 1966. *Entretiens sur les Sciences: Dans lesquels on apprend comment l'on doit étudier les Sciences, & s'en servir pour se faire l'esprit juste, & cœur droit.* Ed. François Girbal et Pierre Clair. Paris: Presses Universitaires de France.

Laslett, Peter. [1960] 1988. Introduction and notes to *Two Treatises of Government,* by John Locke, ed. Peter Laslett. Cambridge: Cambridge University Press.

Lecercle, Jean-Louis. 1982. "Rousseau et Marx." In *Rousseau After 200 Years: Proceedings of the Cambridge Bicentennial Colloquium,* ed. R. A. Leigh. Cambridge: Cambridge University Press.

Lee, James Mitchell. 2001. "Jean-Jacques Rousseau and Bernard Lamy: The Platonic Education of *Amour-propre.*" In *Rousseau and the Ancients/Rousseau et les Anciens,* ed. Ruth Grant and Philip Stewart. *Pensée Libre* (Montreal) 8.

Leibniz, Gottfried Wilhelm. [1686] 1902. *Discourse on Metaphysics.* Trans. George Montgomery. La Salle, Ill.: Open Court.

———. [1702–3] 1988. "Meditation on the Common Concept of Justice." In *Leibniz: Political Writings,* ed. Patrick Riley. Cambridge: Cambridge University Press.

———. [1706] 1988. "Opinion on the Principles of Pufendorf." In *Leibniz: Political Writings,* ed. Patrick Riley. Cambridge: Cambridge University Press.

———. [1710] 1985. *Theodicy: Essays on the Goodness of God, the Freedom of Man, and the Origin of Evil.* Ed. Austin Farrer. La Salle, Ill.: Open Court.

———. 1969. *G. W. Leibniz: Philosophical Papers and Letters.* 2nd ed. Ed. Leroy E. Loemker. Dordrecht: Reidel.

Leigh, R. A. 1964. "Liberté et authorité dans le *Contrat social.*" In *Jean-Jacques Rousseau et son œuvre: Problèmes et recherches,* ed. Jean Fabre. Paris: Librarie C. Klincksieck.

Levine, Andrew. 1976. *The Politics of Autonomy: A Kantian Reading of Rousseau's "Social Contract."* Amherst: University of Massachusetts Press.

Locke, John. [1664] 1997. *Essays on the Law of Nature.* In *Locke: Political Essays,* ed. Mark Goldie. Cambridge: Cambridge University Press.

———. [1690] 1959. *An Essay Concerning Human Understanding.* New York: Dover.

———. [1690] 1988. *Second Treatise.* In *Two Treatises of Government,* ed. Peter Laslett. Cambridge: Cambridge University Press.

———. [1693] 1957. "Letter to Isaac Newton." In Maurice Cranston, *John Locke: A Biography.* New York: Macmillan.

Lovejoy, Arthur. [1936] 1963. *The Great Chain of Being: A Study of the History of an Idea.* Cambridge, Mass.: Harvard University Press.

Luke, Timothy W. 1984. "On Nature and Society: Rousseau Versus the Enlightenment." *History of Political Thought* 5 (2): 211–43.

Lukes, Steven. 1985. *Marxism and Morality.* Oxford: Oxford University Press.

MacAdam, James I. 1963. "Rousseau and the Friends of Despotism." *Ethics* 74 (1): 34–43.

Machiavelli, Niccolò. [1513] 1999. *The Prince.* Trans. George Bull. New York: Penguin Books.

Madison, James, Alexander Hamilton, and John Jay. [1789] 1999. *The Federalist Papers.* Ed. Clinton Rossiter. New York: Mentor Books.

Maguire, Matthew W. 2006. *The Conversion of Imagination: From Pascal Through Rousseau to Tocqueville.* Cambridge, Mass.: Harvard University Press.

Malebranche, Nicolas [1674] 1997. *The Search After Truth.* Ed. Thomas M. Lennon and Paul J. Olscamp. Cambridge: Cambridge University Press.

———. [1685] 1959–66. *Trois Lettres de l'auteur De la Recherche de la Vérité, Touchant la Défense de M. Arnauld contre la Réponse au livre des vrayes et des fausses idées.* In *Œuvres complètes de Malebranche,* ed. A. Robinet. Paris: J. Vrin.

Marcuse, Herbert. 1964. *One-Dimensional Man.* Boston: Beacon Press.

Marks, Jonathan. 2000. "The Divine Instinct? Rousseau and Conscience." Presented at the annual meeting of the American Political Science Association, August 30– September 3, Washington, D.C.

———. 2005. *Perfection and Disharmony in the Thought of Jean-Jacques Rousseau.* Cambridge: Cambridge University Press.

———. 2006a. "The Divine Instinct? Rousseau and Conscience." *Review of Politics* 68 (4): 564–85.

———. 2006b. "Keeping Compassion in Its Place: Rousseau's Account of Compassion." Unpublished paper.

———. 2006c. "Rousseau and the Limits of Compassion." Presented at the annual meeting of the American Political Science Association, August 31–September 3, Philadelphia.

Marmontel, Jean-François. 1767. *Bélisaire.* Paris.

Martinich, A. P. 1992. *The Two Gods of Leviathan: Thomas Hobbes on Religion and Politics.* Cambridge: Cambridge University Press.

———. 1999. *Hobbes: A Biography.* Cambridge: Cambridge University Press.

———. 2002. Introduction and notes to *Leviathan,* by Thomas Hobbes, ed. A. P. Martinich. Ontario: Broadview Press.

———. 2005. *Hobbes.* New York: Routledge.

Marx, Karl. [1843] 1978. "For a Ruthless Critique of Everything Existing." In *The Marx-Engels Reader,* 2nd ed., ed. Robert C. Tucker. New York: W. W. Norton.

———. [1843] 1994. *Toward a Critique of Hegel's "Philosophy of Right": An Introduction.* In *Marx: Selected Writings,* ed. Lawrence H. Simon. Indianapolis: Hackett.

———. [1844] 1987. *Contribution to the Critique of Political Economy.* Vol. 29 of *Karl Marx/Friederich Engels: Collected Works.* New York: International Publishers.

———. [1844] 1994. *Economic and Philosophic Manuscripts.* In *Marx: Selected Writings,* ed. Lawrence H. Simon. Indianapolis: Hackett.

———. [1844–45] 1994. "Theses on Feuerbach." In *Marx: Selected Writings,* ed. Lawrence H. Simon. Indianapolis: Hackett.

———. [1852] 1994. *The Eighteenth Brumaire of Louis Bonaparte.* In *Marx: Selected Writings,* ed. Lawrence H. Simon. Indianapolis: Hackett.

———. [1853] 1978. "On Imperialism in India." In *The Marx-Engels Reader,* 2nd ed., ed. Robert C. Tucker. New York: W. W. Norton.

———. [1857–58] 1973. *Grundrisse.* New York: Penguin Books.

———. [1867] 1977. *Capital.* Vol. 1. Trans. Ben Fowkes. Marx Library. New York: Random House/Vintage Books.

Marx, Karl, and Friederich Engels. [1844] 1967. *The Holy Family.* Ed. and trans. Loyd D. Easton and Kurt H. Guddat. Garden City, N.Y.: Anchor Books.

———. [1845] 1998. *The German Ideology.* Amherst, N.Y.: Prometheus Books.

———. [1848] 1994. *The Communist Manifesto.* In *Marx: Selected Writings,* ed. Lawrence H. Simon. Indianapolis: Hackett.

Masters, Roger D. 1968. *The Political Philosophy of Rousseau.* Princeton: Princeton University Press.

———. 1978. Introduction and notes to *On the Social Contract with Geneva Manuscript and Political Economy,* by Jean-Jacques Rousseau, ed. Roger D. Masters. New York: St. Martin's Press.

Masters, Roger D., and Christopher Kelly. 1994. Introduction to *Social Contract, Discourse on the Virtue Most Necessary for a Hero, Political Fragments, and Geneva Manuscript.* Vol. 4 of *The Collected Writings of Jean-Jacques Rousseau,* ed. Roger D. Masters and Christopher Kelly. Hanover, N.H.: University Press of New England.

McLendon, Michael Locke. 2003. "The Overvaluation of Talent: An Interpretation and Application of Rousseau's *Amour-Propre.*" *Polity* 36 (1): 115–38.

Melzer, Arthur. 1983. "Rousseau's Moral Realism: Replacing Natural Law with the General Will." *American Political Science Review* 77 (3): 633–51.

———. 1990. *The Natural Goodness of Man.* Chicago: University of Chicago Press.

———.1996. "The Origin of the Counter-Enlightenment: Rousseau and the New Religion of Sincerity." *American Political Science Review* 90 (2): 344–60.

Mercer, Christia. 2001. *Leibniz's Metaphysics: Its Origins and Development.* Cambridge: Cambridge University Press.

———. 2002. "Platonism and Philosophical Humanism on the Continent." In *A Companion to Early Modern Philosophy,* ed. Steven Nadler. Oxford: Blackwell.

Miller, Fiona. 2004. "Rousseau's Epicureanism." Presented at the annual meeting of the Midwest Political Science Association, April 15–18, Chicago.

Miller, Fred J., Jr. 1995. *Nature, Justice, and Rights in Aristotle's "Politics."* Oxford: Oxford University Press.

Miller, James. 1984. *Rousseau: Dreamer of Democracy.* New Haven: Yale University Press.

Millet, Louis. 1967. "Le Platonisme de Rousseau." *Revue de l'enseignement philosophique* (June/July).

Montesquieu, Charles de Secondat. [1721] 1964. *The Persian Letters.* Trans. George R. Healy. Indianapolis: Bobbs-Merrill.

Morrow, Glenn R. 1971. "Plato and the Rule of Law." In *Plato II: Ethics, Politics, and Philosophy of Art and Religion,* ed. Gregory Vlastos. Garden City, N.Y.: Anchor Books.

Murphy, Mark C. 1995. "Was Hobbes a Legal Positivist?" *Ethics* 105 (4): 846–73.

Myers, Peter C. 1998. *Our Only Star and Compass: Locke and the Struggle for Political Rationality.* Lanham, Md.: Rowman and Littlefield.

Nadler, Steven. 1992. *Malebranche and Ideas.* New York: Oxford University Press.

Nehamas, Alexander. 2004. "Wisdom Without Knowledge: Socrates Today." *TCU Magazine* 48 (2): 13–15.

Newton, Isaac. [1693] 1957. "Letter to John Locke." In Maurice Cranston, *John Locke: A Biography.* New York: Macmillan.

Nietzsche, Friederich. [1888] 1994. *On the Genealogy of Morality.* Ed. Keith Ansell-Pearson. Cambridge: Cambridge University Press.

Nisbet, Robert A. 1943. "Rousseau and Totalitarianism." *Journal of Politics* 5 (2): 99–114.

Noone, John B. 1972. "Rousseau's Theory of Natural Law as Conditional." *Journal of the History of Ideas* 33 (1): 23–42.

O'Hagan, Timothy. 2004. "Taking Rousseau Seriously." *History of Political Thought* 25 (1): 73–85.

O'Neal, John. 1996. *The Authority of Experience: Sensationist Theory in the French Enlightenment.* University Park: The Pennsylvania State University Press.

O'Neill, Onora. 1975. *Acting on Principle: An Essay on Kantian Ethics.* New York: Columbia University Press.

Panagopoulos, E. P. 1985. *Essays on the History and Meaning of Checks and Balances.* Lanham, Md.: University Press of America.

Pascal, Blaise. [1660] 1966. *Pensées.* Trans. A. J. Krailsheimer. New York: Penguin Books.

Plamenatz, John. [1963] 1992. *Man and Society: Political and Social Theories from Machiavelli to Marx.* Vol. 2. London: Longman.

Plato. 1961. *The Collected Dialogues of Plato.* Ed. Edith Hamilton and Huntington Cairns. Princeton: Princeton University Press.

Plattner, Marc E. 1979. *Rousseau's State of Nature: An Interpretation of the "Discourse on Inequality."* DeKalb: Northern Illinois University Press.

Plutarch. 2001. *Plutarch's Lives.* Ed. Arthur Hugh Clough. New York: Modern Library.

Popper, Karl. 1962. *The Open Society and Its Enemies: The Spell of Plato.* Princeton: Princeton University Press.

Protagoras. 1968. "'Truth' or 'Refutatory Arguments.'" In *Philosophic Classics,* ed. Walter Kaufmann. Englewood Cliffs, N.J.: Prentice-Hall.

Radbruch, Gustav. [1945] 1973. *Rechtsphilosophie.* Ed. Erik Wolf and Hans-Peter Schneider. Stuttgart: K. F. Koehler-Verlag.

Raphael, D. D. 1977. *Hobbes: Morals and Politics.* London: George Allen and Unwin.

Rawls, John. [1951] 1999. "Outline of a Decision Procedure for Ethics." In *Collected Papers,* ed. Samuel Freeman. Cambridge, Mass.: Harvard University Press.

————. 1971. *A Theory of Justice.* Cambridge, Mass.: Harvard University Press.

————. 1993. *Political Liberalism.* New York: Columbia University Press.

Reisert, Joseph R. 2003. *Jean-Jacques Rousseau: A Friend of Virtue.* Ithaca, N.Y.: Cornell University Press.

Riley, Patrick. 1970. "A Possible Explanation of the General Will." *American Political Science Review* 64 (1): 86–97.

————. [1972] 1988. Introduction and notes to *Political Writings,* by G. W. Leibniz, ed. Patrick Riley. 2nd ed. Cambridge: Cambridge University Press.

————. 1982. *Will and Legitimacy: A Critical Exposition of Social Contract Theory in Hobbes, Locke, Rousseau, Kant, and Hegel.* Cambridge, Mass.: Harvard University Press.

————. 1986. *The General Will Before Rousseau: The Transformation of the Divine into the Civic.* Princeton: Princeton University Press.

————. 1993. "The Elements of Kant's Practical Philosophy." In *Kant and Political Philosophy: The Contemporary Legacy,* ed. Ronald Beiner and William James Booth. New Haven: Yale University Press.

————. 1994. Introduction and notes to *Telemachus, Son of Ulysses,* by François de Fénelon, ed. Patrick Riley. Cambridge: Cambridge University Press.

————. 1995. "Rousseau's General Will: Freedom of a Particular Kind." In *Rousseau and Liberty,* ed. Robert Wokler. Manchester: Manchester University Press.

————. 1996. *Leibniz's Universal Jurisprudence: Justice as Charity of the Wise.* Cambridge, Mass.: Harvard University Press.

————. 2001a. "Rousseau, Fénelon, and the Quarrel Between the Ancients and the Moderns." In *The Cambridge Companion to Rousseau,* ed. Patrick Riley. Cambridge: Cambridge University Press.

————. 2001b. "Rousseau's General Will." In *The Cambridge Companion to Rousseau,* ed. Patrick Riley. Cambridge: Cambridge University Press.

Rosen, Allen D. 1993. *Kant's Theory of Justice.* Ithaca, N.Y.: Cornell University Press.

Rosenblatt, Helena. 1997. *Rousseau and Geneva: From the "First Discourse" to the "Social Contract," 1749–1762.* Cambridge: Cambridge University Press.

————. 2002. "On the 'Misogyny' of Jean-Jacques Rousseau: The Letter to d'Alembert in Historical Context." *French Historical Studies* 25 (1): 91–114.

Ross, G. MacDonald. 1984. *Leibniz.* Oxford: Oxford University Press.

Rousseau, Jean-Jacques. N.d. Notes on Plato. [Marginal notations in Rousseau's personal copies of *Divini Platonis: Operum,* trans. Marsilio Ficino. Lugduni: Apud Ioan. Tornaesium, 1550.]

————. [1739] 1964. "La Verger de Madame la Baronne de Warens." In *Œuvres complètes,* ed. B. Gagnebin and M. Raymond, vol. 2. Paris: Pléiade.

————. [1749] 1959. *Le Persifleur.* In *Œuvres complètes,* ed. B. Gagnebin and M. Raymond, vol. 1. Paris: Pléiade.

————. [1751] 1997a. *Discourse on the Arts and Sciences.* In *The Discourses and Other Early Political Writings,* ed. Victor Gourevitch. Cambridge: Cambridge University Press.

————. [1751] 1997b. "Last Reply by Jean-Jacques Rousseau of Geneva." In *The Discourses and Other Early Political Writings,* ed. Victor Gourevitch. Cambridge: Cambridge University Press.

————. [1751] 1997c. "Observations by Jean-Jacques Rousseau of Geneva on the Answer Made to His Discourse." In *The Discourses and Other Early Political Writings,* ed. Victor Gourevitch. Cambridge: Cambridge University Press.

———. [1752–53] 1997. "Preface to Narcissus." In *The Discourses and Other Early Political Writings,* ed. Victor Gourevitch. Cambridge: Cambridge University Press.

———. [1755] 1997a. *Discourse on Political Economy.* In *The Social Contract and Other Later Political Writings,* ed. Victor Gourevitch. Cambridge: Cambridge University Press.

———. [1755] 1997b. *Discourse on the Origin and the Foundations of Inequality Among Men.* In *The Discourses and Other Early Political Writings,* ed. Victor Gourevitch. Cambridge: Cambridge University Press.

———. [1756] 1978. *The Geneva Manuscript.* In *On the Social Contract with Geneva Manuscript and Political Economy,* by Jean-Jacques Rousseau, ed. Roger D. Masters. New York: St. Martin's Press.

———. [1756] 1997. "Letter from J. J. Rousseau to M. de Voltaire, 18 August 1756." In *The Social Contract and Other Later Political Writings,* ed. Victor Gourevitch. Cambridge: Cambridge University Press.

———. [1757] 1969. *Lettres morales.* In *Œuvres complètes,* ed. B. Gagnebin and M. Raymond, vol. 4. Paris: Pléiade.

———. [1757] 2003. "Letter on Virtue, the Individual, and Society." Trans. Arthur Goldhammer. *New York Review of Books,* May 15, 2003, 31–32.

———. [1758] 1960. *Letter to M. d'Alembert on the Theater.* Trans. Allan Bloom. Ithaca, N.Y.: Cornell University Press.

———. [1758] 1967. "Letter to Deleyre." In *Correspondance complète de Jean-Jacques Rousseau,* ed. R. A. Leigh. Geneva: Institut et Musée Voltaire.

———. [1758] 1997. "The State of War." In *The Social Contract and Other Later Political Writings,* ed. Victor Gourevitch. Cambridge: Cambridge University Press.

———. [1761] 1997. *Julie; Or, the New Heloise: Letters of Two Lovers Who Live in a Small Town at the Foot of the Alps.* Trans. Philip Stewart and Jean Vaché. Vol. 6 of *The Collected Writings of Rousseau.* Hanover, N.H.: University Press of New England.

———. [1762] 1979. *Emile, or On Education.* Trans. Allan Bloom. New York: Basic Books.

———. [1762] 1997. *Of the Social Contract.* Ed. Victor Gourevitch. Cambridge: Cambridge University Press.

———. [1763] 2001. *Letter to Beaumont.* In *Letter to Beaumont, Letters Written from the Mountain, and Related Writings,* ed. Christopher Kelly and Eve Grace. Vol. 9 of *The Collected Writings of Rousseau.* Hanover, N.H.: University Press of New England.

———. [1764] 2001. *Letters Written from the Mountain.* In *Letter to Beaumont, Letters Written from the Mountain, and Related Writings,* ed. Christopher Kelly and Eve Grace. Vol. 9 of *The Collected Writings of Rousseau.* Hanover, N.H.: University Press of New England.

———. [1764] 1997. "On Theatrical Imitation: An Essay Drawn from Plato's Dialogues." In *Essay on the Origin of Languages and Writings Related to Music,* ed. John T. Scott. Vol. 7 of *The Collected Writings of Rousseau.* Hanover, N.H.: University Press of New England.

———. [1765] 1986. *Constitutional Project for Corsica.* In *Political Writings,* ed. Frederick Watkins. Madison: University of Wisconsin Press.

———. [1767] 1997. "Letter to Mirabeau." In *The Social Contract and Other Later Political Writings,* ed. Victor Gourevitch. Cambridge: Cambridge University Press.

———. [1768] 1997. *Discourse on This Question: What Is the Virtue a Hero Most Needs and*

Who Are the Heroes Who Have Lacked This Virtue? In *The Discourses and Other Early Political Writings,* ed. Victor Gourevitch. Cambridge: Cambridge University Press.

———. [1769] 1997. "Letter from J. J. Rousseau to M. de Franquières, 25 March 1769." In *The Social Contract and Other Later Political Writings,* ed. Victor Gourevitch. Cambridge: Cambridge University Press.

———. [1771] 1995. *The Confessions and Correspondence, Including the Letters to Malesherbes,* ed. Christopher Kelly, Roger D. Masters, and Peter G. Stillman. Vol. 5 of *The Collected Writings of Rousseau.* Hanover, N.H.: University Press of New England.

———. [1772] 1997. *Considerations on the Government of Poland.* In *The Social Contract and Other Later Political Writings,* ed. Victor Gourevitch. Cambridge: Cambridge University Press.

———. [1776] 1990. *Rousseau, Judge of Jean-Jacques: Dialogues.* Ed. Roger D. Masters and Christopher Kelly. Vol. 1 of *The Collected Writings of Rousseau.* Hanover, N.H.: University Press of New England.

———. [1778] 2000. *Reveries of the Solitary Walker.* Trans. Charles E. Buttersworth. Ed. Christopher Kelly. Vol. 8 of *The Collected Writings of Rousseau.* Hanover, N.H.: University Press of New England.

———. 1959–95. *Œuvres complètes.* Ed. B. Gagnebin and M. Raymond. Paris: Pléiade.

———. 1994a. "Political Fragments." In *Social Contract, Discourse on the Virtue Most Necessary for a Hero, Political Fragments, and Geneva Manuscript,* ed. Roger D. Masters and Christopher Kelly. Vol. 4 of *The Collected Writings of Rousseau.* Hanover, N.H.: University Press of New England.

———. 1994b. "Fragment on Freedom." In *Social Contract, Discourse on the Virtue Most Necessary for a Hero, Political Fragments, and Geneva Manuscript,* ed. Roger D. Masters and Christopher Kelly. Vol. 4 of *The Collected Writings of Rousseau.* Hanover, N.H.: University Press of New England.

———. 1997. *Essay on the Origin of Languages in Which Something Is Said About Melody and Musical Imitation.* In *The Discourses and Other Early Political Writings,* ed. Victor Gourevitch. Cambridge: Cambridge University Press.

———. 2007. "Various Fragments." In *Autobiographical, Scientific, Religious, Moral, and Literary Writings,* trans. and ed. Christopher Kelly. Vol. 12 of *The Collected Writings of Rousseau.* Hanover, N.H.: University Press of New England.

Rubenstein, William B. 2004. "Hiding Behind the Constitution." *New York Times,* March 20, A32.

Russell, Bertrand. 1945. *A History of Western Philosophy.* New York: Simon and Schuster.

———. 1954. *Human Society in Politics and Ethics.* London: George Allen and Unwin.

Schilpp, Paul Arthur. [1938] 1960. *Kant's Pre-Critical Ethics.* 2nd ed. Evanston, Ill.: Northwestern University Press.

Schwarzberg, Melissa. 2003. "Rousseau on Fundamental Law." *Political Studies* 51 (2): 387–403.

Seung, T. K. 1993. *Intuition and Construction.* New Haven: Yale University Press.

———. 1994. *Kant's Platonic Revolution in Moral and Political Philosophy.* Baltimore: Johns Hopkins University Press.

———. 1996. *Plato Rediscovered: Human Value and Social Order.* Lanham, Md.: Rowman and Littlefield.

Shklar, Judith N. 1969. *Men and Citizens: A Study of Rousseau's Social Theory.* Cambridge: Cambridge University Press.

Silverthorne, J. M. 1973. "Rousseau's Plato." *Studies on Voltaire and the Eighteenth Century* 116:235–49.

Simmons, A. John. 1983. "Inalienable Rights and Locke's Treatises." *Philosophy and Public Affairs* 12 (3): 175–204.

Simpson, Matthew. 2006a. "A Paradox of Sovereignty in the *Social Contract.*" *Journal of Moral Philosophy* 3 (1): 47–58.

———. 2006b. *Rousseau's Theory of Freedom.* London: Continuum.

Smith, D. W. 1965. *Helvétius: A Study in Persecution.* Oxford: Clarendon Press.

Sorkin, David. 2003. "Reclaiming Theology for the Enlightenment: The Case of Siegmund Jacob Baumgarten (1706–1757)." *Central European History* 36:503–30.

———. 2005. "Geneva's 'Enlightened Orthodoxy': The Middle Way of Jacob Vernet." *Church History* 74 (2): 286–305.

Starobinski, Jean. 1971. *Jean-Jacques Rousseau: Transparency and Obstruction.* Trans. Arthur Goldhammer. Chicago: University of Chicago Press.

———. 1973. "Rousseau and Modern Tyranny." *New York Review of Books,* November 29.

Strauss, Leo. [1936] 1952. *The Political Philosophy of Hobbes: Its Basis and Its Genesis.* Trans. Elsa M. Sinclair. Chicago: University of Chicago Press.

———. [1953] 1965. *Natural Right and History.* Chicago: University of Chicago Press.

———. 1958. "Critical Note: Locke's Doctrine of Natural Law." *American Political Science Review* 52 (2): 490–501.

———. 1964. *The City and Man.* Chicago: Rand McNally.

———. 1972. "On the Intention of Rousseau." In *Hobbes and Rousseau: A Collection of Critical Essays,* ed. Maurice Cranston and Richard S. Peters. Garden City, N.Y.: Anchor Books.

———. 1975. "Three Waves of Modernity." In *Political Philosophy: Six Essays by Leo Strauss,* ed. Hilail Gildin. Indianapolis: Pegasus.

Strong, Tracy B. [1994] 2002. *Jean-Jacques Rousseau: The Politics of the Ordinary.* Lanham, Md.: Rowman and Littlefield.

Sullivan, Roger J. 1989. *Immanuel Kant's Moral Theory.* Cambridge: Cambridge University Press.

Talmon, J. L. 1955. *The Origins of Totalitarian Democracy.* London: Secker and Warburg.

Tanner, R. G. 1970. "DIANOIA and Plato's Cave." *Classical Quarterly* 20 (1): 81–91.

Taylor, Charles. 1984. "Foucault on Freedom and Truth." *Political Theory* 12 (2): 152–83.

———. 1989. *Sources of the Self: The Making of the Modern Identity.* Cambridge, Mass.: Harvard University Press.

———. 1993. "The Motivation Behind a Procedural Ethics." In *Kant and Political Philosophy: The Contemporary Legacy,* ed. Ronald Beiner and William James Booth. New Haven: Yale University Press.

Thorson, Thomas Landon. 1963. *Plato: Totalitarian or Democrat?* Englewood Cliffs, N.J.: Prentice-Hall.

Torrance, John. 1995. *Karl Marx's Theory of Ideas.* Cambridge: Cambridge University Press.

Trachtenberg, Zev. 2001. "Rousseau's Platonic Rejection of Politics." In *Rousseau and the Ancients/Rousseau et les Anciens,* ed. Ruth Grant and Phillip Stewart. *Pensée Libre* (Montreal) 8.

Tucker, Robert C. 1969. *The Marxian Revolutionary Idea.* New York: W. W. Norton.

———. 1978. Introduction to *The Marx-Engels Reader.* 2nd ed. New York: W. W. Norton.

Vaughan, C. E. [1915] 1962. Introduction to *The Political Writings of Jean-Jacques Rousseau.* New York: John Wiley and Sons.

———. 1960. *Studies in the History of Political Philosophy: Before and After Rousseau.* New York: Russell and Russell.

Vaughan, Sharon Kay. Forthcoming. *Poverty, Justice, and Western Political Thought.* Lanham, Md.: Lexington Books.

Velkley, Richard. 1989. *Freedom and the End of Reason: On the Moral Foundations of Kant's Critical Philosophy.* Chicago: University of Chicago Press.

von Leyden, W. 1954. Introduction to *Essays on the Law of Nature,* by John Locke. Oxford: Clarendon Press.

Watkins, J. W. N. 1973. *Hobbes's System of Ideas.* 2nd ed. London: Hutchison University Library.

White, Morton. 1978. *The Philosophy of the American Revolution.* New York: Oxford University Press.

———. 1987. *Philosophy, the "Federalist," and the Constitution.* New York: Oxford University Press.

Wild, John. 1953. *Plato's Modern Enemies and the Theory of Natural Law.* Chicago: University of Chicago Press.

Williams, David L. 1999. "Dialogical Theories of Justice." *Telos* 114 (Winter): 109–31.

———. 2004. "Justice and the General Will: Affirming Rousseau's Ancient Orientation." *Journal of the History of Ideas* 64 (4): 383–411.

Williams, Howard. 1983. *Kant's Political Philosophy.* Oxford: Blackwell.

Wokler, Robert. 1982. "Discussion." In *Rousseau After 200 Years: Proceedings of the Cambridge Bicentennial Colloquium,* ed. R. A. Leigh. Cambridge: Cambridge University Press.

———. 1994. "Rousseau's Pufendorf: Natural Law and the Foundations of Commercial Society." *History of Political Thought* 15 (3): 373–402.

———. 2001. "Ancient Postmodernism in the Philosophy of Rousseau." In *The Cambridge Companion to Rousseau,* ed. Patrick Riley. Cambridge: Cambridge University Press.

Wood, Allen W. 1980a. "The Marxian Critique of Justice." In *Marx, Justice, and History,* ed. Marshall Cohen, Thomas Nagel, and Thomas Scanlon. Princeton: Princeton University Press.

———. 1980b. "Marx on Right and Justice: A Reply to Husami." In *Marx, Justice, and History,* ed. Marshall Cohen, Thomas Nagel, and Thomas Scanlon. Princeton: Princeton University Press.

Yolton, John W. 1958. "Locke on the Law of Nature." *Philosophical Review* 67:477–98.

Zuckert, Michael. 1994. *Natural Rights and the New Republicanism.* Princeton: Princeton University Press.